D0061353

COMPARABLE WORTH
Theories and Evidence

SOCIAL INSTITUTIONS AND SOCIAL CHANGE

An Aldine de Gruyter Series of Texts and Monographs

EDITED BY

Michael Useem • James D. Wright

COMPARABLE WORTH
Theories and Evidence

Paula England

ALDINE DE GRUYTER

New York

About the Author

Paula England is Professor of Sociology at the University of Arizona. Her research interests include occupational sex segregation, the sex gap in pay, and the integration of sociological, economic, and feminist theories. She is the author of numerous journal articles on these topics, and is the coauthor (with George Farkas) of *Households, Employment, and Gender: A Social, Economic, and Demographic View* (Aldine, 1986). She has testified in federal court as an expert witness in discrimination suits.

Copyright © 1992 Walter de Gruyter, Inc., New York
All rights reserved. No part of this publication may be reproduced or transmitted in any form or by any means, electronic or mechanical, including photocopy, recording, or any information storage and retrieval system, without permission in writing from the publisher.

ALDINE DE GRUYTER
A division of Walter de Gruyter, Inc.
200 Saw Mill River Road
Hawthorne, New York 10532

The paper used in this publication meets the minimum requirements of American National Standard for Information Sciences—Permanence of Paper Printed Library Materials, ANSI Z39.48-1984.

Library of Congress Cataloging-in-Publication Data

England, Paula.
    Comparable worth : theories and evidence / Paula England.
        p.   cm. — (Social institutions and social change)
    Includes bibliographical references and index.
    ISBN 0-202-30348-9 (alk. paper). — ISBN 0-202-30349-7 (pbk. : alk. paper)
        1. Pay equity—United States. 2. Pay equity. I. Title.
    II. Series.
    HD6061.2.U6E54   1992
    331.2'153—dc20

                                                                    92-900
                                                                    CIP

Manufactured in the United States of America

10 9 8 7 6 5 4 3 2 1

331.2153
E58

25 246208
93-0475

To my parents,
Bea England and Bill England

Contents

4 Job Evaluation

5 Pay Equity and the Federal Courts

6 Feminism and Other Philosophical Positions

7 Policy Debates

Preface

Writing this book over the last five years has been both a pleasure and a struggle. I have tried to bring sociologists' and economists' views of labor markets, statistical methods of analyzing national data, job evaluation techniques, legal opinions, feminist theory, and political philosophy into a dialogue with each other around the topic of comparable worth.

To do this, I had to learn things from many fields and find ways to translate between them. I could not have done this without the informal conversations I had with several good friends. The many hours I spent in discussion with them were a crucial, if indirect, contribution to this book. I especially acknowledge five colleagues at the University of Texas—Dallas, where I worked between 1975 and 1989. Nancy Tuana, a philosopher, and Karen Prager, a psychologist, profoundly influenced my thinking/feeling through our monthly feminist reading group. George Farkas helped me integrate recent developments from labor economics and sociology as we hammered out several manuscripts together. Debates with Peter Lewin and Ted Harpham deepened my understanding of the legacies of the classical liberal tradition in economic and political philosophy.

Others provided comments on earlier drafts of chapters. Economists Mark Killingsworth (Rutgers) and Kevin Lang (Boston University) sent constructive criticism of my uses of labor economics. (Kevin may often have wished I had never discovered bitnet!) Peter Kuhn (Economics, McMaster) saved me from error on one point. My understanding of Title VII case law was enhanced by comments from Paul Weiler (Harvard Law School), Douglas Laycock (University of Texas Law School), Robert Nelson (American Bar Association), and Michael Evan Gold (Cornell). My thinking about feminist and Marxist theory was enriched by comments from Beth Anne Shelton (Sociology, SUNY—Buffalo), Ben Agger (Sociology, SUNY—Buffalo), and Nancy Folbre (Economics, University of Massachusetts). Ronnie Steinberg (Sociology, Temple University), Helen Remick (EEO Office, University of Washington), and Richard

Arvey (Industrial Relations, University of Minnesota) shared their academic and practical knowledge of job evaluation with me.

Parts of this research were funded by grants from the National Science Foundation Sociology Program, the Rockefeller Foundation, the Texas Applied Research Program, and the University of Texas—Arlington Women and Minorities Research Center. Betty Demoney and Barbara McIntosh provided word processing through the long series of revisions I undertook, impressing me with their accuracy and good cheer.

Constructing the dataset, "doing the runs" for Chapter 3, and other editorial functions were carried out by the long line of skilled and fastidious research assistants that I have been blessed with at the University of Texas—Dallas and the University of Arizona. I especially thank Melissa Herbert, Irene Browne, Barbara Kilbourne, Lori McCreary-Megdal, Lori Reid, and Jim Emopolos, among whom I understand that I have a reputation for delegating everything that can possibly be delegated. Randy Filer, Randy Hodson, Toby Parcel, and Donald Treiman were kind enough to provide machine-readable data files.

To all those mentioned above, I am grateful. Without their help, the book would easily have taken a decade to research and write.

I dedicate this book to my parents, Bea England and Bill England, both of whose lives have conveyed the message that efforts toward long-term goals yield rich rewards.

Paula England
Tucson, Arizona

1

Segregation and the Pay Gap

I. Introduction

The terms *comparable worth* and *pay equity* refer to a form of sex discrimination that went virtually unrecognized until about 15 years ago. The issue is still little understood. Indeed, its status as a type of discrimination is controversial. Yet evidence abounds that jobs filled mostly by women have pay levels that are lower than they would be if the jobs were filled mostly by men. This is seen as sex discrimination by advocates of the principle of comparable worth.

At first glance, the issue sounds very much like the more familiar issue of "equal pay for equal work," which refers to men and women in the same job, with the same seniority, performing the same work equally well, but being paid differently. Comparable worth is a different issue. It is distinct because it refers to comparisons between the pay in *different* jobs, jobs that differ in that they entail at least some distinct tasks. The comparisons are between one job that is largely male and one that is largely female. (Throughout this book, for brevity, I will use the terms *male job* and *female job* to describe jobs that are *disproportionately* or *predominantly*, but generally not entirely, performed by persons of one sex.) The allegation of discrimination is the claim that the difference between the pay of the two jobs results from gender bias in wage setting rather than from other job characteristics. Needless to say, a thorny issue is how one decides when two distinct jobs are nonetheless comparable in the sense that we would expect them to pay the same in the absence of sex discrimination.

The wage discrimination at issue in comparable worth is also distinct from discrimination in hiring, initial job placement, and promotion (all of which, for brevity, I will refer to as *hiring discrimination*). Hiring discrimination against women seeking to enter traditionally male jobs is one (although not the only) reason for occupational sex segregation. Without segregation of jobs, female jobs could not be given a discriminatory pay level. This is obvious, since, without segregation, there would be no predominantly male and predominantly female jobs! Yet, in my view, engaging in discrimination on the basis of sex in setting the pay levels assigned to male and female jobs is analytically distinct from engaging in hiring discrimination on the basis of sex.

Some examples may help the reader to visualize the sorts of comparisons at issue in comparable worth. In the state of Washington, where female state employees sued over pay equity, the job of legal secretary, a female job, was found by an evaluation study to be comparable in worth to the job of heavy equipment operator, a job filled mostly by men. However, in 1972, heavy equipment operators made about $400 more per month. Stockroom attendants, mostly men, made much more than dental hygienists, who were mostly women. (The above examples are from Remick 1980, pp. 416–417, as cited in Steinberg 1990.) In 1975, nurses in Denver sued the city claiming that their jobs paid less than male jobs such as tree trimmer and sign painter (Blum 1991, p. 49). It would be hard to argue that the latter two jobs require as much skill or are as demanding as nursing. Women workers for the city of San Jose discovered in the mid-1970s that secretaries were generally earning less than workers in male jobs that required no more than an eighth grade education, including, for example, men who washed cars for the city (Blum 1991, p. 60). Eventually, women in San Jose succeeded in getting the city to do a job evaluation study. It showed, to choose some examples, that nurses earned $9120 per year less than fire truck mechanics and that legal secretaries made $7288 less than equipment mechanics (Blum 1991, pp. 82–83). In 1985, the California School Employees Association complained that school librarians and teaching assistants (female jobs) were paid less than custodians and groundskeepers (male jobs) (Steinberg 1990). To take yet another example, in recent years the city of Philadelphia was paying practical nurses (mostly women) less than gardeners (mostly men) (Steinberg 1990). These are not atypical examples. In addition, one is hard-pressed to come up with a single example of a male job paying less than a female job that reasonable people would find comparable in skill, effort, or difficult working conditions. Nor are these differences in pay a result of men averaging more years of experience than women, since in the above comparisons of employers' policies regarding pay levels in the various jobs, a constant level of experience was assumed. (For example, this can be done by comparing starting salaries.)

Recently, the concept of comparable worth or pay equity has been applied to issues of discrimination on the basis of race or ethnicity as well as gender. If a job in a particular organization is filled largely with African Americans or Hispanics, does the pay level tend to be lower than is commensurate with the job's skill level and other demands? We can examine whether the racial or ethnic composition of a job has an effect on its pay level just as we can examine whether its sex composition has this effect. In academic theorizing, as well as in legislation and litigation about *hiring* discrimination, issues of racial discrimination were raised first. They were later extended to sex discrimination. Where comparable worth is concerned, things have happened in the reverse order: The issue was first raised with respect to sex discrimination and has more recently been examined with respect to racial discrimination. In this book, I focus exclusively on comparable worth as an issue of gender discrimination. However, the reader should bear in mind that analogous questions can be raised with respect to race and ethnicity. (See Jacobs and Steinberg 1990a, note 12, on studies that have assessed effects of minority composition on wages. See also National Committee on Pay Equity 1987.)

This book is an interdisciplinary examination of the issue of comparable worth. This chapter sets the stage for the discussion by providing a sketch of the situation of men and women in paid employment in the United States. Twentieth-century trends and contemporary patterns in women's and men's employment, occupations, and pay are described, drawing from research by sociologists, economists, and psychologists. Chapter 2 compares various theories of labor markets from economics and sociology, with attention to how each view explains gender inequality in jobs and earnings, and how it treats the issue of comparable worth. Chapter 3 presents an empirical analysis of aggregate occupational data from the 1980 census that demonstrates the tendency of predominantly female occupations to pay less than predominantly male occupations, even after numerous measures of skill demands, working conditions, and market conditions are statistically controlled. It also demonstrates the penalty for doing nurturant work, a finding I interpret as evidence of indirect gender bias in wage setting. Chapter 4 examines methods of and findings from job evaluation, a technique used to evaluate jobs and assess comparable worth within a single organization. Chapter 5 explains the current legal status of comparable worth in the federal courts. Chapter 6 examines normative debates about gender inequality and comparable worth, drawing on social, political, and economic philosophies, including feminist theories. Finally, Chapter 7 takes the reader through the policy debates surrounding comparable worth, and presents my own view on these controversial issues.

Views of comparable worth hinge, in part, on empirical evidence. Yet such evidence is interpreted differently through the "lenses" of different theoretical models. Views of comparable worth are also affected by normative positions, by values. Although I am a sociologist by training, in this book I also draw upon the disciplines of economics, psychology, law, and philosophy, as well as on interdisciplinary feminist perspectives. Thus, I hope to present a view of the complex and controversial issue of comparable worth that is informed by debates over evidence, theories, and values.

The remainder of this chapter sets the stage for examining comparable worth by summarizing research findings on the situation of women and men in paid employment. For the most part, I will draw upon research from the United States. The situation is similar in other industrial countries, albeit with some variations (Rosenfeld and Kalleberg 1990; Brinton 1988; Blau and Ferber 1986; Roos 1985). This chapter discusses the increases in women's employment in recent decades, the tendency of women to be clustered into a limited number of occupations, changes in the degree of occupational sex segregation, and changes in the sex gap in pay.

II.   Increasing Employment Among Women

Some women have always worked outside the home for pay in addition to working within the home. One often sees the term *working women* used to differentiate women who work for pay from full-time homemakers. This is misleading, of course, since homemakers work as well. To avoid this misleading juxtaposition, I will use the term *employment* or *labor force participation* to refer to paid work typically done outside the home.

A.   Which Women Are Employed?

Women are more likely to be employed if they are single, have fewer children, are black, have considerable education and other job skills, have high potential earnings, or have a husband with low earnings (Killingsworth and Heckman 1986; Desai and Waite 1991; O'Neill 1981). These are each "net" effects, that is, differences that are observed when other things are "held constant" via statistical controls. Yet, since some of these factors are negatively correlated with each other, real women often experience conflicting pulls. For example, consider a woman with a college education, three children, and a husband who is a well-paid manager. The fact that she is married, has children, and has a husband with relatively high earnings all mitigate against her employment. However, her college education increases the earnings she could make in a job, as well as her nondomestic interests, and thus makes it more likely that she will be employed. Marital homogamy, the tendency to marry persons from a similar class and educational background, means that women whose high education and potential earnings mitigate in favor of employment typically have husbands with relatively high earnings, a factor mitigating against employment.

Today, many women remain employed during pregnancy and return to their jobs immediately or within a few weeks or months of birth. Relatively continuous employment around a birth is more common among women who are well educated, are in more skilled jobs, and have higher wages, perhaps because the financial loss from leaving their jobs would be greater for such women (Desai and Waite 1991). However, continuous participation around a birth is also more common among women with more economic need—single mothers or women whose husbands have low earnings (Desai and Waite 1991). Continuous participation is also aided by the availability of a more flexible work schedule or by working in an occupation containing more women with young children (Desai and Waite 1991).

B. Trends in Women's Employment

It was traditionally believed that many women entered and left the labor force numerous times during their lives. Recent research that traces the employment histories of birth cohorts has challenged this view. (A birth cohort is a group of people born in the same year.) This research shows that, while many women left employment at the time of marriage or a first birth, after marriage, every birth cohort in this century has had continuous increases across time in the proportion of women employed (Goldin 1990, p. 22). This implies that while many women spent some years out of the labor force, if they stayed employed or reentered employment after marriage, they generally stayed employed fairly continuously. The reentries were typically after a period of child-rearing. What has been changing most is how many women enter the labor force at all and how early those who leave for childrearing reenter to stay (Goldin 1990).

The proportion of U.S. women who are employed has increased steadily since the early 1800s (Goldin 1990). More and more women have moved from working exclusively in the home to working both in their homes and for pay. As Table 1.1 shows, 19% of women were in the labor force (i.e., either employed or looking for a job) in 1890. By 1950 this figure was up to 30%. It was 35% in 1960, 42% in 1970, 51% by 1980, and 56% by 1987. The only time in this century that a decline in the proportion of women employed has ever occurred was right after World War II.

Table 1.1. shows increases in the proportion employed for both white and black women since 1950. However, the black and white trends differ in that black women did not increase their employment rate between 1890 and 1950; it was already very high (40%) in 1890. As Table 1.1 shows, black women have had higher employment rates than white women during every period, although white women had nearly caught up by 1987.

Married women with small children are still the group with the lowest employment rates. Yet this group has shown the fastest rate of increase, and now has participation rates only slightly lower than women's overall average. Consider, for example, married women who have at least one child under the age of 3. Table 1.1 shows that in 1960, only 15% of such women were in the labor force, compared to 35% of women overall. In 1975, 33% of such women were in the labor force, compared to

Table 1.1. Labor Force Participation[1] of Women by Marital Status, Presence of Youngest Child, and Race, 1890–1987

| | All Women | | | White | | Black[2] | | |
| | | Married[4] | | | | | | Hispanic[3] |
	Total	Total	With child under 3	Total	Married[4]	Total	Married[4]	Total
1890	18.9	4.6	NA	16.3	2.5	39.7	22.5	NA
1950	29.5	23.8	NA	28.5	20.7	37.8	31.8	NA
1960	35.1	30.5	15.3	34.2	29.8	42.7	40.5	NA
1970	41.6	40.8	25.8	40.9	38.5	47.3	50.0	NA
1975	46.3	44.4	32.7	45.9	43.5	48.8	54.0	43.0
1980	51.1	50.2	41.1	50.9	49.3	53.1	59.3	47.4
1985	54.5	54.2	50.5	54.1	53.0	56.5	62.4	49.3
1987	56.0	55.8	54.2	55.7	55.1	58.0	65.1	52.0

Sources: Goldin 1990 (Table 2.1); U.S. Department of Labor 1987b (Tables 1 and 3), 1988, 1989 (Table 6); Lueck, Orr, and O'Connell 1982 (Table A-2); Taeuber 1991 (Table B1–5).
Notes:

[1] Numbers given are percentage of women in the labor force. The labor force consists of those who are employed and those looking for a job. Those out of the labor force include homemakers, students, the retired, and discouraged workers (those who want a job but have given up looking). NA, data not available.

[2] Data for 1890 through 1970 are for all nonwhites rather than for blacks.

[3] Includes all Hispanics, regardless of race. "Hispanic" is a diverse category, including persons whose ancestry is Mexican, Central American, Cuban, and Puerto Rican, and including citizens and noncitizens. Hispanics are also included in "white" and "black" categories according to their race. Figures for Hispanics by marital status not available in government documents.

[4] "Married" includes only married women with husband present.

46% of women overall. However, by 1987, the figure for women with children under 3 was up to 54%, only slightly less than the 56% of all women who were in the labor force.

One might wonder whether the dramatic increase in employment among mothers of young children is mainly an influx into part-time jobs. For the most part, this is not the case. To be sure, mothers are more likely than other women to be employed part-time. For example, in 1988 about one third of women with children had part-time jobs, while only about one fifth of all employed women worked part-time (Barrett 1991). Yet much of the increase in the employment of mothers has been in full-time jobs. This can be inferred from the fact that the proportion of employed women whose jobs are part-time has been relatively constant at around 20% since the early 1960s (Barrett 1991), even while the proportion of employed women who have small children has gone up dramatically.

Perhaps it is surprising, but very few women use part-time employment as a transition between full-time homemaking and full-time employment. It is much more common to move from homemaking to a full-time job (Blank 1989). For some, part-time work is an occasional alternative to full-time employment; for a few it occasionally punctuates nonemployment (Blank 1989). Few women use part-time employment as a transition because part-time jobs are largely dead-end; employers seldom structure jobs to facilitate smooth transitions from part-time jobs to attractive full-time jobs.

C. Explanations of Increases in Women's Employment

What explains the dramatic increase in women's employment since World War II? To examine this, let us separate various specific explanations into two broad claims: (1) those asserting women's increased economic need to be employed, and (2) those asserting their increased opportunities for jobs and higher wages.

Increased Economic Need. Do more women than ever have an economic need to be employed? Yes. This is true in that a growing proportion of women are single or divorced, and more of these women than ever have children. Especially since 1970, the divorce rate has increased, the average age at marriage has gone up, and the proportion of out-of-wedlock births has increased for both white women and women of color (England and Farkas 1986). If we look at families that include children, the proportion of families with no adult male stayed fairly near 10% from 1940 through 1970, but thereafter it began to increase, reaching 16% by 1982 (Norwood 1982). These facts explain some of the increase in

women's employment in terms of economic need. However, they cannot explain the increase among *married* women with husbands present,
except to the extent that more married women than previously are
aware of the risk of divorce and invest in job experience as a form of
insurance (Burkhauser and Duncan 1989).

Can the increase in employment among *married* women be explained
by increased economic need for two incomes? The answer depends, in
part, upon what we mean by "need." The question of what income a
family needs is, at least in part, subjective. However, assuming *any*
constant definition of need, only if the real (i.e., inflation-adjusted) incomes of men have gone down over time can the economic need for a
second paycheck be said to have gone up. Table 1.2 presents data on
men's income. "Income" includes interest, dividends, and government
transfer payments, rather than just earnings from employment. The
figures also include all men, not only those employed full-time year-
round. Since these figures include men who had spells of unemployment, they will show men's incomes going down if annual earnings go
down because more men are unemployed part of the year or because the
average duration of unemployment goes up, as well as if wage rates go
down. Table 1.2 shows that, on average, men's incomes were going up
throughout the 1950s, 1960s, and early 1970s. Since 1973, however,
men's incomes have gone down. They have rebounded since the early
1980s, but by 1988 had only returned to their late 1960s levels. These
trends apply to both white and black men, though in any given year
black men's earnings have been lower than those of white men. (For
discussion of trends in men's earnings, see Levy 1987, 1988; Burtless
1990.) If decreasing male income causes increasing need for wives' employment, one cannot argue that such need was increasing in the 1950s,
1960s, early 1970s, or since 1983, but only between 1973 and 1983.

The reader might question whether increases in the percentage of
earnings paid in taxes would alter this conclusion. Based on data presented elsewhere (Steurle and Wilson 1987; Steurle forthcoming) regarding families at the median income, I have calculated that the percentage
of income paid in federal income tax plus Social Security tax (excluding
the portion paid by the employer) was 7.6% in 1955, 10.8% in 1960,
14.2% in 1970, 17.5% in 1980, and 17.1% in 1990. The increases in federal
taxes in the 1950s and 1960s were not more than increases in male
earnings, and federal taxes have not increased in the 1980s. Thus, the
conclusion that men's incomes have been going up continuously except
between about 1973 and 1983 holds even when federal taxes are considered.

Since 1950, women's employment has gone up continuously, while
men's income went down only between about 1973 to 1983. In sum,

Table 1.2. Median Income of Men by Race: 1950–1988[1]

Year	Total	White	Black[2]	Hispanic[3]
1950	12,615	13,298	7,221	NA
1955	14,823	15,644	8,232	NA
1960	16,306	17,169	9,032	NA
1964	17,734	18,836	10,678	NA
1965	18,864	19,867	10,692	NA
1970	20,337	21,376	12,675	NA
1971	20,164	21,139	12,607	NA
1972	21,085	22,115	13,395	NA
1973	21,465	22,522	13,623	NA
1974	20,281	21,246	13,164	15,461
1975	19,467	20,450	12,226	14,902
1976	19,597	20,660	12,439	14,658
1977	19,762	20,699	12,283	15,221
1978	19,841	20,781	12,449	15,205
1979	19,194	20,051	12,412	14,455
1980	17,989	19,135	11,498	13,867
1981	17,534	18,605	11,063	13,278
1982	17,101	18,080	10,835	12,836
1983	17,414	18,320	10,714	12,893
1984	17,762	18,749	10,757	12,640
1985	18,473	19,494	11,681	12,571
1986	18,473	19,494	11,681	12,447
1987	18,522	19,687	11,679	12,736
1988	18,908	19,959	12,044	13,030

Source: Hensen 1990.
Notes:
[1] All income is in constant 1988 dollars. Thus, these figures are adjusted for changes in the cost of living (as measured by the Consumer Price Index) such that they reflect real trends in pretax purchasing power. NA, data not available.
[2] This category includes black males for 1970–1988. Before 1970, the category includes all nonwhite males.
[3] Includes all Hispanics, regardless of race. Hispanics are also included in "white" and "black" categories according to their race.

while the decade after 1973 saw increases in economic need for a second paycheck, such increases in need have *not* been a *consistent* trend for married women. Thus they cannot be the main explanation of the *consistent* increases in women's employment.

Yet most people I talk to have a clear perception that, in some meaningful way that is missed in the above figures, since the mid-1970s couples have needed two paychecks more than they did in times past.

There is a way to reconcile the kernel of truth in this perception with the figures presented above. My reconciliation hinges on an assumption about how people perceive well-being that comes from research in behavioral economics and social psychology to be discussed in Chapter 2. There is an asymmetry between how gains and losses are perceived. As a result, a decrease in one's income of $5000 reduces one's sense of well-being more than an increase in income over the same income range increases the sense of well-being.

To illustrate, consider the situation of a couple with a nonemployed wife whose husband earns $30,000 a year, but suffers a loss in income of $10,000 due to conditions in the economy at large. Perhaps he worked in an auto plant that closed and the best job he can now find is a non-unionized job paying $20,000. In response to this loss, the wife finds a job that pays exactly the $10,000 that was lost, after expenses such as day care. Later, suppose that the man gets an offer of a better job that will restore him to his original earnings of $30,000 (in inflation-adjusted dollars). The couple had previously felt that this was an adequate income—perhaps not as much as they would like, but high enough to make them decide the wife would stay home and care for their young children. Based on this we would predict that the wife will quit her job when the husband begins his new job. But the data in Tables 1.1 and 1.2 have shown us that when men's incomes rebound after a loss, women's employment does not decrease as the "economic need" thesis would predict. So our task is to understand why our hypothetical wife does not quit even when her husband's earnings had returned to their former level. This could be because she has grown to like her job, but that is not the point I want to emphasize here. If she quits the job, their family income will be exactly where it was before she joined the labor force. However, the asymmetry in how losses and gains affect perceived well-being implies that the original loss of $10,000 lowered well-being more than the rebound of $10,000 increased well-being. Thus, the sense of well-being still dictates the wife's employment. If losses are perceived as larger than gains of the same amount, then permanent increases in women's employment will be spawned in periods when men have even temporary decreases in earnings.

Similarly, the asymmetry in the perception of losses and gains suggests that permanent increases in women's employment will result when earnings inequality among men goes up, even in the absence of declines in men's average earnings. Increased inequality in men's earnings can result from earnings of men in the lower portion of the distribution going down while the earnings of men toward the top of the distribution go up. The asymmetry principle above predicts increased employment among women from this trend. That is, the *losses* in male earnings in the families at the lower end of the distribution will do more to increase their wives' employment than the *gains* in male earnings in the families at the higher end of the distribution will do to lower their wives' employment. Since men's earnings have become substantially more unequal in the last two decades (Levy 1987; Burtless 1990), this may explain some of the increase in women's employment.

Finally, this principle regarding an asymmetry in how gains and losses are perceived helps explain how in recent decades the increases in wives' employment before childbearing make it likely that more wives will continue employment after childbearing than would have been the case in the absence of the prechild employment. Today, unlike in the 1950s and 1960s, most women are employed for several years, if not more, between marriage and the birth of the couple's first child. Consider the example of a woman whose potential wage is $20,000 per year. If she has been employed before having children, she experiences non-employment after childbirth as a loss of $20,000 per year. Had she not been employed before the birth, employment after the birth would be perceived as a gain of $20,000 per year. Since the loss is felt more saliently than the gain of the same amount, women who are employed before childrearing are more likely to be employed afterward than are women who were not employed before the birth, even when the two groups have the same potential postbirth earnings and the same husbands' earnings. Thus, the trend to later childbearing creates an increase in women's employment after childbearing over and above its effect via the higher potential wage of women with more experience.

Increased Opportunities. What about the second explanation of increases in women's employment? Is there evidence that women's employment has increased because of increased opportunities for jobs and higher wages? Since World War II, jobs that had long been sex-typed as "women's work" showed greater increases in labor demand than did jobs overall (Oppenheimer 1970). This growth resulted from a restructuring of the economy that produced declining employment shares in agriculture and manufacturing and increases in service industries (such as retail sales, health, banking, and restaurants) and in service occupations (such as secretary) (Glass, Tienda, and Smith 1988). This has provided women with increased opportunities for employment.

At the same time, real (i.e., inflation-adjusted) wage increases have made the rewards of employment greater. To put it another way, using economist's terminology, the opportunity cost of (i.e., what is forgone by) being a homemaker has increased. Table 1.3 shows that among full-time workers, women's real (i.e., inflation-adjusted) earnings were increasing in the 1950s, 1960s, and early 1970s. This was true for both white and black women, although in any given year black women

Table 1.3. Median Annual Earnings of Women and Men Employed Full-Time, Year-Round, by Race and Hispanic Origin, 1955–1987[1]

	White			Black			Hispanic[2]		
	Women	Men	Ratio[3]	Women	Men	Ratio	Women	Men	Ratio
1955	12,110	21,431	0.565	6,220	11,292	0.551	NA[4]	NA	NA
1960	12,988	21,431	0.606	8,804	14,165	0.622	NA	NA	NA
1965	14,155	24,468	0.579	9,612	15,367	0.625	NA	NA	NA
1970	16,187	27,623	0.586	13,637	19,409	0.703	NA	NA	NA
1975	16,323	27,918	0.585	16,030	21,416	0.748	NA	NA	NA
1976	16,719	28,487	0.587	15,737	20,914	0.752	NA	NA	NA
1977	16,642	28,852	0.577	15,848	20,707	0.765	NA	NA	NA
1978	16,955	28,502	0.595	15,855	22,549	0.703	NA	NA	NA
1979	16,624	28,144	0.591	15,454	21,218	0.728	NA	NA	NA
1980	16,142	27,200	0.593	15,055	19,138	0.787	13,637	19,021	0.717
1981	15,381	26,473	0.581	14,298	18,730	0.763	13,646	18,726	0.729
1982	16,310	26,186	0.623	14,577	18,598	0.784	13,384	18,362	0.729
1983	16,741	26,348	0.635	14,860	18,786	0.791	13,578	18,246	0.744
1984	17,040	27,162	0.627	15,357	18,537	0.828	14,253	18,790	0.759
1985	17,404	27,131	0.641	15,407	18,977	0.812	14,279	18,315	0.780
1986	17,721	27,582	0.642	15,507	19,447	0.797	14,706	17,625	0.834
1987	17,775	27,468	0.647	16,211	19,385	0.836	14,893	17,872	0.833

Source: Figart, Hartmann, Hoytt, and Outtz 1989 (Tables 3 and 4).
Notes:
[1] Earnings are in constant 1987 dollars. Thus, these figures are adjusted for changes in the cost of living (as measured by the Consumer Price Index) such that they reflect real trends in before-tax purchasing power. NA, data not available.
[2] Includes all Hispanics, regardless of race. Hispanics are also included in "white" or "black" categories according to their race.
[3] Ratio of women's annual earnings to men's annual earnings.

earned less than white women. These wage increases for women were fueled by general growth in the economy that provided increases to men as well. During these periods, the rewards of employment went up for women, and this brought into or kept in the labor force an increasing proportion of white and black women (Butz and Ward 1979).

III. The Sex Segregation of Jobs

In the United States, as in most societies, men and women generally hold different jobs. If we use the approximately 500 detailed occupational categories used by the U.S. Census Bureau as a benchmark, approximately 60% of men or women would have to change occupations in order to achieve integration (Blau 1988). "Integration" here refers to a situation in which each occupation has the same sex mix as the labor force as a whole. If we were to use a more detailed classification of job titles and look within firms, we would see segregation to be even more pervasive than these figures indicate (Bielby and Baron 1984). This is partly because some occupations are filled exclusively by men in some firms but exclusively by women in others. For example, many restaurants have either all males or all females waiting tables. Thus, for this occupation, the level of integration implied by national data is misleading as an indicator of how often men and women really work together in the same job within a restaurant. More segregation is seen within firms than in national occupational data for a second reason as well. Organizations often employ more detailed categories than the census categories. Take, for example, a census occupation like physician. The 1980 census shows this to be 14% female. But if we were to use most any clinic's or hospital's more detailed classification by department, we would see that certain specialties, such as pediatrics and psychiatry, contain more than 14% females, while others, such as surgeons, contain fewer (American Medical Association 1986).

Another type of segregation is by industry or firm. The industry one works in is defined by the good or service sold by the firm one works for. For example, one can work in the auto industry or the restaurant industry. Workers in all occupations are included within the industry. Thus, managers, secretaries, production workers, and janitors who work for General Motors are all classified as in the auto industry. Women are more likely than men to work in small firms and in industries with labor-intensive production and relatively low levels of unionization and profit. Yet sex segregation by firms and industries is nowhere near as pervasive as segregation by occupation. After all, most firms and certainly most industries have both male and female workers. In contrast, some occupations (e.g., nursing, secretarial work, plumbing) are filled almost exclusively by one sex or the other.

Segregation means that few jobs are substantially integrated by sex. If sex had no relation to the job one were in, we would expect the sex ratio of each job to approximate the sex ratio of the labor force as a whole, which was slightly over 40% female in 1980. Thus, one way to look at integrated jobs would be to look at what occupations are between, say, 30 and 50% female. According to the 1980 census, out of 503 occupations, this included only 87 occupations. Examples of these integrated occupations are personnel managers, accountants, buyers, physicians' assistants, authors, artists, shoe salespersons, door-to-door salespersons, bartenders, book binders, short-order cooks, ushers, and tailors.

A. What Kinds of Jobs Do Men and Women Hold?

Occupations filled mainly with women include maids, assembly line workers in the electronics industry, clerks in retail stores, secretaries and other clerical workers, teachers (at the grade school through high school level), nurses, real estate agents, social workers, and librarians. Men predominate in the highest status professions (such as doctor and law- yer), in higher levels of management, in blue-collar crafts (such as plumber, carpenter, and electrician), in assembly line jobs in durable manufacturing (such as autos, steel, and tires), and in jobs involving outdoor labor. One can see from these lists that women's jobs are not usually *less* skilled than men's, but women's and men's jobs generally require *different kinds* of skills. There are both male and female jobs at both low and high levels of education. For example, hairdressers (mostly women) and bus drivers (mostly men) each average 13 years of school- ing. Examples of male and female jobs at higher levels of education include electrical engineers and librarians, each averaging 17 years of education. (These examples are taken from the 1980 census data used in Chapter 3.)

Although women's and men's jobs require approximately equal aver- age amounts of formal education received prior to entering the job, women's jobs typically provide less on-the-job training (Corcoran and Duncan 1979; Barron, Black, and Loewenstein 1990). Thus, as the senior- ity of workers increases, women's jobs may *become* less skilled relative to men's.

Female jobs are also attached to shorter mobility ladders than male jobs, thus reducing women's possibilities for promotion (C. Smith 1979; Rosenbaum 1980; Bielby and Baron 1984; DiPrete and Soule 1988). Relat- ed to this is the fact that very few female jobs involve supervision of other workers (Jaffee 1989; Wolf and Fligstein 1979; Hill 1980; Ward and Mueller 1985), especially male workers (Bergmann 1986).

How compatible are women's jobs with family responsibilities? One might think that women would choose jobs most compatible with such responsibilities. To a limited extent this is true. For example, more men than women are concentrated in jobs requiring out-of-town travel, working evenings, or unusually long hours. However, even here there are exceptions. For example, nurses are often required to work eve- nings, nights, and weekends. Overall, on other dimensions, it does not appear that women's jobs are any more compatible with family respon- sibilities than men's. Indeed, one national survey (Glass 1990) found more men than women reporting flexibility of schedules, more unsuper- vised break time, and more paid sick leave and vacation, all of which would be helpful for a parent.

Black women, like white women, generally work in predominantly female occupations. Race discrimination and poverty have limited black women's options even more than those of white women. Thus, more black than white women fill jobs such as maid and nurse's aide. However, much of the convergence between black and white women's earnings during the 1960s and 1970s (seen in Table 1.3) came from black women moving into secretarial work as well as the professions of teaching, nursing, and social work. These jobs had previously been dominated by white women. However, black women in these jobs are more likely than white women to work for the government (local, state, or federal), making their jobs particularly vulnerable to budgetary cuts in this era of fiscal austerity (Higginbotham 1987).

B. Trends in Segregation

If we use the census detailed occupational categories for calculation, the extent of occupational sex segregation among nonfarm occupations declined very slowly and unevenly throughout the century until about 1970 (England 1981; Jacobs 1989a). Starting about 1970, a much faster decline has occurred (Beller 1984; Jacobs 1989a; Blau 1988). Most of the decline since 1970 came from women entering male jobs, rather than men entering female jobs.

The 1970s saw an increasing number of women becoming accountants, bank officers, financial managers, and janitors. These changes contributed heavily to the decline in segregation. Other male occupations that increased their representation of women by at least 10 percentage points during the 1970s include computer programmers, personnel and labor relations professionals, pharmacists, draftspersons, radio operators, public relations professionals, office managers, buyers and purchasing agents, insurance agents, real estate agents, postal clerks, stock clerks, ticket agents, typesetters, bus drivers, animal caretakers, and bartenders (Beller 1984). The decline in segregation was much greater among younger than among older cohorts. The decline was greater in professional occupations than in blue-collar occupations. The overall decline in occupational sex segregation in the 1970s was as great for African Americans as for whites (Beller 1984).

The decline in occupational segregation by sex continued in the 1980s, though at a pace somewhat slower than in the 1970s (Blau 1988). In general, the same jobs that saw large influxes of women in the 1970s did so in the 1980s as well. Examples are computer operators, insurance adjusters, animal caretakers, typesetters, personnel workers, vocational counselors, and public relations workers. There was little integration of women into the skilled blue-collar crafts such as plumbing or carpentry, or into durable goods manufacturing jobs (e.g., auto or steel workers), just as there had been little entry of women into these fields in the 1970s. These facts provide a hint about the reasons for the slowing of desegregation. First, occupations that, for whatever reasons, were the easiest targets for women's entry desegregated first, leaving the "hard cases" to move more slowly later. Second, since the influx of women continues to be largest in those occupations where it began, some initially male jobs have now "tipped" and become disproportionately female. Thus, further increases in the proportion of women in these jobs increase rather than decrease segregation. Examples of such occupations are public relations professionals, personnel and labor relations professionals, and real estate agents.

Thus far the discussion of trends in segregation has been based on research using the detailed occupational categories employed by the Census Bureau. We can think of jobs as specific occupations within a specific establishment (and hence, a specific industry). Such jobs would be the most meaningful categories across which to compute a measure of occupational sex segregation. Unfortunately, such data are not available for the economy as a whole for even one year, much less a number of years. However, as discussed above, we know that national occupational data understate the full extent of job segregation, since men and women in mixed-sex occupations often work in different industries and firms or in different subspecialties within the occupation. But what about *trends* in the sex segregation of these more detailed categories of jobs? Unfortunately, we have little information on this.

One cautionary note to the conclusion that *job* segregation declined in the 1970s comes from case studies of formerly male occupations into which there has been a large influx of women since 1970. In some cases there has been occupational desegregation but not job desegregation. That is, women and men in a newly integrated occupation may often work for different establishments, sometimes in different industries (Reskin and Roos 1990). For example, bus driving has also become integrated, but most of the women work for school districts while men still retain most of the better-paid jobs as city bus drivers. To take another example, the occupation bakers has become integrated as grocery stores have started hiring women for newly created in-store jobs using automated processes to make cakes and cookies. Yet men still dominate the less automated and more highly paid tasks of making bread in nonstore settings. Women are also becoming systems analysts. Yet in this occupation women often work in hospitals, banking, and insurance, while men are more likely to work in manufacturing industries. In each of these cases, women have gone into a formerly male occupation, but into a less desirable subpart of it, at least in terms of pay. Thus, even though an occupation has been integrated, when we use more detailed and industry-specific categories, we see that a new female "ghetto" has been created.

In summary, what can we conclude regarding trends in segregation? Occupational classifications measure the function or task people perform. Occupational segregation increased and decreased sporadically throughout the century, with a very modest net decline between 1900 and 1970. There was a faster pace of decline during the 1970s, and there has been a continued though slowed decline in segregation since 1980. We do not have data on whether segregation in jobs (defined by cross-classifying more detailed job titles and firms) has also decreased since 1970. Doubts about this are fueled by evidence that some of the occupational integration has led to new patterns of segregation within occupations. My conjecture is that some desegregation in jobs *is* occurring, particularly at the managerial and professional level, and will continue, but that the pace of desegregation of jobs is slower than that of occupations.

C. Explanations of Levels and Trends in Segregation

Why are some jobs filled by women, some by men, and few integrated by sex? What explains why levels of segregation change over time? As a way to organize research on these questions, I will divide the factors affecting segregation into those involving *choices* on the part of those entering jobs, and those involving *constraints* faced by job entrants. In making this distinction, we must remember that today's choices may be affected by past constraints, and vice versa. For example, parents or teachers may encourage different job choices for young women and men. This sex-differentiated reinforcement is a constraint that may lead to different job *choices* at the point one declares a college major or applies for a job. The emphasis in this chapter is not on which theory each factor is compatible with. Often a single factor plays a part in several theories, and theories are not my concern in this chapter. (For discussion of how this research forms evidence for particular theories, see Chapter 2.)

Choices. Segregation results, in part, because men and women choose different jobs. But why are these choices different? Some researchers argue that the choices are rational responses to the division of labor by sex in the family. In this view, women choose jobs compatible with their family responsibilities. I see this as playing a relatively minor role in job choices, since, as discussed above, the jobs women hold are generally not more accommodating to parenting than are men's jobs.

A variant of this argument sees the division of labor by sex in the family to cause women's employment to be intermittent, which leads women to choose jobs that maximize lifetime earnings, *conditional* on this intermittent employment. If jobs that provide much on-the-job training have steeper wage trajectories (i.e., higher rates of return to seniority) but lower starting wages, women may avoid such jobs because the gains from steeper wage gains do not outweigh the losses from the lower starting wages. Research on this question is discussed in Chapter 2 as it bears on the ability of human capital theory to explain segregation. In my view, this view is largely incorrect. Consistent with the view, women *are* concentrated in jobs that provide relatively low amounts of on-the-job training (Corcoran and Duncan 1979; Barron et al. 1990), and female jobs do have lower returns to seniority than male jobs (Rosenbaum 1980; Filer 1983). However, no research has ever demonstrated the higher starting wages that are the purported advantage of jobs offering less training. Given this, it is hard to see how women's efforts to maximize lifetime earnings would lead them to choose female jobs.[1]

Thus, if the job choices of men and women differ, I believe these differences are sustained by lifelong socialization that leads men and women to find different jobs interesting, respectable, of value, or consistent with their gendered identities. This is consistent with the view I develop in this book—that it is much more accurate to see men and women in jobs with *different skills,* than with *different amounts* of skill. Preferences for certain kinds of work entail preferences for exercising certain kinds of skills. The socialization that forms these proclivities begins in childhood and continues throughout adulthood. It operates through reinforcement patterns, role models, cognitive learning, sex-segregated networks of peers, and other processes.

These differences in interests can be seen early in life. Even preschool and elementary school children express sex-typed occupational goals (Marini and Brinton 1984). However, the occupational aspirations of boys are more highly sex typed than those of girls (Marini and Greenberger 1978).

Are these differences in job interests a reflection of broader differences in values? Some evidence supports this. Studies decades ago found that males claimed to place more value on money in choosing a job. Studies attempting to assess changes in the job dimensions valued by young adults have found surprisingly little convergence between the sexes (Lueptow 1980; Herzog 1982; Peng et al. 1981; Tittle 1981). Lueptow (1980) compared the occupational values of graduating seniors in 1961 and 1975 and found that in both years men claimed to place more value than did women on status, money, freedom from supervision, and potential for leadership. In both years, the study found that women placed more value on working with people, helping others, using their abilities, and being creative. Other surveys have shown that men place a greater value on autonomy, authority, and promotion possibilities than do women (Brenner and Tomkiewicz 1979; Murray and Atkinson 1981; Peng, Fetters, and Kolstad 1981; Herzog 1982), and these job dimensions have been found to affect men's job satisfactions to a greater extent than women's (Glenn and Weaver 1982; Crane and Hodson 1984; Murray and Atkinson 1981). There is also some evidence that men value taking risks more than women (Walker, Tausky, and Oliver 1982; Subich, Barrett, Donerspike, and Alexander 1989).

Yet we must be cautious in inferring from these studies that sex differences in occupational values explain segregation. Some of the studies surveyed adults already holding jobs. Thus, it is possible that jobs affected values as much as values affected the job chosen. The studies also show some conflicting findings. For example, while a number of surveys find that men claim to value pay more than women, one study found no such difference (Walker et al. 1982), and some studies have found pay to have a greater influence on women's job satisfaction than on men's (Crane and Hodson 1984).

It is also important not to assume that these sex differences show men to be more career or achievement oriented than women. Women may be equally career oriented but focused on different skills or values. One example of such bias in interpretation appears in an article by Brenner and Tomkiewicz (1979), who asked college students to rate job characteristics in terms of their importance to them. Men were found to place more value on income, opportunity to take risks, and supervisory authority. Women placed more value on good relations with coworkers, opportunity to develop knowledge and skills on the job, and intellectual stimulation. The authors conclude from these findings that women give less importance to careers than men. This is certainly not an obvious conclusion from the findings; one might regard an orientation toward continued learning of knowledge and skills, on which *women* placed more emphasis, as the best indicator in the survey of the sort of careerism we would expect employers to care about.

A preference for a sex-typical job does not always reflect values, tastes, or dispositions toward the kind of work in these jobs. It may rather reflect a preference for working with members of one's own sex or for doing work labeled male or female regardless of the content of the work. There is evidence of this sort of preference, especially among males. One experiment (Heilman 1979) divided high school students into two groups that received different information on the projected sex composition of the occupations of lawyer and architect. Students ran-

domly assigned to the first group were told that these jobs were projected to have a high percentage of males in them in coming years, while
those randomly assigned to the second group were told the jobs were
projected to contain a much higher percentage of females. The boys told
that the jobs were projected to have more women in them reported less
interest in going into those jobs. The opposite effect occurred for girls,
although the effect was stronger for the boys.

In my view, gender role socialization and sex-typed choices of jobs
clearly have some role in segregation. But what is their role in the desegregation observed since about 1970? There is evidence that occupational
preferences have shifted substantially among high school students (Marini and Brinton 1984). A decline in sex differences in college majors
occurred during this period as well (Beller 1984; Jacobs 1985, 1989b). Of
course, some of these shifts could be *responses* to changed constraints.
This is suggested by the evidence reviewed above that specific occupational choices shifted more than underlying occupational values. Yet
preferences were undoubtedly shifting for other reasons as well. However, these changes in preferences are probably *not* explained by changing patterns of childhood socialization, since the women who started
these changes in the 1970s were young children in the very traditional
1950s. Thus, to say that socialization is a factor in segregation does *not*
imply that changing patterns of childhood socialization is the only way
for desegregation to occur.

*Constraints Posed by Employers, Male Workers, and Institutional Prac-
tices.* One sort of constraint faced by those seeking jobs is discrimination by employers. Our concern here is not with theories of discrimination, which are reviewed in Chapter 2, but with evidence about whether
hiring discrimination exists. Discrimination in hiring, placement, and
promotion is suggested by experimental studies that present randomly
assigned groups of managers or prospective managers with resumes
that differ only in the male or female names on them. Such studies often
find that men are preferred in typically male jobs (Rosen and Jerdee
1974, 1978; Levinson 1975; Rosen 1982). Sociologists Bielby and Baron
(1986) also found substantial evidence of discrimination in the statements of California manufacturers about their hiring practices.
Milkman's (1987) historical study showed that although many women
went into previously male jobs during World War II, this shifted rather
than eradicated boundaries between men and women's work; employers redivided jobs such that each job was done only by women or
only by men. Women were laid off after the war. As new hires were
made, employers refused to rehire women in the traditionally male jobs
they had held during the war, even when this violated union seniority

rules, and even when the women had more training in the job than the men newly returned from the war.

Employers may discriminate because of beliefs about sex differences in skills, because of values about the roles men and women should play, to create antagonisms that minimize workers' solidarity, or to avoid the disruption that occurs when male workers are faced with a woman entering "their" jobs.

Some women anticipate discrimination and alter their "choices" accordingly. Discrepancies between young women's aspirations and their expectations about future jobs are evidence that women anticipate a constraint. Marini and Greenberger (1978) found that girls expected to end up in occupations that averaged 75% female, but aspired to occupations that averaged 66% female. In contrast they found no difference between the average percentage female of the occupations high school boys said they expected to work in and those to which they aspired. Another survey of high school students showed that 34% of girls but only 22% of boys believed that their sex would prevent them from getting the kind of work they would like to have (Bachman, Johnston, and O'Malley 1980). This is evidence that young women anticipate constraints and this affects their plans.

One constraint women face is the way they are treated by male workers if they enter a male job. In one survey of female blue-collar workers, almost one third of the women reported that male coworkers gave them a hard time and that male coworkers disapproved of women doing craft work (O'Farrell and Harlan 1982). Schroedel's (1985) in-depth interviews with women who entered male-dominated blue-collar craft jobs revealed that many women felt unwelcome as a result of men's derogatory comments, men's attempts to sexualize the relationships (such as touching women while working next to them), and men's unwillingness to teach women the skills they would ordinarily teach a new male coworker. Case studies of occupations that many women entered in the 1970s show that men often tried to keep women out, either for fear that it would lower their wages or because they saw it as a threat to their sense of masculinity (Reskin and Roos 1990). Unionized men have been more successful than others at keeping women out (Reskin and Roos 1990; Hartmann 1976). There are several ways that unions have helped men to keep women out of "their" jobs. Some unionized jobs can only be entered through apprenticeships and one has to be selected by a union member to be an apprentice. Also, prior to the passage of the 1964 Civil Rights Act, which rendered such laws illegal, unions lobbied for laws that prohibited hiring women in particular jobs or for particular shifts.

Institutional inertia plays a role in perpetuating discriminatory constraints. Milkman (1987) examined historical data on a number of manufacturing firms across the century and found that if an industry hires one sex in a certain job at its origin, the sex label generally "sticks" for decades because it gains the weight of tradition.

Institutional inertia perpetuates segregation in yet another way. Many firms have structured mobility ladders, sometimes called internal labor markets. While some jobs are a "dead end" from which one cannot be promoted, others lead to a sequence of jobs through which promotions are common. The jobs at the bottom of these mobility ladders are filled from outside the firm; they may be thought of as ports of entry. Once segregation has occurred in jobs that are ports of entry—for any of the reasons discussed above—the existence of structured mobility ladders will perpetuate segregation up the ladders and through the life cycle of each cohort of workers without a need for further overt discrimination.

Another set of institutional practices that create constraints falls into a category similar to the legal notion of "disparate impact," discussed in more detail in Chapter 5. Job requirements that have a disparate and adverse impact on women are those that, given prior sex differences in experiences, make it more difficult for women to qualify for or remain in the job. These constraints are distinct from direct sex discrimination in hiring. That is, sex is not explicitly being used as a criterion for letting people into the job. Yet other criteria are being used that tend to screen out women. Examples of such criteria that have an adverse impact on women include upper age limits for entering apprenticeships (which disadvantage homemakers returning to the labor force), veterans' preferences (since more men than women have been veterans), limited public advertising of jobs (since more men than women are likely to talk to men who work in the jobs and thus have access to the information), the use of machinery designed for typical male height and strength, and departmental rather than plantwide seniority being credited toward promotions (Roos and Reskin 1984).

It is hard to know how much discriminatory barriers of either an overt or disparate impact variety have changed. My rough sense is that there has been a substantial decline in hiring discrimination, but that a substantial amount remains. Antidiscrimination legislation has had some effects on employers' hiring practices (Beller 1979, 1982a, 1982b; Leonard 1984; U.S. Department of Labor 1984; Burstein 1985; Gunderson 1989). In this sense, the lessening of constraints has been an important factor in desegregation. After legal requirements, Equal Employment Opportunity (EEO) was institutionalized as part of personnel departments in most large firms, thus giving it some inertial force even in the absence of governmental enforcement. The Republican administrations in office since 1980 have been much less aggressive than prior Republican or Democratic administrations about using the Equal Employment Opportunity Commission (EEOC) or the Office of Federal Contract Compliance Program (OFCCP) to sue or fine employers who discriminate against women or people of color.

Women have been helped by changes in some job requirements, whether these changes occurred because of successful lawsuits involving disparate impact (Burstein and Pitchford 1990) or for other reasons. To take an example of the latter, the development of real estate courses at community colleges around 1970 provided a way for women to circumvent apprenticeship systems that had required current brokers (mostly men) to sponsor new real estate agents (Reskin and Roos 1990).

The fact that resistance by male workers to women's entrance into jobs is a factor in discrimination suggests some conditions under which desegregation might proceed. Reskin and Roos (1990) show that women are more likely to enter male-dominated occupations when they are undergoing deskilling, losing autonomy, or their earnings relative to all jobs is going down. Women are more able to enter jobs at such times because men are less concerned with keeping women out when their jobs are losing desirability; in such times men themselves want to leave the jobs. Unfortunately for women, this means it will be easiest to enter those male jobs with declining advantages in terms of earnings, mobility prospects, or autonomy.

Desegregation has also been more likely to occur when there is an expansion in demand in a male occupation and women are found to be cheaper than men (Oppenheimer 1970; Richardson and Hatcher 1983; Cohn 1985).

IV. The Sex Gap in Pay

A. Trends in the Sex Gap in Pay

In the United States, as in most nations, women earn substantially less than men. For manufacturing workers, the female/male earnings ratio moved from 0.35 in 1820, to 0.50 in 1850, to 0.58 in 1930 (Goldin 1990). For all workers, the ratio rose from 0.45 to 0.60 between 1890 and 1930 (Goldin 1990). Table 1.3 shows little change between 1955 and 1980 for whites. During most of this period the ratio was about 0.59. Among blacks, Table 1.3 shows that the sex gap in pay narrowed considerably between 1955 and 1980, with women's relative earnings moving from 0.55 to 0.79. Thus, when it comes to women's pay relative to that of men, there have been eras of progress and eras of stagnation, and the timing of such change has differed by race.

Since 1980, white, black, and Hispanic women have made progress relative to men of their own racial or ethnic group, and relative to white men. As Table 1.3 shows, the sex ratio for whites moved from 0.59 to 0.65 between 1980 and 1987. For blacks the sex ratio moved from 0.79 to 0.84, and for Hispanics from 0.72 to 0.83. For the most part, women made these relative gains because their earnings showed slight (inflation-adjusted) absolute gains during the 1980s, while white and black men's wages were relatively stagnant and Hispanic men's wages declined.

The figures referred to so far (in Table 1.3) are based on annual earnings of full-time workers. Another way to look at trends in the pay gap is

Table 1.4. Female-Male Ratios of Median Usual Weekly Earnings among Full-Time Wage and Salary Workers, by Race, 1967–1989

Year[3]	Unadjusted for Hours Worked[1]		Adjusted for Hours Worked[2]	
	White	Black	White	Black
1967	0.608	0.700	0.676	0.732
1971	0.607	0.707	0.669	0.747
1973	0.606	0.718	0.669	0.756
1974	0.598	0.731	0.659	0.768
1975	0.613	0.751	0.672	0.789
1976	0.615	0.738	0.676	0.781
1977	0.606	0.731	0.669	0.775
1978	0.599	0.732	0.660	0.773
1979	0.611	0.747	0.673	0.790
1981	0.635	0.775	0.694	0.817
1982	0.639	0.794	0.698	0.838
1983	0.646	0.790	0.703	0.832
1984	0.670	0.798	0.731	0.842
1985	0.674	0.829	0.736	0.874
1986	0.679	0.827	0.742	0.866
1987	0.682	0.844	0.745	0.890
1988	0.684	0.830	0.746	0.877
1989	0.693	0.865	0.758	0.914

Source: U.S. Department of Labor 1967–1989.
Notes:
[1] Includes only full-time workers, i.e., those working at least 35 hours per week.
[2] Includes only full-time workers, i.e., those working at least 35 hours per week, and adjusts for sex differences in average hours worked among these workers.
[3] Data for 1967–1978 are for the month of May only.

to examine usual weekly earnings of full-time, year-round workers. Figures in the left two columns of Table 1.4 show these trends for black and white men and women. For some reason the female/male ratios are slightly higher in such data, but they show the same basic trends in the sex gap in pay—steady decreases among blacks and decreases among whites since 1980.

One limitation of the statistics in Table 1.3 and in the left two columns of Table 1.4 is that all workers who work at least 35 hours a week are considered full-time. Yet among these full-time workers, men average slightly more hours per week than women. Thus, when figures on the sex gap in pay are adjusted for differences in hours worked within full-time workers, the ratios are several percentage points higher, although the *trends* in sex gaps are similar, as the right two columns of Table 1.4 show.

One set of statistics that can mislead as an indicator of women's progress is comparisons between the sex gap in pay for different age groups. Table 1.5 gives female/male earnings ratios separately by age group, for

Table 1.5. Adjusted[1] Female-Male Ratios of Median Usual Weekly Earnings among Full-Time Wage and Salary Workers, by Age, 1973–1988

Age	1973	1978	1983	1988
Total, 16 years and older	0.68	0.67	0.72	0.77
16–19	0.86	0.91	0.96	0.93
20–24	0.83	0.80	0.89	0.96
25–34	0.72	0.73	0.80	0.85
35–44	0.61	0.59	0.66	0.75
45–54	0.62	0.59	0.63	0.67

Sources: Figures for 1973 to 1983 from Table 3, O'Neill, June. "The Trends in the Male–Female Wage Gap in the United States." *Journal of Labor Economics* Vol. 3, No. 1, pp. S91–S116. Copyright © 1985. Reprinted with permission. Figures for 1988 from U.S. Department of Labor 1989a (Table 33) and 1989b (Table 41).

Notes:

[1] Adjusted for sex differences in hours worked among workers classified as full-time (i.e., 35 hours/week or more). For 1988 figures only, data on hours used for the adjustments come from a slightly different age group than was used for the figures on earnings because of unavailability of data on narrow age groups in published sources. For 1988, hours for those 25–44 were used to adjust earnings ratios of those 25–34 and 35–44, and hours of those 45–64 were used to adjust earnings ratios of those 45–54.

1973, 1978, 1983, and 1988. The table shows that, in each year, the gap is much smaller among younger workers. For example, in 1988, the female/male earnings ratio among those 20–24 was 0.96, whereas it was 0.85 among those 25–34, and 0.75 among those 35–44. Some interpret this to mean that the sex gap in pay is disappearing. This optimistic interpretation hinges on assuming that the differences in a given year across age groups result entirely from a cohort effect and not at all from a life cycle effect. Another way to put this assumption is to say that each cohort (i.e. people born in a given year) will retain the same sex ratio of pay it currently has as it ages. If this is true, as the older cohorts with the larger sex gap retire, the overall sex gap in pay will decrease. If, on the other hand, we interpret the age differences as entirely a life cycle effect, experienced by every cohort, the figures have no implications as to the future of the sex gap in pay. They simply reveal that the sex gap in pay increases with age. This results in part because the sex gap in experience increases as women go through the childbearing years, and in part because even those women who are employed continuously usually work in jobs low on prospects for mobility and raises. For both these reasons, women's earnings fall further and further behind men's across the life cycle. Further complicating matters is the possibility of period effects. Period effects refer to changes over time, for example, decreases in discrimination, that affect all employed cohorts and age groups approximately equally.

In reality, all three effects (cohort, life cycle, and period) are probably operative, as suggested by Table 1.5 (and by Bianchi and Spain 1986). In each of the years shown, younger workers have a higher female/male ratio of earnings. We can also follow one cohort across the years. To take one example, consider those who were aged 25–34 in 1973, with women earning 0.72 of men's earnings. Ten years later, in 1983, when this same cohort was aged 35–44, the women were earning only 0.66 what men earned. For this cohort, women's relative losses across the life cycle were great enough to override any period gains between 1973 and 1983. But, if we look at the cohort 25–34 in 1978, women earned 0.73 of men's earnings in 1978, but had decreased the sex gap slightly to a ratio of 0.75 by 1988 when the cohort was 35–44. Here the period progress accruing to the cohort appears to have been large enough to override any relative losses of women across the life cycle. This suggests that favorable change in women's relative pay is occurring via both period and cohort effects. However, net of these changes, women's relative position deteriorates across the life cycle. Thus, the progress is not as fast as would be indicated by interpreting all of the age differences in sex ratio for any given year as cohort effects.

B. Explanations of the Sex Gap in Pay

What factors explain the sex gap in pay? Here I will consider evidence for the role of a number of factors, leaving questions of what theories this evidence supports for Chapter 2. Some of these factors have their effects on the sex gap in pay via their effects on segregation.

Sex Differences in Productivity or Effort?   Are women less productive than men? We seldom have measures of productivity, so there is little direct evidence on this. Yet there is much speculation and some indirect evidence. Becker (1985) speculates that, because of their domestic responsibilities, women exert less intense effort on the job, saving energy for domestic pursuits. The fact that women who are employed do more household work than their husbands is well documented (Berk and Berk 1979; Ross 1987; Hochschild 1989). But despite this, tests of differences in effort have, if anything, suggested that women expend *more* effort than men in their paid jobs. Bielby and Bielby (1988) analyzed data from a national survey that asked respondents how "hard" their jobs require them to work, how much "effort, either physical or mental" their jobs require, and how much "effort" they put into their jobs "beyond what is required." Women reported slightly *more* effort than men. One might wonder whether this finding simply results from women "bragging" more than men about their effort level. This is doubtful, since social psychologists' experiments show that men generally overestimate and women underestimate their own performance (Colwill 1982). Evidence on time allocation also suggests that women's effort is higher than men's; national survey data show that women report less time than men in coffee breaks, lunch breaks, and other regularly scheduled work breaks (Stafford and Duncan 1980; Quinn and Staines 1979). Thus, research indicates that sex differences in effort explain none of the sex gap in pay.

Industries and Firms.   While the most obvious form of segregation is at the occupational level, there is some segregation by industry and firm as well, and this contributes to the sex gap in pay. Unlike occupations, many of which are nearly all male or female, almost all firms (and thus industries, since they are a collection of firms all selling the same product) employ both men and women. Yet, although sex segregation by firm and industry is not nearly as extreme as by occupation, there are, nonetheless, systematic tendencies for women to be employed in those firms and industries with low average wages (Blau 1977; Beck, Horan, and Tolbert 1980; Hodson and England 1986; Aldrich and Buchele 1989; Coverdill 1988; Ferber and Spaeth 1984). For example, Blau (1977) examined cases where men and women in the same very detailed occupation (like accounting clerk, payroll clerk, or computer programmer) had different wages, and found that this was usually a matter of women working in a lower-wage firm. Often the entire industry the lower-paying firms were in had lower average wage scales.

However, even when women move to higher-wage firms and industries, their wages do not go up as much as men's do. The wage premium associated with being in a high-wage firm or industry goes disproportionately to male jobs (Aldrich and Buchele 1989).

Amount of Human Capital Investment and Expected Human Capital Investment. Are women in jobs requiring less skill, and, if so, does this affect the sex gap in pay? Here, let us confine our attention to *amount* of skills or training rather than *types* of skill. Amount of schooling, one type of human capital, explains virtually none of the sex gap in pay, since men and women in the labor force have virtually the same median years of formal education, as Table 1.6 shows. Among whites, women had 1.3 years more education than men in the labor force in 1952, and men did not close this gap until 1969. By 1979, white men's median was a trivial 0.1 year more education than white women's. For blacks the trends are somewhat different, but black women have had slightly more education than black men in all years since 1952, as Table 1.6 shows, although by 1983 this female advantage in median education had declined to a relatively trivial 0.2 year.

There *is* a sex difference in another sort of human capital: years of job experience. Because many women spend some years rearing children and keeping house full-time, the average woman in the labor force has fewer years of experience than the average man. Early studies had

Table 1.6. Median Years of School Completed by Men and Women in the Labor Force, by Race, 1952–1983

	White			Black		
	Men	Women	Difference	Men	Women	Difference
1952	10.8	12.1	−1.3	7.2	8.1	−0.9
1959	11.8	12.2	−0.4	8.1	9.4	−1.3
1969	12.4	12.4	0.0	10.8	11.9	−1.1
1979	12.7	12.6	0.1	12.2	12.4	−0.2
1983	12.8	12.7	0.1	12.4	12.6	−0.2

Source: From: O'Neill, J. "The Trends in The Male–Female Wage Gap in the United States." *Journal of Labor Economics* Vol. 3, No. 1, pp. S91–S116. Copyright © 1985. Reprinted with permission.

shown that this difference explains between one quarter and one half of the sex gap in pay (Polachek 1975; Mincer and Polachek 1974, 1978; Sandell and Shapiro 1978).

A 1979 study by Corcoran and Duncan will be discussed in some detail since it is the best available for assessing the effects of various types of human capital on the sex gap in pay. They used a standard method of regression decomposition in which the amount that any variable contributes to the sex gap in pay is a function of (1) the rate of return of the variable (how much an additional increment contributes to earnings for both men and women) and (2) the size of the difference between men and women's average on this variable. They found that the regression coefficients or slopes—the rates of return—to different types of human capital were not terribly different for men and women. Their results do show that the *overall* rate of return to experience is higher for white males than other groups. (Hoffman 1981 also found this.) But when experience is divided into subcomponents according to whether the experience was with one's current employer (called "tenure") and whether it involved on-the-job training, rates of return for the subcomponents did not differ much by race or sex. This implies that the overall group differences in rates of return to experience came from groups spending different proportions of their employed years in different types of experience, which in turn offer varying rates of return. For example, white men are likely to have a higher portion of their experience in a job that provides on-the-job training, and years of tenure during which training was provided have a higher rate of return than other years of tenure in one's current firm or than years of experience in prior firms.

Since coefficients did not vary significantly between groups for most variables, Corcoran and Duncan used white male slopes for the decomposition, and my discussion that follows uses these results. Calculations from Corcoran and Duncan's study (1979) are presented in Tables 1.7 and 1.8. (They include decompositions using other groups' slopes.)

A striking implication of Table 1.7 is the amount of the sex gap in pay among whites that comes from men having more tenure (seniority with one's firm), including periods during which the employer was providing training. The training portion of tenure explains 11% of the gap between white men and white women. Although Table 1.7 shows that this same factor explains 8% of the gap between white men and black women, and 15% of the gap between black men and white men, Table 1.8 shows that on-the-job training is a relatively minor factor in the sex gap in pay between black men and women, explaining only 2%. It is also a trivial part of the pay gap between black women and white women (1%). Whether or not differences between groups in time spent in jobs with

Table 1.7. Percentage of 1975 Wage Gap between White Men and Other Groups Accounted for by Indicators of Human Capital

	Black Men		White Women		Black Women	
Years out of labor force since completing school	0	(0)	6	(5)	3	(−3)
Years of work experience before present employer	2	(6)	3	(1)	1	(−1)
Years with current employer prior to current position	5	(4)	12	(11)	7	(5)
Years of training completed on current job	15	(22)	11	(17)	8	(14)
Years of posttraining tenure on current job	−4	(−5)	−1	(−1)	−1	(1)
Proportion of total working years that were full-time	0	(−1)	8	(7)	4	(2)
Hours of work missed due to illness of others in 1975	−1	(1)	−1	(0)	−2	(−1)
Hours of work missed due to own illness in 1975	−1	(−1)	0	(0)	−1	(0)
Placed limits on job hours or location	0	(1)	2	(1)	1	(−1)
Plans to stop work for nontraining reasons	−1	(−1)	2	(1)	1	(2)
Formal education (in years)	38	(43)	2	(2)	11	(15)
Percentage of total gap explained by human capital	53	(71)	44	(45)	32	(32)
Percentage of total gap unexplained by human capital	47	(29)	56	(55)	68	(68)

Note: The decomposition calculates what percentage of the total gap in the natural log of hourly earnings between white men and each other group arises because of group differences in means on the independent variables, assuming the white male slopes. The calculation is the difference between the two groups' means times the slope. This is then divided by the total log-dollar gap and the quotient multiplied by 100 to convert to a percentage. (The percentages in parentheses are alternative estimates arrived at by using the lower-earning group's slopes.) The total gap is adjusted for whether individuals live in the South and the size of the largest city they live near. Adapted and computed from Corcoran and Duncan (1979, Table 1).

training are themselves explained by discrimination in job assignments or by job choices is a separate question that Corcoran and Duncan's analysis cannot answer.

White women also earn less if they have been out of the labor force. (See also Mincer and Ofek 1982.) This is shown by the net effects on wages of (1) years of work experience before present employer and (2) years with current employer prior to current position. The first of

Table 1.8. Percentage of 1975 Wage Gap between Black Men and Women and between Black and White Women Explained by Indicators of Human Capital

	Black Women and Black Men		Black Women and White Women	
Years out of labor force since completing school	10	(−7)	−8	(14)
Years of work experience before present employer	0	(−3)	−3	(3)
Years with current employer prior to current position	7	(6)	−12	(−12)
Years of training completed on current job	2	(2)	1	(2)
Years of posttraining tenure on current job	2	(−2)	−4	(3)
Proportion of total working years that were full-time	16	(4)	−10	(−6)
Hours of work missed due to illness of others in 1975	2	(−1)	3	(−5)
Hours of work missed due to own illness in 1975	0	(0)	3	(−2)
Placed limits on job hours or location	−3	(1)	−3	(−6)
Plans to stop work for nontraining reasons	3	(5)	−1	(7)
Formal education (in years)	−16	(−20)	76	(97)
Percentage of total gap explained by human capital	25	(−15)	43	(95)
Percentage of total gap unexplained by human capital	75	(115)	57	(5)

Note: The decomposition calculates what percentage of the total gap in the natural log of hourly earnings between the two groups arises because of group differences in means on the independent variables, assuming the slopes of the higher-earning groups, black men in column 1 and white women in column 2. (The percentages in parentheses are alternative estimates arrived at by using the lower-earning group's slopes.) The total gap is adjusted for whether individuals live in the South and the size of the largest city they live near. Computed from Corcoran and Duncan (1979, Table 1).

these two factors explains 3% of the gap between white men and white women (Table 1.7) but has no effect on the sex gap among blacks (Table 1.8). The second factor explains 12% of the sex gap among whites (Table 1.7), and 7% (Table 1.8) of the sex gap among blacks. The proximate cause of these portions of the sex gap in pay is women's lesser employment experience. However, discriminatory job and wage differentials may be behind some proportion of these sex differences in years of employment experience, since women have less motivation to stay employed if they are paid less. It is interesting that none of the measures of experience contribute to the pay gap between white and black women; black women have more experience but lower earnings.

Overall, Table 1.7 shows that Corcoran and Duncan (1979) found human capital (broadly construed to include all measures of education, employment continuity, and labor force attachment) to explain 44% of the pay gap between white men and women and 32% of the gap between white men and black women.

Tables 1.7 and 1.8, taken together, also reveal some facts about the interaction of race and gender. Overall, a much smaller proportion of the sex gap in pay between black women and black men is explained by human capital than is explained for either the gap between black and white women or between black women and white men. In particular, black women's higher average education than black men's makes a large *negative* contribution to the sex gap for blacks. That is, black women have higher education than black men, but lower earnings. In contrast, education makes significant contributions to the pay gap between black and white women (76%), between black women and white men (11%), and between black and white men (38%).

Let us now turn our attention to the question of whether women's *intentions* or *expectations* for less employment continuity at the time they first enter employment might explain some of the subsequent sex gap in pay. To the extent that job experience provides skill accumulation, this can be seen as relevant to the amount of human capital one accumulates. There are two versions of how expectations about continuity of experience might affect earnings. One posits that, if there is a trade-off between starting wages and steep wage trajectories (i.e., high returns to experience and/or tenure), women who plan intermittent employment will be more apt to choose jobs with relatively high starting wages than will either men or women planning continuous employment. This could possibly create an average sex gap in pay, despite the fact that it would produce higher lifetime earnings for women than if they chose jobs similar to men. However, as mentioned above, no study to date has found higher average starting wages for women or in women's jobs, even when other factors are controlled (England 1984; England, Farkas, Kilbourne, and Dou 1988). A milder version of this thesis might say that women will be more motivated to choose jobs with steep upward wage trajectories the longer they plan to be employed. I find this a more plausible claim, although we lack research on how much this has affected women's choices.

A second way that women's plans for intermittent employment may affect the sex gap in pay is via employers' statistical discrimination. (Definitions and theoretical discussion of statistical discrimination appear in Chapter 2.) If women have higher turnover rates, and employers know this, then based on this sex difference in turnover they may engage in what economists call statistical discrimination. That is, employers will be reluctant to hire women in jobs where turnover is especially expensive, particularly jobs that provide much on-the-job training. What evidence is there for this as a factor in the sex gap in pay? First, let us look at the evidence about sex differences in turnover. It is equivocal (Price 1977, p. 40). Several studies based on recent national probability samples of young workers (mostly in their twenties) found no sex differences in turnover, even when wage was not controlled (Waite and Berryman 1985; Donohue 1987; Lynch 1991). At first glance this seems extremely counterintuitive since we know that women leave the labor force for childrearing more often than men. The seeming anomaly is explained by the fact that men change firms more often than women (Barnes and Jones 1974). Other studies find gross differences, with women having higher turnover rates, but after statistically adjusting for wages or wage-related job characteristics, these differences disappear or reverse (Viscusi 1980; Blau and Kahn 1981; Haber, Lamas, and Green 1983; Shorey 1983). In general, workers of any sex or race are more likely to quit a job when it is low paying or has low opportunity for advancement (C. Smith 1979; Osterman 1982; Haber et al. 1983; Shorey 1983; Grounau 1988; Kahn and Griesinger 1989; Light and Ureta 1989). Thus, if women are placed in less desirable jobs through discrimination, this could explain part of their higher turnover in studies that do find gross sex differences in turnover. If this is true, then women's disadvantageous job placements may explain their higher turnover rather than vice versa. However, if the job placements result from statistical discrimination based on real exogenous turnover differences, then statistical controls for job characteristics are inappropriate in studies designed to assess exogenous sex differences in turnover propensity. Thus, the "chicken and egg" question of which is exogenous, the higher turnover or the discrimination, is virtually impossible to assess statistically. My best guess is that, except in the most recent cohorts (to which Waite and Berryman's 1985, Donohue's 1987, and Lynch's 1991 analyses were confined), exogenous sex differences in turnover existed but were very small and not present in all workplaces or occupations. However, it is important to note that among young cohorts in the recent period, turnover differences disappeared. Thus, if employers continue favoring men for jobs providing much training, it cannot be explained rationally via statistical discrimination but must reflect erroneous perceptions or other discriminatory motivations.

Thus far I have discussed how much of the sex gap in pay can be explained by human capital or anticipated human capital at any one point in time. But what of the trends in the sex gap in pay? Can these be explained by trends in human capital? Let us look at this question first in terms of the post–World War II period up until about 1980, a period during which the sex gap in pay was relatively unchanging. Were there trends in human capital that we would expect to have reduced the sex gap in pay? Several studies suggest not. For example, women's education relative to men's has not increased in the last 50 years (Goldin 1990; Smith and Ward 1984). Thus, based on education trends, we would not expect the sex gap in pay to change. Of course, during all this time, both men's and women's levels of education were increasing, and women had as much or more education than men (Jacobs 1989b). Thus, the point is not that at any one time education can explain the sex gap in pay, but rather that trends in the sex gap in education were not changing favorably to women, so we would not expect a change in the sex gap in pay on the basis of trends in education alone.

Similarly, prior to 1980, women's experience did not increase relative to men's (Smith and Ward 1984; Goldin 1990). At first this seems counterintuitive. One might think that as the percentage of women who are employed increases, this would lessen the sex gap in experience. But, in fact, the upward surge in women's employment affects the average experience of employed women in two conflicting ways: (1) On the one hand, the fact that fewer currently employed women have left the labor force (at all or for as long a time) increases the average experience of employed women. (2) On the other hand, the entrance of new female workers with little experience depresses the average years of experience of employed women. Thus, whether the average experience of employed women goes up, down, or stays the same as women's employment increases depends upon the relative strength of these two conflicting forces. Recent research (Smith and Ward 1984; Goldin 1990) suggests that they canceled each other out, so that women's average experience did not rise, and the sex gap in experience did not begin to close, until about 1980. Since 1980, however, women's relative experience has increased, and this is one factor in the declining sex gap in pay (Smith and Ward 1984; Goldin 1990; O'Neill 1985). However, this does not mean that experience completely "explains" the sex gap in pay. As we have seen, experience explains less than one half the sex gap in pay at any particular point in time.

Values and Preferences.   Do women's values and preferences help explain the sex gap in pay? In one sense, I have already considered this question above. I argued that gender-specific socialization orients both men and women toward kinds of jobs and skills typical for their gender. Insofar as women's jobs then pay less, values have played a part in the sex gap in pay. In a formal analysis of this type, Filer (1983) uses a large number of measures of tastes and personality characteristics to predict earnings and finds that they explain some of the sex difference in pay.

Much of this, I would argue, is an indirect effect. Values are affecting occupational choice and occupations are affecting earnings, but Filer's (1983) study does not make clear the mechanism through which occupational characteristics affect earnings. One such mechanism is the sort of wage discrimination against female jobs at issue in comparable worth, to be discussed below.

A thesis claiming a more direct causal line from values to earnings posits that men simply place a higher value on earnings when they decide which occupation to select, while women trade these off for other job characteristics. A number of studies have asked people what they value in jobs, and find that men rank earnings more highly than women (Brenner and Tomkiewicz 1979; Lueptow 1980; Peng et al. 1981; Herzog 1982; Major and Konar 1984). However, one study by Walker et al. (1982) found no such difference. Moreover, research on job satisfaction has found that women's satisfaction is *more* affected than is men's by the pay in their job (Glenn and Weaver 1982; Crane and Hodson 1984). In addition, studies of turnover find that the extent to which wage increases affect whether women will quit a job is as large or larger for women than for men (Shorey 1983; Kahn and Griesinger 1989; Light and Ureta 1989). Thus, if we look at responses to job characteristics, it appears that women may place more importance than men on earnings. In short, existing evidence provides no clear answer to the question of whether or not there is a sex difference in the value placed on money contributing to the sex gap in pay.

Sex Composition Effects. The call for comparable worth is based on the finding that a job's sex composition affects its wage level. This is a very consistent finding coming from a wide range of studies. Here I review this research, dividing studies into three types: those taking occupations as units of analysis and using national data, those taking individuals as units of analysis and (generally) using national data, and those taking jobs as units of analysis using data from a single organization or employer.

One type of study has taken U.S. Census detailed occupational categories as units of analysis and used national data. Such studies have controlled for occupational characteristics such as average requirements for education, and an array of occupational demands, with measures typically taken from the Dictionary of Occupational Titles (DOT). In general, such studies have found that, net of these measures, both men and women earn less if they work in a predominantly female occupation. This has been found for 1940, 1950, and 1960 with controls for education (Treiman and Terrell 1975b), for 1970 with controls for education, DOT skill measures, and other variables (England and McLaughlin

Table 1.9. Summary of Studies Examining the Effect of Occupational Sex Composition on Earnings and the Sex Gap in Pay

| Study | Data Source[1] | Measure of Earnings | Pay Ratio (Female/ Male) | Estimated Coefficients of Sex Composition[2] | | Percentage of Sex Gap Explained by Sex Composition[3]: Coefficients | | | Unit of Analysis[4] | Control Variables[5] Included in Regressions |
				Female Equation	Male Equation	Female	Male	Average		
Ferber and Lowry (1976)	1970 census	Median annual		−1438	−5008				Weighted occup. (n = 260)	1, 2
Snyder and Hudis (1976)	1970 census	Median annual		−2070	−3900				Unweighted occup. (n = 212)	1, 2, 7, 11, 27
Treiman and Hartmann (1981)	1970 census	Median annualized[6]		−1630	−2960				Unweighted occup. (n = 499)	1
England, et al. (1982)	1970 census	Median annual for full-time year-round	0.54	−1682	−3005	21	38	30	Weighted occup. (n = 387)	1, 26, 27, 29, 30, 31, 32
Aldrich and Buchele (1986)	1980 NLS	Hourly	0.64	−0.586	−0.686	9	11	10	Weighted occup. (n = 192)	1, 2, 4, 5, 6, 7, 12, 13, 14, 26, 27, 33
O'Neill (1983)	1980 CPS	Log hourly	0.68	−0.158 (0.049)	−0.148 (0.049)	12	11	11	Weighted occup. (n = 306)	1, 2, 6, 7, 11, 18, 27, 28, 36, 37, 38, 39
Johnson and Solon (1984)	1978 CPS	Log hourly	0.66	−0.090 (0.014)	−0.168 (0.015)	11	21	16	Individual n_f = 19,412 n_m = 24,056	1, 2, 3, 6, 7, 8, 9, 10, 12, 13, 15, 26, 27, 28, 36
U.S. Bureau of Census (1987)	1984 SIPP	Log hourly for full-time workers	0.70 nhs[7] hs	−0.340 (0.067) −0.211 (0.033)	−0.241 (0.060) −0.225 (0.026)	43 28	30 30	37 29	Individual n_f = 5,555 n_m = 8,167	1, 4, 5, 7, 8, 9, 10, 12, 13, 16, 17, 18, 19, 20, 21, 22, 23, 24,

36

| Sorensen (1989b) | 1984 | PSID | Log hourly | 0.65 | col | −0.417 (0.061) −0.230 (0.033) | −0.189 (0.056) −0.239 (0.040) | 38 | 17 | 28 | 23 | 23 | 24 | 28 | 23 | Individual $n_f = 2{,}411$ $n_m = 2{,}616$ | 25, 34 | 1, 2, 4, 5, 6, 7, 8, 9, 10, 12, 13, 15, 19, 23, 24, 26, 27, 28, 35 |

Source: Adapted from Sorensen 1989b (Table 4.1).

Notes:

[1] Abbreviations: NLS = National Longitudinal Survey, Center for Human Resource Research, Ohio State University. CPS = Current Population Survey, U.S. Government. SIPP = Survey of Income and Program Participation, U.S. Government; PSID = Panel Study of Income Dynamics, Institute for Survey Research, University of Michigan.

[2] All measured as the proportion of workers in an occupation who are female except Aldrich and Buchele, which is percentage female. Standard errors are in parentheses when available.

[3] Blanks exist because data were unavailable to calculate these figures or unweighted occupations were used as the unit of analysis and thus individual inferences could not be made. The percentage of the pay gap accounted for by the sex composition of an occupation using the male coefficient was calculated as follows: $b_m(X_m - X_f)/w_m - w_f)$. X_m and X_f are the sample means of the proportion of women in an occupation for men and women, respectively. w_m and w_f are the sample means of earnings for men and women. b_m is the male regression coefficient for the proportion of women in an occupation. To derive the figure using the female coefficient b_m is replaced by b_f.

[4] Weighted occup.: each observation is an occupation weighted by the proportion of the female or male work force in the occupation; unweighted occup.: each occupation counts equally; individual: each observation is an individual worker; n = number of observations; n_f = the number of women; n_m = the number of men.

[5] Independent variables included were (1) sex composition of an occupation, (2) education, (3) potential work experience, (4) actual work experience, (5) tenure (job and/or employer tenure), (6) region, (7) urban, (8) race, (9) marital status, (10) children (number and/or presence), (11) hours of work, (12) union status (membership and/or coverage), (13) government employment, (14) industry dummies for core/periphery distinction, (15) two-digit SIC code industrial categories, (16) firm size, (17) involuntarily left last job, (18) turnover, (19) health/disability, (20) blue-collar occupation, (21) high school curriculum, (22) attended private high school, (23) obtained advanced degree, (24) obtained college degree, (25) various fields of study in college, (26) general education development (DOT), (27) specific vocational preparation (DOT), (28) DOT measures of working conditions, (29) DOT measures of cognitive skills, (30) DOT measures of perceptual skills, (31) DOT measures of manual skills, (32) DOT measures of social skills, (33) race composition of an occupation, (34) usually work full-time, (35) part-time last year, (36) part-time this year, (37) employed five years earlier, (38) license or certification required, and (39) self-employed. DOT refers to measures from the Dictionary of Occupational Titles.

[6] Median annualized earnings = (median annual earnings · 2080)/mean annual hours.

[7] nhs: not a high school graduate; hs: high school graduate; col: college graduate. Separate analyses done by educational level.

37

1979; England, Chassie, and McCormick 1982), and for 1980 with similar controls (Parcel 1989). The one study that does not find this net negative effect of occupational percentage female (Filer 1989) used a very extensive list of controls. I will argue in Chapter 3, in conjunction with my analysis of this genre using 1980 census data, that Filer may have included inappropriate variables and "overpartialed" the effect. To foreshadow, my analysis in Chapter 3 finds a negative effect on wages of the percentage female in an occupation, under more rigorous controls than most previous studies have used for skill demands as well as characteristics of the firms and industry people in given occupations typically work in.

A second type of study takes individuals as units of analysis, and examines the effects of occupational sex composition by mapping this contextual variable onto each individual's record according to the occupation s/he holds. Controls for various other occupational characteristics are mapped on in the same way as contextual variables. Such studies find a net negative effect on both men's and women's wages of being in an occupation that is predominantly female (Johnson and Solon 1986). One advantage of such studies is that they employ controls for individuals' human capital. One study (England et al. 1988) found this negative effect of occupational percentage female using longitudinal data and a "fixed-effects" model to control for any unmeasured differences between unchanging pay-relevant attributes of those individuals in predominantly female and male occupations.

Sorensen (1989b) has assembled most of the published studies investigating the net effect of occupations' percentage female. (She includes studies using either census occupations or individuals as units of analysis.) These findings are summarized in Table 1.9. In general, these studies find that moving from an all-male to a comparable all-female occupation is associated with a wage penalty equivalent to between 10 and 30% of the sex gap in pay.

A third type of study employs data from one organization or employer. These studies show similar findings. One advantage of these studies is that they often employ more detailed job categories than do national studies. A second advantage is that they allow us to see the potential effects of comparable worth at the level at which they would occur in the version of the reform generally advocated—within a single employer or organization. A disadvantage of such studies is that they are limited to the public sector, where data on pay are more readily available. A number of states have done job evaluation studies for comparable worth purposes in the last ten years. Invariably, these studies have found that, net of measures of job skill or worth, female jobs pay less (Remick 1984; Rothchild 1984; Steinberg, Haignere, Possin, Chertos, and Treiman 1986; Acker 1989; Orazem and Matilla 1989). The job evaluation techniques used in such studies are discussed in more detail in Chapter 4.

Another study of public sector employment examined pay in the California state civil service. Baron and Newman (1989; forthcoming) found "smoking gun" evidence of discrimination in pay setting. A 1934 memo (Becker 1934) said that pay in jobs is set, among other things, according to the "age, sex, and standard of living of employees normally recruited for the given job." Baron and Newman's (1989; forthcoming) analysis of the California civil service data found higher pay levels in predominantly male jobs, even when controlling for the broader occupational category into which each more detailed job falls, and for the education and experience required of persons entering the job. Their study did not have the sort of measures of skill demands common to job evaluations. However, the validity of their conclusions is further buttressed by the fact that changes in the sex composition of jobs between 1979 and 1985 were associated with changes in a job's pay level such that a job's becoming more female depressed wages and becoming more male increased wages (Baron and Newman 1989). If we assume that any changes in jobs' skill demands were uncorrelated with changes in sex composition, then their findings about change effectively "hold constant" any unmeasured skill demands of the jobs.

Other studies that have also analyzed how change over time in jobs' sex composition affects change in their pay find that when a job changes its sex composition, the wage for both men and women goes up if more males come into the job, and the wage for both men and women goes down if more women come into the job (Ferber and Lowry 1976, p. 384; Pfeffer and Davis-Blake 1987). We cannot be sure if the changing sex composition affected the wages, as these authors suggest, if the change in wage affects sex composition (as suggested by Reskin and Roos 1990), or if both effects are operative.

Types of Skills and Working Conditions in Jobs: Indirect Gender Bias. Another factor affecting the sex gap in pay is the kind, rather than amount, of skills and working conditions jobs require. Some view this as a part of the comparable worth issue. The studies above implicitly do not. That is, they take as given the returns to different job characteristics, and, controlling for these factors, estimate the adverse effect on wages of being in a predominantly female occupation.

However, the types of skills common in women's jobs may have lower returns than the types of skills common in men's jobs *because* of gender discrimination. That is, if a type of skill or working condition has traditionally been associated with women's work in either the household or paid employment, it may come to be devalued via stigma that gets institutionalized into wage systems, so that this skill or working condition comes eventually to carry a low rate of reward, or a penalty, whether it appears in a male or female occupation. However, since such skills and working conditions are more common to female occupations, this devaluation has a disparate and adverse impact on women's wages. Many view this as a part of the discrimination at issue in comparable worth, as will be discussed in Chapter 4 as an issue in job evaluation studies, in Chapter 5 as an issue in legal proofs of discrimination, and in Chapter 6 as an issue of feminist theory. There is substantial evidence that women's concentration in jobs with different kinds of skills affects the sex gap in pay. Daymont and Andrisani (1984) show that one's college major has an important effect on pay, and women are in the majors associated with lower pay. Women are more often than men in jobs involving nurturant social skills, and these not only have lower returns than other skills, but actually have net negative returns (Kilbourne, England, Farkas, and Beron 1990; Steinberg et al. 1986; Jacobs and Steinberg 1990a; Steinberg 1990). The fixed-effects model used by Kilbourne et al. (1990) allows an assessment of the effect of doing nurturant work on earnings while controlling for all unchanging, unmeasured differences between individuals in nurturant and other jobs. Even under these stringent individual controls, as well as controls for factors computed from DOT measures and occupational sex composition, the penalty for nurturance is found. My analysis in Chapter 3 will show this penalty for doing nurturant work as well. The adverse working conditions typical in some women's jobs (such as interpersonal stress, exposure to death and suffering, or exposure to blood, urine, and feces) are often given fewer points in job evaluations used to set pay than are the kinds of adverse working conditions (such as exposure to dirt and the out-of-doors) more typical in men's jobs (Steinberg 1990). Even those adverse working conditions typical to male jobs seldom have a large effect on earnings, however.

Overall, I conclude that the *kinds* of skills traditionally exercised by women are valued less in wage determination than are traditionally male skills. This more indirect form of gender bias is seen by many advocates as part of the discrimination to be redressed by comparable worth.

C. Consequences of the Sex Gap in Pay

What are the consequences of the sex gap in pay? A person doubting the importance of the issue might argue that if marriage is nearly universal and husbands and wives pool their income, the sex gap in pay has little consequence for the economic well-being of either women or children. This would be a mistaken conclusion, however. The sex gap in pay has important consequences within marriage as well as for those women who are not married.

Not all women marry, and some women divorce. Many never-married and divorced women have children. Indeed, rates of both divorce and out-of-wedlock births have increased dramatically. About half of the cohort born in the early 1950s (Cherlin 1981; Preston and McDonald 1979), and two thirds of those marrying today (Martin and Bumpass 1989) are projected to experience divorce. Many divorced women have children. Out-of-wedlock births rose from 5% of all births in 1960 to 18% in 1980 (Preston 1984). Unmarried women with children—whether divorced or never married—typically have custody of their children and must support them on some combination of their own earnings, any child support they receive from the children's fathers, and government subsidies. Child support awards are typically small. For example, awards to divorced women averaged $2500 per year per family in 1981, and less than half the mothers received the full amount awarded (U.S. Bureau of Census 1983b). While it is true that many divorced women remarry, both age and the presence of children inhibit women's remarriage probabilities (Mott and Moore 1983), so a significant minority of women with children do not remarry (Preston 1984). Thus, the sex gap in pay, in combination with the fact that divorced and never-married women generally have financial responsibility for their children after divorce, is a crucial part of why such a high proportion of female-headed families is in poverty (McLanahan, Sorensen, and Watson 1989, p. 120).

There is a paradox here. To some extent the increase in divorce is probably itself a result of women's increased economic independence (England and Farkas 1986, pp. 64–65). The fact that more women than previously have jobs means that more can afford to leave marriages they consider unhappy and at least minimally support themselves and their children. Yet, because of the continued sex gap in pay and men's failure to support their children after divorce, the economic consequences of divorce for women and children are still grave (Preston 1984).

But what of marriages that remain intact? For married women, does the sex gap in pay have adverse consequences? Yes. A long line of research on marital power (reviewed in England and Kilbourne 1990c) has shown that women's employment and the relative earnings of husbands and wives affect the balance of power in marriages. When women's earnings are lower, even when they are making valuable contributions in the form of home management and child rearing, their bargaining power vis-à-vis their husbands is substantially lower than that of women with higher earnings. The fact that women's economic fate is more adversely affected by divorce than men's is part of why men can retain disproportionate bargaining power within marriages. The ability to leave a relationship with relatively few losses implies the power to hold out for a better bargain without risk of a big loss. Thus, the sex gap in pay has profound consequences for the degree of informal democracy in marriages. It adversely affects women's ability to negotiate for what they want in marriage on a wide range of issues, including intimacy, purchasing decisions, the sharing of household work, and geographical moves. The sex gap in pay is a part of what prevents equality in husbands' and wives' bargaining power over all these issues.

V. Conclusion

This chapter has presented an overview of women's and men's positions in paid employment. The chapter began by exploring explanations for the unabated increase in women's employment. One factor is the increasing proportion of women who are single, many with children. These women need jobs because, whether they are divorced or never married, they usually have the major responsibility for the support of themselves and any children they have. Among married women, increased potential wages have drawn more women into employment, as has a restructuring of the economy that brought disproportionate increases in labor demands in fields already labeled "female." I argued that couples today may perceive a greater need for two earners than previously despite the fact that, on average, male earnings have greater buying power today than in the 1950s or early 1960s. I speculated that this increase in perceived need can be reconciled with trends in men's earnings if a decrease in income is perceived as larger than a gain of the same amount over the same income range. The last 20 years have seen fluctuations in men's earnings because of recessions and recoveries, and increasing wage inequality among men. The asymmetry in the perceptions of losses and gains of the same size may explain why women who enter paid labor to buffer reductions in men's earnings often stay even after their husband's earnings have rebounded. Also, as the norm becomes for women to be employed before childbearing, couples get used to two incomes and want to avoid the loss that would occur if women did not return to their jobs shortly after childbearing.

The unabated increase in women's employment makes the issue of comparable worth more important: As employment becomes the norm for most women most of the time, the consequences of facing discriminatory wage penalties increase. The importance of comparable worth also results from occupational sex segregation. If there were no disproportionately female or male jobs, there would be no problem of comparable worth, at least as an issue of gender inequality. There might still be concerns about whether the pay levels of jobs were set in a consistent manner, or about whether the racial or ethnic composition of jobs had discriminatory effects. But without the sex segregation of jobs, comparable worth would not be the important women's issue it is today.

Occupational sex segregation has declined since about 1970, although it is still substantial. Yet even as national data show a decline in segregation, we also see sex segregation of subfields within occupations women have recently entered, and some occupations show desegregation and then resegregation, as they move from being mostly male to integrated, and then "tip" and become segregated female enclaves.

Occupational sex segregation is partly explained by social forces operating upon women's and men's choice of jobs. These social forces include influences of parents, educational institutions, peer groups, and other social networks. Discrimination by employers in hiring is also a factor, as is the resistance of male workers to women's entrance into their occupations. Finally, historical and institutional factors also contribute to segregation; if a job starts out as female or male, considerable inertia develops around that initial label. Also, if entry level jobs are of one sex or the other, this segregation will be perpetuated over time and up the mobility ladders that comprise internal labor markets.

Segregation more often takes the form of women and men exercising *different kinds* of skills than of women's concentration into less skilled jobs. This is precisely why the issue of comparable worth is so poignant; women are often being paid less for equally demanding, though different jobs. This fact also makes it more comprehensible that women's own choices could be one factor in job choices. When we focus upon the low wages and low mobility prospects of typically women's jobs, it appears that no rational woman would choose such jobs. But when we see that often equally high levels but different kinds of skills are exercised in female jobs, it is more plausible that reasonable people would find such work interesting and meaningful. This, however, does not imply that women want or agree with the low pay accorded their jobs.

This chapter also examined research on the sex gap in pay. Education and effort, the two "all-American" routes to economic success, do have payoffs for both men and women. Yet neither is particularly relevant to the sex gap in pay since women have as many years of education as men, and studies show women expend as much or more effort as men on their jobs. Women's fewer years of seniority and overall employment experience, and the intermittency of such experience, explains some proportion (between one quarter and one half) of the sex gap in pay.

Much of the sex gap in pay results from segregation itself. Some of this segregation is interfirm, with women concentrated in lower-paying firms and industries. This aspect of the sex gap in pay would not be touched by comparable worth reforms unless we envisioned a national wage setting board whose authority spanned the entire economy, something no American advocates of comparable worth have suggested.

A large component of the sex gap in pay comes about because women are segregated into lower-paying occupations within every firm. Proponents of pay equity reforms allege that at least some portion of the pay differences between male and female jobs arise *because* the jobs are filled by women or entail skills that are traditionally female. Evidence abounds that, controlling for a number of measures of skill and other occupational requirements, jobs with more women in them offer lower wages to both men and women than do jobs containing more men. I refer to this as direct gender bias in wage setting. There is also evidence that, net of this direct effect of jobs' sex composition, kinds of skills traditionally done by women, such as nurturant social skills, have lower (sometimes even negative) returns than other kinds of skills (such as cognitive skills). I refer to this as indirect gender bias in wage setting. Comparable worth is about both of these types of gender bias in wage setting: direct gender bias based on the sex composition of the job, and indirect gender bias in which the returns to jobs' requirements for various types of skill and working conditions differ according to whether the job characteristic is traditionally associated with women's or men's spheres.

This chapter has focused on empirical regularities rather than how these are interpreted by theories or help us to evaluate theories. The next chapter will focus on scientific theorizing, examining how a number of bodies of theory view labor markets, gender inequality, and, most specifically, comparable worth.

Note

1. The evidence is mixed on whether women with more traditional family plans are more likely to choose female occupations. Waite and Berryman (1985) find that young women who aspire to have more children and less continuous employment are more apt to choose female occupations. In contrast, Lehrer and Stokes (1985) find that young women's plans to be employed at age 35 and expected family size affected the skill level of the occupation aspired to, but *not* its sex composition. Even if Waite and Berryman's finding is correct, this does not demonstrate that female occupations lead to higher lifetime earnings than male occupations for those who have intermittent employment. It may simply mean that the wage disadvantages of female occupations are taken into account more in occupational choices of women who plan more continuous employment.

2

Theories of Labor Markets

I. Introduction

This chapter considers competing theories of how labor markets work, and their implications for gender inequality and comparable worth. The theories to be discussed include orthodox neoclassical economics, a new neoclassical institutionalism, and framing models from behavioral economics that blend well with findings from experimental social psychology. I also consider Marxist views in sociology and economics, as well as other sociological and institutionalist perspectives. Finally, I propose an interdisciplinary view that draws selectively upon the theories reviewed.

I give a disproportionate amount of space to the neoclassical view for two reasons: First, the internal coherence of the neoclassical view makes it possible to spell out its implications clearly. Second, the neoclassical "market wage" argument has come to dominate arguments against comparable worth policies. I find some merit in neoclassical theories. Yet, in contrast to the view of most neoclassical economists, I believe that comparable worth policies could have salutary effects on women and address a very real form of discrimination. It is important to my argument to explain why I hold this view despite its tension with neoclassical thinking.

This chapter focuses on theories about how labor markets operate to produce wage differences between women and men, and between female and male jobs. In contrast, Chapter 6 focuses on *normative* theoretical questions about how rewards, including wages, *should* be allocated to men and women and across jobs. Of course, these positive and normative questions are never entirely separate, though some bodies of theory emphasize one aspect over the other. Both positive and normative issues underlie policy debates over comparable worth, to be discussed in the concluding Chapter 7.

45

II. The Orthodox Neoclassical View

A. Basic Neoclassical Concepts

The starting point of neoclassical economics is a vision of rational individuals who *optimize* or *maximize*, i.e., who make choices that yield the greatest amount of utility, given their constraints. *Utility* refers to happiness, satisfaction, or well-being, subjectively construed. The assumption of rationality is usually seen to have two components: First, preferences are transitive. This means that if I prefer A to B and prefer B to C, I will also prefer A to C. Second, individuals are assumed to make accurate calculations about the outcomes that can be expected to result from their actions, subject to the availability of information that is needed for the calculations. Economists traditionally have made the simplifying assumption that people have perfect and costless information with which to make calculations, and some economic models still assume this, even though no one really believes it to be true. Recently, however, economists have emphasized the importance of the costs of gathering and disseminating information. The notion of optimization now includes calculating what resources it is worthwhile to spend on information. These developments are referred to as the "new information economics." (See Stigler 1961, 1962; Arrow 1974; Lippman and McCall 1976; Diamond and Rothschild 1989.)

In economic models, *endowments* and *tastes* are both typically assumed to be exogenous inputs. That is, they are assumed to be explained by something causally prior to economic processes, rather than by economic models. Endowments are the resources one acquires from biology, from one's family of origin, or from other gifts (Becker 1976, 1981, pp. ix–x). An individual's *tastes* (sometimes called preferences) determine the amount of utility provided by different combinations of leisure, job conditions, consumer goods, household arrangements, and other factors. These tastes determine one's *utility function*. Economists do not generally attempt to explain the origin of these tastes, nor do they believe that tastes change. However, to say that tastes do not change does not deny that a person will make different consumption choices as his or her income changes. For example, the optimal house to buy when one earns $30,000 a year is different than the optimal choice when one earns $60,000, even if one's tastes do not change. Stigler and Becker (1977) have argued that whether tastes are exogenous is moot, since there is little variation in tastes across persons or time. Thus they argue that most behavior can be explained by endowments or by variations in the economic constraints of prices.

We often think that economics deals with behavior directed toward gains that are pecuniary (i.e., relating to money), whereas sociology deals with behavior in which nonpecuniary tastes for things such as social approval are prominent. This is not true in principle, even if it is somewhat true in the practice of the two disciplines. Economists recognize that individuals often trade pecuniary compensation for the nonpecuniary rewards of interesting work or leisure. This is embodied in the notion of compensating differentials in labor markets (Flanagan, Smith, and Ehrenberg 1984, pp. 179–196), to be discussed later in this chapter, and in the contention that individuals maximize utility or "full income," not merely money income (Schultz 1981, Chapter 4). More fundamentally, the importance of nonpecuniary rewards is clear from the fact that, to economists, money is merely a medium of exchange used to buy goods or services that are enjoyed for the subjective utility one experiences from them. Since the ultimate goal of money is utility, forgoing a gain of money in order to experience utility directly from a nonpecuniary benefit is fully consistent with the paradigm.

Yet, despite their formal recognition of both pecuniary and nonpecuniary goals, economists seeking empirical predictions from their theory *sometimes* add the auxiliary assumption that actors maximize only money. This avoids the sticky problem of measuring utility and allows more determinate predictions.

Economics is concerned with relations of exchange within markets. When we apply the rationality assumption to exchange, we conclude that an individual will undertake an exchange when the anticipated outcome is preferred to that from any other *available* option. Of course, the social class into which one is born affects one's endowments, and thus the amount of resources available to one to use in exchange. Since economists recognize endowments as exogenous inputs to their models, they implicitly recognize these effects of social class background.

The results of an exchange are defined as *Pareto-superior* to the preexchange situation if at least one party's utility increases from the exchange while neither party to the exchange thereby loses utility. When all possible Pareto-superior moves have been made in a market, a Pareto-optimal equilibrium has been reached. Economists do not analyze which of the two parties "got more" from an exchange because of their assumption that interpersonal utility comparisons are impossible (Hirshleifer 1984, pp. 476–477; Gibbard 1986). Thus, Pareto-optimality, rather than equity or equality, is the type of efficiency that is generally taken by economists to be the yardstick for outcomes.

Economists make no use of the notion of coercion within market relations. For them, coercion involves appropriating something owned by someone else without compensation agreed to by both parties

(Hirschleifer 1984, p. 12). Theft is an example. But capitalist property rights do not qualify as an example of coercion, no matter what the political or social consequences of such rights, and no matter how great the resulting inequality. For economists, market relations are never coercive; rather, coercion and power result from barriers to free market competition. Some of the actions of democratically elected governments in taxing and regulating the economy are viewed as non-Pareto-optimal. When economists do advocate such policies, they are defended on the basis of equity or of "market failures" that are seen as exceptions to the general rule that markets produce Pareto-optimal results (Thurow 1983; Averitt 1988).

Because individuals enter exchanges whenever it will make them better off, market systems generate constant pressure toward equilibrium via price adjustments to changes in supply or demand, discussed below.

B.   Supply and Demand in Labor Markets

The concepts of supply and demand can be applied to wage determination in competitive labor markets, and thus are relevant to discussions of comparable worth. Labor markets are seen as competitive as long as there are many potential employers that might be interested in each employee and vice versa. Neoclassical theory has clear implications for why some jobs pay more than others. What labor will be paid in a given job (i.e., what a particular skill type of labor will be paid) hinges on the intersection of supply and demand curves, as seen in Figure 2.1.

An employer's demand curve for a particular job (skill type of labor) is a bivariate relationship between the wage rate and the person-hours of labor the employer will choose to employ. Demand is a curve or line, *not* a single number. This is because the quantity of labor an employer is willing to hire depends upon the price of labor. Demand curves generally slope downward because the more an employer has to pay for each unit of labor, the less s/he will hire. In competitive labor markets, the demand curve is the same as the marginal revenue product (MRP) curve.[1] Any one employer's demand curve reveals how much the employer is willing to pay per unit of labor for any given quantity or, looking at the same bivariate relationship the other way, how many workers will be hired at any given market wage. An employer hires labor at the going rate until a number of workers is employed that, through diminishing marginal returns, causes MRP to fall to equal the wage. At that point no more labor is hired.

A profit-maximizing employer will pay no *more* than the market clearing wage because there is no need to do so and no gain from doing so.

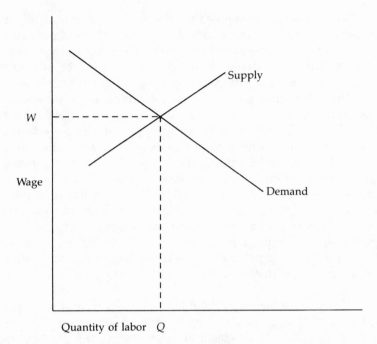

Quantity of labor   Q

Figure 2.1.   The supply and demand for labor. The horizontal axis gives the
   quantity of labor supplied for the supply curve, the quantity of labor demanded for the demand curve, and the quantity of labor supplied, demanded, and employed at the point of intersection. With these supply and
   demand curves, the wage will be W and the quantity of labor employed will
   be Q in equilibrium.

(We will see that this notion gets modified in the efficiency wage models
of the new institutionalism, discussed below.) Competition with other
employers for the same workers forces the employer to pay no *less* than
the market wage. Thus, neoclassical theorists argue that each employer
is a "price taker," paying the market wage.

   The marketwide demand curve for a particular job (or skill-type of
labor) is the aggregation of all relevant employers' demand curves.
When there is discrimination against women, the aggregate market demand curve for women of a given skill type is below that for men, even
when MRP is the same for male and female labor. This reflects the fact
that employers are unwilling to pay as much for females as for equally
qualified male labor. However, for reasons discussed below, most economists view the persistence of discrimination in competitive labor markets as an anomaly for neoclassical theory.

The other half of the economic model is supply. Like demand, supply is a curve or line, not a single number. The marketwide supply curve for a job (or skill type of labor) is a bivariate relationship between the wage rate and the number of person-hours of labor that will be offered in the job. In general, the higher the wage in a job, the more people willing to work in this job, although at some point a high wage may lead individuals to choose fewer hours of work. The location of the supply curve for a particular job will be affected by opportunities outside this job for people with the same skills (e.g., wages of alternative jobs), by how much investment in training the job requires, and by whether the marginal worker finds doing the work in the job a "disamenity"— an unpleasantness—or an amenity. The theory of human capital implies that jobs requiring more investment will have to pay more, or workers will not be motivated to make such investments. The notion of compensating differentials posits that jobs the marginal worker finds unpleasant will have to pay more to be filled. If they do not, workers will choose other jobs with the same pay but more pleasant working conditions.

Above I said that neoclassical theorists believe employers pay the market wage. Having discussed both demand and supply curves, we are now in a position to discuss how they believe this market wage is determined. The supply-demand model implies that the market wage (read off the vertical axis in Figure 2.1) and the quantity of labor employed (read off the horizontal axis in Figure 2.1) are determined by the point at which the marketwide supply and demand curves intersect. This intersection point defines the only wage at which the quantity demanded (a single number on the demand curve) equals the quantity supplied (a single number on the supply curve). In this sense, markets move toward equilibrium (equating the quantity of labor supplied with the quantity demanded) via wage adjustments. Prices (wages) are the mechanism of equilibration.

Once equilibrium is achieved, further changes in prices will occur only if there is an exogenous shift in either the supply or demand curve. For example, a fall in prices for one industry's product would cause a downward shift in the MRP and labor demand curves for occupations over-represented in that industry. This would cause movement down the unchanging supply curve to a new lower price and lower quantity employed, defined by the intersection of the new demand curve with the unchanged supply curve.

Summarizing Figure 2.1, the neoclassical model says that a job will pay more if it has either a higher demand curve or a higher supply curve on the vertical dimension.[2]

C. Human Capital Theory

In this section I explain the theory of human capital and review research flowing from this theory that seeks to explain occupational sex segregation and the sex gap in pay. A later section applies human capital theory more specifically to comparable worth.

The neoclassical theory of human capital posits that individuals invest in their stock of skills by paying and/or forgoing something in the present for the sake of some future gain. For example, schooling is often undertaken to increase one's future wages. Schooling involves the direct cost of tuition, and the opportunity cost of forgone wages and forgone opportunities to use one's time in homemaking or leisure. Human capital investment could also include learning how to cook so one will be a better homemaker, or getting a doctorate in English so as to find a more satisfying job. In principle, the scope of the theory of human capital is not limited to investments that yield later *earnings*, although this is by far the most common application.

In neoclassical theory, whether one will undertake an investment (in human capital or anything else) depends in part upon one's "discount rate," the way in which present compared to future utility is valued. One's discount rate is part of one's tastes. The lower a person's discount rate, the more one defers gratification, and the less present-oriented one is. Whether one invests also depends upon the rate of return one can expect from the investment. This rate of return could, in principle, include nonpecuniary returns, though most research has focused on pecuniary returns.

Three kinds of investments relevant to earnings are emphasized by human capital theorists: One is education (schooling). A second is that subset of on-the-job training, formal or informal, that produces knowledge not only applicable to this firm, but that makes one potentially more productive in many other firms as well. Learning a common computer program on the job would be an example of this. Both of these kinds of investments are called general, rather than firm specific. This is because the investments should increase productivity and hence earnings in either one's current firm or working for another employer. A third type of human capital investment is the on-the-job training (formal or informal) that teaches firm-specific knowledge, i.e., things that are unique to this firm. This is called firm-specific human capital investment. Most on-the-job training is a mixture of the second and third type. Where on-the-job training is offered, human capital theorists presume that employees will pay for at least a part of its costs by accepting lower starting wages (Hashimoto 1981).

Human capital theory has been used to explain occupational sex segregation and the sex gap in pay, as explained below. These explanations
have not focused on formal education because men and women in the
U.S. labor force scarcely differ in their average years of educational
attainment, as discussed in Chapter 1.

Human Capital and Occupational Sex Segregation.   Uses of human capital to explain occupational sex segregation have not focused upon the
simple fact that employed women average substantially fewer years of
employment experience than men. At first glance, one might think
that the absence of women in male jobs requiring many years of experience reflects the unavailability of women with sufficient years of experience to enter these jobs. This may indeed explain a part of the absence of
women from jobs at the top of lengthy promotion ladders that had
plenty of women in the jobs from which the promotions usually occur.
Yet this cannot be a *major* factor in segregation since entry-level positions
themselves are very segregated by sex, despite the fact that, at entry
level, men and women are equal in lacking any experience.

Applications of human capital theory to occupational sex segregation
have focused on how differences in men's and women's initial *plans* for
job experience will lead to different investments and job choices. Polachek (1979, 1981, 1984) suggests that women who plan breaks from
employment for homemaking will choose jobs that have low depreciation of human capital during years of homemaking. Since many more
women than men plan years of homemaking, he sees these supply-side
choices as generating segregation. "Depreciation" refers to the atrophy
or obsolescence of job skills occurring during periods of homemaking
that leads one to have a lower real wage upon returning to employment
than one had prior to leaving a job. Most tests of this hypothesis have
not supported it (Corcoran, Duncan, and Ponza 1984; England 1982,
1984; Abowd and Killingsworth 1983; England et al. 1988). (See Polachek
1984 for a counterargument.) Research shows that women do not experience any more wage depreciation while out of the labor force if they are
in male jobs than if they are in traditionally female jobs. Thus, those
who plan spells of homemaking do not have the economic incentive to
avoid male jobs that Polachek suggested.

Human capital theorists also argue that women who plan noncon-
tinuous employment will choose jobs with relatively high starting wages
but flat experience-earnings curves over jobs with lower starting wages
but steeper wage increases with experience (Zellner 1975). Recalling the
neoclassical view that low initial wages are an investment in the human
capital received from on-the-job training, economists see the choices of
jobs with higher starting wages and flatter trajectories as a choice to

invest less in human capital formation. Such a choice would make sense for women who do not plan to be employed long enough for steep wage increases to make up for initially lower wages. However, studies show that this is *not* a cause of segregation. This is shown by the fact that women are not in jobs with higher starting wages than men's jobs requiring comparable education and skill. Indeed, women are in jobs with *lower* starting wages (Greenberger and Steinberg 1983; England 1984; England et al. 1988). Thus, women's jobs do not have the benefit of higher starting wages that human capital theorists see as motivating women's choice of these jobs.[3] In sum, the evidence does not support the explanations of segregation from human capital theory.

Human Capital and the Sex Gap in Pay. Chapter 1 reviewed trends in the sex gap in pay, a gap that is still significant. Findings from Corcoran and Duncan's (1979) study of the contribution of human capital to the sex gap in pay were also reviewed in Chapter 1. Here I consider the question of how the findings support or cast doubt on the ability of human capital theory to explain the sex gap in pay.

Corcoran and Duncan found that the number of years of education explains virtually none of the sex gap in pay among whites, and "negatively" explains the sex gap in pay among blacks. This is because, although education has a positive rate of return for all groups, black women average a fraction more of a year of education than black men, and white men and women have virtually the same average level of education.

A novel feature of Corcoran and Duncan's (1979) analysis lies in their use of measures of the subcomponent of one's total employment experience that was with one's current employer, and the subcomponent of this experience with the current employer that involved training. Length of on-the-job training was measured by asking individuals how long they think it takes a person in their job to be fully trained after hire. A major finding of the study is that experience with one's current employer, including the training portion, explains more of the sex gap in pay than prior experience. Clearly, the breaks women take for homemaking lower their seniority with their employers and this explains some of the sex gap in pay. Overall, however, less than half of the sex gap in pay was explained by human capital and other indicators of labor force attachment.

Explanations of the sex gap in pay in terms of human capital are often juxtaposed to explanations in terms of discrimination. While both forces may be present at any one time, they are separate forces in the sense that a given share of the sex gap in pay explained by one force at any one time is thereby not explained by the other. However, if we take a more dynamic view, it is important to recall that if women are discriminated against, they will have less incentive to invest in human capital. For example, if they receive lower wages, this gives them less incentive to stay in the labor force, and job experience is one form of human capital. Thus, some of the share of the gap explained by current sex differences in seniority or experience may actually be explained by past discrimination that led women to gain less seniority. This brings up the question of the theoretical status of discrimination within economic theory, to which I now turn.

D. Discrimination

Chapter 1 reviewed substantial evidence of discrimination against women in hiring and pay. Although the long-term persistence of discrimination by employers in competitive markets is an anomaly for neoclassical theory, economists have developed a number of models of discrimination. Models of discrimination are reviewed below, followed by an explanation of why theorists believe that discriminatory employers will gradually disappear from competitive markets. The discussion is summarized in Table 2.1.

Taste Discrimination. Neoclassical discussions of discrimination generally begin with Becker's (1957) taste model, which posits that employers, workers, or customers may have a taste for discrimination. Such a taste refers to a preference in favor of or against hiring, working with, or buying from a group such as women. (His discussion generally referred to race discrimination, but the model can be applied to sex discrimination as well.) To economists, whether one is willing to pay an extra amount of money for something is indicative of whether one has a taste for it. Thus, a taste for discrimination implies that discriminators are willing to pay more to hire the group that is preferred than they are willing to pay for equally productive members of the disfavored group. Becker (1957) saw tastes for discrimination as explained by premarket factors, following the usual neoclassical assumption that tastes are exogenous to economic models.

An employer with a taste for discrimination against women is unwilling to hire women *unless* they offer themselves at a wage enough below the wage paid to men that it completely offsets the distaste they experience by employing women. How low this wage must be will depend upon the extent of the employer's taste for discrimination. Thus, to economists, there is an inextricable link between discrimination in wages and hiring; they are not distinct types of discrimination.

Table 2.1. Types of Discrimination

Type	Motivation	Characteristics of the Type According to Neoclassical Theory	
		Creates Group Differences in Earnings?	Erodes by "Arbitrage"?
Taste	Nonpecuniary individual gain in utility	Yes, unless based upon employee tastes, in which case leads to segregated firms but not segregated occupations and not group differences in earnings	Yes, unless altruism in employer's tastes leads to paying the favored group above MRP,[1] or unless discrimination is based upon customer tastes (but this should only affect jobs involving customer–employee interaction)
Statistical	Pecuniary individual gain through saving screening costs and obtaining more productive employees for the wage		No
	Subtype of statistical discrimination—based on group differences in:		
	Mean productivity	Not in excess of average productivity differences	No
	Variance in productivity	If employers risk averse	No
	Reliability of screening devices	If employers risk averse or via effects on groups' human capital investments	No
Error	Perceived (but at least partially illusory) pecuniary individual gain through saving screening costs and obtaining more productive employees for the wage	Yes	Yes
Monopoly	Pecuniary group gain through "dividing and conquering" of workers	Yes	Yes, unless ways of enforcing monopoly against free riders is successful

Note:
[1]MRP, marginal revenue product.

Some employers discriminate, not because of their own tastes, but as a response to their customers' tastes. Yet we would not expect customer discrimination throughout the economy; rather it should occur only in service firms (e.g., stores) where employees meet customers. In manufacturing and extractive firms, and even in many service firms, customers do not know the race or sex of workers, so customer-induced taste discrimination should not be pervasive.

Employers may also discriminate in response to their workers' tastes. For example, male workers may object to working with women (Bergmann and Darity 1981), requiring a higher wage to do so.

Statistical Discrimination. Models of statistical discrimination are a part of the new information economics, the key insight of which is that it is costly to gather information relevant to decisions. These models focus on the fact that employers make decisions about hiring in the absence of full information about each applicant's productivity. This is because it would be too expensive and perhaps impossible to get full information on each individual. There are several models of statistical discrimination. I will discuss models based on average differences between women and men on productivity, those based on differences in the variances of men's and women's productivity, and those based on differences between women and men in how reliably or accurately screening instruments (such as tests) predict their productivity.

Let us consider the model of statistical discrimination in which hiring decisions are made on the basis of race or sex group *averages* on ability to be productive in the job (Arrow 1972, pp. 96–97; Phelps 1972, p. 60; Lloyd and Niemi 1979, p. 11). These models assume that it is too expensive for the employer to measure each individual's ability, but that group differences in *average* productivity are correctly known. Thus, members of the group with a higher average productivity are preferred.

Since men and women have overlapping distributions on virtually all characteristics, using a group's average to estimate characteristics of individuals who are members of the group results in mistaken predictions about individuals who are qualified in a way unusual for their sex. However, since sex can be observed almost costlessly, in the absence of other cheap screening criteria, it may improve the average productivity of an employer's work force to choose all workers from the sex group with the higher average. This model does not imply that sex group differences are innate; it simply implies that they were not created by the employer who is engaging in the statistical discrimination.

Thurow (1975, p. 172) confuses the issue when he says that statistical discrimination "occurs whenever an individual is judged on the basis of the average characteristics of the group or groups to which he or she belongs rather than upon his or her own characteristics." Thurow is correct that the use of group averages is one of the defining characteristics of this model of statistical discrimination. However, Thurow's implication that nondiscriminators use "individual characteristics" rather than "group averages" makes no sense unless we are to consider virtually all hiring decisions discriminatory. All individual characteristics (e.g., test scores, education) define groups (e.g., the group with SAT scores over 1100, the group of college graduates). Thus, there is no operational difference between basing decisions on individual characteristics or on group means. Productivity is always estimated from individual characteristics of applicants that define groups, whether these groups are defined by achieved characteristics, such as education, or characteristics ascribed at birth, such as sex. The only exception to this is the case where the relevant individual characteristic *is* a direct measure of productivity on the job. But on-the-job productivity is virtually never measured before hire. It is the fact that *group averages* are used that makes us call a screening process *statistical* (whether an ascribed criterion such as sex or an achieved criterion such as education defines the group). It is the fact that *ascribed* criteria such as sex or race define the groups for which averages are compared that makes us label the process *discrimination*.

Is there evidence that supports the model of statistical discrimination based on sex differences in averages as an explanation of gender discrimination in hiring? The mean sex difference most often invoked by economists in discussions of statistical discrimination is women's allegedly higher turnover rates. (For examples, see Landes 1977; Bulow and Summers 1986; Barron et al. 1990; Kuhn 1991.) Such discrimination should be particularly likely in jobs offering on-the-job training. If women stay less long, then the cost of the initial training per year of employment is greater for women, on average. Thus, after these larger per year training costs are subtracted from their productivity (assuming that before the subtraction it is equal to men's), the net productivity per year of women workers is less as a result of the higher probability of turnover. Yet, as reviewed in Chapter 1, overall, studies do not provide unequivocal support for the idea that women have a higher propensity to quit jobs that is exogenous to their treatment by employers. The evidence can be read as either rejecting or supporting exogenous sex differences in turnover, since whether one should control for variables such as one's wage depends upon one's theoretical assumptions.

Less discussed in the literature, but probably more realistic, is the possibility of mean sex differences in specific kinds of learned abilities that are relevant to specific jobs but costly to measure. An example might be men's greater knowledge of auto mechanics or women's greater knowledge of how to operate sewing machines. Statistical discrimination might help explain the preference for one sex in such jobs where sex differences in averages exist on job-relevant skills.[4]

But can the model of statistical discrimination based on average difference in productivity-related characteristics explain discriminatory wage differentials disadvantaging women as a group? Aigner and Cain (1977) argue that it cannot, claiming that statistical discrimination based on averages does *not* reduce the *average* earnings of the race or sex group with the lower average productivity. They point out that since group means on productivity are the basis of hiring and pay decisions, groups will receive an average level of pay commensurate with their average productivity. For example, if women are 10% less productive at some jobs, employers will be unwilling to hire any women in such jobs unless they will work for 10% less than is paid to men. The "error" involved in statistical discrimination is that individuals who are atypical for their group will be paid more or less than their individual productivity, although, on average the group will be paid commensurately with its productivity. For example, the woman who, compared to the average woman, knows an unusually large amount about auto repair will not find a job as a mechanic or she will have to settle for a lower wage than she would in the absence of statistical discrimination. This is because all women will be treated like the average woman, and all men will be treated like the average man (holding constant observed indicators of productivity such as schooling). In sum, absent other forms of discrimination, statistical discrimination based on group averages might lead to occupational segregation, but it should not lead to group differences in *average* earnings in excess of average productivity differences (Aigner and Cain 1977).

A second type of statistical discrimination hinges on race or sex group differences in *variances* rather than averages (Phelps 1972; Aigner and Cain 1977). Suppose that women have the same average as men on a productivity-relevant characteristic, but the women's distribution has a larger variance, indicating more women than men at both extremely high and extremely low scores. If the cost of finding a better indicator of productivity and using it to screen each individual applicant is prohibitively high, will it pay employers to prefer the group with the smaller variance? The answer to this question depends upon whether employers are risk averse (Aigner and Cain 1977). If they are not risk averse, the expected value of productivity for women and men will be determined by the respective means of the two groups, and if they are the same, it is not rational to engage in statistical discrimination. However, if the employer is risk averse, the group with the smaller variance will be preferred even when group means are equal.

The relevance of risk aversion to preferring a group with a smaller variance can be seen by making an analogy to how people decide what stock investment to make. Suppose you have two investment possibilities, and each has an expected payoff of 9% in the next year. Your generally accurate broker tells you that investment A has an expected return of 9%, and the return is unlikely to fall outside the range of 8–10%. She estimates that investment B also has an expected return of 9%, but sees a reasonable chance of either losing all your money or making a huge return on B. The more risk averse you are, the more likely you are to pick investment A over B, although they have the same "average" (i.e., expected) return. Likewise, in hiring, the risk-averse employer is more likely to engage in discrimination against a more internally variable group because there is more risk of hiring an especially bad worker from this group. Unlike statistical discrimination based on means, if employers are risk averse, statistical discrimination based on variances *can* produce sex differences in average earnings that are in excess of sex differences in average productivity.

Is there any evidence that the realities of sex discrimination fit this model of statistical discrimination based on variances? I know of no evidence that women's distribution on unobserved productivity indicators is generally more variable than men's. There may be greater heterogeneity among women than men in turnover rates, and this might explain some statistical discrimination by risk-averse employers even if women's average turnover is not lower. However, this is a speculation; I know of no research documenting that this is the source of discrimination.

A third model of statistical discrimination posits race or sex differences in the degree of accuracy with which ability is measured by tests or other selection devices (Phelps 1972; Aigner and Cain 1977; Borjas and Goldberg 1978; Lang 1988; Lundberg and Startz 1983). For one group, the "error term" in a regression predicting productivity from the selection device is larger, and the R^2 (explained variance) is smaller. Thus the selection device has lower reliability for the group with the larger error term. This does *not* mean that productivity is systematically underestimated for the group for whom the screening device is less reliable. Most models assume that men and women with any given score on the selection device have the same average productivity, but there is more variability or dispersion around the regression line for women. And there is no assumption of *any* difference in the male and female distributions on productivity; both means and variances may be equal between the sexes. If the cost of finding and using a more reliable indicator of productivity is prohibitively high, will it pay employers to prefer the group for whom the available indicator has greater predictive power? As with models of statistical discrimination based on differences in variances in productivity, risk-averse employers will discriminate. (Even in the absence of risk aversion among employers, it is possible for this sort of discrimination to create discriminatory wage differences through creating incentives for groups for whom selection devices are worse predictors to invest less in unobservable forms or more in observable forms of human capital or other "signals" of productivity. See Lundberg and Startz 1983; Lang 1988.)

Is there evidence that the model of statistical discrimination based on differential reliability of selection devices for men and women explains a significant amount of sex differences in occupational placement or pay? I know of no evidence about sex differences in predictive validity of selection instruments, so the application of the model to gender differences remains speculative.

Error Discrimination. Error discrimination is a term I use to describe the situation where employers underestimate the relative average productivity of a group and, based upon this mistaken belief, are unwilling to hire group members or will hire them only for a lower wage. The error about group averages may entail believing that men and women differ in productivity for some job when in fact no group difference exists. Alternatively, it may entail an exaggeration of the size of an actually existing difference. Error discrimination has in common with statistical discrimination that the employer has no nonpecuniary distaste for employing women in the job, but rather is discriminating in an effort to hire a more productive work force. Error discrimination differs from statistical discrimination based on means in that the former involves erroneous estimates of group averages whereas the latter involves correct estimates of group averages (although even statistical discrimination causes erroneous predictions for individuals who are atypical for their group). Most economists ignore the possibility of error discrimination because they presume that such errors would eventually be corrected as employers accumulated experience. Some authors (Lloyd 1975, p. 17; Blau and Jusenius 1976, Note 33; Blau 1984; Bielby and Baron 1986) include what I am calling error discrimination in their definition of statistical discrimination. I prefer to distinguish the two because, as discussed above, statistical discrimination based on mean differences should not produce discriminatory group differences in average pay, whereas error discrimination will.

Monopoly Models of Discrimination. Monopoly or monopsony models of discrimination involve members of a group formally or informally colluding, acting collectively rather than as competing individuals. Monopsony is defined as a situation where there is only one buyer, in this case one employer buying female labor. (Monopoly is defined as a market with only one seller; but often the term *monopoly* is used to refer to either monopsony or monopoly.) Madden's (1973) monopsony model and Hartmann's (1976) and Strober's (1984) theories of patriarchy all posit that women are kept out of good jobs by collusion among men, as husbands, employers, legislators, and workers. It is clear that such a "cartel" or "gentlemen's agreement" benefits men *as a group* at the expense of women as a group. Indeed, members of any group will make relative gains if they can exclude nonmembers from opportunities.

Madden's monopsony model takes as an unexplained fact that men have substantial power over women's decisions to accept jobs. For example, women's options were limited in the past by laws barring them from some jobs. Even today they are limited by patriarchal customs in which husbands have the right to dictate in which city a couple will live. This creates a monopsonylike power for employers who hire women. The real situation is not so extreme that all women face a single employer, but the model's insight is to work out the implications of a situation where, because of various forms of male power, women are closer to being in a situation of having only one potential employer than are men. Monopsonistic employers can pay lower wages to women than they would be able to if they were in competition for female labor. The classic example of monopsony power is the labor market for nurses in small towns that only have one hospital.

Seen through neoclassical lenses, the Marxist notion of "divide and conquer" is also a monopoly model. This conception holds that employers discriminate to create divisions or hostilities between groups of workers. The purpose of discrimination is to prevent workers from organizing cohesively enough to threaten profit levels by raising wages through unionization, strikes, or more radical political action (Gordon 1972, pp. 71–78; Edwards, Reich, and Gordon 1975, pp. xiii–xiv; Bonacich 1976; Bowles and Gintis 1976, p. 174; Humphries 1976; Roemer 1979; Reich 1981; Stevenson 1988). Every employer has a material interest in preventing such solidarity of workers. Yet, in a neoclassical view, one employer cannot get away with limiting women to worse jobs unless other employers do too; otherwise women would leave the discriminating firm for other firms. Thus, the strategy of divide and conquer via gender discrimination works only if employers collude. It is the fact that employers *collude* to keep women's opportunities worse than men's, making the situation to some extent as if there were only *one* employer, which places the divide-and-conquer model of discrimination into the broader category of monopoly models when looked at through a neoclassical lens.

The Demise of Discrimination in Competitive Markets.   Most neoclassical economists believe that discrimination sows the seeds of its own destruction because it costs money. Becker (1957) realized that this was a tension in his discrimination theory (Arrow 1973). The erosion of many types of discrimination should happen as long as labor markets are "competitive," by which economists mean that there are a number of possible buyers of labor for each seller of a particular type of labor and vice versa. Product markets need not be competitive for the conclusion to hold. Let us examine the process by which economists believe discrimination should eventually disappear.

Suppose that the discrimination is based on employers' tastes, but employers differ in the strength of their discriminatory tastes. Some employers' tastes not to hire women will be so strong that they will hire no women, regardless of how cheaply women offer to work. At the other extreme are employers we will call "nondiscriminators": They are indifferent between men and women, so they are open to hiring either men or women, or both, and paying them equal wages. Employers with an intermediate level of discriminatory tastes are willing to hire some women, but only if the women will work for a lower wage than they are willing to pay men. How much lower the wage would have to be to make them indifferent between men and women is a measure of the severity of their discriminatory taste.

How does this relate to supply and demand? Suppose, for simplicity, that we are dealing with a job that has average requirements for qualifications, and with equivalently qualified men and women. The labor demand curve for any type of labor is the sum of the labor demand curves of all the employers in the market. Since at least some employers are taking sex into consideration, we need to think of two different marketwide demand curves, one for men and one for women. The more discriminators there are in the market, and the greater the wage differential that discriminators require to make them indifferent between hiring men and women, the farther the labor demand curve for women will lie below the labor demand curve for men. Thus, if men had a supply curve identical to that of women, the market wage for men and women would differ because the two identical supply curves would intersect the lower female demand curve at a lower wage. This will yield a single marketwide wage for women and one for men (in the particular occupation in question). Neoclassical notions of supply and demand imply that any single employer can hire as many women (men) as s/he wants at the female (male) market wage, but cannot hire any at a lower wage. (The recognition of search costs modifies this to allow for some dispersion of wages because of information costs, but the basic principles of the model remain.)

In such a setting, what will the nondiscriminators who are indifferent between men and women do? Since women are available at a lower wage than men despite equivalent productivity, they will choose to hire the cheaper women. Employers will hire all men if their tastes for discrimination are so extreme that they are unwilling to hire women no matter how low the price. Employers whose tastes for discrimination are intermediate will hire women if the difference between the female and male market wage is great enough to offset their distaste, but will hire men if it is not. Employers whose taste (by coincidence) requires exactly the same wage differential to make them indifferent between men and women as the difference between the female and male market wage may hire some of each sex. These employers will pay men the male market wage and women the female market wage.

In this scenario, nondiscriminators are taking advantage of the exploited status of women, paying them a lower wage than men are making at other firms. Thus, in one sense, we might not want to call them nondiscriminators. Economists, however, label them nondiscriminators because, if other employers' discriminatory tastes had not provided them with cheapened labor, they would have been willing to pay men and women the same wage. Further, these nondiscriminators who hire women cheaply are not the source of women's discriminatory low wage; indeed, they are part of the mechanism of the erosion of discrimination. Such employers are like arbitrageurs in stock markets who buy up stocks that others are undervaluing.

Such nondiscriminators contribute to the demise of discrimination because their relatively low labor costs give them an advantage in competitive product and capital markets. Because they can sell their products for a lower price and/or offer higher returns on investments in the firm, such firms should come to sell an increasing share of the product market and hire an increasing share of the labor market in their industry. Because of their higher labor costs, employers with more taste for discrimination may go bankrupt. Alternatively they will be bought out by employers with less or no taste for discrimination. Eventually, the theory predicts, only the least-discriminatory employers will be left. By this point, the expansion of employment in the least-discriminating firms should have bid up the job opportunities and wages of women, leading women's wage and job distributions to converge toward men's. At this point, the wage at which women must offer to work to get hired is only as low as consistent with the tastes of the least-discriminatory employer. Through this process, competition is said to bring about the demise of taste discrimination in the long run. Of course, the length of the "long run" is an empirical question that theory cannot specify.

This economic reasoning implies that the *eventual average* amount of discrimination in the economy depends not on the *average initial* level of discriminatory tastes, but upon the amount of discriminatory taste held by the *least*-discriminatory employers. This latter amount will be the *eventual average* level of discrimination after the "arbitrage" has occurred.

As long as there are some employers with *no* discrimination in their tastes, arbitrage will erode all discrimination.

The description above of the demise of discrimination applies generally if the discriminatory tastes belong to employers. It will not occur in the case of customer tastes causing discrimination since customers do not go out of business for paying to indulge their tastes. However, the sex of those who work in a job is generally not visible to customers. So the neoclassical model would predict noneroding taste discrimination based on customers' tastes only in service jobs where customers interact with workers. In the case of discrimination based on workers' tastes, the erosion process should lead to enduring sex segregation by firm. However, this segregation by firm should not generate occupational segregation within firms or wage differences between men and women.

Analogous logic explains how the erosion of error discrimination would occur via market forces. Nondiscriminating employers who do not have erroneous estimates of women's abilities for particular jobs will get labor at a bargain price and can thus come to represent a larger share of their markets. Error discrimination should be even less likely than taste discrimination to persist since employers might correct their erroneous perceptions through observation. But even if no employers change their erroneous perceptions, the fact that there is some dispersion in the degree of employers' error about women's productivity implies that discrimination should eventually diminish to be consistent with the proclivities of the least-discriminatory employers. Eventually employers whose judgments are the least clouded by error should employ the whole work force.

From within the neoclassical camp, Goldberg (1982) has pointed out an important exception to the notion that taste discrimination will necessarily erode in competitive labor markets. (His discussion refers to race discrimination; I have adapted it to sex discrimination.) The argument hinges on the distinction between two types of taste discrimination: antifemale discrimination in which women are paid less than MRP while men are paid MRP, and promale discrimination, in which men are paid more than MRP while women are paid MRP. The distinction is depicted in Figure 2.2. Promale discrimination involves selective altruism toward men because the employer finds employing them rewarding in a nonpecuniary sense. Goldberg (1982) argues that antifemale discrimination will eventually erode in competitive markets (to the level of the least-discriminatory employer) by the process described above. However, his point is to show that the discrimination I call altruistic promale discrimination need not erode in competitive markets. The argument is that employers engaging in altruistic promale discrimination can survive in the long run if the nonpecuniary utility they get from altruistically pay-

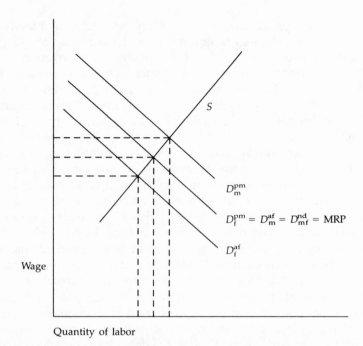

Figure 2.2. The demand for labor by nondiscriminators, antifemale discriminators, and promale discriminators. Key: D_f, demand for females; D_m, demand for males; D_{mf}, demand for males or females (where no distinction is
made between them), af by antifemale discriminator, pm by promale discriminator, nd by nondiscriminating employer; MRP, marginal revenue
product; S, supply of labor, assumed the same for males and females.

ing men more than MRP makes them willing to take a lower-than-mar-
ket profit rate. This nonpecuniary gain leads them to reject buy-out bids
from owners who are less (or non-) discriminatory, and thus could run
the business more profitably. In contrast, if one is engaging in antifemale
discrimination, the same buy-out offer from a less (or non-) discriminatory employer *will* be compelling because there is no offsetting nonpecuniary utility to be derived from keeping the firm.

The two models of taste discrimination, antifemale and altruistic
promale, are similar in several senses, but crucially different in their
ability to survive in competitive markets. Both types of discriminators
are willing to take less profit than the maximum possible in order to
indulge their taste for discrimination. That is, both antifemale and promale models of taste discrimination take the notion of nonpecuniary
motives seriously and thus assume that firm owners may maximize

utility (money profit plus nonpecuniary reward), not merely money profit. Both models feature employers that are willing to sell or buy a firm for the discounted present value of the expected stream of future utility from owning the firm. The critical difference between the two models is that in the altruistic promale model, the value of the firm is greater to one with more rather than less (or non-) discriminatory tastes, so nondiscriminators cannot buy out discriminators. In the antifemale model, the pecuniary gain that a nondiscriminator can make (at least temporarily) from hiring women at their cheapened wage makes it possible that the firm is more valuable to the nondiscriminator than the discriminator. This is because, if women are hired at their market price, the two employers have the same profit level but the antifemale discriminator suffers nonpecuniary disutility due to the antifemale taste. The nondiscriminator does not suffer this nonpecuniary disutility. Goldberg (1982) points out that Becker (1957) incorrectly assumed that the two types of taste discrimination, antifemale and promale, are identical with respect to their tendency to erode in competitive markets.

The concept of statistical discrimination has had great appeal to economists because it seems more capable than other models of discrimination of explaining the anomaly of the persistence of discrimination in competitive markets. Unlike taste or error discrimination, it is pecuniarily rational for employers to engage in statistical discrimination if the costs of the error it creates in predicting individuals' productivity are less than the expense of developing and administering screening instruments with greater predictive power. The latter costs exist because of limitations in the "technology" of personnel administration. They are examples of what economists call information or search costs. Because of these costs, there is no pecuniary advantage to ceasing statistical discrimination, as there is for taste or error discrimination. Why would an employer want to abandon a cheap method of estimating productivities when it is expensive to develop screening devices that allow one to find those individuals whose productivities are above the average of their sex? If employers are already using the most effective screening technology that is cost-effective, statistical discrimination will endure in competitive markets because it does not cost money. Thus, statistical discrimination is distinct from the other types of discrimination in that it cannot erode entirely through the pure market forces of arbitrage as the others can. However, it is important to remember that only those models of statistical discrimination involving variances or the reliability of screening instruments can produce group wage differentials in excess of productivity differentials. Models of statistical discrimination based on different group means will not produce such differentials. No compelling evidence of gender differences in variances or reliabilities of screening devices exists in the literature, so it is not clear that this is a factor in gender differences in pay.

What of the monopoly models of discrimination? How do economists think that discrimination involving the noncompetitive feature of group monopolies can disappear, since the very competition through which market forces work is suspended by the monopolistic collusion? As long as the restrictions against hiring a group, such as women, are successfully enforced by law, informal sanctions, or group loyalty, economists concede that the discrimination will not diminish. But economists focus on the difficulties of enforcement. The instability of such monopolies inheres in the pecuniary incentive each *individual* employer has to be a "free rider" on the colluding group. For example, a free rider would hire cheap female labor while the rest of the group continued to collude in the monopoly that is refusing to hire women and is thus providing the free rider with the cheapened female labor. Similarly, each individual consumer has a pecuniary incentive to buy from a firm that has hired cheaper female labor because of the lower prices of goods sold by such firms. Male workers do not have such an incentive to free ride on the monopoly, but individual employers and consumers have a pecuniary incentive to sabotage workers' efforts to enforce the monopolistic restrictions. Thus monopolies are unstable because they give many members of the dominant group an individual incentive not to follow the restrictions that benefit the group as a whole. As a result, monopolistic discrimination should erode unless the collectivity finds sufficient motivation and effective methods of enforcement against free riders.

One might try to counter this argument for the instability of monopolies by positing that employers and consumers in the dominant group have a group loyalty (e.g., to their fellow males) strong enough to make them cooperate with the restriction despite the pecuniary loss this decision entails. Undoubtedly this is often true. But such a group loyalty can be seen as a *taste* that one is willing to risk having to pay for. Thus, if the monopolistic restrictions are adhered to by all group members *only* out of loyalty, we really have a special case of taste discrimination, and the arguments above about how and whether taste discrimination can persist apply.

To summarize, most forms of discrimination, whether based on tastes, error, or group monopolies, tend to self-destruct in competitive labor markets in the long run, according to orthodox neoclassical reasoning. Taste discrimination should erode from arbitragelike markets forces alone unless it is altruistic promale discrimination that entails paying men above MRP. Error discrimination should erode from arbitrage as well as from updated information. Discrimination based on a group monopoly should erode from free riding, unless means of enforcement are found to avoid this. Statistical discrimination based on variances or differential reliability of screening devices will not erode through arbitragelike market forces alone. These theoretical deductions explain why neoclassical economists respond in stylized ways to evidence of persistent job and wage differentials by race and sex that cannot be explained by available measures of human capital or compensating differentials. Some see persistent discrimination as an anomaly for their theories, for which they do not yet have an explanation (Arrow 1973). Others concede only statistical discrimination, the persistence of which is viewed as least anomalous (Fuchs 1988). The discrimination described by the promale altruism model, while as likely to persist as statistical discrimination, is nonetheless less popular among economists because they generally do not presume altruism in market relations. Others deny that any significant amount of market discrimination still exists, positing supply-side explanations that hinge upon unmeasured group differences in preferences or human capital. Some of those who deny discrimination will concede that premarket (i.e., familial or societal) discrimination or past market discrimination may explain these supply-side differentials (Polachek 1984). Others see supply-side choices hinging on biological differences between men and women in comparative advantage in childrearing (Becker 1981).

E.   Comparable Worth and the Neoclassical View

Are wage differentials between predominantly male and female jobs discriminatory, as proponents of comparable worth claim? What are the likely effects of comparable worth policies? Here I consider how these two questions are approached from within a neoclassical view.

Neoclassical theory is couched in terms of the constraints faced and decisions made by individuals and firms, not in terms of aggregates such as jobs. Yet implications of neoclassical theory for wage differences between jobs can be teased out, as I suggest below. To move toward job-level conclusions, let us first consider how neoclassical theory implies that the work to be done in a firm is divided into distinct jobs. If firms seek to maximize profits, firm owners will adopt a division of labor that is most efficient *for profitability*. That is, they will choose the division of labor that gets the greatest output for the least costs of labor and other inputs. Efficiency, in this sense, does not deal merely with technical issues of production, but could also include organizing work in such a way that workers are less able to organize a union or other collective action.

Human Capital.   Human capital theory has clear implications about the wages offered in various jobs. Employers can fill jobs requiring substantial prior investments in training only if they pay high enough wages to induce workers to make these investments. This is a fact about the supply side of labor markets. The relevant fact about the demand side of labor markets is that better-trained workers will be hired only in some jobs, even if they are more productive in all jobs. Employers will not spend the extra money required to hire more highly trained workers except in those jobs where they calculate that the benefits exceed the costs of the higher wages they must pay (Lang and Dickens 1988). Thus, although human capital theory is often described as a supply-side theory, it has a demand side as well.

Suppose we take the skill level of a job to be a rough measure of how much productivity in that job is increased by investment in schooling or other training. In this case, human capital theory predicts that jobs with higher skill levels will pay more. Applying the theoretical reasoning above, this is true for two reasons: First, on the demand side, employers are willing to pay more because of the greater effects on profits of using better-trained workers in these jobs compared to other jobs. Second, because of supply-side constraints, employers must pay more to attract persons who have invested in obtaining the relevant skills.

Thus, before concluding that pay differentials between male and female jobs are discriminatory, a neoclassical economist wants to be sure that differences between the jobs in human capital requirements do not explain these wage differences. Since there are many types of human capital that are not well measured in available data, economists often suspect that *unmeasured* aspects of human capital actually explain group differentials.

Compensating Differentials. Suppose that male and female occupations with equal human capital requirements differ in pay, even after temporary disequilibria from shortages or gluts are remedied. Such differences are sometimes explained by the notion of compensating differentials. Other things equal, jobs that workers find more onerous have to offer higher wages in order to be filled. Equivalently, jobs that workers find more desirable because they are interesting, safe, pleasant, or otherwise satisfying can be filled for lower wages than if they were more onerous.

However, a wage premium will be unnecessary if a sufficient number of workers are indifferent to or even prefer the putatively onerous job characteristics in question. That is, compensating differentials depend on the tastes for nonpecuniary amenities and disamenities of the *marginal* rather than the *average* worker (R. Smith 1979). An example illustrates the point. Most of us think that collecting garbage would be awful because of the associated smells. Thus, many of us would have to be paid more to agree to collect garbage than to take a less onerous job requiring an equal investment in human capital. We might expect, then, that garbage collecting carries a compensating wage differential and pays more than other jobs at similar skill levels. However, suppose that the economy needed less than 1% of workers to be garbage collectors, and that 5% of workers were indifferent to the smells of garbage. In this case, because the *marginal* worker found no disamenity to the job, it would not carry a compensating differential, even though the *average* worker found the job distasteful. The marginal worker is the "last" worker hired. However, the theory does not construe "last" in a temporal but rather a metaphorical sense. To see this, imagine that workers are lined up in the order of their disutility for garbage, with those liking to collect garbage the most at the head of the line. Hiring will start at the head of the line. As we move down the line, we come to workers who require a higher wage to collect garbage. It is in this metaphorical sense that neoclassical theory sees the tastes of the "last" or marginal worker hired determining the wage paid to all workers in the job.

An interesting aspect of the theory of compensating differentials is that it shows us the inappropriateness of a sharp dichotomy between work and leisure, or of a definition of work as an activity undertaken only for pecuniary reward. If a job is enjoyable, one is willing to do it for less money. If we define leisure as activities we will undertake without pecuniary motivation, then enjoyable work can be seen as part leisure, where the leisure component need not be paid.

Empirical applications of the theory of compensating differentials by labor economists have focused on testing whether *physical* disamenities are associated with higher wages. In principle, however, the theory applies to nonphysical amenities or disamenities as well. For example, if the marginal worker likes authority, jobs with authority should pay less than jobs not requiring authority, other things equal. But if the marginal worker dislikes authority, jobs with authority should pay a wage premium. Similarly, if exercising a particular kind of skill is a disamenity to the marginal worker, jobs requiring this skill should pay more. The theory is particularly difficult to test because workers vary in their tastes regarding job characteristics. Thus, even when we can comfortably assume, based on commonsense knowledge, that the average person dislikes a job characteristic, we still cannot be sure whether the marginal worker likes or dislikes the characteristic. This makes a theory-based prediction of whether a given job characteristic should have a positive or negative effect on wages difficult to make. Hence, the theory of compensating differentials is less falsifiable than most theories. Given this, it is hard to evaluate the extent to which evidence supports the theory.

My reading of available studies is that they provide only sketchy support for the theory of compensating differentials. Robert Smith (1979) reviews such studies and notes that not even a majority show the predicted positive effects on wages for alleged disamenities such as physical work, repetitiveness, lack of freedom, and job insecurity. One study found that jobs involving physical discomfort and hazards paid compensating differentials (i.e., higher wages) to male but not to female production workers (Barry 1985). However, another study found little evidence of a compensating differential for hazardous work for either women or men, black or white (Kilbourne et al. 1990; Kilbourne 1991). Positive compensating differentials have been found fairly consistently for jobs involving a risk of death (R. Smith 1979; Olson 1981; Duncan and Holmlund 1983), but findings for other physical disamenities are very mixed (Brown 1980). The studies referred to above generally used national probability samples, and thus cast doubt on the theory of compensating differentials for the economy as a whole, most of which is made up of the private sector. Jacobs and Steinberg (1990a, 1990b) review findings from a number of job evaluation studies done in the public sector. In general, these studies find a net *negative* return for onerous physical working conditions they presume to be disamenities to workers, such as hazards and demands for physical effort. If these job characteristics are really disamenities to the marginal worker, we would expect them to have net positive returns if the theory of compensating differentials is true.

Usually the notion of compensating differentials refers to wage premiums or penalties that compensate for *nonpecuniary* aspects of work. But if we allow the notion to apply across both pecuniary and nonpecuniary costs and benefits of a job, then even the theory of human capital is subsumed within the theory of compensating differentials (Rosen 1986). In human capital theory, the reason jobs requiring more skill pay more is to "compensate" for the disamenity (mainly the opportunity cost of forgone earnings) required to attain the necessary skill. Such disamenities that one "pays" before taking the job are investments. Other compensating differentials refer to nonpecuniary disamenities endured in an ongoing way as the job is performed; these are compensated by the wages in a "pay as you go" fashion. Despite this difference in when the worker gets paid for the disamenity, and whether it is pecuniary, the principle of equalization at the margin remains the same in both views.

If female jobs pay less than male jobs, net of human capital requirements, a neoclassical view suggests that the male jobs have disamenities (as perceived by the marginal worker) that are being compensated for by the higher wage (Killingsworth 1984, 1985, 1986, 1990; Filer 1985, 1989, 1990a). One study has found the effect of sex composition on wages to disappear under controls for job characteristics intended to measure compensating differentials (Filer 1989). (See Jacobs and Steinberg 1990a, 1990b for a criticism of the study and Filer 1990a for a reply.) However, most studies controlling for multiple job characteristics find that female jobs have lower wages even *net* of these characteristics (Jacobs and Steinberg 1990a; England et al. 1988; Kilbourne et al. 1990). Thus, most studies suggest that compensating differentials do not *entirely* explain the pay gap between female and male jobs. (Chapter 3 contains my own empirical analysis of compensating differentials and comparable worth.)

Crowding. The crowding hypothesis is one view of the origins of the lower pay of predominantly female occupations. Bergmann's (1974, 1986) version of the crowding thesis invokes hiring discrimination. (Bergmann's model builds on an idea advanced by Edgeworth in 1922.) It contrasts with other neoclassical explanations of occupational pay discussed above, none of which involve discrimination. Although it uses neoclassical reasoning about the *consequences* of hiring discrimination, the crowding model's assumption of such discrimination is in a tension with neoclassical claims that discrimination cannot persist in competitive markets.

In Bergmann's (1974, 1986) crowding model, employers prefer not to hire women for some jobs. Some women manage to get hired in these jobs anyway by working for a lower wage than men. But many women take female jobs because there is less or no discriminatory resistance to their entry into these jobs. Female jobs will thus have an artificially high supply of labor. The large supply is artificial in the sense that, for any given wage, the amount of labor supplied to female jobs is greater than it would have been in the absence of the discrimination against women in male jobs. This amounts to saying that the exclusion of women from male jobs shifts the labor supply curve facing female jobs outward (i.e., downward and to the right in Figure 2.1). This lowers the market wage in female jobs below what it would be in the absence of discrimination in the male jobs. As noted above, in neoclassical views, discrimination in hiring and discrimination in wages arises from a single source. But, via crowding, this discrimination within male jobs will affect women's wages in female jobs, even when employers are neutral regarding hiring women or men into these female jobs.

Bergmann's (1974, 1986) crowding model posits a devaluation of female labor when employers are hiring for male jobs, a devaluation that leads them to refuse to hire women or to hire them only at a lower wage than paid to men. But the model ignores the possibility of an analogous devaluation of the work in female jobs, leading to a lower wage for female jobs. Rather, her crowding model posits that the lower wages in female jobs occur entirely because devaluation of females when they seek male jobs leads to "excess" supplies of labor to female jobs.

A kind of crowding can also arise without discrimination. Increases in female labor force participation for reasons other than rising wages will produce an outward shift of supply curves to female occupations if most women select traditionally female jobs. This outward shift in the supply curve will lower the wage in female occupations, although it is not artificial as in the discriminatory case above.

Effects of Comparable Worth Policies.   Many economists are skeptical of comparable worth policies because neoclassical theory implies that raising the wages in female jobs will disemploy women,[5] the very group the policy is designed to help (Oi 1986; Roback 1986; Killingsworth 1990). Some of them believe there is little sex discrimination in labor markets. Others subscribe to Bergmann's (1974, 1986) version of the crowding thesis, yet reject comparable worth wage policies that would force employers to raise the relative pay of female jobs. These economists generally favor prohibiting hiring and wage discrimination in male jobs. According to the crowding thesis, this would eventually lead to higher pay in female jobs as the artificially high supply of labor to these jobs was thereby decreased.

Why do economists believe that raising wages in female jobs will disemploy people? Recall that the downward slope of demand curves indicates that the number of workers that employers will choose to employ in a job (the "quantity demanded") is negatively related to the wage they must pay. Thus, faced with a requirement that they pay a higher wage than previously in female jobs, neoclassical theory says that employers will either lay off workers or hire fewer workers than they otherwise would have hired in these jobs. This would be depicted in Figure 2.1 as an upward and leftward movement along an unchanging demand curve. Thus, persons who would otherwise have been in these female jobs may end up either unemployed or out of the labor force because their next-best job offer is undesirable enough that they decide against employment.[6] Either outcome is referred to as *disemployment.* Since comparable worth makes labor in female jobs more expensive relative to capital than previously, one mechanism of disemployment is that employers may now choose to automate processes done in female jobs, substituting capital for labor. At the same time that a mandated higher wage in female jobs is decreasing the quantity of labor demanded, the existence of higher wages in female jobs will increase the quantity of female labor supplied by bringing more women into the labor force to look for jobs, deterring some women from leaving the labor force, and encouraging both men and women who would otherwise have sought male jobs to seek female jobs (Nakamura and Nakamura 1989). This increase in the quantity of labor supplied would be depicted in Figure 2.1 as an upward and rightward movement along an unchanging supply curve. Thus, following neoclassical theory, we would expect comparable worth to create an imbalance between the amount of labor demanded and supplied to female jobs, thus creating disemployment. The argument is similar to economists' arguments about the disemployment caused by minimum wage laws.

If employers' *overall* wage bill is increased by comparable worth policies, i.e., if the raises in female jobs are not compensated for by reductions in wages in male jobs, then we would expect some disemployment to result, as described above. If the overall wage bill is increased, we would also expect increases in the prices of goods and services produced by firms covered by the policy (Killingsworth 1985). However, in the longer run, money spent on comparable worth adjustments might result in smaller raises in male jobs than would otherwise have been awarded. To the extent that this is true, the effect on the total wage bill and hence the *amounts* of theoretically predicted disemployment and price increases are smaller.

Why would neoclassical theory predict that the disemployment resulting from comparable worth policies would fall largely on women? It is female jobs in which the mandated pay raises should lead to a quantity of labor supplied that exceeds the quantity demanded. We would expect it to be largely women who are laid off from the female jobs, or who apply but are not hired in female jobs. However, women might respond to potential disemployment by seeking male jobs (Kahn 1986). Thus disemployment will fall less disproportionately on women to the extent that women seek male jobs and are not met with hiring discrimination in these jobs (Kahn 1986).

Killingsworth (1990) provides estimates of disemployment effects of several implementations of comparable worth. (For earlier studies see Gregory and Duncan 1981; Kahn 1986; Ehrenberg and Smith 1987; and Gregory, Anstie, Daly, and Ho 1989.) In the United States, there is no national policy of comparable worth covering either the private or public sector. As discussed in Chapter 5, some lawsuits have attempted to persuade federal courts to interpret the major federal antidiscrimination law, Title VII of the Civil Rights Act of 1964, to require that employers use wage-setting principles of comparable worth. However, most of these cases have been unsuccessful. Comparable worth policies in the United States have been limited to states and localities passing legislation demanding comparable worth wage setting in their own public sector employment. Thus, Killingsworth uses one state, Minnesota, and one locality, San Jose, California, as two of his cases. His third case is

Australia, where minimum wages for specific jobs are set by a national board affecting private and public sector employers. This board had long explicitly discriminated against women's jobs in wage setting, but adopted comparable worth–like policies in the 1970s, although it has since backed away from them.

Estimating the magnitude of disemployment effects is made difficult by the need to hold other factors affecting employment levels constant except change induced by the comparable worth adjustments. Killingsworth (1990) uses a two-step process: First he estimates how employment levels respond to changes in wages by using data on variation in wages and employment levels across time and occupation within each of his three cases. This step assesses the wage elasticity of demand. In the second step, he estimates the magnitude of wage increases in female jobs from the pay adjustments. Then the wage elasticities of demand are applied to the wage increases to estimate disemployment.

Using this method, Killingsworth estimates that in San Jose the amount of female employment growth typical for one year was lost due to comparable worth pay increases. However, a study by Kahn (1986) of the San Jose case found no disemployment in targeted female jobs. (For a discussion of differences in the two studies' methods, see Ehrenberg 1989.) In Minnesota, Killingsworth estimates that the amount of female employment growth typical for three years was lost. However, another analysis of the Minnesota case, using somewhat different methods, found substantially less disemployment than this (Sorensen 1991a, 1991b). Whether one views such effects as small or large is a matter of judgment. Killingsworth points out that in neither of these cases was pay in women's jobs raised all the way to the pay of the male jobs to which the job evaluation studies showed them comparable. Thus, he concludes that under a more stringent comparable worth policy, the disemployment effects might be substantially larger. In Australia there were larger disemployment effects initially, but virtually no disemployment effects after the policy had been in force several years. (For a criticism of Killingsworth's analysis of the Australian case, see Sorensen 1991a.) The small effects after several years must, however, be weighed against the fact that there was no net improvement in wages in women's compared to men's jobs several years later when this later assessment of disemployment was made. Overall, then, Killingsworth (1990) provides some evidence of a disemployment effect of comparable worth, although there is debate about its magnitude.

Some neoclassical economists have suggested that, in addition to causing disemployment, comparable worth policies could lower some women's wages, quite the opposite of the intent of the policy (Oi 1986; Smith 1988). This is a possible prediction from neoclassical theory *if* the policy covers some firms but not others. Suppose, for example, that small firms were exempted or, as a practical matter, that the law was seldom enforced against them even though it applied. Such firms would become an uncovered sector absorbing the overflow labor disemployed from the covered sector. With the existence of such an uncovered sector, workers disemployed from the covered sector would not all become unemployed or leave the labor force, as would be more likely if all sectors were covered by the policies. Rather, some workers disemployed from the covered sector would crowd into the uncovered sector, and the crowding would lower wages. To the extent that those ending up in the uncovered sector were disproportionately women, the sex gap in wages could increase. At the least, the amount that the sex gap in pay decreased as a direct result of the comparable worth policies would be reduced. Since comparable worth has not been adopted on a large scale anywhere but Australia, we do not yet have evidence of what the economywide effects would be on women's earnings.

III.   The New Neoclassical Institutionalism

A new development within economics purports to explain various anomalies to neoclassical theory, but to remain within the neoclassical tradition. This development is called *the new institutionalism*. It includes models of implicit contracts and agency (or bonding) models (Baily 1974; Azariadis 1975; Akerlof and Miyazaki 1980; Lazear 1981), the transactions cost economics of Oliver Williamson (1975, 1981, 1985, 1988), and efficiency wage models (Akerlof and Yellen 1986; Katz 1986; Dickens and Katz 1987; Krueger and Summers 1988). These ideas provide possible explanations for otherwise theoretically anomalous realities such as unemployment, interindustry wage differentials between workers with equal human capital in the same occupation, golden parachutes for early retirement, and wage trajectories that do not equal marginal revenue product in each time period.

A.   Implicit Contracts, Specific Capital, Agency, and Transaction Costs

The term *implicit contract* refers to a situation in which there is no formal, legally binding, written contract, yet things are structured in such a way as to create incentives for employers and employees each to engage in behavior in which the other party has an interest. Sometimes the term has been used to describe a narrower subset of economic models that are distinct from models of specific capital, bonding, and trans-actions costs. I will use the term here in a broader sense that encom-passes all these developments.

The notion of implicit contracts, broadly construed, was fore-shadowed by Becker's (1962) discussion of firm-specific human capital (often referred to as simply specific capital), discussed previously. What are the costs and benefits of this training to the employer and employee? Costs may include expenses for materials or teachers. But even when the training is informal and the costs less visible, there are still costs. An example is the opportunity cost of forgone productivity while an experi-enced worker teaches a new worker. Gains include higher productivity that results from the training and higher wages. Hashimoto (1981, p. 475) summarizes the standard analysis this way:

> (T)he worker invests in specific human capital by accepting a wage lower than his *(sic)* alternative wage, and receives a return on his *(sic)* investment during the post-investment periods in the form of a wage higher than his *(sic)* alternative wage. The employer invests in specific capital by paying the worker a wage larger than the value of his *(sic)* marginal product, and receives a return on the investment in subsequent periods by paying a wage smaller than the value of his *(sic)* marginal product.

Although at the end of a worker's career with the firm, s/he is earning less than MRP, this is nonetheless more than the worker could make elsewhere since we are discussing training with applicability only to this firm. So, compared to a worker's alternatives elsewhere, wages are lower initially but higher later in the firm providing the specific training. Although Hashimoto (1981) does not use the term *implicit contract*, he describes what is, in essence, an implicit contract between employer and employee. The wage trajectory, which makes employees pay their share of training costs initially, gives the employee an incentive to stay with the firm, which the employer wants in order to avoid the costs of train-ing a new worker. The fact that the employee makes less than MRP late in the career gives the employer an incentive not to fire the worker. Thus the wage trajectory creates incentives for both parties to act as if they were honoring a contract to keep the relationship intact. We can think of this as an implicit contract.

But would it not be better for both parties to write a legal, binding contract stating that the employer will provide training and a specified wage trajectory and that the employee will stay long enough for the employer to recoup search and training costs? In a sense, in proposing the implicit rather than such an explicit contract, Becker (1962) was foreshadowing the transactions cost models introduced by Williamson

(1975, 1981, 1985, 1988). One of the insights of transactions cost models is relevant to labor markets: In the presence of both a joint investment (the training) and prohibitive costs of transacting an explicit contract, implicit contracts are often the solution.

In jobs with specific training, both employer and employee have invested in an asset, firm-specific human capital, that benefits both parties most if the employee continues to work at this firm. It benefits the employer in that the worker is more productive than workers who might be newly hired, since they would not have this specific training. It benefits the employee in that s/he is more productive here than at firms for which s/he has not received specific training, and thus will get paid more here than elsewhere. Williamson (1988) calls this a situation of "asset specificity." It leads both employer and employee to want a contract to guard their specific asset. But why not a formal, written, legally binding contract that spells out each party's rights and obligations under all contingencies? This is what economists call a *perfect contingent-claims contract*.

What would either party want such a contract to cover? Employees would want such contracts to promise future wage increases, promotion chances, pensions, and layoff protection. Employers would wish such contractual promises to be contingent upon both the employee's performance and the economic conditions confronting the firm. For example, if the firm experienced an unexpected increase in the cost of raw materials, or a decline in the price it receives for its product, the employer would want these facts to condition whether s/he had to give raises, or could lay off workers. Employers would also want a promise from employees to stay with the firm to safeguard the firm's investment in on-the-job training, or to compensate the employer for the cost of the training if the employee quit before a specified amount of time had passed. Employees would wish any such agreement to be contingent upon the offers available to the employee in other firms, and upon the inflation rate.

Perfect contingent-claims contracts would have to cover a myriad of contingencies. While explicit contracts exist in unionized jobs and some others, contracts as detailed as those described above are unheard of. Such detailed contracts are impractical because of their excessive transactions costs (Williamson, Wachter, and Harris 1975; Wachter and Williamson 1978). Transactions costs include the time it takes to bargain over the contract, the costs of obtaining information about whether the contingencies of the contract have been met (e.g., whether the employee's performance has been adequate), and the costs of enforcement of the contract (perhaps including lawyers' fees). These costs are quite high relative to the benefits of such contracts. As a consequence of these transactions costs, elaborate contingent-claims contracts are rare. Yet something like a contract arises in at least some jobs. According to the new institutionalists, in the presence of both transactions costs and the asset specificity constituted by specific capital, the real-world outcome is often implicit contracts (Williamson et al. 1975; Wachter and Williamson 1978; Nalebuff and Zeckhauser 1981; Okun 1981; England and Farkas 1986, Chapter 6; Rebitzer 1989). What these contracts include varies, but they may include raises, promotions, protection from layoffs, seniority-based callbacks from layoffs, and pensions, depending on the richness of the contract involved.

The term *implicit contract* also has a narrower use, as I said above. Here it refers to models that do not add the complications of firm-specific human capital, although it is clear that the desire for such a contract by either party would be greater in the presence of specific capital. The narrower use refers to models I will call "insurance" models of implicit contracts. These models see implicit contracts as providing a kind of insurance scheme to protect workers from unwanted layoffs or wage reductions and to protect employers from unwanted quits. Orthodox theory predicts that reductions in the demand for a firm's product will lower MRP and lead to layoffs or, if conditions are better elsewhere, quits that anticipate such layoffs. If the reduction of MRP is economywide, then the market wage will fall.

This class of implicit contract models posits that firms offer "contracts" that amount to a kind of insurance that risk-averse workers "buy" from their employers in the form of a lower but predictable wage. The insurance protects them against later layoffs in the event of reductions in demand for the firm's product (Baily 1974; Gordon 1974; Azariadis 1975; Azariadis and Stiglitz 1983). In essence, employers have entered the insurance business and the employee is paying a small insurance premium deducted from every paycheck. Such contracts are seen to function in the aggregate to improve matches between workers and firms.

Another "insurance-based" implicit contract model posits insurance against unemployment and wage reductions as well, but only after some seniority is built up (Azariadis and Stiglitz 1983). Here, the implicit contract states that any layoffs undertaken will be seniority-based, with seniority-based callbacks, but that wages will not be reduced (Okun 1981) or will only be reduced temporarily, while conditions facing the firm are bad (Hall and Lilien 1979; Grossman and Hart 1981; Grossman, Hart, and Maskin 1983).

Because implicit contracts have no explicit mechanisms of enforcement, Okun (1981) has referred to them as the "invisible handshake." What protects employees from employers who renege? If the employer lays off workers after the worker has paid for insurance in the form of a lower wage, or lowers wages when the contract promises this will not be done, there is little the employee can do about it. Indeed, such events occur. However, there is one long-term incentive for employers not to renege on the contract. This incentive stems from the fact that the firm's reputation as an employer who treats employees well affects whether good workers will sign on with the firm, and affects the turnover rate among its recently trained workers (Lazear 1981; Azariadis and Stiglitz 1983; Bull 1983; Yellen 1984).

Those contracts in which the implicit promise is that wages will not be lowered and that any layoffs when times are bad will be seniority-based have an additional protection for the worker from the employer reneging. The "moral hazard" problem that would otherwise result from asymmetric information (i.e., the fact that employers observe decreases in product demand, but workers do not) is avoided in such arrangements.[7] This is because employers may have an incentive *at any time* to lie and declare that times are bad for the firm so they can lower the wage, but they do not have an incentive to lay workers off except when times are really bad for the firm. Thus, layoffs, combined with seniority rights of protection from them, are less likely to be seen by workers as a violation of the contract than are wage reductions (Okun 1981). Alternatively, an implicit contract might permit temporary wage reductions but only when in conjunction with layoffs. Here again, since the firm has no incentive to lay people off except when demand for their product is falling, moral hazard is avoided (Hall and Lilien 1979; Grossman and Hart 1981; Grossman et al. 1983).

What is to prevent employees from reneging on the implicit contract? If an employee takes a job with a lower wage as insurance against bad times, but times are good later and a higher wage could be earned at another firm without such insurance premiums, what keeps the employee from quitting? Reputation effects are one possibility, but they seem a less plausible answer for employees than for employers (Azariadis and Stiglitz 1983; Holmstrom 1983). After all, it is much more feasible that each employee checks on the reputation of the few firms s/he is thinking about joining than that an employer checks out the reputation of every prospective employee with respect to quit record. This led to the idea that perhaps the "insurance payment" is "front loaded," i.e., paid mostly in the early period of employment (Azariadis and Stiglitz 1983; Holmstrom 1983). This gives employees an incentive to stay with the firm since it is only in the later period that they may be able to make more in this firm than in alternative firms. Another way to think of the same arrangement is that the employee puts up a "bond" (paid in the form of a lower starting wage) to be repaid later in the form of higher wages and/or protection from layoffs. This assures the employer that the employee has a motivation to stay with the firm.

Such front-loaded versions of the insurance implicit contract model feature wage profiles like those in the specific capital model in that both models see workers as initially earning less than their alternative wage in other firms. In the case of the specific capital model, workers were paying for part of their training in this period, while in front-loaded implicit contract models, workers pay their insurance premium in this early period rather than spread out across the life cycle. In the specific capital model the later wage is higher than the worker's alternative elsewhere because the training has increased the worker's productivity in this firm but not in others, although the later wage is still less than MRP (Hashimoto 1981). In front-loaded versions of insurance implicit contract models, later wages are often higher than either MRP or what the worker could make elsewhere. This part of the contract is what motivates the employee to stay through the initial period of low wages (Azariadis and Stiglitz 1983; Holmstrom 1983; Bull 1983). Thus both models feature a steep wage trajectory in which wages are not equal to MRP at each time point, although they do equal expected MRP across the entire life course. A model that includes *both* firm-specific human capital *and* insurance implicit contracts should have an even *steeper* trajectory with even lower starting wages and even higher later wages. To the extent that there is a competitive market in jobs with implicit contracts, it is a market for long-term contracts and an expected lifetime wage. Market forces have to work exclusively at the point of entry to the firm.

So far the implicit contract models that have been considered are all motivated, from the employer's side, by a concern that workers not quit. Some of these models have led to a wage trajectory that pays less than MRP or the worker's alternative wage in the early period and provides greater benefits of one form or another in the later period. Lazear (1979, 1981) proposes a model in which employers offer a similar wage trajectory based, not on concerns about quits, as above, but on concerns about the level of effort put forth by employees. His model is commonly referred to as an "agency" model. The name refers to the fact that employers (the "principals") are trying to use wage profiles to get workers to act faithfully as their "agents" in the sense of putting forth effort and not engaging in malfeasance. Lazear (1979, 1981) suggests that workers can be motivated to put forth more effort by making initial wages lower than MRP and later wages higher than MRP. This way they have to perform well enough not to get fired in order to reach the period where rewards are higher than what they could make elsewhere. Thus, in

Lazear's agency model, as in some other implicit contract models, expected lifetime wages equal expected lifetime MRP, but the shape of the trajectory is changed to lower initial wages and raise later wages. The incentive system created by the wage trajectory makes workers act as if they are honoring a contract to put forth diligent effort. Although he does not label this an implicit contract model, his model features the same wage trajectory as the front-loaded implicit contract models discussed above, and involves arrangements that create incentives in place of an explicit contract. Thus, under the broader definition I am using here, it can be considered an implicit contract model.

How can we apply the notion of implicit contracts to illuminate gender differentiation in labor markets? From those implicit contract models that feature a low starting wage and steep wage trajectory one can derive a supply-side explanation of occupational segregation that has the same predictions as the human capital theory of sex segregation explained above. Indeed, if the implicit contract model in question is the specific capital model, the explanations are the same. In this view, women planning intermittent employment are well advised to avoid jobs with implicit contracts since these jobs have lower starting wages. One who plans only a short spell of employment will maximize earnings by choosing a job with higher starting wages, despite its less steep trajectory, since a short spell of employment affords one little of the gain from the steep wage trajectory. However, the evidence does not support this explanation of segregation, since women's jobs do not have higher starting wages than male jobs of the same skill level (Greenberger and Steinberg 1983; England 1984; England et al. 1988).

A second possible application of implicit contract theory would emphasize demand-side statistical or error discrimination. If women have higher or more variable quit rates than men, this may lead employers to discriminate against women in jobs offering substantial amounts of on-the-job training or to organize jobs already filled by women to exclude such training. Since implicit contracts are particularly likely in jobs with provision of firm-specific training, it would seem at first glance that this could explain the fact that women are typically not in jobs with steep wage trajectories (England et al. 1988). However, this explanation would only make sense within a neoclassical model if women's turnover rates are higher or more variable than men's, and the evidence reviewed in Chapter 1 casts doubt on this commonly made assumption.

While the models of implicit contracts featuring low starting wages and steep trajectories propose reasons why women's wage trajectories have a less steep *slope* than men's, they do not provide an obvious explanation for the lower wage *levels* of women and of female jobs *across the entire life cycle.* I want to suggest one rather unorthodox application of implicit contract theory that I believe *can* illuminate the slow erosion of discrimination in labor markets, and thus the lower wages of women and of female jobs over the entire life cycle (England et al. 1988). I should be clear, however, on the fact that this has *not* been suggested by economists writing in the literature on implicit contracts. Many implicit contract models amount to giving experienced workers more privileges than less-experienced workers, by providing them with raises and promotions, and by protecting them from wage decreases or layoffs. These strategies discourage the replacement of experienced men by cheaper women. But such replacement would speed the arbitrage process discussed above, which neoclassical theorists believe erodes discrimination in competitive markets (England et al. 1988; Jacobs 1989b). Thus, in jobs with implicit contracts, most of the competitive forces that should otherwise erode discriminatory wage differentials are reduced to operating at the discrete time points of each worker's entry to the firm. It is at this point that employers offering greater lifetime earnings will be motivated to choose the cheapest available workers with the greatest productive potential without discrimination. Because this "precontract" point is affected by competitive forces, economists generally presume that the usual conclusions about erosion of discriminatory wage differentials still hold in a model including implicit contracts. Despite the fact that the new neoclassical institutionalism can be given this conservative reading, it also has implications consistent with a notion of demand-side discrimination and segmentation in labor markets. When the competitive forces of labor markets impinge primarily on the initial moment in an individual's career with a firm, as is implied by implicit contract theory, their effects are much less swift and powerful than the orthodox neoclassical view suggests (England et al. 1988). Although many economists still resist these implications, I believe they provide one possible explanation for the failure of discrimination to erode in competitive markets.

B. Efficiency Wage Models

Efficiency wage models provide one possible explanation for wages being higher in some jobs than others in a way that is "uncompensated" by either nonpecuniary disamenities or demands for human capital. The key insight of efficiency wage models is that paying higher wages may induce behavior in workers (or prospective workers) that increases rather than decreases profits. The behavior desired by employers may be working hard (in the shirking or gift exchange model), staying with the firm (in the turnover model), joining the firm if one is of high quality (in the adverse-selection model), not unionizing (in the union threat model), or applying for or accepting a job with the firm (in the recruiting model). Efficiency wage models differ from orthodox neoclassical models in asserting that such worker behavior is endogenous rather than exogenous to the wage. In such a situation, it may be profit maximizing for employers to raise wages above the market-clearing level implied by the usual supply-demand model. Wages will be raised as long as they lead to revenue increases greater than the cost of the wage increase.

Below I review several efficiency wage models. Each proposes a different rationale for why, within some range, profits might be a positive function of the wage offered to workers of equivalent human capital. Each model suggests different hypotheses about the types of firms, industries, or occupations in which above–market efficiency wages are most likely to be present. (For an overview, see Katz 1986.) Then the models are examined to see whether they can illuminate gender inequality in labor markets.

One efficiency wage model is the *shirking* or *effort elicitation* model (Bulow and Summers 1986; Shapiro and Stiglitz 1984; Bowles 1985). Here the focus is on potential costs of workers' engaging in malfeasance (such as sabotaging equipment) or putting forth low levels of effort, and on the costs of detecting such shirking. Even with minimal surveillance, workers know that there is some probability of losing their jobs for shirking. If they are paid more than they could make at other firms, they will have a motivation to avoid shirking so as to avoid the wage drop they would experience if they were caught and fired, and had to procure a job at a firm not paying above–market efficiency wages. In some situations it may be cheaper to reduce shirking through raising the wage above the market level than to spend extra money on technology or personnel for more thorough surveillance. The model predicts that above–market efficiency wages are more likely where the elasticity of effort with respect to the wage is greater, and this elasticity may be greater where monitoring costs are higher.

A second efficiency wage model focuses on *turnover* (Stiglitz 1987). Here above-market wages lower turnover. This reduces the costs that firms expend in screening and training new employees. This model suggests that above–market efficiency wages will be found in occupations, industries, or firms where hiring and training costs are larger.

A third efficiency wage model is the *adverse-selection* model. Firms that pay higher wages are more likely to have their offers accepted by applicants of higher quality on dimensions that are not possible to observe and screen. This is true if workers who are better on such unobservables have higher reservation wages. A worker's reservation wage is the smallest wage below which s/he will turn down the job. Higher reservation wages among better workers might occur for two reasons. If "good" workers are also better, on average, at either homemaking or self-employment, then they will have higher reservation wages since their alternative to taking the job is more valuable (Weiss 1980). If we introduce imperfect information and search costs, there is a second reason why workers who are better on qualities that are unobservable at hire might have higher reservation wages. This is because such workers know that if they get a high-wage job (an "efficiency wage" job) they are unlikely to be fired for malfeasance, and thus it is more worth the continued search costs for them to hold out for a high-wage job than is true for other workers.

A fourth efficiency wage model is the *union threat* model (Dickens 1986). In this model nonunionized firms that face a threat of unionization pay union or near-union wages to avoid unionization. We would expect this model to apply where unionization is a more likely threat.

A fifth efficiency wage model is a *recruiting* model (Lang 1991; Montgomery 1991; Weitzman 1989). Here the focus is on the costs to firms of an insufficient number of applicants or of workers turning down their offers. Such costs include the costs of screening and processing applications of additional workers, and costs of physical capital that goes unused while positions are empty. By having an above-market wage that is publicized, firms can get more applicants and have more of them accept their offers. Where the costs avoided exceed the extra wage paid, profit-maximizing firms will adopt this strategy. We would expect such a strategy to be especially likely in jobs where employees work with much physical capital. This is because the capital increases workers' productivity, and thus increases the forgone costs of the position being vacant.

A final efficiency wage model is the *gift exchange* model (Akerlof 1982, 1984). In this model, a wage above the market-clearing level is perceived by workers as a gift and as compliance by the employer with norms of fairness. This increases workers' morale and hence their effort, also offered as a gift and as compliance with norms of fairness. Akerloff's efficiency wage theory departs form neoclassical orthodoxy in a way that the other efficiency wage models do not in not assuming entirely selfish actors, but assuming some altruism among both employers and employees. Each offers an altruistic gift—one a higher-than-market wage, the other a higher-than-minimal effort. Perhaps for this reason, economist Akerlof (1982, 1984) refers to this gift exchange model as "sociological," because the mechanism linking wages and productivity involves norms of altruism and fairness affecting group morale.

If employers in all sectors benefited from gift exchange efficiency wages to an equal extent, the notion would have little relevance to the explanation of why some jobs pay more than others. But workers' norms of fairness may include the notion that firms should pay higher wages when they have a greater "ability to pay," i.e., when they have higher profit levels. If so, then firms with higher profit levels will gain more in workers' morale and productivity from paying above-market wages than will other firms (Katz 1986). Thus, the gift exchange model offers one explanation of why industries' profit rates affect wages (Seidman 1979), a finding that is otherwise an anomaly for neoclassical theory. Orthodox theory implies that investment in less-profitable sectors will eventually cease and the sectors will disappear unless their return on investments equals other sectors, and thus that economic profit rates between industries should not differ in the long run.

Overall, efficiency wage theory provides possible explanations for two common findings that have been regarded as anomalies for orthodox neoclassical theory. One is the presence in the economy of unemployed workers willing to work for less than the wage of employed workers of equal productivity, but unable to get jobs by offering themselves for this lower wage. Efficiency wage theory explains this by the dual role being paid by the wage. The same wage cannot clear the market for new hires (which implies paying as little as competition allows, and thus predicts wage decreases rather than unemployment during recessions), while simultaneously altering the behavior of current employees or applicants in the direction employers wish to alter it. Efficiency wage theory and implicit contract theory are alternative, competing explanations of why wages do not fall sufficiently during recessions to allow the economy to absorb unemployed workers, as orthodox theory would predict.

Efficiency wage theory also provides one possible explanation for persistent interoccupational, interfirm, and interindustry wage differentials that cannot be explained by differences in workers' human capital or by compensating differentials. Efficiency wage theory challenges the orthodox contention that, through competition and attendant mobility, interjob wage differences will disappear, except those needed to compensate for human capital investment or nonpecuniary disamenities of jobs. In this sense, efficiency wage models are a greater departure from neoclassical orthodoxy than are implicit contract models. Implicit contract models maintain the notion of a lifetime wage that is just that needed to compensate for human capital investment and nonpecuniary disamenities, but allow the timing of pay increases to deviate from the time path of MRP. In efficiency wage theory even the lifetime wage is decoupled from MRP. This is because wages cannot simultaneously play the market-clearing function of equalizing differentials between sectors accorded them in orthodox theory, while still staying high enough to affect workers' behavior in the efficiency-producing ways specified by the theory. Since individual profit-maximizing employers have more stake in the latter, the "invisible hand" of competition does not produce the former.

One critique of efficiency wage theory asks why employers cannot motivate the desired behavior with the implicit contract scheme discussed above, in which early low wages and high later wages motivate the behavior efficiency wages are supposed to accomplish (Carmichael 1985, 1990). This is called the "bonding" critique, and applies to three of the efficiency wage models, the shirking, turnover, and adverse-selection models (Katz 1986). Would not the higher-than-market wages in the later portions of the career that are featured in some of the implicit contract models provide as effective an incentive against shirking and turnover? Would not wage profiles with lower starting wages and rewards later serve to self-select better workers (since they know they are unlikely to be found wanting enough to be fired)? If so, why would neoclassical theorists prefer an efficiency wage model that makes the wage above market for the entire career, rather than a competitive market lifetime wage that is sequenced so that bonding (a lower wage) is present in the early period but the wage is higher than MRP later? Clearly the former is a greater departure from neoclassical orthodoxy. Efficiency wage theorists choose the model with a lifetime wage above the competitive wage because of their belief that, as a practical matter, employers cannot set starting wages low enough to pay for the later above–market efficiency wages (Katz 1986, pp. 243–246). In the extreme, this might require a negative starting wage! Minimum wage laws and imperfect capital markets on which workers could borrow this bond may explain why such a solution is impractical. Thus, all efficiency wage models retain a greater anomaly for orthodox theory than do either Lazear's (1981) agency model or other implicit contract models. The anomaly is interjob lifetime wage differentials between workers in various industries, firms, or occupations that cannot be explained by human capital or compensating differentials.

Can efficiency wage models help us to understand gender differences in wages? It is hard to think of a supply-side reason that women would avoid jobs with efficiency wages. Do the models suggest any reason that employers would be more likely to discriminate against women seeking to enter jobs with efficiency wages, and/or be less likely to pay efficiency wages in predominantly female occupations?

In the shirking model, some firms find it cheaper to reduce shirking by increasing the wage than by increased surveillance. However, if women have higher quit rates, then the cost to women of losing the job would be less than the cost to men, since the women would forgo the above-market wage for only the limited time period they intended to stay. Thus, a high efficiency wage would do less to deter women's than men's shirking (Bulow and Summers 1986; Aldrich and Buchele 1989). Put another way, it would take a higher wage increment to deter women's than men's shirking. Given this, if women have higher quit rates than men, the model predicts statistical discrimination against women in jobs with high monitoring costs and efficiency wages (Goldin 1986). As discussed in Chapter 1, the evidence is not clear on whether women's quit rates are higher than men's beyond what can be explained by job placements that result from discrimination (other than merely statistical discrimination). Thus, the relevance of this model to explaining segregation and the sex gap in pay remains questionable.

In the turnover model, above-market-clearing wages exist to deter turnover. Since firms that pay such wages are those in which turnover is especially expensive, they may also not want to hire women if women have higher turnover. If employers are risk-averse, then they may avoid hiring women because female turnover is more variable than men's, even if it is not higher. Thus, this model also suggests that in hiring for jobs with efficiency wages there will be statistical discrimination against women based on beliefs in sex differences in turnover (Aldrich and Buchele 1989). However, if women's turnover rates are *more* sensitive to their wage than are men's, this might be a mitigating factor throwing the rationality of statistical discrimination against women in such jobs in doubt even if women's turnover is higher or more variable. Two studies have shown a greater wage elasticity of women's than men's quits (Kahn and Griesinger 1989; Blau and Kahn 1981). Thus, it is not clear that it *is* rational for employers to discriminate against women in jobs where they are trying to deter turnover.

The adverse-selection model says that efficiency wages designed to attract better workers (presumed to be those with higher reservation wages) are most likely in jobs where it is particularly difficult to observe worker quality in advance of hire. Presumably this strategy would work to attract either male or female workers of high quality, and hence should have no implications for discrimination. But Aldrich and Buchele (1989) claim that the very screening costs that lead firms to adopt efficiency wages under the adverse-selection model also lead to statistical discrimination based on women's higher turnover rates. An objection to this is parallel to the objection I have raised about applications of all the models to gender differences via statistical discrimination: Based on the evidence reviewed in Chapter 1, it is not clear that women have turnover rates that are higher than men's for reasons exogenous to discriminatory practices.

The union threat model suggests that efficiency wages are less likely in female jobs *if* such jobs do not exhibit as realistic a threat of unionization as male jobs. It is often assumed that women are harder to organize than men, presumably because they plan to stay in their jobs less long. However, little evidence is ever presented that women are harder to organize, and, as argued above, the alleged difference in exogenous turnover rates is not firmly established.

The recruiting model suggests efficiency wages are most likely in capital-intensive jobs because the opportunity cost of letting a position go vacant is greater in such jobs. It is not obvious from the model why firms using this strategy would be any more or less likely to discriminate against women than other firms.

In sum, it seems that none of the efficiency wage models reviewed above is very helpful in explaining why employers with efficiency wages would be particularly motivated to engage in sex discrimination. Where such implications have been suggested, they hinge on assuming that women have higher turnover rates. Yet Chapter 1 showed that we lack compelling evidence that women have higher turnover rates that are exogenous to discriminatory treatment by employers.

The gift exchange efficiency wage model has more promise in explaining gender-relevant differences, although this application was not discussed by Akerlof (1982, 1984). The model says that group norms will affect wage differentials because workers put forth more effort when they see that employers are following the norms. It follows, then, that if prevailing norms are sexist in that they devalue traditionally female jobs and skills, the model predicts lower wages for female jobs. However, this would only be true if women as well as men hold sexist norms, or to the extent that efficiency wages in male but not female jobs increased men's productivity more than it lowered women's.

IV. Framing Models

Psychologists and social psychologists (whether within the discipline of sociology or psychology) have long used laboratory experiments to test theory. In recent years some psychologists and economists have begun to use the method of laboratory experiments to test assumptions of and predictions from neoclassical theory. This enterprise is referred to as *behavioral* or *experimental economics*. Some of the experimental results support neoclassical theory. However, one body of this experimental research finds what can be interpreted as violations of the rationality assumption in the form of "framing effects" (Kahneman and Tversky 1979; Tversky and Kahneman 1987; Kahnamen and Thaler 1991). A *frame* refers to features of the situation surrounding a decision that affect what an option is compared to, and thus affect how the option is valued.

Whether a choice looks good or bad depends on what it is compared to, on what else is in the frame. The frame seldom contains all the available options, thereby leading to something other than a rational decision. Framing effects involve something more than *random* errors in cognition, which would pose little threat to neoclassical theory. Rather, frames affect decisions in *systematic* ways that distort rationality. Framing models also suggest endogenous tastes, a violation of neoclassical assumptions.

How might framing effects apply to comparable worth? They suggest that employers may use present wage levels as a frame for deciding appropriate future wage levels. This will perpetuate any initially erroneous estimates of the relative MRP of jobs, and perpetuate effects of any past discrimination in the pay of female jobs, whether it was based on cognitive error or other factors, such as tastes or collective action. Studies by experimental social psychologists have shown that, in assessing the fairness of their pay, people generally compare their pay to that of those in the same or a similar occupation and to those of the same sex (Major and Forcey 1985; Hegtvedt 1989; Major 1989). Also, one's own past pay tends to frame an evaluation of one's current pay (Hegtvedt 1989; Major 1989). Since women are often segregated in low-paying jobs, these framing effects mitigate against employees' (male or female) or employers' ability to see the pay as discriminatory.

Major (1989), a social psychologist, emphasizes that what is in the frame for comparison affects norms of entitlement as well as one's cognitive evaluation of alternatives. Since norms can be thought of as tastes, we can regard these findings as challenging economists' notion that tastes are exogenous to economic processes. This leads to a paradox that social psychologists concerned with norms of distributive justice have noted: Distinctions between what is, what one expects, and what is seen as fair tend to blur over time (Jackson 1989; Major 1989). Existing arrangements come to be expected and seen as fair. Thus the low pay of female occupations comes to be expected and seen as fair over time, regardless of how overtly discriminatory the origin of the differentials. While even the victims of the discrimination themselves internalize this belief, I suspect that they generally hold it with more ambivalence and doubt than those who gain from the discrimination.

So far, the implications of framing models I have discussed have been quite pessimistic about the possibility of achieving comparable worth reforms voluntarily, highlighting how the status quo perpetuates itself through providing the frame. However, framing models have more optimistic implications about how people would respond to the reform once instituted. If employers are required to make wage adjustments based on principles of comparable worth, these adjusted wage levels will become part of the frame for future wage setting, thus making comparable worth wages seem more reasonable to both employers and employees.

Another aspect of how evaluations and decisions are framed, called loss aversion (Tversky and Kahneman 1987), has implications for comparable worth. This refers to the fact that the negative response to a loss (relative to what one now has or expects to have) is more extreme than the positive response to a gain of the same amount. That is, people behave in ways that imply that they perceive the displeasure of losing a sum of money to exceed the pleasure of gaining the same amount. This principle of asymmetry is observed in experiments in discrepancies between the amount of money people say they are willing to pay for something and the larger amount they would require to give it up if they already have the good. The asymmetry in the perception of losses and gains implies that opportunity costs and out-of-pocket costs are not treated alike, as assumed by neoclassical theory. In a similar vein, experimental social psychologists have found that affective or behavioral responses to a punishment (defined as losing a benefit one already had) are much greater than to a reward of the same size (Gray and Tallman 1987; Molm 1991).

As suggested in Chapter 1, this asymmetry principle provides a hypothesis about why women's employment would rise when men's wages go down, but women's levels of employment would not fall when some or all of these male wage losses are regained. I also used the asymmetry principle to explain why increasing inequality in husbands' incomes may increase wives' employment, as the income losses of men at the bottom create more women's employment than the gains of men at the top do to reduce it.

This same principle of asymmetry in perceptions of and responses to losses and gains of the same objective size also provides predictions of probable responses to comparable worth. It suggests that wage losses by men will be fought with more intensity than will forgone gains. Thus, achieving gender equity in part through slower raises in male jobs than would otherwise ensue will entail less resistance than will lowering wages in male jobs.

V. Marxist Views

I start with an overview of Marxism, discuss how orthodox and revisionist Marxists have approached questions of gender discrimination, and end by considering how Marxist perspectives can illuminate comparable worth. In Marxist literature the distinction between sociology and economics is scarcely relevant, since Marxists in both disciplines are following a common, though not monolithic, paradigm. (See Marx [1844] 1975; [1852] 1963; [1867] 1967; [1885] 1967; [1894] 1967; Tucker 1978; Burawoy 1990.)

A. Basic Concepts of Orthodox Marxism

Fundamental to a Marxist analysis of modern capitalist societies is the notion of a conflict of interest between two classes, capitalists and workers. This conflict is seen as inherent to a capitalist society. Classes are defined by their relationship to the means of production. Those who own capital (i.e., factories, equipment, or other nonhuman infrastructure necessary to production) are able to reap profits and to have managerial authority over workers. Workers must make a living by selling their labor. Thus, capitalists earn profits even if they do not work, while workers must work for wages.

Marx saw work (i.e., transforming nature into something of use) as what is most essentially human. His labor theory of value contended that everything of value is created by work.[8] In this view, capitalists' profits are inherently exploitative because they are not a result of work but are taken from value created by workers' labor.

Marxists see change as the result of conflicts of interest. Change comes from the resistance that capitalism's oppressions engender in workers. Workers resist capitalism because they would prefer that profits not be taken from their wages. Yet financial exploitation is not the only reason that workers resist capitalism, in a Marxist view. The hierarchical division of labor is alienating to workers because decision-making authority over many work processes is given to managers rather than workers, and because workers cannot see the whole product they produce.

Marxists assert that struggle ensues within capitalism when workers gain "class consciousness." This means they come to see that their interests are distinct from those of capitalists, that capitalism is exploitative, and that collective action is the appropriate response.

The elusive concept of dialectics is important to Marxist theory. A dialectical view is one in which the same features of the system that encourage one outcome also encourage the opposite effect. Let us take the power of capitalists as an illustrative example. In one sense, the more their power, the more stable the system of capitalism is, because with more power capitalists are better equipped to defeat workers' acts of resistance through such actions as strike breaking, hiring lobbyists, and transferring production abroad. Yet in another sense, the greater

capitalists' power the more oppressive the system will become for workers, and the more resistance is developed, thus raising the likelihood of
change. The notion that capitalists' power has these two contradictory
effects is an example of dialectical thinking.

The dialectic posits contradictions that resolve into some synthesis,
which itself may embody new contradictions. Since each of the two
contradictory elements is simultaneously affecting the other before the
synthesis emerges, a dialectical relationship also implies something
other than one-way causation. In mature capitalism, the *social relations of
production* are seen by Marxists to be in a contradictory relationship with
the *forces of production*. The social relations of production refer to the
hierarchical division of labor and the fact that some make profits while
others sell their labor. The forces of production include both the infrastructure of machinery, called capital, and human capacities and
skills, called labor power. The idea is that the social relations of capitalism hold back the development of the full potential for productivity
inherent in the forces of production. For example, Marxists claim that
private ownership of capital and a hierarchical division of labor make an
industrial economy less productive than it would be under a true socialism, which most North American and Western European Marxists do
not believe has ever existed anywhere in the world.

Marx's vision was not entirely dialectical in that he believed that, with
the coming of communism, all significant exploitation and conflict
would end. This vision (unlike that followed by the Soviets, for instance)
entailed nonhierarchical social relations in work. It also entailed an end
to the private ownership of the means of production and, hence, an end
to private profits.

Marxist theory is materialist in asserting the causal primacy of the
mode of production (which includes the social relations of production)
in influencing other features in society. Marx distinguished between the
material base and the superstructure of a society. The base refers to the
mode of production, for example, industrial capitalism. The superstructure refers to other institutions of society such as the state, churches,
and schools. The superstructure also includes the realm of ideas—
culture, ideology, and religion. In general, Marxists believe that institutions of the superstructure will serve the interests of capital, although
they will also be a locus of struggle between capital and labor. Materialism also implies that the ideas that predominate in an era are more
determined by the mode of production than vice versa. In this view, a
religion or ideology could hardly change the world. Rather, those religions or other belief systems that make current arrangements of economic power seem legitimate are the ideas that those in power will allow
to survive. In short, to Marxists, materialism means that the mode of

production has causal primacy over other institutions and over ideas.

However, developments in the post–World War II period have "softened" the materialism or "economism" of Marxist theory. For example, the critical theorists who are intellectual descendants of the Frankfurt School (Held 1980; Benhabib 1986) reject the traditional base/superstructure model, not only in seeing greater causal weight for the latter than Marxists traditionally have, but also in seeing culture as a material force in its own right. They see the confrontation of cultural and personal forms of domination as a necessary part of any progressive struggle, rather than something that contradictions in the material relations of productions will automatically bring about.

Other lines of Marxist thought have also deepened this emphasis on the role of ideas. Gramsci (1971) developed the idea of domination through "hegemony," referring to the way in which the ideas that come to be taken for granted reproduce the domination of capitalism. Althusser (1970, 1971) extended this, arguing that internalized ideology, propagated by the "ideological state apparatus," has an important causal role in perpetuating domination, although he retained the belief that the economic base is determinative "in the last instance." Poulantzas (1974, 1978) furthered this development by collapsing the base/superstructure distinction, so that ideology, the state and the "economic base" are seen as one complex unity. Poststructuralist Marxists, such as LaClau and Mouffe (1985), reject even the "in-the-last-instance" version of materialism. Overall, these developments have increased the importance given to ideas and noneconomic institutions by contemporary Marxists (Bergesen 1988).

B. The Hierarchical Division of Labor and Class Categories in the Modern Occupational Structure

Marglin (1978) argues that the hierarchical division of labor in early capitalism arose out of efforts to control work processes and markets rather than to achieve technical efficiency. (See also Gorz 1978.) Marglin contrasts a worker's role in the division of labor of a factory or office to the role of an artisan who buys materials, makes a product, and markets it. In an economy of self-employed artisans, there is no capitalist controlling the labor process and extracting surplus value; every artisan is an independent producer. Marglin concedes that the modern factory is a more technically efficient form of production than decentralized artisanship, in the sense that more product can be produced for the same dollar inputs of capital, labor, and raw products. Nonetheless, Marglin (1978) argues that the usual rendering of economic history in which the hierarchical division of labor arose because this greater technical efficiency could increase profits is false. Rather, he argues that the hierarchical aspect of the process developed first, within the system of putting-out, before the efficiencies of the factory were developed. While still using the system of putting-out, large capitalists increasingly divided the tasks entailed in making a product between different self-employed "workers" who got materials from capitalists and performed production at home. Allocating the tasks needed to make a single product to various workers was begun, according to Marglin, so that the large capitalists would have a necessary role and thus be positioned to take profits. In the short run, control was a higher priority than maximizing profits.

Marxists deemphasize the way that jobs within a hierarchical division of labor differ in skill. Rather, they see a long-term trend to deskill all jobs, thus producing increased homogeneity in the working class (Braverman 1974). They also argue that the modern bureaucratic division of jobs into graduated authority and status levels serves to divide and conquer workers by leading them to focus on status competition with each other rather than on unified class consciousness and action (Edwards et al. 1975).

Some Marxists also see occupational differences in authority as indicating contradictory class location. For example, Wright (1978) argued that one's class is determined by whether or not one (1) owns the means of production, (2) has control over the production process, (3) has control over the labor power of others via supervision, and (4) has control over one's own labor power via autonomy. This leads to two clear class locations (capitalists and nonsupervisory workers) and a contradictory class location for managers and supervisors. Capitalists have all four advantages. Workers without supervisory or managerial functions have none. However, managers and supervisors are a contradictory class location in that they do not own companies (though some high-level managers have stock options as part of their compensation) but often have substantial amounts of the other three types of control.

The relatively high earnings of managers and supervisors is interpreted by Wright, Costello, and Sprague (1982) as a result of this class position, rather than as a result of managerial skill. The most pronounced difference that Wright et al. (1982) found between women and men's placement across these categories is that women are much less likely than men to be managers or supervisors. Recall from Chapter 1 that this is a finding common to researchers within and outside the Marxist tradition. This difference, which Wright et al. (1982) interpret as differential class location, explains a portion of the sex gap in pay. But how do women and men come to be differentially distributed across job categories, whether the categories differ in class location or not? One possibility is discrimination, so it is important to see how Marxists have interpreted such discrimination.

C. Discrimination as a Capitalist Strategy to Divide and Conquer Workers

Here I examine contemporary applications of Marxist ideas to understanding labor market discrimination and comparable worth. However, it is important to recognize that Marxist theory sees the structured inequalities between workers and capitalists as much more central than inequalities between groups of workers such as men and women. The relevance of discrimination to orthodox Marxist theory is that it is interpreted as a divide-and-conquer strategy by capitalists to weaken working class solidarity.

In this view, employers discriminate by race or sex to create divisions or hostilities between groups of workers that will prevent workers from organizing cohesively enough to threaten profit levels by unionization, strikes, or more radical political action (Gordon, 1972, pp. 71–78; Edwards et al. 1975, pp. xiii–xiv; Bonacich 1976; Bowles and Gintis 1976, p. 174; Humphries 1976; Reich 1978, 1981; Stevenson 1988). Capitalists, as a class, have a material interest in preventing such solidarity of workers.

As discussed above, through neoclassical lenses, the problem with this view is why free riding employers do not subvert the class "monopoly" to lower their individual wage bill by hiring women in jobs for which other employers are paying more for men. It is at least plausible that individual capitalists could lower their overall wage bill more effectively by hiring women (or whatever group is discriminated against) at their lower market wage in all the jobs generally reserved for the favored group than by the divide-and-conquer strategy. But free rider behavior that advantages the individual capitalist will undercut the strategy of the capitalist class to keep workers divided. The fact that Marxists have had little to say about this makes clear that most Marxists implicitly assume *collectively* self-interested action by a class. In contrast, neoclassical theory posits that each capitalist acts to maximize *individual* self-interest. (The relatively new analytic Marxism, by contrast, assumes individual self-interest. See Roemer 1979, 1988.)

While it is difficult to document whether divide and conquer is the *motive* for most employers' discrimination, one can investigate whether discrimination has the *effect* of impeding working-class gains. Reich (1978, 1981) provides some evidence in favor of the divide-and-conquer thesis; he shows that states in which black/white relative income is lower also have more disadvantaged white working classes, net of other factors. (See Szymanski 1976 for related evidence.) Another study did not support the thesis; Beck's (1980) time series analysis did not find unionism to be negatively related to blacks' relative income. But if the subordination of blacks serves to divide and thereby weaken the power of the working class, Marxist theory predicts a negative relationship between blacks' relative status and union power. These studies provide conflicting findings about whether racism subverts progress for the working class. A Marxist perspective on comparable worth would suggest that discriminatory segregation and discriminatory wages in female jobs are part of a strategy to divide and conquer workers. Whether these mechanisms of sexism serve to divide and conquer the working class has not been well studied.

D. Socialist-Feminist Views

Socialist feminists accept the broad contours of a Marxist analysis of class relations, but reject the tendency of orthodox Marxists to see sexism as merely a by-product of capitalist class relations. The view of sex discrimination described above, which sees sexism as part of capitalists' strategy to divide and conquer the working class, is an example of seeing sex inequality as a derivative of class relations. Socialist feminists argue that without preexisting sexism, capitalists could not get workers to see gender as a salient enough issue to be able to engage in a strategy of divide and conquer.

Socialist feminists see patriarchy to be as important a form of women's oppression as capitalism. One difference between the two types of oppression is that with patriarchy the beneficiaries of oppression are men of all classes (though perhaps some more than others), whereas with capitalism, the beneficiaries are the much smaller number of (male or female) capitalists. Some socialist feminists see "capitalist patriarchy" as merged into one system. Other socialist feminists espouse a view that sees capitalism and patriarchy as analytically distinct, coexisting systems of oppression. Some socialist feminists see capitalism and patriarchy as mutually reinforcing while others see them as contradictory. (These positions are reviewed in Walby 1986; Shelton and Agger forthcoming.)

In what institutions do socialist feminists believe that patriarchy operates? Shelton and Agger (forthcoming) note the tendency of some socialist feminists (e.g., Delphy 1984) to see class relations as relevant to wage labor and patriarchy as relevant only to sexuality and the household. In contrast, Hartmann (1976, 1981) is a socialist feminist who sees *both* capitalism and patriarchy as structuring the family *and* the realm of wage labor. Thus the analytical distinction Hartmann makes between capitalism and patriarchy does not mean that there is a separate institutionalized sphere in which each operates. Patriarchy in the household is exemplified by men's ability to control women's labor and sexuality, to get women to do onerous childrearing and household work, and to meet men's sexual needs regardless of their own needs. Hartmann (1976) documents how patriarchal organization is also present in the paid workplace; male workers have been active in efforts to keep women in lower-paying, segregated jobs. One can also see male workers' resistance to comparable worth, and their ignoring and minimizing of the skills involved in women's jobs, as part of patriarchy.

In the socialist-feminist view, discrimination against women in labor markets may occur because of either a class-based divide-and-conquer strategy, the collective patriarchal efforts of men, or both. In addition, many socialist feminists acknowledge the Marxist-feminist argument that women are disadvantaged in competing in labor markets because capitalists have encouraged a system in which women perform reproductive labor in the home without pay. Such reproductive labor is generally taken to include the emotional services wives perform for husbands, which makes them able to perform another day of alienated labor, as well as the socialization of children, who are the next generation to provide wage labor. This arrangement frees capitalists of having to pay as much as they otherwise would need to for the reproduction of the labor force upon which they rely (Shelton and Agger forthcoming).[9] Capitalists may encourage the arrangement in many ways, including paying low enough wages to women that they need husbands, and encouraging patriarchal ideologies. All these may contribute to women's disadvantage, in the socialist-feminist view.

In sum, while socialist feminists share with orthodox Marxists a belief that women's disadvantage may sometimes stem from the divide-and-conquer strategies of capitalists, and share with Marxist feminists the belief that women's disadvantage in labor markets may sometimes arise from capitalists' interests in women doing reproductive labor in the home, they depart from these views in insisting that there is also an independent causal role for patriarchy in explaining women's oppression. At least for some socialist feminists such as Hartmann (1976, 1981), this causal role of patriarchy is at work in the labor market as well as in the home.

VI. Other Sociological and Institutional Views

In this section I relate gender inequality and comparable worth to three somewhat overlapping theoretical positions within sociology:

functionalism, conflict theory, and social structural views. I also include a discussion of a nonneoclassical institutionalist tradition within economics because of its closer connection with sociological than neoclassical views.

It is more difficult to write an overview of theories of labor markets for sociology than economics because there is less consensus within sociology. Economics has a paradigm, and most economists agree upon many of its implications. Fifteen years ago, most sociologists saw the two major competing sociological theories to be functionalism (associated with Talcott Parsons) and conflict theory (in either a Marxist or Weberian variety), the two traditions to be discussed below. Some would have included symbolic interactionism as a third competing tradition. Today, sociology is much more fragmented. Few identify themselves as functionalists, though there is some interest in what Alexander (1985) calls "neofunctionalism." As I see it, conflict theory has won out in that it is widely acknowledged that functionalism underemphasized power and overemphasized consensus as a basis for order. There is also increasing agreement that arrangements cannot be explained simply because of their functionality for some "whole," but have to be constructed by specific social groups with both the power and motivation to do so. But the version of conflict theory that has won out in the mainstream of the profession is not orthodox Marxism with its rather specific predictions and prescriptions about the contradictions of capitalism. Indeed, even the Marxist tradition has become increasingly fragmented, as discussed above. The relative importance of the base and the superstructure are under debate, the new analytic Marxists have questioned whether capitalists may not free ride on class interests, and socialist feminists insist that women's oppression derives from patriarchy as well as class relations. Thus conflict theorists today agree on only the most general propositions. What results is a view in which the possible bases of power are multiple, and the possible outcomes of inequalities are not determinant in a way easily summarized by a theory. Another way to describe the situation is that the distinction between functionalism and conflict theory has blurred. Alexander (1985) comments that neofunctionalist theories are often about conflict. Marxist writers now talk about ideological hegemony, acknowledging that subordinated groups often hold beliefs that support their oppression. Given this increased blurring, the debate between functionalism and conflict is no longer at the forefront of the discipline. Because of this, other debates, such as those about the relationship between "micro" and "macro," and between the individual and the structural, have received increased attention. Thus, structuralist views are also discussed below.

A. Functionalism

The functionalist theory of stratification (Davis and Moore 1945) posits that, in order to adapt and survive, societies must give higher rewards to occupational positions that are most functionally important. The incentives provided by higher rewards are seen as necessary to ensure that the positions are filled, and filled with sufficiently qualified persons. Being more "functionally important" is not precisely the same thing as contributing more to marginal revenue product (MRP) in neoclassical theory, since the functionality is to the entire society, whereas MRP refers to the contribution to profit of individual firms. However, Parsons's version of functionalism saw what is functional for each institution in society contributing to the functionality of the whole, and neoclassical economists, following Adam Smith, believe that an economy made up of selfish profit maximizers leads, via the invisible hand, to growth for all. Given this, the functionalist claim is similar to the neoclassical claim. One difference is that in functionalism the mechanism is consensus on internalized values. In contrast, in the neoclassical case it is the invisible hand of competition that generally creates efficient outcomes despite each individual's self-interested behavior.

How does this view compare with the implicit view of reward systems in the literature on comparable worth? Job evaluation as a method of achieving comparable worth, discussed in Chapter 4, shares basic assumptions with functionalism. It is a method that purports to determine the relative value of jobs to organizations. Both functionalism and job evaluation posit that average rewards in a job depend most directly upon the characteristics of a position that determine its functional importance, and only indirectly upon individual characteristics. Thus, both functionalism and job evaluation focus on the position as the fundamental unit of analysis. In that limited sense, they are both structural views. This point is sometimes obscured (e.g., in Horan 1978) when status attainment research (e.g., Blau and Duncan 1967; Treiman and Terrell 1975a; Featherman and Hauser 1978) is taken as the main exemplar of functionalist research, because the focus of status attainment research is on how individual characteristics affect access to highly rewarded occupations. However, functionalist theory also contains a structuralist claim about how the functional contribution of *positions* affects their reward levels.

Despite these links, research on comparable worth also undermines some functionalist assumptions. Research shows that women's jobs are generally paid less (relative to men's jobs) than is commensurate with their value to the organization, as assessed by job evaluation (Remick 1984; Rothchild 1984; Steinberg et al. 1986; Acker 1987; Orazem and Mattila 1989). (Of course, critics of comparable worth would dispute that job evaluations measure value to the organization.) Studies using national data, reviewed in Chapter 1, generally reach the same conclusion. Such research disputes the claim that a functionalist theory tells the whole story of how jobs are paid. If the factors used in job evaluation are proxies for functional worth to an organization, it is clear from such studies that functional factors explain much of interjob variance in pay, but equally clear that women's jobs are relatively underpaid in a way that functionalism cannot explain.

Functionalists would have to strain to come up with a functional explanation for such pay differences between male and female jobs. Parsons's writings on gender differentiation described a gender-based division of labor, with husbands emphasizing the "instrumental" realm through their jobs, while wives emphasize what he called the "expressive" realm of childrearing and creating emotional solidarity in the family (Parsons 1954, 1966; Parsons and Bales 1955). The nonemployment of women was seen as functional because it created a differentiated and specialized role for socialization and familial solidarity, and because it reduced solidarity-threatening competition between husbands and wives. In the more recent context where a majority of married women are employed, functionalists see sex segregation of jobs with women in different and lower-paying jobs to be functional to reduce competition between husbands and wives (Gross 1968). (See Oppenheimer 1982 for a critical discussion.)

However, functionalism also posits that it is adaptive for societies, in an evolutionary sense, to become increasingly universalistic. Universalism refers to using a consistent set of criteria to make decisions about people. This implies nondiscrimination by sex in hiring and in setting the wages for jobs. In this sense, sex discrimination is an anomaly for functionalism as it is for neoclassical economics. Thus, it would seem more consistent with a functionalist view to posit that women self-select out of jobs that could be construed as competing with their husbands, rather than to posit discrimination by employers. Little research has tested whether women do this as a conscious strategy, although Oppenheimer (1982) interprets some results this way. But even if this is true, it would lead to the question of why functionalism does not predict eventual universalism in role assignment in the family as well as the labor market. (For a defense of functionalism by a feminist, see Johnson 1989, forthcoming.)

B. Institutionalist Economics

The institutionalist school of economics traces its origins to turn-of-the-century writers such as Thorstein Veblen, John Commons, and John

Dewey, as well as midcentury writers such as Clarence Ayres. The school still has adherents today, although institutionalism, like Marxism, is marginal in American economics. (For an overview of contemporary institutionalism, see Tool 1988.)

The views of institutionalists share much with those of functionalist sociologists. Both views emphasize consensual cultural values and the distinction between instrumental and expressive or ceremonial behaviors. This may surprise sociologists who have noted a similarity between functionalist sociology and neoclassical economics (Horan 1978) in their conservative political overtones, as well as a similarity between institutionalists among economists and nonfunctionalist sociologists in their left-leaning politics. As an example of the divergence of institutionalist from neoclassical views, the 1984 special issue of the institutionalist journal, *Journal of Economic Issues,* was devoted to comparable worth, and was made up entirely of articles sympathetic to the notion that there is institutionalized sex discrimination in labor markets. As discussed above, for most neoclassical economists, persistent discrimination (with the exception of statistical discrimination) is a theoretical anomaly. The acceptance by institutionalists of the notion of sex discrimination also points out a difference between institutionalism and functionalism. To institutionalists, norms are often dysfunctional, irrational traditions from *formerly* functional institutional practices. The idea that culture and institutions lag behind what is functional is less accepted in sociological functionalism.

Central to institutionalist thought is the dichotomy between *instrumental* and *ceremonial* aspects of behavior and institutions. The instrumental side of life involves knowledge, skills, and technology. It is the tendency to evaluate things in terms of their consequences. Instrumentalism is seen as the source of economic progress in a society because it is adaptive to the environment. Because of this emphasis, institutionalism is sometimes called evolutionary economics.

Institutionalists implicitly ascribe greater value to the instrumental than the ceremonial aspects of institutions. This valuation is in the same spirit as the implicit valuing of optimizing and efficiency by neoclassical economics. Institutionalists differ from neoclassical economists, however, in recognizing a more ritualistic, habitual, and inertial aspect to institutions that is often denied in neoclassical theory. In a neoclassical view, what institutionalists call the ceremonial realm is relegated to the realm of tastes, and is seen as more relevant in consumption than in production. This is because firms are generally assumed to be profit maximizers. The neoclassical view that tastes for discrimination cannot persist indefinitely in competitive labor markets is an example of this view. Thus, while institutionalists share with both neoclassical economists and functionalists a privileging of instrumentality, institutionalist thought nonetheless differs from the neoclassical view in its emphasis on the inertial drag of institutions.

The institutionalist view suggests that habits are a result of instrumental values but then become ceremonial when they no longer serve their original purpose but remain institutionalized. A similar view of habits is found among some sociologists (Camic 1986). In an institutionalist view, habits of discrimination are seen as a ceremonial lag in the system. Thus, institutionalist theory is consistent with what appear to be anomalies in neoclassical labor market analysis (Greenwood 1984).

C. Conflict Theory

Modern conflict theory has varied strands, but all emphasize the non-consensus and conflict of interests between societal groups. The domination of some groups over others is seen as the force holding society together, as well as the source of change through the conflict it engenders (Collins 1975; Kerbo 1983, Chapters 4 and 5). What functionalists consider to be common values are, in the eyes of conflict theorists, the values of those with power. If subordinate groups do internalize these values, this may reflect the power of elites to control the institutions of socialization. Marxist versions of conflict theory, discussed above, see power as based primarily on the ownership and control of property. Here I discuss a more eclectic conflict view. This view sees a multidimensional set of possibilities for bases of conflict, does not assume that material relations always have primacy, and has a less clear view of the destination toward which processes of change point than is present in most Marxist views.

Thus, in such a view, gender becomes one among many possible vectors for conflicting interests and collective action (Folbre forthcoming). Men's collective efforts to keep women out of male jobs and to keep male jobs evaluated as more worthy is thus consistent with conflict theory. Notions of discrimination reviewed above based on taste or group monopoly are also consistent with conflict theory. Sociological conflict theory does not explain the origins of the subordination of women, but it provides one framework for understanding the processes by which women have been kept out of some jobs, and work performed by women has been devalued and assigned a lower wage. However, the emphasis on devaluation is a relatively new development within conflict theory.

Another literature within conflict theory that can be appropriated for its relevance to gender inequality is Bordieu's theory of cultural capital (Bourdieu 1977; Bourdieu and Passeron 1977; DiMaggio 1979). The theory is about one mechanism through which class advantage is re-produced intergenerationally. It suggests that cultural capital—certain skills, knowledge, tastes, and life-styles—is passed on intergenera-tionally within a class through socialization. Elites make holding such capital a prerequisite of rewards even when such capital does not con-tribute to the "bottom line" of production and profit. In doing this, elites engage in a symbolic struggle to impose the definition of the social world most in conformity with their collective class interests.

Bordieu does not discuss how this might apply to gender inequality. However, extending this idea to gender inequality in labor markets, one could see skills and interests that men are encouraged to develop as a form of cultural capital that is reproduced among men and arbitrarily rewarded in labor markets. This could be applied to understanding gen-der differences in access to occupations as well as comparable worth. With respect to access to positions, it is in men's interest that those qualifications that men typically have more of be weighted more heavily in deciding whom to hire. For example, consider the fact that experience managing a home or in voluntary organizations often counts less than military experience in getting a job. This could be interpreted as valuing men's cultural capital over that of women in a way that cannot always be justified by differential relevance to skills needed in the job. Requiring years of experience for promotions might be explained as differentially valuing forms of capital men have more of, rather than in terms of the relevance of learning on the job the ability to handle the new position. I know of no empirical research that has tried to assess whether cultural capital or necessary skills explain job requirements that favor men. Such research would be relevant to what in the law is called discrimination on the basis of disparate impact. Here a criterion is applied neutrally to men and women. However, this "neutral" application favors men since they have more of this type of capital. If the type of capital is shown not to be relevant to performing the job well, discrimination has been found un-der the doctrine of disparate impact. Otherwise, the differential is not seen as discriminatory. (See Chapter 5 for a discussion of disparate im-pact proofs of sex discrimination in employment.)

Feminist critics of current job evaluation practices charge that the choice of factors and weights is biased in favor of men (Shepala and Viviano 1984; Hartmann, Roos, and Treiman 1985; Acker 1987; Steinberg and Haignere 1987). This criticism can be viewed as harmonious with theories of cultural capital. (See England and Dunn 1988 for an interpre-tation of studies by Barrett 1980; Phillips and Taylor 1980; Dex 1985; Acker 1987; and Reskin 1988 in this vein.) The contention is that the skills or tasks that typify female jobs will receive lower positive or even negative returns (weights) in comparison to skills and tasks typical to men's jobs. For example, physical strength, supervisory or managerial power, and mathematical skills may be highly valued because men are often in jobs requiring these. On the other hand, finger dexterity, verbal skills, and skills in nurturant human relations may receive low or negative returns precisely because female jobs are more likely to require them. Using the vocabulary of cultural capital, we could say that jobs that require typically male cultural capital are rewarded more than jobs that require typically female cultural capital, even if the female jobs contribute as much to firms' profits.

Kilbourne et al. (1990; Kilbourne 1991) draw from both cultural-feminist theory and the cultural capital view to make a similar argument. (Cultural-feminist theory is discussed more fully in Chapter 6.) The argument is that male power and biases in the culture lead to a devaluation not only of women, but also of all work done by women, and of the skills and activities typically performed by women. This would give rise to women's disadvantage in labor markets in ways that will often not appear to be overt discrimination simply because the criteria themselves are stacked in the interests of men. They show, for example, that there is a negative return to working in a job requiring nurturing social skills, even when cognitive and physical skills are held constant (Kilbourne et al. 1990, Kilbourne 1991).

However, even with the biases built into job evaluation systems, most of them find women's jobs underpaid, as discussed in Chapter 4. This finding, too, would be seen by conflict theorists as evidence of the exercise of male and/or employers' power. Conflict theory suggests that women's groups will have to organize and struggle to persuade employers and governments to raise the relative pay of female jobs. Establishing pay equity is not merely a matter of finding a technocratic way to measure job worth "objectively." The opposition being waged against pay equity initiatives by groups such as the U.S. Chamber of Commerce and the Eagle Forum (an organization of the new religious right) illustrates this point.

One unresolved debate within conflict theory is germane to comparable worth. This is the question of who benefits from sex discrimination: male workers, employers (generally capitalists, but sometimes governments), or both? Bonacich's (1972, 1976) theory of split labor markets discusses ethnic stratification with principles that might be generalized to gender stratification. She argues that the dominant group of workers benefits and capitalists lose from keeping minorities out of desirable jobs. Applying this logic to gender stratification suggests that men gain from segregating women into lower-paying jobs and from assigning low wages to women's occupations because employers who devalue women or the work they do can pay more to men. Some socialist feminists also hold this view. An alternative Marxist view, discussed above, sees sex discrimination increasing profits by a divide-and-conquer strategy that makes women's wages lower than men's, but *both* men's and women's wages lower than they would be in the absence of discrimination against women. In this view, what men would otherwise gain from discrimination is more than offset by the effects of discrimination on worker solidarity leading to lower wages for all workers. That is, if there were no discrimination, men would see that their interests are united with those of women, since both groups are workers, and through collective class organization, both men and women could gain wages higher than under discrimination. In this view, only capitalists gain from discrimination; it increases the rate of profit. As indicated in the discussion of Marxist views above, this is an important but empirically unresolved question within conflict views of discrimination.

D.   Structuralist Views

In this section I combine two sociological views that have a structural focus in that they emphasize the causal effects of *positions* on individuals' outcomes. Unfortunately, the term *structuralism* now has so many meanings that it no longer carries much information about theoretical positions. (For a discussion of the various meanings of the term *structural* within sociology, see Wilson 1983, pp. 40–62.) Some see a structural analysis as one in which all concepts must be properties of systems (e.g., societies, organizations) rather than of their parts (e.g., occupational positions or their individual incumbents). Others do not see an analysis as structural unless all the concepts are defined relationally (as in some forms of network analysis, or as in a Marxist as opposed to a continuous view of class). Some see a structural analysis as one in which characteristics of positions held by individuals have causal effects on their behavior and rewards, even *net* of the characteristics of these individuals before they entered the positions. Here, I will use this latter definition. I will draw upon two distinct traditions that are structural in this sense, applying each to gender and labor markets. The first, the "new structuralism" in stratification research, deals with how job characteristics affect wages net of the race, sex, and human capital of the individuals in the positions. I then link this to a discussion of the "social structure and personality" school of social psychology, which emphasizes how structural positions, such as jobs, affect individuals' habits, preferences, and behavior. When we combine these two structural views and apply them to questions of gender inequality, they suggest a pattern of feedback effects between gender inequality in jobs and in households that helps explain the perpetuation of discrimination and its effects.

The new structuralism in stratification research arose as a reaction against the exclusive focus of status attainment research on individual and familial characteristics, and its neglect of how structural positions within labor markets affect rewards. The status attainment tradition (Blau and Duncan 1967; Featherman and Hauser 1978) showed how the socioeconomic status (education and occupational status) of one's father as well as one's own education affects one's occupational attainment and earnings. Variations on the model included other social-psychological characteristics that might be picked up in the home or neighborhood.

Initially, new structuralists borrowed heavily from theories of economic (Averitt 1968) and labor market (Doeringer and Piore 1971) segmentation being developed by institutionalist and radical economists. The literature on economic segmentation is often called the *dual economy* thesis. The notion is that the economy is divided into two sectors, often called *core* and *periphery*. The core contains large (sometimes multinational), unionized, oligopolistic firms with capital-intensive production, high profit rates, and high wages. These firms have internal labor markets that make promotions and wage increases with seniority likely. Firms that manufacture durable goods are mostly in the core. The periphery contains smaller firms with less unionization, more competition in product markets (i.e., many firms selling the same product), labor-intensive production, low profit rates, low wages, and dead-end jobs for many workers. (For reviews of the theory by sociologists see Beck, Horan, and Tolbert 1978; Wallace and Kalleberg 1981; Althauser and Kalleberg 1981; Hodson and Kaufman 1982; Farkas, England, and Barton 1988.)

As work in this tradition developed, it became clear that a unidimensional dualism is an inadequate representation of the segmentation at issue (Zucker and Rosenstein 1981; Coverdill 1988; Tigges 1988). That is, not all the proposed indicators of whether industries are marginal are highly correlated, not all have effects on earnings, and the cutting point between core and periphery is somewhat arbitrary. Thus, recent research has generally used multiple continuous indicators of sectoral marginality and advantage (Baron and Bielby 1980; Hodson 1984; Kalleberg, Wallace, and Althauser 1981).

To oversimplify and ignore many debates about how concepts should be operationalized, new structuralist research has shown that wages are generally higher in firms that are larger, more capital intensive, unionized, and more profitable (Beck et al. 1978; Tolbert, Horan, and Beck 1980; Kalleberg et al. 1981). The contention of the theory that *rates of return* to human capital are greater in more advantaged sectors has been supported much less consistently (Zucker and Rosenstein 1981; Hauser 1980).

Applications of this view to gender inequality have shown that part (most estimates are between 5 and 15%) of the sex gap in pay arises from women's concentration in marginal industries (Beck et al. 1980; Hodson and England 1986; Coverdill 1988). Yet women's concentration in marginal industries is much less important to the wage gap than is occupational sex segregation, segregation that exists in firms in all sectors.

How is the new structuralist view related to the literature on comparable worth? On the one hand, the focus is very different: Comparable worth addresses intraorganizational pay differences, while the new structuralism focuses on interindustry and interfirm variations in pay. The part of the gender gap in pay that new structuralist research has explained by men's and women's differential placement across industries cannot be reached by intrafirm job evaluations of the sort proposed by pay equity proponents. Yet the fact that sex *composition* is a characteristic of positions rather than of individuals renders comparable worth a structural issue. In addition, comparable worth shares with the new structuralism the contention that some structural positions have lower pay that is "uncompensated" (Farkas et al. 1988), i.e., not balanced by lower requirements for human capital or for working conditions requiring compensating differentials. That is, they share a claim that the neoclassical doctrine of "equalization at the margin" does not hold. Thus, in this more abstract sense, claims of comparable worth discrimination are very much in the spirit of the new structuralist view in their challenge to the neoclassical view and in their emphasis on effects of characteristics of positions. The literature on comparable worth also shares with the new structuralism an emphasis on pay differences for which there is no obvious explanation in functionalist theory.

This structural view of labor markets can be combined with a social-psychological view of the sort advanced by the "social structure and personality" school (e.g., Kohn and Schooler 1983; Kanter 1977). The labor market contains structural positions characterized by different kinds of work and by uncompensated advantages and disadvantages. Once sex discrimination gets started, effects of women's and men's structural positions in labor markets on their job and household behavior helps perpetuate the concentration of women in disadvantaged jobs. This combined view differs from the neoclassical view by insisting that institutional inertia and feedback effects between supply and demand sides of labor markets allow discrimination and its effects to persist indefinitely, despite market forces operating to erode discrimination (England and Farkas 1986).

Feedback effects are social-psychological consequences of discrimination that create new discrimination, or perpetuate groups' disadvantages that resulted originally from discrimination. Table 2.2 presents a

Table 2.2. A Typology of Feedback Effects from Discrimination

	Effects on	
Effects on	A. *Employees' Behavior That Affects Rewards*	B. *Employers' Propensity to Discriminate*
I. *Effects of Discrimination on Current Adults*		
1. Rational responses	I.A.1	I.B.1
2. Skills	I.A.2	I.B.2[2]
3. Habits, tastes, or cognitions	I.A.3[1]	I.B.3[1,2]
II. *Effects of Discrimination on Next Generation*		
1. Rational responses	II.A.1	II.B.1[2]
2. Skills	II.A.2	II.B.2[2]
3. Habits, tastes, or cognitions	II.A.3[1]	II.B.3[1,2]

Notes:
[1] Violates assumptions of neoclassical economic theory. "Habits" imply nonrationality, a violation of the rationality assumption. The notion that discrimination alters tastes violates the assumptions that tastes are unchanging and exogenous to economic models. The notion that cognitions are other than correct challenges the rationality assumption.
[2] Violates usual neoclassical conclusion that discrimination will eventually disappear from competitive market forces alone.

typology of such effects. The structuralist contention is that the *position* (in this case, job) one holds molds one's rational responses, as well as one's skills, habits, tastes, and cognitions. The last three of these five types of effects are incompatible with neoclassical theory.

Let us consider first the effects of discrimination on employees who are the victims of the discrimination (cells I.A.1–I.A.3 of Table 2.2). These effects of discrimination on jobs and earnings endure even if discrimination has declined. They involve alterations in employees' behavior caused by the demands and expectations of the jobs they hold. One such effect, rational responses to constraints (cell I.A.1 of Table 2.2.), is entirely compatible with neoclassical theory. For example, if discrimination steers women into jobs with little reward for seniority, frequent turnover is a rational response. The resultant lack of seniority will adversely affect later earnings, even if discrimination lessens. Similarly, sex discrimination makes it more rational for couples to emphasize the man's career and assign domestic responsibilities to the wife. This, in turn, limits the woman's later career prospects.

Discrimination may also affect the training and skills one attains on the job, and this affects future earnings (cell I.A.2 of Table 2.2.) Examples of this kind of effect abound. Women are concentrated in jobs offering less on-the-job training and such training has large effects on future earnings (Corcoran and Duncan 1979). When placement into the initial job is discriminatory, this sequence is a feedback effect from discrimination. Thus the common distinction between portions of group differences in earnings due to discrimination and portions due to human capital investment is blurred when discriminatory employers decide whose human capital to develop. Even when the "training" aspects of jobs are invisible, sociologists have shown that jobs with greater cognitive demands increase the intellectual abilities of jobholders, while jobs with less demands erode such abilities, and that this affects future job attainment (Kohn and Schooler 1983). Such effects undoubtedly exist for other kinds of skills as well.

This structuralist view of social psychology also posits that discrimination may affect the habits, tastes, or cognitions of current employees (cell I.A.3 of Table 2.2.) By "habits" I refer to behavioral patterns that are learned, perhaps initially because of their adaptive advantage, but that persist when they are no longer helpful and are even harmful. Habits have been emphasized by nonneoclassical institutionalist economists as well, as noted previously. The notion of habits that are harmful to an actor's own interests contradicts the neoclassical rationality assumption but is consistent with institutionalism in economics. The notion of "tastes" here is like that of economists; they refer to the preferences for experiences that give one "utility" (i.e., satisfaction or happiness). However, the notion that experiences in labor markets can affect workers' tastes is inconsistent with the usual neoclassical assumption that tastes are unchanging and exogenous to economic models (Lang and Dickens 1988). It is, however, consistent with framing models, discussed above. These models assert that one's cognitive evaluation as well as how much satisfaction one gets from a particular reward level is framed and thus affected by one's past rewards, themselves a function of one's structural position. Thus, the structuralist version of social psychology is incompatible with neoclassical economics in arguing that one's *position* can affect habits, cognitions, and tastes.

How might such effects of position on tastes and habits work to perpetuate effects of discriminatory job placements? If women are discriminatorily assigned to jobs demanding the social skills of nurturing rather than authoritative managing, this may cultivate women's preferences and habits toward nurturing work and men's toward managerial work (Kanter 1977).

Feedback from discrimination may also involve *intergenerational* effects such that the children of current employees are disadvantaged when they reach employment age because of consequences of discrimination against the previous generation of their race or sex group (cells II.A.1–

II.A.3 of Table 2.2). These intergenerational effects may involve rational responses, skills, tastes, cognitions, or habits. Developing any cognitions other than the "correct view" violates the rationality assumption. The possibility of habits the actor herself would define as "bad" violates the neoclassical rationality assumption. The idea that parents' jobs affect their children's tastes is inconsistent with the neoclassical assumptions of exogenous tastes, unless the family sphere in which the changes in tastes occur is considered exogenous to economic models (England and Kilbourne 1990a, p. 165).

So far we have examined feedback effects acting upon current or next-generation employees (cells I.A.1–I.A.3 and II.A.1–II.A.3 of Table 2.2). These involve perpetuation of the *disadvantage* that arises from discrimination rather than the perpetuation of discrimination itself. They are an example of what Feagin and Feagin (1978) call effects of past discrimination in the present. But since none of them involve the perpetuation or creation of discrimination itself, none of the effects in the A column of Table 2.2 challenge the neoclassical view that discrimination will erode in competitive markets. It is the effects involving employers (cells I.B.1–I.B.3 and II.B.1–II.B.3 of Table 2.2) that challenge this view.

When employers discriminate they create differences in the skills and habits of groups of employees, as discussed above. This in turn creates the conditions for statistical discrimination as a rational response (cell I.B.1 of Table 2.2). Further, if employers or their managers discriminate long enough, their "skills" in selecting applicants on the basis of merit may fail to develop or may atrophy, making continued discrimination likely (cell I.B.2 of Table 2.2.). In addition, the practice of discrimination may be self-perpetuating through inculcating discriminatory habits and tastes and through providing a frame for cognitions and tastes that make discrimination appear to be the right course of action (cell I.B.3 of Table 2.2). For example, consider the practice of discriminatory placement, which encourages occupational sex segregation. Such segregation may create a sufficient "taste" of male solidarity that male managers decide to collude with male workers rather than being the "free-riding arbitrageurs" who would contribute to the erosion of discrimination. All these effects may be intergenerational as well, such that the next generation of employers and managers grows up with reasons to engage in statistical discrimination, and the skills, tastes, cognitions, and habits compatible with other types of discrimination (cells II.B.1–II.B.3 of Table 2.2).

In sum, using Table 2.2, I have explored the implications of the social-structural view that sees positions as affecting the individuals who hold them, and have applied this view to the perpetuation of women's disadvantage. I began with a discussion of the causal cycle with discrimination. This does not mean that I believe that the demand side is always the "prime mover" in gender inequality. Rather, my goal was to show that a structural view implies that discrimination can beget both future disadvantage for women and future discrimination, even in competitive markets. Many of the mechanisms implied by this view are denied by neoclassical theory. These feedback effects between gender inequality in households and in labor markets are one key implication of a sociological view (England and Farkas 1986).

VII. Adjudicating Between Theories

In this section I identify and try to resolve five issues upon which the theories discussed above disagree. The issues are (a) whether deviations from rationality are random or are systematic in theoretically specified directions, (b) whether actors follow the interest of groups to which they belong even when it violates selfish interests, (c) whether preferences are exogenous or endogenous to economic outcomes, (d) whether the sort of discrimination at issue in comparable worth is merely a result of hiring discrimination, and whether any discrimination can persist in competitive markets, and (e) the probable effects on women's well-being if comparable worth policies were to be instituted. For each of these issues, I discuss how the issue is dealt with by those theories for which it is relevant, and then present my own view.

A. Rationality

The theories reviewed in this chapter differ in the degree of rationality they assume of actors in labor markets. The aspect of rationality at issue here is the process of making calculations and inferences regarding which means will best meet one's ends. Neoclassical theory assumes strict rationality. Employers are presumed to know how much the marginal worker in each job is contributing to the firm's profit. Workers are presumed to know the earnings trajectories in various occupations and the returns to various levels and types of human capital. While the costs of collecting data to make such computations are acknowledged by the new information economics, such costs are generally seen to lead to *random* rather than *systematic* errors.

Other theories posit systematic rather than merely random distortions in perceptions and calculations, biases that are a violation of strict rationality. Experimental work in behavioral economics and social psychology has shown systematic effects on decisions of how the options are framed. One's perception of benefits or costs of a choice are influenced by the context in which the decision occurs. These findings of systematic departures from rationality are relevant to comparable worth in several ways. First, because information on those who are socially similar to oneself enters the frame of wage comparisons particularly strongly, comparisons are likely to be made with others of the same sex and in a similar occupation, making devaluation of female occupations hard for anyone to see. Second, since past earnings are in the frame for evaluating current earnings, past wages in women's and men's jobs influence what is seen as an appropriate present wage by employers and employees. Both of these implications are examples of how, once discrimination starts, powerful forces of cognitive distortion by both workers and employers operate to keep it from being corrected.

Conflict theories, including Marxism, assume a basic tendency toward rationality, with two caveats: First, they posit collective rather than individual rationality, a point to which I return in discussing selfishness versus group self-interest below. Second, conflict theorists focus on power differentials, believing that those with greater resources will utilize those resources in part to disseminate communications that favor their positions. For example, since the U.S. Chamber of Commerce has more resources with which to disseminate its position on comparable worth than does the women's movement, this skews the information available to the public.

The social-psychological portion of the structuralist sociological view sketched above challenges the rationality assumption in yet another way. This view posits that one's structural position affects habits. For example, job roles can engender habits that make job mobility unlikely, even when such mobility is desired. The notion of a habit assumes a lack of reflection that allows one to persist in self-defeating behavior. In such cases, habits are irrational.

While all theories reviewed assume a basic orientation toward rationality among actors, all except the neoclassical theory specify circumstances under which cognition is systematically distorted. But relaxing the rationality assumption makes theories less able to generate determinate predictions than is possible from neoclassical theory. In my view, actors generally intend rationality, but often have their perceptions and calculations biased in systematic rather than merely random ways. The exceptions to rationality posited by behavioral economics, social psychologists, conflict theory, and the structuralist view of social psychology have important implications for comparable worth. They all suggest that discrimination and its effects are harder to root out than is suggested by the neoclassical view, in which market forces driven by rational actors are sufficient to reduce discrimination.

B. Selfishness versus Group Self-Interest

If rationality entails calculating the most efficient means to one's goals, a theory using rationality to generate predictions must also specify whether goals are set "selfishly." Alternatively, actors may see their interests in a collective fashion, and rationally pursue what is in the interest of the group, even when it conflicts with selfish individual interests. In those cases where collective and selfish interests diverge, a collective orientation amounts to selective altruism toward members of one's group. Such altruism in no way implies lack of rationality, but rather a different unit (the group rather than the individual) to which rationality is applied. The theories reviewed above differ in their assumption on this issue.

In a formal sense, neoclassical theory assumes self-interest, not selfishness, and self-interest does not necessarily preclude altruism (Friedman and Diem 1990). However, when economists discuss behavior in markets they generally presume interest to be pursued at the individual level (England forthcoming). This is sometimes made explicit by assuming that actors' utilities are not interdependent (Folbre forthcoming). This amounts to an individual selfishness assumption. (Yet, curiously, economists often see these same actors to be altruistic within the family.)

Sociologists who are functionalists often see elites as altruistic, leading to the apt criticism of functionalism that it does not recognize self-interested exercises of power.

Conflict theory, including its Marxist variety, presumes the eventual development of group consciousness and often ignores conflicts of interest between individuals within groups. For Marxists the relevant group is a class. Once class consciousness is achieved, members of classes are seen to operate in the interest of the class. For example, discrimination pursued by capitalists is seen as a divide-and-conquer strategy. But neoclassical theory points out the individual interest each capitalist has in being a free-riding arbitrageur on this collusive arrangement. A free rider would secretly sabotage fellow capitalists by hiring women in men's jobs for bargain wages made available by the colluders. If all capitalists acted as free riders, there would be no collusion from which to have benefits. Although this is seldom made explicit by Marxists, their notion of class consciousness presumes self-interest at the group level *and* selective altruism by individuals toward members of their class. Individuals are seen as altruistic enough to other members of their class to cooperate with them and resist a selfish free-rider stance. Yet they are self-interested enough on behalf of the class as a whole to lack any altruism or solidarity toward those outside the class.

This assumption of altruism toward in-group members but self-interest on behalf of one's group is implicit in non-Marxist varieties of conflict theory as well. However, in these theories, groups other than classes may be the collective on behalf of which one is assumed to renounce both individual selfishness vis-à-vis in-group members *and* any altruism felt toward out-group members. Non-Marxist conflict theorists see many potential groups other than classes as possible bases of collective action. These include gender, racial, cultural, or ethnic groups. I find this a more realistic view than the Marxist view that effectively sees classes as the only collectives whose members subordinate individual selfishness to group self-interest. However, one indeterminacy of such non-Marxist conflict theories is a difficulty predicting which of the various groups to which each individual belongs will engage her or him in collective action.

I believe that both selfishness and altruism abound in labor market institutions, and it is extremely difficult to make broad a priori assertions about which will prevail when. I find the neoclassical view that individual selfishness always overrides collective interests in market behavior to be implausible. But I am also unconvinced by the particular mix of selfishness and selective altruism assumed by Marxists and some other conflict theorists. Sometimes individuals are selfish in a way that undercuts their class or group, and sometimes they are moved by altruism for those outside their class or group. Neither of these two possibilities is recognized by conflict theorists, and the second is generally assumed out of existence by neoclassical economists. I believe that there are conflicting pulls toward both individual self-interest and group consciousness with which theories must contend (Elster 1979). For example, when do men transcend class or race barriers to engage in collective action that disadvantages women? This indeterminism makes generating predictions very difficult.

C. Preferences

What is the source of the preferences of actors in labor markets? Neoclassical theorists refer to preferences as tastes, and would include what sociologists call values or norms in this category as well. Neoclassical theory sees tastes as exogenous to economic models. That is, none of the variables in economic models are seen to affect tastes. Thus, the outcome of market processes (e.g., what job and wage one gets) cannot affect tastes, in this view. Efficiency wage models (part of the new neoclassical institutionalism) depart from orthodox theory in seeing employees' productivity as endogenous to their wage. For example, the shirking model sees how hard one works as affected by one's wage in comparison to the market wage that could be earned in another firm. However, even here, *tastes* are not made endogenous to the wage; it is not the *taste* for shirking that is altered by the wage in the model, but rather the opportunity cost and thereby the probability of shirking. Thus, efficiency wage models do not break with the neoclassical assumption that tastes are exogenous; this is true of other parts of the new neoclassical institutionalism as well.

Other theories see tastes as affected by economic processes and outcomes. Behavioral economics can be interpreted as seeing tastes to be framed just as cognitions are. For example, models of loss aversion posit that decreases of a reward are seen to be worth more than increases of the same amount. One's valuation of a reward, which is a taste, is framed by one's current resource level.

The Marxist notion of false consciousness refers, at least in part, to what in neoclassical terminology would be called endogenous tastes. For example, Marxists would see the taste or gender group loyalty involved in sex discrimination by male coworkers as false consciousness induced by employers' efforts to divide and conquer the working class.

Sociological functionalism sees values as endogenous to the social structures of the society. On this functionalists agree with conflict theorists, including Marxists. However, functionalism differs from conflict theory in seeing prevailing values as functional for the whole society rather than in the narrower interest of powerful groups. Here functionalists ignore the fact that power is often used in a self-interested way, while conflict theorists ignore the possibility of altruistic behavior on the part of elites toward nonelites.

Institutionalists among economists discuss how institutional practices that were once functional become ceremonial tastes that have inertia even when they are no longer rational. Thus, institutionalists also see the possibility of endogenous tastes.

While some structuralist sociological views seek to make tastes entirely irrelevant, the view of structuralism I presented sees tastes as affected by the structural role one holds.

In my view, tastes are often affected by economic processes and outcomes in ways described by each of the models other than the neoclassical model. This is relevant for comparable worth in two ways. First, it explains how a discriminatory environment perpetuates itself, in part, through creating tastes in women and men, and in employers and employees, that perpetuate segregation, the low pay of female jobs, and discrimination. It also suggests that if comparable worth policies are instituted, they will affect what wages employers and employees come to think of as fair. Through changed values, this will create effects of the policy that are more salutary for women and that last longer than would be predicted by neoclassical theory.

D. *The Nature and Persistence of Discrimination*

The theories reviewed in this chapter differ in their notions about the nature and persistence of discrimination. Of particular interest here is the nature of the discrimination at issue in comparable worth. Neoclassical writing insists that if wages in predominantly female jobs are discriminatorily low, this must be because there are discriminatory barriers keeping women from entering male jobs, and this in turn leads to an artificially high supply of labor to female jobs, thus driving their wages down. Other views of the discrimination at issue in comparable worth, particularly in sociological and feminist writing, see a devaluation of jobs because they are filled by women and/or because they require skills traditionally seen as feminine. This is seen to lower the wages in female jobs relative to male jobs, irrespective of whether there is an artificially high supply of labor to female jobs.

I believe that there is an inconsistency in the neoclassical view that crowding is the sole source of discriminatory wages in women's jobs. In this view, employers devalue female *labor* for certain jobs such that they will not hire women unless they work for a lower wage than would be offered men. The devaluation of female labor is generally seen as motivated by tastes, statistical generalization, or group collusion. Yet, in seeing this as the sole discriminatory source of low wages in women's jobs, neoclassical writers implicitly reject the possibility that employers devalue certain jobs or job characteristics because of their present or historic association with women. But surely if the first devaluation is plausible, the second is as well. If employers tend to underestimate the value of women's labor for a given job in the hiring process, surely it is likely that they also tend to underestimate the contribution of the work done in women's jobs to the organization's productivity. Much of the radical/cultural-feminist view to be discussed in Chapter 6 centers on the fact that spheres of human endeavor associated with women have been systematically deprecated in Western thought and institutions. This devaluation is consistent with a cultural capital version of sociological conflict theory as well. I believe that both the devaluation of female labor for particular jobs (acknowledged by neoclassical theorists) *and* the devaluation of particular jobs or job characteristics because they are done by women or are seen as feminine (denied by neoclassical theorists) occur in labor markets.

These disagreements about the nature of sex discrimination have implications for the appropriateness of comparable worth policies. In a neoclassical view, comparable worth wages do nothing to eradicate what is seen as the underlying discrimination against women seeking entry to male jobs. Hence, they also do nothing about the crowding in female jobs. The view of discrimination I have advocated also recognizes the devaluation of jobs and job characteristics because they are presently done by women or traditionally associated with· women. In this view, mandating higher relative wages in female jobs is precisely germane to the nature of the discrimination.

A second issue on which theories disagree regards whether discrimination can persist in a market economy. Most neoclassical theorists see the persistence of discrimination as an anomaly. The anomaly arises because market forces should erode discrimination as employers with a lesser propensity to discriminate take over more of product and labor markets because of their lower wage bill and higher profits. Neoclassical economists concede that statistical discrimination can persist in competitive markets, but do not believe that other kinds of discrimination can persist. Goldberg (1982) adds the caveat that taste discrimination could persist, *if* it involved the promale altruism of paying men more than MRP. But most neoclassical economists ignore this because they assume selfishness in market behavior.

I suggested that implicit contract theory (part of the new neoclassical institutionalism) can be used to explain how the process of the erosion of discrimination is slower where there are implicit contracts and internal labor markets. This is because in such settings competitive market forces operate only at moments of entry to firms, rather than throughout employees' life cycles. However, most neoclassical implicit contract theorists have ignored this implication of their theory.

Marxist models assume that discrimination will persist as long as capitalism does since it is rational for the capitalist class to divide and conquer workers. In my view, orthodox Marxists exaggerate the extent to which all sex discrimination is derivative of class relations.

Models from behavioral economics and structuralism in sociology offer discussions of how one's current position affects tastes, cognitions, and habits. Some of these claims are at odds with neoclassical assumptions of exogenous tastes and rationality, and thus help explain the persistence of discrimination and its effects.

Taken together, nonneoclassical perspectives provide ample theoretical reason to believe that discrimination is as self-reinforcing as it is self-destroying. Neoclassical theory sees only the latter. I believe that the arbitragelike market forces operating against discrimination posited in neoclassical theory *are* present. However, given the other effects discussed, they are usually not decisive. Thus, discrimination, including the sort at issue in comparable worth, is unlikely to disappear without governmental or other collective action.

E. Trade-offs between Gains and Losses from Comparable Worth Policies

Comparable worth policies are designed to remedy the wage inequality resulting from discriminatorily low wages for women's jobs. Would such policies do this? What would be the side effects? The theories reviewed above differ in the answers they suggest to these questions.

Neoclassical theory implies that wage gains some women make through comparable worth will lead to either disemployment or wage losses for others, and these others will be disproportionately female. I believe that this possibility of disemployment or crowding into un-covered sectors should not be ignored. However, the magnitude of the effect is an empirical question.

Other theories discuss effects that the elevated wages in female oc-cupations would have that are ignored by neoclassical theory, effects that increase the benefits of comparable worth policies. Framing models suggest that higher wages in female occupations would start to remedy cognitive errors, norms, or tastes that devalue jobs held by women, and would start to create perceptions that higher relative wages for female/male occupations are fair. This would affect future wage setting practices even in the absence of continual enforcement efforts. These salutary effects should not be ignored in considering the benefits of such a policy, but they are ignored in neoclassical theory. On a more pessi-mistic note, conflict theorists remind us that the powerful groups be-hind discrimination will not change their practices without a serious struggle, a struggle for which they have disproportionate resources.

VIII. Conclusion: An Interdisciplinary View

I conclude this chapter by presenting an interdisciplinary view of labor markets, gender differentials, and comparable worth that draws upon those portions of the theories reviewed that I find most defensible. I certainly do not settle all points of disagreement between theories here, but focus on what a viable theory of labor markets would say about those questions most relevant to comparable worth: causes of occupa-tional sex segregation and the sex gap in pay.

First, let us consider the question of what factors affect sex differences in the occupations in which men and women work. While the neo-classical theory of human capital does have some explanatory power explaining individuals' allocation to occupations (e.g., that education affects the job one obtains), it is of little use in explaining occupational *sex* segregation. Women and men in the labor market scarcely differ in average years of education, and at entry level they do not differ in experience, yet typically they are employed in very different jobs. Those applications of human capital theory that see differences in occupational choice hinging upon differences in *expected* experience have not generated predictions consistent with the data; women's occupations offer neither higher starting wages nor lower wage drops during time out of the labor force.

I believe that two factors explain occupational sex segregation, and they reinforce each other. Discrimination is the relevant demand-side factor. Employers prefer to hire men in some jobs and women in others. This type of discrimination may arise from indulging male workers' desires to exclude women. It may be based upon believing that it is improper for women to do some jobs, and men others. Or discrimination may be based on erroneous beliefs about women's abilities or turnover propensities. It may be based on women's larger variance on turnover. It may be based on divide-and-conquer attempts by employers. I do not have a strong view as to the relative contribution of these types of discrimination.

Neoclassical theorists argue that discrimination should not be able to persist in competitive markets. These arguments are ultimately unconvincing. The market forces specified by neoclassical theory do exist but are seldom decisive against forces articulated by other theoretical perspectives. For example, if discrimination is based on employers' taste for selective in-group "altruism" toward men, Goldberg (1982) has shown that it will not erode in competitive markets. Another reason that discrimination may not erode in competitive markets is because competitive forces impinge only upon hiring in entry-level jobs in firms with implicit contracts and internal labor markets. It may not erode because of institutional inertia via habits, or because discrimination has caused employers' skills for nondiscriminatory selection to atrophy.

A second factor in explaining men's and women's different occupational positions is sex role socialization. This is a supply-side factor, but relatively unrelated to the usual derivations from human capital theory. One could put sex role socialization into the language of human capital theory and say that women invest in different kinds of human capital than men, leading to different kinds of jobs. Girls may take secretarial courses while boys take "shop" and learn welding. College women major in nursing while men major in chemistry. But these are not issues of women investing in *less* human capital than men. Rather, they are issues of different kinds of investments reflecting the different interests or aspirations into which men and women have been steered by the socialization process. Women may often not realize the adverse implications on their future earnings of the decisions they are making, because information about earnings in jobs is often scarce. Although sex role socialization is a supply-side factor, to use the language of economics, it would be incorrect to see socialized job preferences as what economists would call exogenous tastes. Social-psychological research has shown that what one observes is often converted into what one thinks is morally proper. Thus, the distribution of women and men across occupations is an important input into the socialization of the next generation's values and tastes. This renders these tastes endogenous to economic outcomes at the system level. Socialization should also be seen as a lifelong process. If a woman enters a male job and is ridiculed and isolated by the men in the job, this may change her tastes to "preferring" a female job.

In sum, occupational sex segregation is established and perpetuated through the two processes of discrimination and sex role socialization.

What about the sex gap in pay? How is this explained? Three main factors are relevant: First, women, on average, have fewer years of seniority and labor force experience than men, and this explains somewhere between one quarter and one half of the sex gap in pay. This part of the explanation is consistent with human capital theory. The educational dimension of human capital is not very relevant, because men and women average approximately equal years of education.

What of the portion of the sex gap in pay not explained by human capital? It results mainly from the different jobs men and women hold. But what about these jobs leads women's jobs to pay less? Part of this may be that women are concentrated in jobs that are low on some of the skills or disamenities that neoclassical theories predict to affect wages. Another portion of the gap comes from the wage discrimination at issue in comparable worth. Jobs are discriminatorily assigned low wages when they are filled by women. This results in part from employers' sense of the propriety of paying men more. One could think of this as a taste, selective altruism toward male employees, or collusion with them. Second, the discriminatorily low pay in female jobs results from systematic cognitive errors in assessing the contribution that the work done in female occupations makes to organizations' profits or other goals. Neoclassical theorists reject both of these explanations, arguing that if discrimination is relevant at all, it must operate through barriers to women's entry into male jobs, which indirectly depress the wages in female occupations via crowding. I accept that crowding may occur, but as I have argued above, I think it inconsistent to believe that employers devalue women's *labor* when they engage in hiring decisions but do not also systematically devalue women's *jobs*. I believe that the *persistence* of this wage discrimination becomes plausible when we think about framing effects (discussed by social-psychologists and behavioral economists). This helps us to understand how errors in cognition about the value of women's jobs might persist, since present pay is in the frame used to assess the appropriateness of future pay. This also helps us to realize why it is difficult for women to develop a sense of injustice that might lead them to change jobs or to engage in collective action in favor of comparable worth.

All theorists agree that comparable worth policies would raise the relative wages of women in covered jobs. However, several of the theories other than neoclassical economics provide reasons to think that the policy, once instituted, would have long-term effects in this direction even in the absence of its continued enforcement—through its effects on the frame within which people evaluate the appropriateness of the wages of jobs and through institutional inertia. I suspect that the disemployment effects economic theory predicts would and do occur. While they will not affect only women, they will disproportionately affect women. Thus, the net assessments of benefit to women of the policy should take this possibility into account. Because changes in frames and institutional inertia make the potential benefits of such policies larger than would otherwise be the case, I make a more optimistic assessment than most neoclassical theorists of the potential gains for women of comparable worth. This is not to minimize the political difficulty of obtaining comparable worth wage adjustments of a nontrivial magnitude (see Steinberg forthcoming; Blum 1991; Acker 1989). It is rather to say that if these political hurdles can be overcome, the potential benefits to women are great.

One major conclusion of this chapter is that there is theoretical warrant for believing that the sort of discriminatory devaluation of women's jobs at issue in comparable worth is a salient and persistent feature of labor markets. I turn in Chapter 3 to a more detailed empirical analysis that provides evidence for this assertion.

Notes

1. Technically speaking, the labor demand curve is equivalent to only the *downward-sloping* portion of the MRP curve, i.e., the portion in the range after marginal returns begin diminishing. Also, note that I use the term MRP rather

than the traditional marginal product (MP) or value of marginal product (VMP) because the latter two terms are appropriate only where product markets are competitive. In this case they equal MRP. However, MRP is the more general case; even where labor markets are competitive but product markets are not, the labor demand curve equals the downward-sloping portion of the MRP curve.

2.   This statement presumes, for expositional simplicity, that we can hold the supply and demand in one job constant while varying them in another job. In reality, supply and demand in each job are affected by the wage in the other job. For example, if one job becomes more lucrative, the number of people supplied to the other job at any given wage may be reduced, i.e., the location of the other job's supply curve shifts inward and upward. Also for simplicity, I have ignored the fact that supply or demand curves may differ in slope or elasticity as well as in level.

3.   The observation that predominantly female occupations have flatter wage trajectories *and* lower starting wages is possible to reconcile with neoclassical theory if (1) lack of on-the-job human capital investment explains the lower trajectories, which, other things equal, we would expect to be accompanied by higher starting wages, while (2) compensating differentials explains the lower starting wages. However, in one analysis that introduced a large number of job characteristics to control for compensating differentials, female jobs were still found to have lower starting wages (England et al. 1988). Another possible reconciliation is suggested by Kuhn (1991).

4.   However, we should not leap to the conclusion that all sex discrimination is statistical. In their analysis of 1960s and 1970s data from approximately 300 businesses in California, Bielby and Baron (1986) found that many employers openly stated that they reserved some jobs for one sex or the other. In many such jobs, the skills required were *not* skills on which there are commonly known sex differences in average attainment (as might be argued, for example, for upper body strength). Thus, the thrust of Bielby and Baron's argument is to minimize the importance of statistical discrimination based on real group differences in means. Rather, they stress that segregation derives mainly from other forms of discrimination, such as what I call taste or error discrimination. They also stress that these forms of discrimination may perpetuate stereotypes, leading to further discrimination, and sometimes becoming self-fulfilling prophecies leading to later statistical discrimination.

5.   There is one exception to the statement that neoclassical theory predicts comparable worth policies to cause disemployment. If a monopsony model of discrimination is assumed, disemployment will not necessarily result (Kahn 1986; Ehrenberg and Smith 1987). Competitive employers can hire all the labor they want at the market wage, and none at a lower wage. By contrast, a monopsonistic employer faces the entire market's labor supply curve, and thus has to pay *all* workers hired a higher wage in order to increase the quantity employed. Put another way, since a monopsonist is the entire demand side of the labor market, s/he can only hire more workers by increasing the wage paid to all workers. Thus, for monopsonists, the cost of the marginal worker is more than his or her wage. As a consequence, many monopsonists employ fewer workers than they would prefer at the existing wage, and thus would cut back fewer workers than would a competitive employer in the face of a required increase in the wage in female jobs.

6.   U.S. government statistics distinguish between those who are unemployed and those who are out of the labor force. The unemployed are those who

do not have a job but are actively looking for one. Those not looking for a job are instead counted as out of the labor force. This includes homemakers, retirees, students, and those who have become discouraged and given up looking for work. A mandated wage increase in female jobs might add people to both categories. The term *disemployment* is used by economists to refer to increases in either category.

7. *Moral hazard* is a term used by economists to refer to incentive systems, particularly those involving insurance of any sort, that reduce the incentives for "good" behavior. For example, from the point of view of insurance companies, the moral hazard problem about auto insurance is that once the insurance is bought, people's individual self-interest-based incentive to drive carefully is reduced.

8. The "new analytical Marxism" rejects the labor theory of value, but retains the conclusion that workers are exploited under capitalism (Roemer 1988). In this view, the basis of exploitation is unequal initial endowments of property; those with little or no property are exploited whether those who own more property hire them as workers or whether they rent the property owners' capital to engage in self-employment. Under the orthodox labor theory of value, the latter would not entail exploitation.

9. In a Marxist-feminist view, homemakers perform reproductive labor, which benefits capitalists in re-creating the current generation of workers and producing the next generation. This labor contributes to surplus value formation. Thus, the innovation of Marxist feminists was to deviate from the orthodox Marxist contention that homemakers are not, technically speaking, exploited by capitalists, because surplus value is not extracted from their labor. Most socialist feminists agree with the Marxist-feminist contention that homemakers are exploited by capitalists. However, because they recognize patriarchy as an independent system, socialist feminists also see homemakers as oppressed by the men they live with. Thus, the difference between socialist feminists and Marxist feminists on questions of domestic labor is parallel to the difference between socialist feminists and orthodox Marxists on questions of sex discrimination in paid labor. In each case, socialist feminists refuse to accept the contention that women's disadvantage is *simply* a derivative of capitalist class relations. In each case, socialist feminists argue that it is at least partly a result of patriarchy. See Chapter 6 for further discussion of the issue.

3

Pay in Female and Male Occupations: Findings from National Data

I. Introduction

Across the national economy, female jobs (i.e., jobs filled primarily with women) usually pay less than male jobs. What explains this lower pay in female jobs? In particular, how important a factor is the sort of wage discrimination at issue in comparable worth? What other factors are operative in explaining why some occupations pay more than others, and, more specifically, in explaining why female occupations pay less than male occupations? This chapter explores these questions, using 1980 census data. I will not be concerned here with explanations of why men and women get into the occupations they hold, nor with lack of equal pay for men and women in the same job, topics discussed in earlier chapters. Here I narrow the focus to an empirical analysis directly relevant to comparable worth: whether an occupation pays less if it is "women's work."

Among full-time year-round workers in the United States, the 1980 census showed a sex gap in pay of \$3.39/hour, with men averaging \$8.59/hour compared to women's \$5.20/hour. This overall gap is not the same as the pay gap between female and male occupations, since not all women are in female occupations, nor are all men in male occupations, and since there is also a sex gap in pay within occupations. However, a portion of this overall sex gap in pay *is* due to female jobs paying less than male jobs. In general, the higher the percentage of females in an occupation, the less the job pays either men or women. For example, in the census data used in this chapter, when summarized as a linear relationship, pay and sex composition are related such that those in occupations that are virtually all male earn approximately \$1.00/hour more than those in occupations that are virtually all female. This relationship holds both for men and women, so that men as well as women have lower wages if they work in a predominantly female occupation.[1] This relationship between sex composition and earnings contributes to the sex gap in pay. My interest here is to determine how much of the overall sex gap in pay, and of the pay gap between male and female occupations, can be explained by the sort of between-occupation wage discrimination at issue in comparable worth. This requires a statistical analysis that controls for characteristics of occupations that influence their wages for reasons other than gender bias.

What are the major explanations of why female occupations pay less than male occupations? Thinking about logical possibilities will suggest what variables need to be included as controls in the analysis, and what variables' effects will index gender-based wage discrimination. Several possibilities must be considered:

1. Women may be concentrated in occupations that require less cognitive, social, or physical skills. The idea that the skill level required by a job affects its wage is consistent with the functionalist theory of stratification as well as with human capital theory in economics (both discussed in Chapter 2).

2. A lower proportion of women than men may be in jobs involving supervisory social skills. Marxist theory (discussed in Chapter 2) predicts that jobs involving managerial or supervisory authority pay more, not due to their skill requirements, but due to their class location.

3. Men may be concentrated in occupations with less pleasant or more onerous working conditions (such as danger, dirt, or stress); and employers may have to pay a wage premium to fill jobs with greater nonpecuniary disamenities or less nonpecuniary amenities. Economists' theory of compensating differentials, discussed in Chapter 2, predicts this.

4. Women may be concentrated in jobs that require less effort. If expending effort is onerous to workers, then the theory of compensating differentials would predict effort to affect wages positively.

5. Female occupations may be concentrated in industries or firms that have lower wage scales for some reason other than the fact that women work in them. Theories of efficiency wages proposed by economists as well as the new structuralism in sociological stratification research suggest the importance of such factors in wage determination. (See Chapter 2.)

The discussion so far suggests that an analysis to detect wage discrimination against female occupations in the economy at large must adjust out of any estimates of such discrimination differences in pay due to skill demands, working conditions that tap required effort and other amenities and disamenities, and industrial and firm characteristics.

6. In addition, women's occupations may have lower wages because they are crowded. This will result if hiring discrimination keeps women out of male occupations, and this creates an artificially large supply of labor to the jobs in which employers will hire women. This oversupply or crowding of female jobs may then explain their lower wages, according to economist Bergmann's (1974, 1986) crowding thesis, discussed in Chapter 2. Unfortunately, I know of no way to disentangle this portion of the wage gap from the estimate of direct wage discrimination against female occupations.

7. Female occupations may have their wages lowered by the direct sort of wage discrimination at issue in comparable worth. What I term direct gender bias occurs when employers respond to an occupation's sex composition in setting its wage level. If an occupation is filled largely by women (for whatever reasons, discriminatory or not), employers may discriminate in wage setting by offering lower wages to (both male and female) workers in the occupation. This direct gender bias will be assessed by estimating the effect of occupations' percentage female on the wages they offer, net of control variables designed to capture effects involved in other explanations.

8. Women's occupations may require kinds of skills, such as nurturant social skills, that have lower or negative rates of return compared to the skills typically required by men's jobs. This indirect sort of gender bias in occupational wage determination is also part of what is at issue in comparable worth. It will be assessed by comparing the returns to nurturant social skills, the one clear example of a type of skill associated with women's traditional sphere, to returns for other skills (such as physical, cognitive, or supervisory skills) more commonly required by male occupations. Both direct and indirect gender bias in occupational wage setting are plausible predictions from those conflict theories in sociology that deal with gender, including Marxist and feminist views. (See Chapter 2.)

9. Women's jobs may also employ more racial or ethnic minorities, and this may depress the wages in such jobs as a result of racial or ethnic bias in wage setting. Just as there could be a devaluation of a job leading to lower wages because the occupation is predominantly female, such bias in wage setting could exist for jobs with concentrations of African Americans and Mexican Americans as well. Various conflict theories in sociology suggest that both the race and sex composition of jobs may affect their earnings.

II. Data and Variables

A. Units of Analysis

The analysis to follow uses a dataset in which 1980 census detailed
(three-digit) occupations are the units of analysis. All jobs have been
categorized by the Census Bureau into 503 occupational categories.
There are 403 of these occupations that do not have missing values on
any of the variables. All regressions, means, and decompositions presented in this chapter are based on these 403 occupations.[2]

The Census Bureau's detailed occupational classification is used because it provides the most detailed categories for which national data on
earnings are available. However, these categories are less detailed than
the job titles used within many firms. Thus, some of the sex gap in pay
within these occupational categories may arise from sex segregation of
more detailed job categories. This portion of the pay gap will not get
counted in the estimates I provide of how much of the overall sex gap in
pay is explained by gender bias in occupational wage settings. Thus,
estimates provided here could be underestimates of direct gender bias in
wage setting.

B. Description of Variables

Variables used in the regression analyses reported in this chapter are
described below. I first describe the variables in groups discussed together for conceptual reasons. In the next section, I discuss the data
sources for the variables. All variables used in any of the regression
models to be presented are listed in Table 3.1, which also gives the data
source for each variable. As the discussion proceeds, I will identify each
variable with a short, descriptive name, given in capital letters.

The independent variables are included as measures of factors that
may affect the earnings that occupations offer. I am particularly interested in the effect of sex composition on earnings. Other variables
that are correlated with sex composition may also provide partial explanations for why male occupations generally pay more than female occupations.

In dividing variables into groups, I distinguish between indicators of
skill demands and indicators of amenities or disamenities. The former
are relevant to predictions from human capital theory. The theory suggests that, insofar as any kind of skill has costs (even opportunity costs)
of acquisition, occupations requiring more of it will pay more, controlling for other factors. Measures of amenities and disamenities are

Table 3.1. Description of Variables Used in Regression Analyses[1]

Variable	Description	Source	N^2
Sex composition			
% FEMALE	% Female of all FTYR wkrs in occ	U.S. Census 1980	503
Race composition			
% BLACK	% Black of all wkrs in occ	Census P.U.M.S.	503
% MEXICAN	% Mexican of all wkrs in occ	Census P.U.M.S.	503
Cognitive skill and training demands			
COMPLEXITY W/ DATA	Complexity of task w/ data	DOT	495
GEN'L EDUC	General education (schooling)	DOT	495
INTELLIGENCE	Intelligence	DOT	495
NUMERICAL APTITUDE	Numerical aptitude	DOT	495
VERBAL APTITUDE	Verbal aptitude	DOT	495
FEM EDUC	Mean education in years of women in occ	Census P.U.M.S.	502
MALE EDUC	Mean education in years of men in occ	Census P.U.M.S.	503
FEM PERCENT COLLEGE	% Women w/ 4 or more years college	Census P.U.M.S.	502
MALE PERCENT COLLEGE	% Men w/ 4 or more years college	Census P.U.M.S.	503
VOC OR OJT TRAINING	Vocational or OJT time, in months	DOT	495
LEARN NEW THINGS	Need to learn new things on the job	Filer, QES	432
COGNITIVE FACTOR	Factor created with above 11 variables; principal-components factor analysis	Created by author	430
FEM EXPER	Mean estimated wk experience of women in occ	Filer, NLS, Census	431
Social skill demands			
AUTHORITY	Dummy variable for whether occ involves supr or mgr authority over other wkrs	Coded by author	503
NURTURANCE	Dummy variable for whether occ involves nurturance toward clients or customers	Coded by author	503
COMPLEXITY W/ PEOPLE	Complexity of task in relation to people	DOT	495
DEAL W/ PEOPLE	% Wkrs req to deal w/ people beyond give/take instructions	DOT	495

(continued)

tail changing their slopes, then this group of industrial and organizational variables, as a whole, explains about 7% of the sex gap in pay.

V. Conclusion

The central finding of this chapter is that the sex composition of an occupation affects the pay it offers, such that both men and women earn less if they work in a predominantly female occupation. That this relationship held up under the stringent set of controls used here is evidence that the wage discrimination at issue in comparable worth is pervasive in the U.S. economy. After adjusting for cognitive, social, and physical skill demands, amenities, disamenities, demands for effort, and industrial and organizational characteristics, jobs pay less if they contain a higher proportion of females. If comparability is defined as having the same predicted wage based on all the variables in the analysis besides sex composition, then I have shown that female jobs pay less than comparable male jobs.

The magnitude of the effect of sex composition is smaller in this analysis than many past studies. Here it explains between 5 and 11% of the sex gap in pay, depending on the model and decomposition method used. (See Table 3.9.) Past studies reviewed by Sorensen typically showed sex composition to explain between 10 and 30% of the sex gap in pay. The smaller figure obtained here is probably due to the more numerous and varied control variables used. Part of what shows up here as indirect gender bias—the devaluation of types of skills such as nurturance because they are associated with women—may show up as direct bias in wage setting in those analyses. One lesson from this analysis, then, is that the more detailed the variables included in a job evaluation, the more important that comparable worth strategies include indirect gender bias as part of what they correct.

I interpret the coefficient on sex composition as evidence of direct wage discrimination against predominantly female occupations. The effects are such that moving from an all-female to a comparable all-male occupation leads to a loss of between 40 cents/hour and $1/hour. The analysis cannot reveal the mechanisms through which this discrimination operates. Such mechanisms may include making cognitive errors in assessing the contribution of female jobs to organizational goals, including profit, or normative devaluing of work done by women. Other mechanisms of the effect may include the practice of using past wages within the organization or present wages in other organizations ("the market") to set jobs' pay levels, thus perpetuating an employer's own past discrimination as well as other organizations' discrimination.

Neoclassical skeptics disagree with this interpretation of the net negative effect of occupations' percentage female on wages. Ardent believers in the notion that discrimination cannot persist in competitive markets would argue that with enough control variables, the effect of sex composition will disappear. Chapter 2 explained my reasons for believing that discrimination often persists even in competitive markets. For some, all evidence is irrelevant since unmeasured variables will be invoked to avoid the conclusion of discrimination. Other economists concede discrimination, but only in access to positions and wages within jobs. These economists agree with me in seeing effects of sex composition on wages indicating discriminatorily low wages in female occupations. However, they see the mechanism as an unwillingness of employers to hire women in male occupations for the same wages paid to men, which leads to crowding and hence lower wages in female occupations. I argued in Chapter 2 that it makes little sense to accept the possibility of discrimination in hiring and wage setting within jobs but not in between-job wage setting. While I agree that hiring discrimination exists, I believe that any "excess supply" caused by the extent to which women's jobs are more crowded than men's has probably been offset by the disproportionate increases in labor demand in predominantly female jobs as the service sector has grown and bureaucratization has necessitated more clerical workers. Thus, I interpret the coefficient on sex composition as resulting entirely from wage discrimination in between-occupation wage setting. However, my analysis was not able to separate this from any possible effects of crowding. Thus, the coefficients on sex composition may capture a combination of any crowding that exists and the discriminatory assignment of wages to occupations based on their sex composition.

The second major finding is that being in a job requiring nurturing carries a net wage penalty of between 24 cents/hour and $1.71/hour, depending on the model. (See Table 3.5.) This penalty cannot be explained by nurturant jobs requiring less cognitive or physical skill, by their lack of requirements for managerial authority, by their lack of disamenities or surplus of amenities, by the type of firm or industry in which such jobs occur, or even because the jobs are currently held largely by women, since all these factors were controlled in the models assessing this penalty. I interpret this as evidence that nurturant work is devalued in markets because of its traditional link with women's work in the home and in labor markets. Once this devaluation has occurred, it affects both female and male jobs.

Effects of other job characteristics on earnings were of interest because, given sex differences in means on these variables, they may explain some of the sex gap in pay. In the summary of these findings to follow, I will use the estimates of the percentage of the pay gap explained that are an average of the estimates obtained using the male and the female slopes.

Race composition makes no contribution to the sex gap in pay (Table 3.9). Occupations containing a higher percentage of African Americans and Mexicans pay less (though not significantly so in all models); however, since the race composition of the jobs men and women are in does not differ substantially the effect on the sex gap in pay is nil.

Occupations requiring more cognitive skill and training offer higher wages. Yet, despite large returns to this factor, it explains only 2% of the sex gap in pay. This is because the jobs in which men and women work differ only slightly on requirements for cognitive skill and training. (See Table 3.6.)

Two types of social skill, authority and nurturance, differ drastically in their returns. Net of all else, occupations involving authority over other workers pay between 37 cents/hour and $1.37/hour more. Occupations involving nurturance pay between 24 cents/hour and $1.71/hour less than comparable jobs that do not involve nurturance (Table 3.5). As discussed above, I interpret the penalty for nurturant skill to indicate indirect gender bias in wage setting. Since men are more apt to be in occupations involving authority than women, while women are more apt to be in occupations involving nurturance, these two factors together explain 6 to 7% of the sex gap in pay (Table 3.9).

Physical skill demands explain between 4 and 5% of the sex gap in pay (Table 3.9). This arises largely because of the positive return to physical strength combined with women's lesser representation in jobs requiring such strength. Most of the other physical skill demands do not have significant positive returns.

Amenities, disamenities, and effort, taken together, contribute nothing to the sex gap in pay. In fact, they make a negative contribution (Table 3.9). That is, women's job distribution is slightly more favorable to wages than men's on these variables. In general, coefficients on these variables have the signs predicted by the theory of compensating differentials in the regressions (Table 3.5). With some exceptions, when effects are significant, nonpecuniary amenities lower wages, disamenities raise wages, and requirements for effort raise wages. This suggests the operation of compensating differentials in labor markets. However, none of the *physical* disamenities offer positive compensating wage premiums. Moreover, these results do *not* support the notion that compensating differentials explain the pay differences between men's and women's jobs. There is no systematic tendency of women's jobs to require less effort, to have more nonpecuniary amenities, or to have fewer nonpecuniary disamenities or variables with significant effects.

My conclusions about compensating differentials hinge on a priori assumptions that I made about what variables are amenities and disamenities. Recall from Chapter 2 that the theory of compensating differentials is only testable with assumptions about the tastes of the marginal worker. Some economists might conclude from the negative returns to nurturance and positive returns to authority that the former is an amenity and the latter a disamenity to the marginal worker, and thus that the theory of compensating differentials explains the 6–7% of the sex gap in pay that I attributed to type of social skill required. However, since I think there is little evidence to suggest that more workers prefer nurturance than authority, to conclude this would be to assume the truth of the theory of compensating differentials a priori. For this reason, I reject this interpretation.

Differences between male and female occupations in their typical industrial and organizational settings explain 7% of the sex gap in pay. Contributing to this gap are the fact that women's occupations often involve government employment, which lowers wages, and that men's occupations are more likely to be unionized or in industries that are higher paying because of foreign dividends or for other reasons.

This chapter has presented a policy-capturing job evaluation at the national level to provide an overview of the factors, including gender bias, contributing to the relatively low pay of female occupations. However, job evaluation is generally carried out at the organizational level. I turn now, in Chapter 4, to discussing methods of job evaluation and the merits and pitfalls of using them to rid organizations' wage systems of gender bias.

Notes

1. The figure of $1.00/hour was arrived at in the following way: women's average hourly pay in the occupation was regressed on the percentage of females in the occupation across the 503 1980 detailed census occupational categories weighted by their numbers of women, with no control variables. The coefficient times 100 tells us that a woman changing from an occupation that is 0% female to one that is 100% female would lose $1.30/hour, on average. Running the same regression with men's average hourly pay as the dependent variable and weighted by occupations' number of men shows that, for men, moving from an occupation that is 0% female to one that is 100% female would lead to losing $0.63/hour. Thus, regardless of the individual's sex, those in female occupations earn less. The analogous figures for the 403 occupations without missing values on any variables used in the regression analyses presented later in this chapter were $1.25 and $0.83/hour.

2. The sex gap in pay across all 503 occupations is $3.39/hour. The sex gap in pay across these 403 occupations is very similar, $3.50/hour. Even though miss-

ing values led to a loss of almost 20% of the occupations, this only entailed a loss of 10% of the full-time year-round labor force because the missing occupations employed fewer people on average. Also, a nearly identical proportion of labor force was lost for men and women (within one percentage point of 10%). Thus, we can be quite confident that the conclusions drawn here apply to the labor force as a whole.

3. To avoid multicollinearity, some variables were dropped due to correlations of above 0.75 with other variables to be included in the model. Where I had a choice about which of two variables to drop, I used two criteria. Variables measuring the interests or preferences of the typical worker in a job were seen as less germane as indicators of skills or amenities/disamenities than were other variables, so these were dropped. Also, if there were alternative measures more similar to one variable, or one variable was seen as less likely to be compensated, it was dropped. A measure of the extent to which workers in the job prefer working with data was dropped because of its high correlation with INFLU-ENCE. This was a measure of preferences, and the dataset provided other better measures of skills in using data. A measure of the extent to which workers in the job prefer working with machines was dropped because of its high correlation with PRECISION, a measure of the percentage of workers in an occupation who must do work requiring the precise attainment of set limits, tolerances, or standards. A measure of the extent to which workers in the job prefer working with things was dropped due to its high negative correlation with VERBAL APTITUDE and with the two variables making up the SOCIAL COMPLEXITY SCALE, COMPLEXITY W/ PEOPLE and DEAL W/ PEOPLE. A measure of the percentage of workers in the job required to talk or hear was deleted since this is quite a minimal requirement that seemed unlikely to be compensated, and because of its strong correlation with DEAL W/ PEOPLE. A measure of the percentage of workers in the job required to see was also dropped since this seemed quite a minimal requirement that is not likely to be compensated. A measure of the extent to which workers in the job prefer working for the good of people was dropped due to its correlation with COMPLEXITY W/ PEOPLE. A measure of the extent to which the job requires form perception was dropped because of its correlation with SPATIAL APT (the job's requirement for spatial aptitude). A measure of the percentage of workers in the job who prefer routine tasks was dropped because of its correlation with REPETITION, a measure of the extent to which the job actually involves repetitious work. The percentage of workers in the occupation who work for a private firm was dropped because of the negative correlation between this variable and % GOVT. Since the percentage self-employed was also included, roughly speaking, one can interpret coefficients on % GOVT as the effect of being employed for government in comparison with working for a private firm.

4. I am grateful to Donald Treiman of the Sociology Department, University of California-Los Angeles, for providing me with a machine-readable data file with these aggregate occupational measures computed from P.U.M.S. data. These measures pertain to all workers in an occupation, not just those employed full-time year-round.

5. I am grateful to Donald Treiman, who provided me with these data as well.

6. The NAS file provides DOT variables for some occupations in categories more detailed than three-digit occupations (industries within occupations). In such cases, a weighted average was computed to get one score for each variable

for each 1970 occupational category before merging the DOT variables onto the individual file.

7.   I am grateful to Randall Filer of the Economics Department at Hunter College, City University of New York, for providing me with these variables coded to 1980 census occupational categories. These measures pertain to all workers in the occupation, not just those employed full-time year-round.

8.   I am grateful to Randy Hodson of the Sociology Department at Indiana University for providing me with these data coded to three-digit 1970 census industrial categories.

9.   The census matrix contains only 447 occupational categories rather than the full 503. This results mainly from grouping several small three-digit categories into one in several instances. In this case, I assigned the occupational mean for the broader matrix category to each of the several constituent detailed categories on the final occupational file. In a few cases, the matrix broke a detailed census occupational category into two or more categories on the matrix. In this case, I used an average across the several matrix categories. Thus, no missing variables on the ultimate occupational file were created by this mismatch between the occupational categories of the matrix and detailed census occupational categories. However, the final occupational file does have missing values for some industrial variables. This occurred when there was an occupation all of whose incumbents work in industries that were scored with missing values on the industrial dataset obtained from Hodson. This is particularly likely for occupations involving government work.

10.   It is also possible to use individuals as units of analysis and test for effects of occupations' sex composition. In this latter case, the % FEMALE and other occupational characteristics are contextual variables appended onto each individual's record according to the % FEMALE of her or his occupation. In this case, results can be generalized to the population of employed persons. With the strategy of taking occupations as cases, results are generalized to occupations. However, when *all* variables in the individual analysis are contextual, it should give roughly the same results as this analysis with occupations as cases, as long as occupations are weighted by the numbers of persons employed in them, as they are in this analysis. In my view, individuals are preferable units of analysis only if more detailed measures of types of human capital are available on the individual datasets for which occupational averages are not available. Examples might be years of general experience and seniority with current firm. For a similar analysis on individual data, see England et al. (1988). For a discussion of the similarity of findings between studies using individuals and occupations as units of analysis, see Chapter 1 and Table 1.9.

11.   When job evaluation is done within organizations, as discussed in Chapter 4, this problem does not arise and one equation is sufficient. This is because the dependent variable in such policy-capturing regressions is the starting, highest possible, or midpoint (not average or median) pay in the job. This wage is attached to a job by policy. It is not the actual average wage earned. Thus, within-occupation sex differences in actual pay do not thereby affect the coefficient on sex composition or the height of the male job or female job line. In contrast to job evaluation for a single employer, in the national data analyzed in this chapter, there is no way to measure employers' "policies" except by the actual wages paid.

12.   I have described this process as if predicted earnings on the basis of all other variables are calculated first and then % FEMALE is added. In fact, how-

ever, effects of each variable are calculated while simultaneously netting out the others. The coefficient on each variable is its effect as if it were added last.

13.   While we cannot use the difference in intercepts as a measure of discrimination here, in job evaluations for a single employer where the dependent variable is starting, midpoint, or highest wage in an occupation (as set by policy), with separate regressions for male and female jobs, intercept differences *can* be seen as the additive effects of being in a male versus female job, holding constant the other variables in the equations. In such job evaluations, intercept differences are not affected by within-occupation differences in pay, as they are in the present analysis of national data. (This is because the top, bottom, or midpoint of a policy-set wage band for the job is the dependent variable in a job evaluation, whereas in these national data we are using actual mean male and female earnings.) Thus, in such job evaluations, the intercept differences are one measure of the net, additive effects of jobs' sex composition, the same measure you would get by using one equation for all occupations and taking the coefficient on a dummy variable for female-versus-male occupations as the measure of the effect. One weakness of the measure is that it has thrown away precision by dichotomizing sex composition. To avoid this, a single equation could be used for job evaluation, with % FEMALE (as a continuum) added as a variable. Then, analogous to the analysis here, the coefficient on % FEMALE would measure the net, additive effect of sex composition on earnings. The job evaluation analysis would not require two separate equations, as is required for the data analysis reported here, because, as discussed previously, the coefficient on sex composition is not affected by within-occupation sex differences in actual earnings in the job evaluation because policy-set wages for the job are the dependent variable.

A key thing to remember is that intercept and sex differences in coefficients are affected by within-occupation sex differences in earnings when actual earnings are the dependent variable. However, coefficients within each sex-specific equation are not so affected because, by using an equation for each sex, sex is held constant.

14.   Of course, a job that is 0% female has no women in it, and an occupation that is 100% female has no men in it. However, these extreme values are used to illustrate the effects of going from an occupation that is *virtually* all male to one that is *virtually* all female.

4

Job Evaluation

I. Introduction

Job evaluation is a technique used by many large employers to help determine and legitimate the relative pay of jobs. The most popular method of job evaluation involves giving points to jobs for such things as education, various skills, difficult working conditions, and responsibility. Job evaluation has become intimately linked with the comparable worth debate in two somewhat contradictory ways: On the one hand, proponents of comparable worth argue that job evaluation has been biased against predominantly female jobs, thus contributing to women's lower pay. On the other hand, job evaluation is seen as a tool to achieve equitable pay for women's jobs. Indeed, Remick (1984, p. 99) defines comparable worth as the "application of a single, bias-free . . . job evaluation system within a given establishment across job families, both to rank jobs and set salary."

Despite this link between job evaluation and comparable worth, the use of job evaluation predates the comparable worth debate by decades. In the 1940s a number of firms began to use job evaluation because they found that it reduced disputes with unions (Northrup 1980; Patten 1987). Job evaluation provided a technical means to rank jobs so that the *relative* pay of jobs was not subject to negotiation unless the content of a job changed. Thus, while employers still had to bargain about overall pay levels, job evaluation saved them from negotiating about each job individually. When the content of a job changed, evaluation provided the means to decide the new rank order of the job. Job evaluation also got a boost from events during World War II. Concerns about national security led to more than the previously accepted amount of regulation of the economy, and the National War Labor Board mandated that many firms use job evaluation. For these and other reasons, job evaluation has been in common use by many large employers since World War II.

What proportion of firms use job evaluation today, and what proportion of employees work in such firms? Among large firms responding to one survey, 56% used job evaluation for managerial jobs and 67% used it for nonsupervisory office jobs (Akalin 1970). Small firms are less apt to use job evaluation (Schwab 1984). The federal government and most state governments use job evaluation, while local governments vary in whether they use it. Overall, Belcher (1974) conjectures that two thirds of U.S. workers are in jobs where wages are affected by job evaluation, while Schwab (1984) offers the more conservative estimate that over half of workers are covered. Whatever the proportion of employers who use job evaluation, it has seldom been adopted with pay equity between male and female jobs as a goal. This use of job evaluation is a phenomenon of the last 15 years and is limited almost exclusively to job evaluations mandated by states or localities for their public sector employees. A few corporations have undertaken job evaluation with pay equity between male and female jobs in mind, but they are the exception (Bernstein 1986). Yet, job evaluation has an importance for comparable worth far beyond the pervasiveness of its current use. This is because proponents of pay equity want to see job evaluation practiced much more universally, as a strategy to correct sex bias in the relative pay of jobs.

II. Methods of Job Evaluation

There are four major methods of job evaluation: ranking, classification, factor comparison, and point-factor (sometimes called "point"). The first three have decreased in popularity because they leave many decisions implicit that are made explicit in the point-factor system (Treiman 1979). In all methods of job evaluation, it is the requirements of the *job* that are evaluated, *not* the performance of a given *individual* within the job. It is taken for granted that within any one job, different individuals are paid different amounts because of differences in merit or seniority. However, each job generally has a pay range within which such individual variation is confined. For example, the pay in one job may range from $800 to $11,000/month, while in another it ranges from $950 to $12,500/month. The second job has a higher pay level, whether defined by the bottom, midpoint, or top of the pay interval. Job evaluation is a way of deciding which jobs will have a higher pay level than others according to a standardized way of evaluating the demands of the job.

Whatever method is used, the process of job evaluation is generally controlled by managers, often guided by consulting firms. In addition, nonmanagerial employees, union representatives, and/or citizens (in the case of the public sector) sometimes participate in the process. Obviously, the outcome may be affected by who participates in the process, so this is one source of political contestation when job evaluation is to be used to achieve pay equity for women and/or minorities (Steinberg and Haignere 1987; Acker 1987).

A. Ranking

Ranking is the simplest of the four systems. Here jobs are simply ordered by their payworthiness. The question of what things about jobs make them payworthy is not explicitly addressed or measured. Allocating jobs into ordinal pay grades 1 through 10 by an overall judgment of their comparative worth would be an example of ranking.

B. Classification

Classification is a slightly more sophisticated technique than ranking. Classification in federal government jobs began with the Classification Act of 1923 (Collett 1983). (Today, however, most federal jobs are evaluated with point-factor systems.) To use classification, several compensable "factors" are identified. Factors refer to pay-relevant characteristics of jobs. For example, knowledge, responsibility, and harsh working conditions are the factors in many evaluations. In classification, those making the decisions are to consider all factors in arriving at a decision to classify a job into one of a number of ordinal pay grades. However, separate points for each factor are not given explicitly. In this system, it is difficult to classify a job that is high on one factor and low on another. The decision entails deciding whether the factors count equally in weight (and thus simple averaging will do) or whether one factor is much more important. Yet this decision about weights is left implicit (Treiman 1979). Suppose, for example, that one is comparing the jobs of nurse's aide and supervisor of custodians. Suppose that they require about the same amount of knowledge, but nurse's aide entails harsher working conditions (exposure to urine, fecal matter, smells, disease, etc.) whereas the supervisor of custodians requires taking more responsibility. In this case, which job one will rank higher depends upon the relative weight given to responsibility and working conditions. Yet, because assigning a weight to the factors is not an explicit step, there is nothing in the method that ensures that one will be consistent in the weights given these two factors as a large number of jobs are rated.

Because the ranking method does not break up jobs into their constituent factors, and neither the ranking nor classification method explicitly
determines the relative weights of the factors, these two methods are
called "qualitative" or "whole job" systems.

C. Factor Comparison

The factor comparison method involves a number of steps:

1.   Choose a subset of jobs as "key" (or "benchmark") jobs. These
should be jobs about which there is agreement that the pay is correct.
2.   Choose compensable factors.
3.   Rank-order the jobs separately on each factor.
4.   Make a judgment of how much of the total wage now paid to each
key job comes from each factor. This is done separately for each key job.
5.   Attempt to rectify the conclusions about each key job's ranking on
each factor arrived at from steps 3 and 4. For example, if secretary ranks
higher than messenger on the factor *knowledge*, but messenger was determined to receive $2.00/hour of its total pay from this factor, whereas
secretary was determined to receive $1.75 from this factor, this is a
discrepancy. Resolving discrepancies can be achieved by changing rankings in step 3, changing dollar amounts in step 4, or dropping some jobs
from the list of key jobs. This step is an implicit way of assigning weights
to factors.
6.   For each factor, give each nonkey job the number of points associated with the key job to which it is most similar on that factor.

Because it features neither the simplicity of a simple ranking scheme
nor the sophistication of the point-factor system, the factor comparison
method is seldom used today. (On factor comparison systems, see
Benge 1941, 1984; Livy 1975.)

D. The Point-Factor Method

The point-factor method makes explicit many of the decisions that are
implicit in the other methods. The systems used by the well-known Hay
and Willis consulting firms are examples of point-factor systems. The
Position Analysis Questionnaire (PAQ) is also a point-factor system (Mc-
Cormick, Jeanneret, and Mecham 1972). Recently the federal government has been moving to a point-factor system called the Factor Evaluation Systems for its white-collar jobs (Katz 1984). Point-factor systems
are the most common choice in the private sector (Schwab and Wichern

1983; Akalin 1970) and have been used in most of the pay equity studies done by states and localities.

Using the point-factor system entails several steps: job description, choosing compensable factors, rating jobs on compensable factors, assigning weights to the factors to get total points for each job, and using points to set pay. These steps are discussed below.

Job Description. The first step is to assemble written descriptions of each job (Beatty and Beatty 1984). There are several ways to gather information for the descriptions. One survey of job evaluators found that 90% talked to supervisors to obtain information, 60% talked to incumbents, and 44% observed the job being performed (Schwab and Heneman 1986). Steinberg and Haignere (1987) suggest the use of surveys of incumbents. Such surveys were used in the New York State pay equity study (Steinberg et al. 1986).

Whatever method is used to assemble the information, the general purpose of a job description is to describe the actual tasks performed in each job, as well as the skills, effort, responsibilities, and working conditions associated with the job. This could include what education and prior experience are required to work in the job. It may include how much of one's time is spent on various tasks. It may include the number of employees, clients, or dollars of budget for which job incumbents are responsible. Overall, the intent is to provide an accurate description of what is demanded of one holding the job.

Choosing and Assigning Weights to Compensable Factors and Assigning Points to Jobs on Each Job. The next step in a point-factor job evaluation is to choose the compensable factors and to rate each job on each factor. While plans differ in how many factors they use, most tap skill, effort, responsibility, and working conditions. As an example, the Hay system uses three factors: know-how, problem solving, and accountability. (Each factor has two or three subfactors.) When manual jobs are being evaluated, Hay adds a fourth factor of working conditions. *Working conditions* refers to unpleasant, stressful, or dangerous aspects of performing the job.

In order to move from a score on each factor to total points for each job, one needs to decide how to assign weights to factors. The relative weight given to a factor will determine the relative dollar return to increments of that factor if the job evaluation is used to set pay. There are two ways to determine the weights of factors: the *a priori* and *policy-capturing* methods.

In a priori systems (such as the commercial Hay or Willis plans) the weights of factors are determined in advance by management or consultants. The weights are often hidden, implied in the scoring systems.

Consider an example where there are four factors, each factor has the same maximum possible number of points, and total points are calculated by adding the points from each of the four factors. Such a scoring system amounts to assigning equal weight to each factor.[1] On the other hand, if one factor ranges from 0 to 10 while the other three range from 0 to 5, and total points are calculated by adding up points on each factor, this amounts to giving a weight to the first factor that is twice as large as the other three. Because they involve explicit decisions about which factors are to count more in setting pay, a priori systems provide an opportunity for employers to individualize a job evaluation system to their unique organizational priorities. For example, a retail service industry might decide to give more weight to human relations skills than a goods-producing industry. In practice, however, such customizing seldom occurs. Firms and governments that use a priori systems often use commercial systems from major consulting companies such as Hay or Willis. Most consulting companies use the same implicit weights for all their clients. These are weights that they have found to "fit" general market realities.

Policy-capturing systems determine the weights of factors *empirically* using current pay practices of the employer as the criterion. This is generally done with a multiple regression analysis that predicts jobs' pay from their points on all the factors. Minimum, midpoint, or highest pay in each job can be used as the dependent variable for the policy-capturing regression analysis, although this choice may affect the weights (Treiman 1979). The regression analysis is used to estimate coefficients for each factor from the firm's pay policies. The coefficient for each factor reveals the weight it is being given in the employer's current pay practices. This is the sense in which this type of job evaluation "captures policy" with its empirical analysis of how existing pay corresponds to factor scores.

Policy-capturing regression analyses may use all jobs in the establishment as observations in the analysis. Alternatively, the analysis may use only "key" or "benchmark" jobs as observations. Key or benchmark jobs include those in which hiring is done from outside the organization, as well as those that are most comparable to jobs in other organizations (Schwab 1980; Schwab and Wichern 1983). These are the jobs most directly affected by external labor market conditions. Because of this, through using key jobs, policy-capturing systems of determining weights are affected by the relative weights given to various compensable factors in the external labor market.

How does one determine the total points for each job? This is calculated by plugging the score on each factor for a given job into the regression equation obtained from the policy-capturing regression analysis and calculating predicted pay. The equation contains one constant and a weight (also called the *slope* or *coefficient*) for each factor. (These calculations are discussed in more detail below in the section on using job evaluation to correct sex bias in pay.)

Setting Wages. The final step is to use the job evaluation to help determine pay. Often a scattergram is drawn of total job points against pay. Pay is generally measured with the bottom, top, or midpoint of the pay interval set by policy for each job. Each point in the scattergram represents one job. The location of the point from left to right is determined by the number of total points the job was given in the job evaluation. The vertical location of the point is determined by the job's current pay. The best-fitting line through the scatter of points is called the *policy line* or *pay line*. This is illustrated in Figure 4.1. There will always be some scattering of points, but in general the points cluster around a line, indicating that there is a substantial correlation between points and pay. Jobs above the line are those that are paid more than average *for their number of points*. Jobs below the line are paid less than average *for their number of points*. At this point the employer decides what pay changes to make as a result of the job evaluation. What do employers do about jobs substantially above or below the line? If the pay in each job is moved to the line, this entails raising pay in some jobs and lowering it in others. However, it is not conventional to lowering existing workers' wages. Sometimes jobs above the line are "red-circled" for slower raises and/or

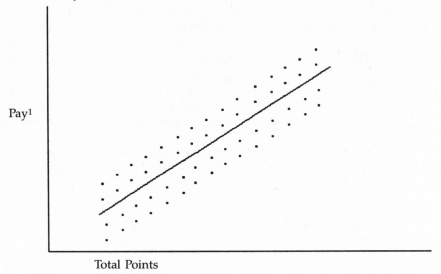

Figure 4.1. Scattergram plotting job pay against job's total points from job evaluation.

[1] Can be starting pay in the job, maximum pay, or midpoint of this interval. Units of analysis are jobs.

for two-tier wage systems in which new hires in the job are paid according to the policy line while current incumbents are paid the old, higher
wage. The two systems then gradually converge through differential
raises and/or attrition. The special issues presented when the purpose of
the job evaluation is pay equity between male and female jobs are discussed in a later section.

Often employers divide jobs into different job families, each with a
different pay plan (Bellak 1984). Each plan uses a separate point-to-dollar
conversion (and sometimes even separate factors or factor weights). For
example, a firm may have three plans: exempt (usually professional and
managerial jobs), clerical, and production (blue-collar). In such a system,
blue-collar production workers whose jobs have points equal to those of
clerical jobs may earn much more, but these differences will be consistent with the job evaluation since it is used to make comparisons within
but not between pay plans.

III.   Reliability

Like all measures, job evaluation is vulnerable to two types of problems in measurement: lack of reliability and lack of validity. Since psychologists have contributed most to developing methods for
establishing reliability and validity, it is not surprising that industrial
psychologists have done the bulk of the empirical work to ascertain the
reliability and validity of job evaluation. A burst of studies dealt with the
issue after World War II, when many employers had just begun using
the technique. After that, although job evaluation continued to be widely used, there was virtually no research on its psychometric properties
until the issue of comparable worth renewed interest in whether job
evaluation can be used to detect sex bias in pay. In this section I consider
the reliability of job evaluation.

A system of job evaluation is more reliable if it is *consistent* in the
ratings that different raters (sometimes called judges) give each job. That
is, a system of guidelines for how to rate jobs is more reliable if two
judges agree on the rating for any given job. A second concept of reliability (sometimes called *internal lack of bias*) relates to whether the correlations between the various factors used in the job evaluation, as well as
between each factor and total job points, are the same for male as for
female jobs.

The first of these is called *interjudge* or *interrater* reliability. It refers to
how much two or more judges (raters) agree in that they give similar
scores to any given job. An interjudge correlation of 1 would indicate

perfect reliability—that the two judges agreed completely. In contrast, an interjudge correlation of 0 would indicate no reliability at all—that there was no tendency for jobs that one judge scored higher to be scored higher by the other judge as well. Studies vary in the correlations they find between the job evaluation ratings of pairs of judges, but they are generally between .60 and .90 (Lawshe and Wilson 1947; Ash 1948; Chesler 1948; Jones 1948; Lawshe and Farbo 1949; Anderson and Corts 1973; Arthur Young and Company 1981; Doverspike and Barrett 1984; Madigan 1985). Whether this is "high enough" is a matter of judgment. Judges disagree about working conditions more than other factors (Schwab and Heneman 1986). In general, total scores are more reliable than scores on any one factor. If correlations between the averaged scores of groups of evaluators (instead of individual evaluators) are computed, total scores are quite reliable, with intergroup correlations above .90 (Schwab and Heneman 1986).

The issue of interjudge reliability can also be approached with *generalizability analysis*. This technique uses analysis of variance to determine what proportion of the variance across jobs in total points is to be attributed to jobs, separate factors, and individual raters. Generally very little of the total variance is attributed to the raters (Doverspike, Carlist, Barrett, and Alexander 1983; Fraser, Cronshaw, and Alexander 1984; Eulberg 1987), thus indicating high interjudge reliability.

The second kind of reliability concerns the correlations between the factors on which jobs are scored, or between scores on any one factor and total points. If these correlations are the same within the subset of male jobs as within the subset of female jobs, this is taken as evidence that the internal structure of the evaluation is consistent across jobs irrespective of their gender label. Such interfactor and factor-to-total correlations are generally approximately the same for female and male jobs (Doverspike and Barrett 1984; Eulberg 1987), with some exceptions. In particular, for female and male jobs human relations skills correlate differently with other factors and with total scores (Eulberg 1987). This could indicate differential reliability of ratings for male and female jobs. However, it may simply indicate differences in the job characteristics that tend to occur together in male and female jobs, and thus not indicate lack of reliability.

IV. Validity

Are job evaluation scores valid? A score is valid if it measures the intended concept. This raises the question of what underlying concept job evaluation is intended to measure. Most employers want job evaluation to measure (1) how much the work in the job, when done at a satisfactory level, contributes to the productivity of the organization, and (2) how much the job requires skills or has other demands (e.g., that onerous working conditions be endured) that need to be compensated to ensure an adequate supply of labor. Yet because productivity and supply are so difficult to measure, there are virtually no studies of these questions in psychology, economics, or sociology.

A. Concurrent or Convergent Validity

Investigations of the validity of job evaluation generally involve an indirect approach called *concurrent* or *convergent validity*. A method of job evaluation is said to have convergent validity if its ratings of jobs correlate highly with ratings from another system applied to the same jobs. Such a correlation tells us how much different methods agree in their results, so it is also called *method convergence*. In general, correlations between .50 and .95 have been found (Chesler 1948; Atchison and French 1967; Robinson, Wahlstrom, and Mecham 1974; Gomez-Mejia, Page, and Tornow 1982; Snelgar 1983; Madigan 1985; Madigan and Hoover 1986). (For a table summarizing some of these results, see Schwab 1985, p. 40.) Most of the methods compared in these studies are variations of the point-factor system discussed above. Whether such correlations are large enough to indicate validity is a matter of judgment. They certainly indicate substantial agreement between methods. However, Madigan and Hoover (1986) caution that even relatively high correlations between two job evaluation systems can entail quite different dollar predictions of the appropriate salary for particular jobs.

One issue of validity is whether there is a tendency for job evaluations to produce lower (or higher) relative ratings for female jobs than they merit. High convergent validity is no guarantee against such sex bias, since if two methods both contain bias against female jobs, this will actually increase the intermethod correlation! The issue of sex bias in job evaluation is an aspect of validity so crucial to the topic of comparable worth that I devote the next section to it.

B. Lack of Validity Due to Sex Bias

The question of validity of greatest concern for comparable worth is whether job evaluation is tainted by sex bias. Advocates of comparable worth point out that job evaluation, as currently practiced, is often tainted by sex bias. Despite this, they advocate the use of an unbiased system of job evaluation to correct sex bias in wage setting. If, through sex bias, women's jobs are given fewer total points than they merit, then the effect of using job evaluation to set wages will generally be to set lower wages in women's jobs than would be the case absent such bias. (For exceptions to this general rule see Schwab and Wichern 1983.)

To preview, the major sources of sex bias in job evaluation involve (1) giving women's jobs less points on given factors than they deserve, (2) assigning larger weights to those factors emphasized in men's jobs than those emphasized in women's jobs (at the extreme, completely ignoring skills and demands typical to women's jobs), and (3) using different pay plans (with different weights and/or higher ratios of pay to points) in job groups containing mostly men's jobs. Below I examine how sex bias may occur at each of these stages of job evaluation. (For overviews, see Arvey 1986 and Steinberg and Haignere 1987.)

Giving Women's Jobs Less Points on Factors Than They Merit. As discussed above, most job evaluators use a point-factor method in which each job is given points on each of a number of predetermined compensable factors. When evaluators assign points to each job, is there sex bias in the number of points jobs are given? This could happen in two ways: either because those who write job descriptions of female jobs tend to describe them as less demanding than they are (Steinberg and Haignere 1987), or because, even with accurate descriptions, raters tend to give fewer points to female jobs than they merit.

Some argue that our culture devalues women and the skills they have traditionally practiced. This is a major tenet of cultural feminism, discussed further in Chapter 6. If this is true, then a phenomenon psychologists call the "halo effect" may help explain low ratings given to female jobs. The halo effect operates when people or jobs who are labeled as good on some important dimension are surrounded with a positive aura or halo, which causes other positive qualities to be ascribed to them (McArthur 1985). If maleness is valued in employment contexts, then male jobs might receive the benefit of the doubt in job evaluations.

One example illustrates the problem. The analyses in Chapter 3 made use of the skill measures developed by the U.S. Department of Labor in the fourth edition of the *Dictionary of Occupational Titles* (DOT). In examining the third edition of the DOT, Witt and Naherny (1975) found some traditionally women's jobs undervalued to such an extreme extent that the measures lacked that most commonsense type of validity called *face validity*. For example, attendants at dog pounds and parking lots (usually men) were rated more highly than nursery school teachers, and zookeepers more highly than day care workers (Steinberg and Haignere 1987). Here the bias against female jobs is obvious. Attempts were made to correct such bias in the fourth edition. But is such bias against women's jobs routine in job evaluation?

Research on the question of sex bias in assigning job evaluation points is scarce and has produced conflicting findings. Three experiments found no such bias against female jobs, but a fourth did find bias. The approach of these studies was to have subjects evaluate jobs from job descriptions. In each case information about the sex of those in the jobs being evaluated was the experimentally manipulated variable.

Arvey, Passino, and Lounsbury (1977) had student subjects evaluate the job of administrative assistant using a point-factor system. The students saw a slide presentation in which a person appearing to be a job incumbent described the job. One group of subjects saw a female incumbent on the slides, and the other saw a male incumbent. The two groups did not differ in the average ratings they gave the job. In this design, information on jobs' sex composition was indirect, to be inferred through the sex of the incumbent shown in the slides. One problem with the design is that if subjects knew that most administrative assistants are women, this may have lowered the ratings of both groups equally, an effect that cannot be discerned from comparing the two groups.

Grams and Schwab (1985) had student subjects evaluate three jobs (loan commitment specialist, banking representative, and loan collateral auditor) on three factors. Gender composition was experimentally manipulated (i.e., varied between the two groups) only for the job of banking representative. Subjects in one group were told that 3 of the 20 banking representatives were women, while subjects in the other group were told that 3 out of 20 were men. The two groups were given identical job descriptions. The two groups did not differ significantly in the ratings they gave the job, indicating that no sex bias was present. Schwab and Grams (1985) repeated the experiment using compensation specialists instead of students as subjects, and found no evidence of sex bias in ratings here either.

However, one experiment did find evidence of direct sex bias (McArthur and Obrant 1986). Student subjects evaluated the jobs of public relations professional and purchasing agent. The subjects saw a videotape where a person presumed to be the job incumbent provided information about the job. Information about the sex of those in the job was manipulated in two ways: First, in each of the jobs, one group saw a female incumbent and the other group saw a male incumbent on the videotape. The group seeing a male incumbent gave the same job more points, on average, on factors called responsibility, job criticality, job structure, and persuasive ability than did the group that saw a female incumbent on the videotape. A second way in which information about the sex of those in the job was manipulated was to tell subjects how many men and women worked in the job—either two men and eight women, five and five, or eight and two. This was found to have no effect on the job ratings. However, a postevaluation questionnaire showed that many of the subjects did not remember what they had been told about the job's sex composition, so this could not have been taken into account even if subjects were predisposed to sex bias. This being the case, whatever inference subjects made about the sex composition of the job probably came from the sex of the hypothetical incumbent on the videotape. The fact that the sex of this person affected ratings suggests the presence of sex bias in ratings.

These studies illustrate a methodological dilemma, a trade-off between internal validity and the applicability of findings to real-world job evaluation (external validity). All four studies chose jobs that do not have clear sex labels in the public mind, either because they are more sex integrated than most jobs or because they are jobs many people know little about. Choosing such jobs is necessary if the researcher is to manipulate the independent variable of incumbent's sex or job's sex composition in a way that is believable to subjects while holding job title and content constant. To illustrate the point, suppose the job titles of secretary, nurse, carpenter, or plumber were chosen. These are well-known jobs, and almost everyone knows that most secretaries and nurses are women while most carpenters or plumbers are men. If an experiment manipulated sex composition of these jobs by telling one group that the company's secretaries are 90% female while telling a second group they are 90% male, the second group might not find the hypothetical information believable. It is also unrealistic to manipulate incumbents' sex through slides or videos in jobs with well-known sex labels. For example, seeing one male secretary is unlikely to change one's belief that most secretaries are female. This explains why the experimental researchers chose little-known or relatively integrated jobs. However, it also points up a dilemma. If sex bias does affect real-world job evaluation when the jobs being evaluated are known to be mostly male or female, experimental research using jobs with mixed or ambiguous sex compositions may not show us this. This challenges the relevance of the experimental studies since, within organizations, most jobs are made up largely of one sex or the other (Bielby and Baron 1984).

What, then, can we conclude thus far about direct sex bias in job evaluation points? (1) The bulk of the experimental evidence finds no sex bias in ratings, although one out of four studies did find bias. But (2) there may be an inability of experimental studies to tap bias that only pertains to jobs well-known for their sex composition, and such jobs are a high proportion of all jobs in the economy.

Given these limitations of the experimental studies on sex bias in job evaluation, it makes sense to look at more indirect evidence. Another group of studies provides more indirect evidence of one way in which sex bias in assigning points to job factors may arise. This occurs if the pay of a job affects the points it is given and if the pay of female jobs has been influenced by sex discrimination (perhaps in market wages). The literature reviewed in Chapter 1 and my own analysis in Chapter 3 provided evidence of such sex discrimination in pay. Further, several experimental studies find that jobs will be given more points if subjects are told or otherwise believe that the job pays more (Grams and Schwab 1985; Schwab and Grams 1985; Mount and Ellis 1987; Rynes, Weber, and Milkovich 1989). McArthur (1985) argues that this is another instance of the halo effect discussed above. In this view, the fact that a job pays well casts a positive halo over evaluators' perceptions of the worth of the job. These facts together make sex bias in assigning points probable. Schwab (1985, p. 45) argues that "the implications of this finding for wage fairness are potentially profound. For if there is sex bias in current wage structures, replicated evidence that wage rates influence evaluations suggests that bias could enter evaluation results even though salaries are not used as an explicit external criterion in validating the system."

Another larger body of experimental research has indirect relevance for the question of whether there is sex bias in evaluating women's jobs. This research pertains to sex bias in other kinds of personnel decisions, particularly performance evaluation and selection of persons for jobs. The general format of these experimental studies is for subjects to read a resume and/or a description of a person's performance. Then subjects make a hypothetical personnel decision about whether to hire, promote, or give some reward to the person. Individuals are assigned randomly to one of two groups. Both groups evaluate a resume or performance description. The evaluated materials given to the two groups are identical except for whether a male or female name is given for the hypothetical person under evaluation. A majority of such studies find that males are judged to perform better and to be more deserving of hire, promotion, or a job reward than women with identical qualifications. (For a review of such studies, see Arvey 1979 and Nieva and Gutek 1980.) The bias against women is stronger when less information is provided on credentials or performance (Deaux 1985). Luck is more often seen as the reason for high performance by women, whereas high performance by men is more often attributed to skill (Deaux and Emswiller 1974). Another experimental tradition, this one within sociology, also suggests that women are perceived by members of our culture to be less competent at most tasks. This literature is associated with *expectation-states theory* (Berger, Cohen, and Zelditch 1972; Berger, Conner, and Fisck 1974). It provides evidence that these widespread cultural biases lead the contributions of men to be listened to more and evaluated more highly in small groups (Ridgeway forthcoming). All the studies discussed in this paragraph deal with evaluating *individuals,* whereas job evaluation involves evaluating *jobs.* In the absence of definitive conclusions from research on bias in job evaluation, these findings of sex bias in evaluating individuals suggest the hypothesis that sex bias is also present in evaluating jobs.

In summary, the question of whether sex bias affects job evaluation is not fully resolved; however, it is likely that women's jobs are given fewer points than they merit.

Sex Bias in Choosing Factors and Setting Factor Weights. To use a point-factor system, one needs to choose the factors on which jobs will be evaluated and set the weights for each factor, using either an a priori or a policy-capturing approach, as discussed above. Sex bias can occur in choosing factors and setting factor weights. Factor weights indicate the relative size of the return in total points to each incremental unit of the various factors. If the kinds of skills and demands typical of jobs held by women are assigned lower weights, or not even included as measured compensable factors, this will adversely affect the total points given to women's jobs. This is an example of what in previous chapters I have referred to as indirect gender bias in wage setting.

If kinds of skills and demands typical of women's jobs are not tapped at all by the factors chosen, and/or not even mentioned in the job descriptions, then women's jobs will receive no points for them. This is a special case of setting factor weights, where the omitted factor is effectively given a weight of zero. Steinberg and Haignere (1987, pp. 168–169) argue that the following job characteristics are common to women's jobs but are often overlooked and thus given no weight in job evaluation: finger dexterity, having responsibility for confidential information, sitting for long periods of time, communication stress (from dealing with upset people), stress from distractions, stress from visual concentration (e.g., on video display terminals), stress from exposure to sick and disabled persons, stress from receiving work from numerous people, and stress from working in an office where people come and go. Except for the first of these characteristics, which is a skill, and the second, which is a measure of responsibility, this is a list of difficult working conditions. The most common job evaluations in use in industry and government have only a small number of factors, and only one (if any) factor for working conditions. In many job evaluation systems, this factor taps only those onerous working conditions typical to men's jobs, such as exposure to dirt or physical danger. This has an adverse impact on the number of total points women's jobs receive. However, the *magnitude* of the bias introduced in this way is usually limited because factors measuring cognitive skill and authority contribute the most to pay in virtually all job evaluation systems; the working conditions factor generally has a low weight and thus does not contribute very much to pay.

Ironically, the inclusion of difficult working conditions common to women's jobs in a *policy-capturing* analysis may actually *hurt* the relative pay of women's jobs if the job evaluation is used to set pay. This is because there are negative returns for some working conditions common to women's jobs. This was found in the New York State pay equity study and in a number of other state and local job evaluation studies (Steinberg et al. 1986; Jacobs and Steinberg 1990a, 1990b).

Even more consequential in affecting women's wages is the low weight attached to social skills and the negative weight attached to nurturing social skills. Often this is not measured in job evaluations, but those studies that have measured nurturing social skill have found it to have a net negative return (Jacobs and Steinberg 1990a). This has been found in national data as well (Kilbourne et al. 1990), and was seen in the analysis of 1980 census data I presented in Chapter 3.

The issue of how much bias has affected factor weights is difficult to discern statistically. When a policy-capturing system is used, weights will be set empirically according to how much various skills actually affect pay in the organization. The question as to whether such weights contain sex bias depends on whether employers have valued certain kinds of skills more *because* they are done by men. If the organization has been following market wages, at least in key jobs, then the bias may reflect devaluation of demands common to women's jobs by other employers, since, in the aggregate, other employers create market wages. Here, we could ask whether this market devaluation was because of the association of the job characteristics with women. Unfortunately, however, I see no statistical way to discern what the weights for various factors *would have been* in the absence of sex bias, and thus to measure the exact extent of bias in currently used factor weights. However, if using weights that do not have a disparate impact on female jobs is a policy goal, a priori approaches to job evaluation can be used to give higher value to skills often found in female (or minority-dominated) jobs (Treiman 1979).

Sex Bias through Using Multiple Pay Plans. Many employers divide all their jobs into several job "families," each of which has a separate pay plan. Clerical jobs may be in one family while blue-collar jobs are in another. The city of Dallas, for example, uses eight separate pay plans. The federal government has two major plans, the General Schedule (GS), mostly white-collar, and the Federal Wage System (FWS), mostly predominantly male blue-collar jobs. Sometimes a separate job evaluation (meaning separate lists of factors or different factor weights) is used for each family. For example, some plans reward human relations skills more when they occur within managerial jobs than in other jobs (Steinberg and Haignere 1987). Other times a common set of factors and weights is used for all families, but each family has a separate pay line. In this case one job family's pay line will have a higher intercept and/or slope. The effect is that two jobs with virtually the same characteristics may receive different pay because they are in different families (Acker 1989, p. 71). Frequently, job families contain disproportionate numbers of men or women, and the families containing many female jobs are those with lower pay lines. Because of its adverse effect on women's wages, Hartmann and Treiman (1983) have called this the "multiple plan problem."

The reason firms use different job families is generally to obtain some compromise between following external market wages and internal equity. With multiple plans, internal equity is confined to comparisons *within* job families, where pay is according to points, but the market is allowed to dictate differences in pay lines *between* job families. The choice of what jobs will be clustered together into families may be affected by a tendency to lump women's jobs together as much as by functional similarity of the jobs. Sometimes a lower pay line is chosen for predominantly female job families *because* they are female. Alternatively, the lower line may be chosen because it reflects what the jobs in the job family are commonly paid in the market. If the market realities reflected in the different lines themselves result from sex bias in other employers' wage systems, then the use of multiple job families is discriminatory in its effect. Because of the likelihood of sex bias inherent in multiple plans, Remick (1984) has included the requirement of one plan per establishment in her definition of comparable worth.

V. Using Job Evaluation to Identify and Correct Sex Bias in Pay

Above I have explored the ways in which job evaluation may embody sex bias. Yet it is seen by advocates of comparable worth as an antidote to sex bias in wage setting as well. This is because, whatever biases exist in job evaluation, if a single job evaluation plan is used to set pay throughout a firm or government, *it nearly always gives women's jobs higher wages relative to men's than most employers currently pay.* That is, female jobs generally pay less than male jobs that job evaluations find to have the same number of total points. Our best evidence on this comes from the pay equity studies mandated by many state legislatures in the last decade. All of these have found that female jobs systematically pay less than male jobs with the same total points, usually by 5–20%. Such findings occur whether an a priori or policy-capturing method is used. (See Pierson, Koziara, and Johannesson 1983, 1984; Orazem and Mattila 1987, on Iowa; Remick 1984, on Washington; Rothchild 1984, on Minnesota state and local governments; Acker 1987 and 1989, on Oregon; Steinberg et al. 1986, on New York; and Dresang forthcoming, on Wisconsin.)

Even though many large firms use job evaluation, there is little publicly available data on the results of evaluations in the private sector. However, the national findings reviewed in Chapter 1 and my analysis of national data in Chapter 3 suggest that the same underpayment of female jobs obtains in the private sector. Anecdotes suggest the same. Executives with Hay Associates have stated that in their experience most private sector firms pay female jobs less than male jobs scoring the same points on the Hay system (Bureau of National Affairs 1981). In particular, female clerical jobs are generally paid less than male blue-collar jobs that have fewer total points. However, these differentials are entirely compatible with the plans installed by Hay since Hay encourages different pay lines for different job families.

How can findings from a job evaluation be used to show whether wages in female jobs are depressed by discrimination? We can use the various statistics that are generated from job evaluation to determine whether pay is being awarded to male and female jobs in a consistent way, and whether skills and demands more typically found in female jobs have lower returns (weights). Here I ignore the very real possibility that the job evaluation itself contains bias in the points given to women's jobs on each factor. Instead, I ask how, taking these scores on individuals as valid, we can use job evaluation to assess whether an employer is paying comparable male and female jobs equally. Systematic departure from such equality will be taken as evidence of sex discrimination in pay—a kind of discrimination that job evaluation can correct if an employer chooses to set wages by following the job evaluation rather than either the market or tradition. As in previous chapters, I will distinguish here between what I call direct sex bias in wage setting, ascertained by an effect of sex composition on jobs' pay, and indirect sex bias, for which there is evidence if those factors on which women's jobs have high scores are given lower or even negative weights.

A. Statistics Used in Job Evaluation

The discussion of how to use job evaluation statistics to assess discrimination involves intercepts, slopes, and the additive and interactive

effects of jobs' gender composition. Any point-factor system of job evaluation (whether a priori or policy capturing) can be used to write the
following equations that describe the pay line that relates pay to points
on various factors and total points:

$$PAY = a + b_1F_1 + b_2F_2 + \cdots + b_nF_n \tag{1}$$

$$PAY = a + b_0T \tag{2}$$

where

$$b_0T = b_1F_1 + b_2F_2 + \cdots + b_nF_n \tag{3}$$

PAY refers to the pay of each job. (As discussed previously, one can use
minimum, midpoint, or maximum pay allotted to the job.) The F refer to
the compensable factors on which each job is scored; the $b_1, \ldots, b_n$
refer to the weights for the factors (whether given a priori or empirically
through policy capturing). If weights are set by policy capturing, this
implies estimating the a and b as coefficients from a multiple regression
analysis in which PAY (the amount the firm's policy dictates paying in
the job) is the dependent variable and the F are the independent variables. In a priori systems the b are implicit in the scoring system, so that
the points given a job on any factor n would be b_nF_n for that factor. The
term b_0T in Equation (2) is the total points calculated from taking each
factor times its weight (b), and then adding these products, as shown in
Equation (3). Thus, Equation (2) defines the pay line relating total points
to pay, as seen in Figures 4.1, 4.2, and 4.3. The intercept of the pay line
[a in Equation (2)] defines where the pay line crosses the vertical axis
(providing the predicted wage in the hypothetical case of a job scoring
zero points). The slope of the pay line indicates the dollar value of each
additional point. The height of the pay line affects the total wage bill,
while the relative points for individual jobs determine their relative pay.

B. Assessing Direct Sex Discrimination in Pay against Female Jobs

When a job evaluation is first done, an employer will seldom be paying jobs exactly according to the pay line. There will generally be a
scatter of jobs around the line as shown in Figure 4.1. To test for underpayment of female jobs, one needs to separate jobs into those that are
primarily male and female. (It is arbitrary what cutoff is used to define a
job as female or male, but 70% is a common choice.) If female and male
jobs are both equally distributed above and below the line, there is no
evidence of direct sex discrimination in jobs' pay, as shown in Figure 4.2.
Three possibilities are shown in the figure, all of which would indicate

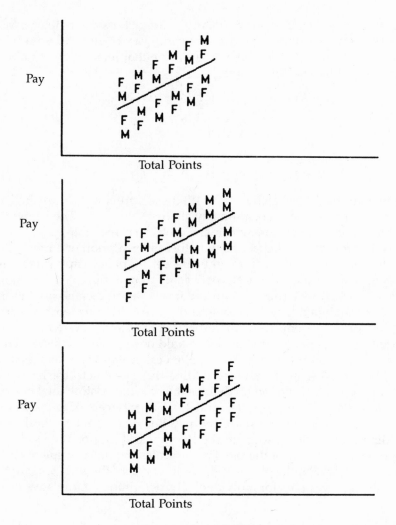

Figure 4.3. Hypothetical scattergrams plotting job pay against total points, where there is direct sex discrimination in assigning pay to jobs and/or an interaction.

Note: "F" denotes predominantly female job; "M" denotes predominantly male job. Units of analysis are jobs.

no direct discrimination on the basis of the sex makeup of jobs. In the top panel of Figure 4.2, female and male jobs merit about the same average job points and are equally likely to be below the line. In the middle panel of Figure 4.2, female jobs average less points than male jobs, but again female jobs are no more likely than male jobs to be below the line. In the bottom panel of Figure 4.2, male jobs average less points than female jobs, while again there is an equal tendency of male and female jobs to be below the line. If we assume that the job evaluation is not biased, then none of these three cases show direct pay discrimination against female jobs in the sense of inconsistent standards being used for wage setting in male and female jobs. However, these cases are not typical of what is found.

When a single evaluation is used for an establishment, the typical finding is that most female jobs are below the line while most male jobs are above the line. This is depicted in the top two panels of Figure 4.3. Another way to describe this situation is that there is a female line and a male line. When the female jobs are systematically below the overall pay line, this implies that female jobs generally pay less than male jobs that were assigned the same number of job evaluation points.

If the two lines (for male and female jobs) are parallel but the female line is lower (as in the top panel of Figure 4.3), then the distance between the two lines is the difference between their *intercepts*. The amount of difference between the intercept of the male job line and female job line is a measure of how many dollars on average it costs one to be in a female rather than male job—when comparing jobs with the same total points. *This is a dollar measure of the average amount of direct wage discrimination against female jobs.* In more statistical terms, the difference between the two intercepts is a measure of the net, additive effect of being in a male (as opposed to a female) job. We could achieve the same result if the regression equation [Equation (1)] were run on all male and female jobs together (omitting mixed jobs) with a variable coded 0 and 1 for male and female jobs, respectively, entered in the equation. The coefficient of this dummy variable would be the same as the difference between the intercepts of the male and female job line.

The female job line and the male job line may also differ in their slopes. If the male job line has a steeper slope and is above the female job line all across the existing range of job points, this also indicates discrimination against female jobs. This situation is shown in the middle panel of Figure 4.3. This contrasts to the case of parallel male and female lines that differ only in intercept (shown in the top panel of Figure 4.3): Parallel lines mean that the benefit of being in a male versus female job is the same at every level of points. In the case of male jobs having a point-to-pay line that is everywhere above the female job line and has a higher slope, in jobs with relatively low levels of points, there is some advantage to being in a male versus female job, but in jobs with more points, the advantage of being in a male versus female job is even greater.

In statistical terms, different slopes for male and female jobs mean that there is an interactive effect of the sex composition of jobs and points on pay. However, it is not the existence of an interaction effect in itself, but rather the fact that the female job line is below the male job line at every

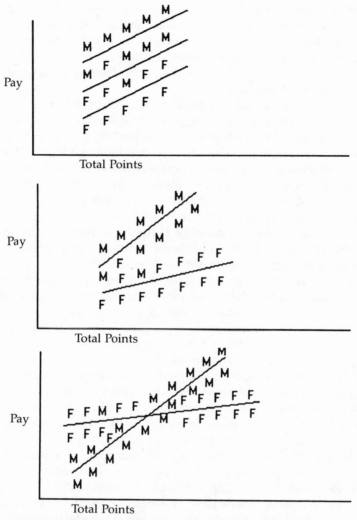

Figure 4.3. Hypothetical scattergrams plotting job pay against total points, where there is direct sex discrimination in assigning pay to jobs and/or an interaction.

Note: "F" denotes predominantly female job; "M" denotes predominantly male job. Units of analysis are jobs.

level of points (as it is in the example of the interaction effect in the middle panel of Figure 4.3) that indicates discrimination against female jobs. As I argued in Chapter 3, interaction effects do not have an unambiguous interpretation vis-à-vis discrimination. To see this, consider the hypothetical example in the bottom panel of Figure 4.3. Here, too, there is an interaction effect such that the returns to job points are higher in male jobs. However, here the two lines cross midway through the existing range of points, so the interaction effect results in female jobs having higher pay than male jobs in lower ranges of points, while male jobs have higher pay than female jobs in higher ranges of points. One might conclude here that male jobs with low points are being discriminated against whereas female jobs with high points are being discriminated against. As I argued in Chapter 3, when one group (in this case male jobs) has higher returns, whether this is an advantage or disadvantage depends upon the point level we focus attention upon. Results like those in the bottom panel of Figure 4.3 are rare. My purpose in showing this hypothetical possibility is to clarify the point that it is the lower *level* of the female job line, not the presence of an interaction effect itself, that indicates discrimination against female jobs. This lower level can be present with either additive or interactive effects of jobs' sex composition.

A related method of estimating direct wage discrimination against female jobs adds the percentage female of a job to the regression equation. Equation (1) thus becomes

$$\text{PAY} = a + b_1 F_1 + B_2 F_2 + \cdots + b_n F_n + b_{n+1} P \tag{4}$$

where P is the percentage female of a job. This method has two advantages: First, sex composition is treated as a continuum rather than the dichotomy implied in comparing male versus female jobs in the method discussed above. Second, data from all jobs can be used to calculate the pay line; integrated jobs need not be excluded. If scores on compensable factors were used consistently to set pay in jobs at all levels of sex composition, the effect of percentage female would be zero. If there is direct wage discrimination against predominantly female jobs, the coefficient on percentage female will be negative. The coefficient on percentage female tells us the amount of money that one loses for each percentage point increment in percentage female, when comparing jobs with the same total points. This is the approach I used in Chapter 3.

The second advantage of including percentage female in Equation (4) is that it corrects the weights (slopes) of the other compensable factors for direct gender bias. To illustrate, consider this example. Suppose that female jobs are more likely than male jobs to require finger dexterity, but that there are some male jobs that require some finger dexterity. If female jobs pay less due to direct sex discrimination, this, rather than a devaluation of finger dexterity, would give rise to a low positive or even negative coefficient on finger dexterity in a regression analysis that excludes percentage female. By including (and thus controlling for) percentage female, this bias is removed from each of the factor weights. Controlling for percentage female leads the weight for each compensable factor to be calculated such that it reveals the increase in pay associated with an increase of each unit of the factor across occupations with a common sex composition. However, this technique will not remove the bias that comes from a factor (such as finger dexterity or nurturance) being devalued such that it now has a low or negative return in *either* male or female jobs as a result of its traditional association with the female sphere. This indirect sort of wage discrimination against female jobs is discussed in the next section.

In Equation (4), percentage female has an additive effect. To test whether there are also interactive effects, we can add interaction terms (percentage female times the factor) for each factor to Equation (4). A negative coefficient on an interaction term would indicate lower positive returns (or more negative returns) for the factor the more heavily female a job is. As discussed above and in Chapter 3, the interpretation of such interaction effects vis-à-vis discrimination is ambiguous. If female jobs have less positive or more negative returns to most compensable factors, some might see this as evidence of discrimination. I question this interpretation. An interaction effect between percentage female and a factor may describe a situation in which there is a crossover point (some number of factor points) above which jobs with a lower percentage female pay more than those with a higher percentage female, but below which jobs with a higher percentage female pay more. (This is like the situation shown in the lowest panel of Figure 4.3.) In this case, whether being in a less female job is an advantage depends upon how many points the job has on the factor involved in the interaction. Thus, I think it best to define discrimination against female jobs as a case where jobs with a higher percentage female pay less than jobs with fewer females but with the same points. That is, it is the *level* of pay for female versus male jobs, not the slope of points-to-pay for female versus male jobs, that determines whether there is discrimination against women's jobs. This means that, if interaction effects are present, further calculations of predicted pay at various levels of factors and sex composition must be made to determine whether occupations with a higher percentage female have lower pay at each level of factor points. If so, then direct wage discrimination against female jobs is present. If not, then there is some range in which female jobs are discriminated against and some range in which male jobs are discriminated against.

C.   Assessing Indirect Sex Discrimination in Pay against Female Jobs

By "indirect sex discrimination in pay against female jobs" I refer to a situation where those kinds of skills and other demands typical to female jobs are given lower positive or even negative returns to earnings. In Chapter 3, I argued that the net negative return to nurturant skill is an example of such indirect bias. However, it is more difficult to reach consensus on a technical way to estimate the magnitude of indirect sex bias than direct sex bias. In ascertaining direct sex bias, as discussed above, we take the returns or weights for each factor as given and not under suspicion for sex bias. Based on them, we are able to assess whether female jobs pay less than male jobs with the same predicted pay from the regression. If there is sex bias, we can estimate exactly how much by the size of the coefficient for jobs' sex composition. But how can we tell whether the weights for compensable factors [the coefficients in regression Equation (4)] contain bias? What do we use as the nondiscriminatory baseline to assess what the weights would be in the absence of such bias? Unfortunately, I know no clear way to estimate the exact dollar magnitude of this indirect gender bias because it is not clear how we can come up with an estimate of what the returns to these deprecated skills and demands would have been in the absence of such indirect sex bias in wage setting. Nonetheless, attention to indirect gender bias is warranted.

D. Possible Sources of Error in the Assessment of Sex Discrimination

What are the limitations of using job evaluation to assess direct wage discrimination against female jobs? As with all techniques, several possibilities for error are present.

One possibility for error involves lack of reliability, discussed above. What effect will this have on our assessment of direct sex discrimination? Arvey, Maxwell, and Abraham (1985) caution that differences in either the slopes or pay lines for male and female jobs can possibly arise from low reliability of job scores, even in the absence of pay discrimination. In general, unreliability of a measure reduces the slope. However, this will not create different slopes for male and female jobs unless the scores for female jobs are less reliable than for male jobs. Unreliability for both male and female jobs can produce differing intercepts for the male and female line. But it should not tend to make the female pay line lower than the male pay line in a way that appears systematically across most all studies. Rather, the effects of such unreliability should be random across studies in whether it leads to lower intercepts for male or female jobs. Thus, I conclude that unreliability may explain an occasional finding of a lower intercept or slope for female pay lines, but it cannot explain the systematic tendency for job evaluation studies to find that female jobs have lower pay lines. I take this near universality of lower female pay lines to be indicative of direct sex discrimination against female jobs in wage setting. This may arise from employers treating female and male jobs differentially, or from employers following market wages that aggregate the results of many other employers' decisions to treat female and male jobs differentially.

A second possible source of error is sex bias in the procedure that assigned points to each job, also discussed in an earlier section. Let us look at the circumstances under which this will cause us to underestimate or overestimate direct wage discrimination against female jobs. As mentioned above, if there is sex bias adversely affecting the number of points women's jobs are given on each factor, such bias will be built into the evaluation, and thus the statistical approach suggested above will underestimate the amount of direct wage discrimination against female jobs. If men's rather than women's jobs were systematically given too few points, then bias against men's jobs would be built into the evaluation, and the approach suggested above would overestimate direct wage discrimination against female jobs. However, past research suggests that this direction of bias is unlikely.

A third possible source of error involves what statisticians refer to as omitted-variable bias. Suppose that there are job characteristics that affect wages, some of which are not included as compensable factors in the evaluation. If these omitted job characteristics are correlated with jobs' sex composition, then the coefficient on jobs' percentage female, which I suggest as a measure of direct wage discrimination against female jobs, will itself be biased. If two pay lines, one for male jobs and one for female jobs, are computed, this bias will affect the intercepts for the two equations, rendering it invalid to use the difference between the intercepts of parallel male and female lines as a measure of direct wage discrimination against female jobs.

What will be the direction of omitted-variable bias? If the omitted job characteristic has a positive return to earnings and male jobs score higher on it, or if it has a negative return and male jobs score lower, then its omission will cause the methods suggested above to overestimate the amount of direct sex discrimination against female jobs. If, on the other hand, the omitted job characteristic has a positive return to earnings and female jobs score higher on it, or if it has a negative return and female jobs score lower, then its omission will cause the method suggested above to underestimate the amount of direct sex discrimination against female jobs. The existence and severity of this bias hinges on the size of the correlations between (1) jobs' sex composition and the omitted variable and (2) the omitted variable and pay. The lower either correlation, the less the effect of the omission of the job characteristic on the accuracy of the estimate of direct sex discrimination in interjob wage setting.

Another possible source of error in using a job evaluation to assess direct sex bias in interjob wage setting flows from how the dependent variable of jobs' pay is measured. In Equation (4), the dependent variable of pay is generally the starting or highest wage of the wage interval set by policy for the job. In some instances, the midpoint of this interval is used. Two problems may arise from these choices.

First, consider a situation where there is no direct sex discrimination in the policy-set wage bands for each job, but the employer actually discriminates in placing more individuals toward the top of the band in male jobs for reasons unrelated to merit or seniority. This discrimination will not be discerned by a job evaluation using policy-set minimum or maximum wage as the dependent variable. This discrimination *will* be discerned if Equation (4) takes actual mean or median pay of persons in the job as the dependent variable. However, this introduces other problems. For example, two jobs that have the same total job evaluation points will differ in average actual pay even under nondiscrimination if the average seniority of those in one job is higher. Thus, if actual mean or median pay is to be used as the criterion, the analysis must adjust for interjob differences in average seniority or merit of job incumbents.

Another type of discrimination can be missed if starting pay is used as the criterion. Consider a situation where male and female jobs with the same job evaluation point have the same starting salaries, but the male jobs have a higher maximum wage. This will not be discerned unless the maximum wage is used as the criterion in the job evaluation.

These considerations suggest that using actual, minimum, or maximum pay as the criterion in a job evaluation each has its uses in discerning different types of interjob sex discrimination in pay-setting practices.

E. *Using Job Evaluation to Correct for Direct and Indirect Sex Bias in Wages*

Most pay equity studies find that female jobs pay less than male jobs rated with the same number of points. Substantial struggle generally ensues over what changes are to be made. First, let me consider correcting for what I have called direct sex bias in wage setting. The solution favored by most pay equity advocates is to bring female jobs up to the male job pay line. (Review Figure 4.3.) Employers may resist this because it increases the overall costs of payroll. In Minnesota it cost approximately 4% of payroll to bring female jobs up to the male job pay line (Rothchild 1984). Sometimes female jobs are not all brought precisely to the male line, but rather the scatter around the male line is retained. This is accomplished by giving each female job a raise the size of the distance between the female and male line. This results in pay to each female job that is the same distance above or below the male line that it was above or below the female line. The state of Wisconsin used this approach (Dresang forthcoming). Alternatively, in San Jose, the city only brought underpaid female jobs' pay up to a certain distance below the male line, rather than all the way up to the line. That is, the city removed some but not all of the discrimination in pay against female jobs. This is a typical outcome from public sector pay equity efforts. Few employers have lowered wages in male jobs. However, pay equity efforts may result in men's jobs—or all jobs—getting smaller raises in future years than they otherwise would have, with these forgone raises used to pay the bill of comparable worth (Acker 1989).

The underpayment of female jobs could also be resolved by using the overall pay line rather than male and female lines. One option is to raise the pay of female jobs to the overall line while not changing the pay in male jobs. This option is opposed by most advocates of pay equity since it raises female jobs to a line that most male jobs are above. Thus, male jobs continue to pay systematically more than female jobs, although the differential is reduced; this option removes some but not all of the underpayment of female jobs. A second option is to move the pay of all jobs to that dictated by the overall line. This will generally be costless to employers if it only brings female jobs up to the overall line, not the higher male line, while it reduces pay in male jobs to the level of the overall line. However, employers seldom lower wages as a result of job evaluation. Employers do sometimes red-circle jobs that are significantly above the line. These are usually male jobs. The current wages of incumbents in the red-circled jobs are not lowered, but new entrants are paid the lower wage dictated by the evaluation, and raises are curtailed in the red-circled jobs until raises in other jobs move the pay line up to the level of the red-circled job. Advocates of pay equity generally oppose this practice, in part because of the opposition to pay equity it may arouse in male workers. (For a comparison of the costs to employers of these various strategies, see Arvey and Holt 1988.)

How can statistics from job evaluations be used to correct for what I have called indirect sex discrimination, i.e., sex discrimination in the weights given to compensable factors? As stated above, it is hard to know what each weight would have been in the absence of sex bias. Nonetheless, one possible approach has been suggested by Jacobs and Steinberg (1990a). At the very least, they suggest that workers should not be *penalized* for being in jobs that, although just as high on highly valued job factors as other jobs, *also* have demands for devalued skills and demands with negative returns. They suggest that any skill or demand that a policy-capturing job evaluation finds to have a negative slope should not be counted in computing total points, and hence in setting jobs' pay. Effectively this means that the slopes that are negative should be set to zero in calculating the new wage for each job. This approach was taken in the New York State pay equity program, but only after pressure from the union representing state workers. However, setting slopes of devalued characteristics to zero may be an overly conservative approach to correcting for discrimination in slopes. It does not correct for cases where demands more common to women's jobs have lower but still positive returns compared to demands common to men's jobs. Nor does it bring above zero the returns to devalued skills and demands. This strategy will lead to increases in pay for *both* male and female jobs, though larger increases for female jobs (Jacobs and Steinberg 1990a). This is a sensible, albeit minimal, approach to indirect gender bias when reasonable people can agree that the negative return does not reflect a compensating differential for a nonpecuniary amenity, and thus indicates indirect gender bias.

VI. Job Evaluation and Market Wages

Two opposite claims have been made about the relationship between job evaluation and markets. On the one hand, job evaluation has been said to do little more than replicate market wages. This is problematic if market wages in female jobs are discriminatorily depressed. On the other hand, opponents of comparable worth claim that job evaluation sets wages by a criterion of internal equity that completely ignores the market realities of supply and demand. Two such opposite views cannot both be true. The truth lies somewhere between. To find it we need to examine the ways job evaluation within an organization is affected by wages in the external labor market.

Let us first consider the strategy of an employer who does not use job evaluation, but seeks to follow market wages. How does this process work? We might speculate that small employers find out the market wage for a particular skill type of labor by a strategy of trial and error. They initially set wages at the lowest level they think the market will bear, and if positions cannot be filled with labor of the appropriate quality, they raise them a little at a time until positions can be filled. Larger firms are more likely to use surveys to find out what other employers in the labor market pay in various jobs. In theory, such surveys should tell the employer the market wage in each job so that the firm can attract and retain employees of the desired quality at competitive costs (Ehrenberg 1979). However, industrial psychologists have pointed out that using market wage surveys is considerably more complex in the real world than economists' models would suggest. There is no one market wage in a job, but a dispersion. Decisions about the appropriate market wage to pay in a job will depend on whether local or national data are used, whether the survey reached small as well as large firms, and where in the existing range of wages found for a given job the firm decides to place its wage (Rynes and Milkovich 1986). Thus, the real-world operationalization of "paying the market wage" involves measurements and judgments. This ambiguity should be kept in mind when the term *market wages* is used below.

Now let us consider how market wages affect pay setting in firms that pay market wages in key jobs and use a policy-capturing job evaluation to set wages in other jobs. As discussed above, a regression analysis of the (market) wages in key jobs sets the weights for how much each compensable factor counts. Thus, if the market rewards some skills (compensable factors) at a higher rate than others, this is reflected in the weights of the job evaluation (Williams and Kessler 1984). This led Schwab (1980, p. 76) to conclude that policy-capturing "job evaluation does not measure worth beyond its definition in market wages." (Jaussaud 1984 argues this as well.) This is true in the limited sense that the weights for each compensable factor are market driven. To the extent that indirect gender bias causes factors traditionally associated with women's sphere to be devalued, this bias will be present in the weights obtained from a policy-capturing analysis. However, even accepting these weights, job evaluations generally find women's jobs to be underpaid, as discussed above. That is, women's jobs are generally found to be paid less relative to male jobs in actual practice than would obtain if the job evaluation were used to set pay. Thus, policy-capturing approaches to job evaluation bring in some market information, specifically factor weights, but do not have the same result as paying market wages in each job. They neither build all of the market's discrimination into job evaluation, nor ignore market wages.

On the surface it would appear that a priori applications of the point-factor system would be less market based than policy-capturing applications, since in a priori systems, market data are not used to set the weights for each compensable factor. This is true in theory; a priori job evaluation can be used to correct the indirect gender bias that has led to lower weights for factors traditionally practiced by women such as finger dexterity and nurturant human relations skills. However, a priori systems can also be instruments of bias against women's jobs if lower weights are systematically set for factors more common to female jobs. In actual practice, most firms or governments that use a priori job evaluation use the services of a consulting company. Such companies have a "canned" set of weights implicit in their scoring systems. They have chosen weights that "fit" market realities. Thus, these weights are usually, in practice, as market driven as those from policy-capturing approaches.

Job evaluation systems that build in the greatest amount of market wage information (and thus of any bias present in market wages) are those that involve multiple pay plans. As discussed above, many firms and governments have several different job families, each with a distinct pay plan. For example, there may be a plan each for exempt (usually professional and managerial), clerical, and blue-collar jobs. These separate plans may entail different factors or different factor weights. Alternatively, they may use the same factors and weights but a different pay line. If job families contain jobs with mostly one sex label, and if there is sex discrimination against female jobs in the market, then letting market wages dictate differences in the pay line between families of jobs will build this discrimination into the wages set by the multiple-plan job evaluation. For example, clerical jobs may pay much less for a given number of points than either exempt or factory jobs precisely because the wages of all clerical jobs are depressed due to sex discrimination. Such plans let in much more market information, including market discrimination, than do single-plan policy-capturing or single-plan a priori systems. They redress discrimination (to the extent allowed by the weights) *within* but not *between* job families.

To summarize, different methods of job evaluation incorporate different amounts of market wage information. Wage and salary surveys (not usually seen as a job evaluation method) are the most market based. Policy-capturing point-factor systems use market values for weights and intercepts. If followed, they pay male and female jobs consistently according to these market-derived weights. This will generally lead to higher relative wages for female jobs than most employers currently pay. In principle, a priori systems could contain different weights for factors than the market. In practice, however, most commercial a priori systems work about like policy-capturing systems. This is because consulting firms have set factor weights that, in their experience, are typical in industry. Job evaluation systems bring in more market information, including bias, when there are separate pay plans for various job families within an organization. The more pay plans there are, the more similar this will be to simply using wage survey results to set pay in each job. The greater the tendency of job families to contain all male or all female jobs, the more sex bias in pay the use of multiple plans will bring in from market wages. Indeed, I believe the prevalence of multiple pay plans is the single most important reason that the common practice of job evaluation has done little to close the sex gap in pay.

VII.   The Politics of Using Job Evaluation for Pay Equity

In this section I discuss how advocates of comparable worth would like to see job evaluation used to combat sex discrimination, and some of the political debates that often arise in implementing pay equity.

Advocates of comparable worth believe that Title VII of the Civil Rights Act of 1964 should be interpreted to prohibit the form of sex and race discrimination in wage setting identified by comparable worth. That is, advocates believe that failure to pay the same amount to female and male jobs, when a single bias-free job evaluation used across the entire establishment has shown them to be comparable, should be a prohibited form of discrimination. Since Title VII applies to the private as well as public sector, the requirement of pay equity in wage setting should apply to both private and public sectors as well. This would mean that job evaluation results could be used in a trial as evidence for proving the presence or absence of discrimination. If this interpretation prevailed, more employers would begin to do job evaluation and to follow it in wage setting to avoid legal liability. Chapter 5 will discuss how the courts have dealt with this interpretation. In general, courts have required more than this kind of statistical evidence to be convinced of discrimination, even though in *hiring* discrimination cases they have sometimes allowed reliance on statistics alone to show discrimination. If the courts will not interpret Title VII to require comparable worth wage setting, then advocates of pay equity support alternative legislation as well as voluntary uses of job evaluation by employers. A few companies have voluntarily instituted job evaluation for gender pay equity (Bernstein 1986).

The major political energy behind pay equity has gone into introducing legislation in states and municipalities to do job evaluation studies and use them to correct discriminatory pay differentials among public sector workers. Eastern and midwest states have led in pay equity efforts, and states that have ratified the ERA and have a more unionized public sector have been more likely to institute pay equity (Chi 1986). Table 4.1 shows the activities of the states as of 1989. (For short case studies on what states and localities have done, see Cook 1985, 1986.) The job evaluations done for pay equity differ significantly from those used previously (if any) primarily because they do not use separate pay lines for various job families. Legislation has been passed twice in the U.S. House of Representatives to institute a pay equity study for the federal civil service. However, the bills have not gotten out of committee onto the floor of the Senate because of stiff opposition in the Senate committees.

Table 4.1.   State and Local Government Pay Equity Activities as of 1989

State	Research/Data Collection	Pay Equity Study	Pay Equity Adjustments	Number of Local Gov't Actions
Alabama	X			0
Alaska				0
Arizona	X			1
Arkansas				0
California	X		X	97
Colorado	X			1
Connecticut	X	X	X	8
Delaware				1
District of Columbia		X		
Florida	X	X*	X	1
Georgia	X*			0
Hawaii	X	X	X	1
Idaho				0
Illinois	X		X	2
Indiana	X			1
Iowa	X	X	X	1
Kansas	X			0
Kentucky	X			0
Louisiana	X			0
Maine	X	X	X	1
Maryland	X	X		2
Massachusetts	X	X	X	32
Michigan	X	X	X	8
Minnesota	X	X	X	1392
Mississippi	X			0
Missouri	X			0
Montana	X	X		5
Nebraska	X			0
Nevada	X			0
New Hampshire	X			0
New Jersey	X	X	X	1
New Mexico	X	X	X	1
New York	X	X	X	74
North Carolina	X			0
North Dakota	X	X		0
Ohio	X	X		1
Oklahoma		X		0
Oregon	X	X	X	11
Pennsylvania	X*		X	4
Rhode Island	X		X	1
South Carolina	X			0
South Dakota		X	X	0
Tennessee	X			0
Texas	X			1

(continued)

Table 4.1.   (Continued)

State	Research/Data Collection	Pay Equity Study	Pay Equity Adjustments	Number of Local Gov't Actions
Utah	X			0
Vermont	X	X	X	1
Virginia	X			4
Washington	X	X	X	37
West Virginia	X	X		16
Wisconsin	X	X	X	33
Wyoming	X	X		0
Totals	44	23	20	1739

Notes:
*Activity conducted by a union, individual state legislator, women's organization, or other nongovernmental entity. All other activity indicated has been sanctioned by a governor, state agency, or legislature.
Source: National Committee on Pay Equity 1989.

The question of what will be done with wages in male jobs after a pay equity study raises the possibility of a divide-and-conquer strategy by employers (Flammang 1986). For example, Hutner (1986) recounts that when the union representing San Jose city workers struck for a general raise and pay equity adjustments, the city offered the comparable worth adjustments for women's jobs but no general increase. The union leadership was dominated by women in female jobs, especially librarians. The women refused to "sell out" the male workers and continued to strike until a general raise was offered along with pay equity adjustments. The price of this was incomplete pay equity adjustments. The possibilities for divisiveness between male and female workers are clear. Yet this has not proved to be the prominent divide in the politics of comparable worth.

The politics of comparable worth features business groups and academic economists opposing the concept, while feminist groups and those unions dominated by female workers are the most active supporters. Business groups opposing the concept include the National Association of Manufacturers, the Chamber of Commerce, Business Roundtable, National Public Employers Labor Relations Association, and the Equal Employment Advisory Council (Hutner 1986). Business groups oppose any increase of governmental regulation of their affairs, in this case since it lessens managerial control of wages and may increase their total wage bill (Williams and Kessler 1984). Many economists have denounced comparable worth policies because of a generalized belief in market solutions or for other reasons discussed in Chapter 2. Feminist groups supporting comparable worth include the National Organization for Women and the National Women's Political Caucus. Prominent among the unions supporting comparable worth is the American Federation of State, County, and Municipal Employees. Despite all the possibilities for divisiveness between male and female workers, male-dominated unions have generally not mobilized against comparable worth. Indeed, the mostly male AFL-CIO has endorsed the concept of pay equity (Northrup 1980), although it took some struggle by women members to achieve this, and endorsing comparable worth does not mean that the union has expended considerable resources to achieve it. (For more detailed discussions of the politics and implementation of comparable worth in the public sector, see Steinberg forthcoming; Blum 1991; Acker 1989; Evans and Nelson 1989.) The substance of debates over pay equity will be the topic of Chapter 7.

VIII. Conclusion

Job evaluation is a technique that allows employers to use a set of criteria consistently to set wage levels in jobs. Many large employers had already used it for decades when the issue of comparable worth came to public attention in the 1980s. Job evaluation methods show reasonable levels of reliability and validity. However, they are not immune to sex bias, and they are likely to incorporate some of the sex bias present in market wages. This is particularly true when different pay lines are used for different job families. However, even with their possible incorporation of sex bias, job evaluation techniques are able to detect some sex discrimination against female jobs in wage practices. This is why advocates of comparable worth encourage employers in the public and private sectors to use job evaluation for wage setting.

Notes

1. Equal ranges imply equal weights as long as the factors have similar means and variances as well as the same range. Otherwise, the implicit factor weights may not be equal even though the possible ranges of the factors are equal. Consider an example where two factors both have a hypothetical range from 0 to 10, but the first factor has as mean of 2.5 and only one job out of 1000 scores above 5 on the factor, while the second factor has a mean of 5 and jobs are normally distributed around this mean. Here, a decision to get total points by a simple unweighted addition of the two factors is implicitly giving a higher weight to the second factor.

5

Pay Equity and the Federal Courts

I. Introduction

In the last decade cases alleging sex-based wage discrimination involving dissimilar but purportedly comparable jobs have been litigated under Title VII of the Civil Rights Act of 1964. This chapter explores the views of the federal courts on these cases, which I call "comparable worth cases."[1] I sketch developing legal precedents and issues still unresolved. I also criticize the circuit court decisions, and discuss the conservative drift of decisions since 1980. I conclude that comparable worth is unlikely to make much headway in the federal courts in the current climate.

I begin with a very brief primer on legal terminology and the federal court system for unfamiliar readers. Cases alleging violations of federal laws begin in federal district courts, also called trial courts. These courts are charged with reaching decisions based on an assessment of the facts and how the law applies to these facts. After a district court issues its decision, either side may appeal to the circuit court of appeals. The nation is divided into twelve geographical circuits, each of which has such an appellate court. What circuit courts have decided on a given issue constrains trial judges in districts within the circuit unless the circuit court's ruling is contradicted by a ruling of the Supreme Court. After a circuit court has made a decision, either party may ask the U.S. Supreme Court to hear the case. The Supreme Court decides which of the cases it will hear. Agreeing to hear a case is called *granting certiorari.* If the Supreme Court does not hear a case, the decision of the circuit court stands. When the Supreme Court agrees to hear a case, it agrees to do so to decide one or more specified issues on the basis of which either the plaintiff or defendant has requested certiorari. The Court's decision sets precedent that must be followed by lower courts with respect to these issues.

The U.S. Supreme Court and the circuit courts decide only points of law, leaving the determination of questions of fact to the trial (district) courts. For example, neither the Supreme Court nor a circuit court would ever decide whether manager Smith really told applicant Jones that he never hires women as sales representatives because clients prefer men. Higher courts always take the district court's determination of the facts as given. They are limited to ruling on questions of law. Questions of law involve how the relevant federal statute or Constitutional provision is to be interpreted. These questions include which party has what burden of proof and what type of evidence parties have to show to meet their burden of proof.

Discrimination law comes under what is called "civil" rather than "criminal" law. Television shows have made it common knowledge that, in criminal trials, the prosecutor, representing "the people," has the burden of proof, and must prove guilt of the defendant beyond a reasonable doubt. In civil law, however, things are somewhat different. The two parties are referred to as the *plaintiff* (the person bringing the case alleging that s/he was wronged in violation of some law) and the *defendant*. Plaintiffs may bring either individual or class action suits (although the latter require a preliminary class certification hearing). Many comparable worth cases are class action suits. Different civil laws allocate the burdens of proof various ways. However, the standard of proof in civil law is never "beyond a reasonable doubt" but rather "preponderance of the evidence." That is, if the judge or jury concludes that there is considerable doubt but more evidence supports the defendant's argument than the plaintiff's, the ruling is to be for the defendant, and vice versa. Thus, whenever I say below that one side has the burden of proof on a given issue, this should be taken to mean that party has the responsibility to prove what is in question by the standard of preponderance of the evidence.

Discrimination cases seldom involve juries. They are usually decided by judges. The written document explaining the reasons behind a court's decision on as case is an *opinion*, written by a judge.

In most of this chapter I speak in a "lawyerly" rather than a social scientific voice. That is, I review what the courts have decided, with attention to the legal reasoning by which they reach such decisions based on the statute and, where relevant, higher courts' interpretations of it. I rely exclusively on Supreme Court and circuit court opinions. I do not discuss decisions on points of law made by district trial courts since they are not binding on any future cases. Later in the chapter, I reassume the voice of a social scientist. I criticize the circuit courts' unwillingness to interpret Title VII in a way that remedies the sort of discrimination at issue in comparable worth. Even lawyers believe that court decisions are somewhat affected by the social and political context.

But in the discourse of law (much as in scientific discourse) it is normative for judges and lawyers to remove discussion of any political criteria that may be affecting their decisions from the written record. Nonetheless, I include a section in which I speculate about the social and political factors affecting the negative reception plaintiffs' comparable worth claims have received in the federal courts, and what this means for the future of comparable worth. (For other overviews of federal court treatments of comparable worth, see Williams and Bagby 1984; Heen 1984; U.S. Commission on Civil Rights 1985; Reichenberg 1986; Barnett 1986; Pinzler and Ellis 1989.[2])

The most general conclusion of this chapter will be that the courts are extremely reluctant to find for plaintiffs in comparable worth cases. The burden of proof given to plaintiffs makes it nearly impossible to prove discrimination in the setting of wages for dissimilar jobs unless there is a "smoking gun," such as a statement by employers that they set jobs' wages on the basis of the sex of those doing the work. In part, this reflects a less sympathetic treatment by the courts of comparable worth cases compared to cases involving other types of discrimination. However, it also reflects a conservative drift of the courts over the last decade that is affecting all areas of discrimination law, as well as other areas of the law.

II. The Equal Pay Act and Title VII of the Civil Rights Act

There are two major pieces of federal legislation that affect sex discrimination in employment: the Equal Pay Act of 1963 and Title VII of the Civil Rights Act of 1964. Below, I provide background by reviewing these statutes as well as court precedents established under them before comparable worth cases arose.

A. The Equal Pay Act of 1963

The Equal Pay Act of 1963 deals exclusively with the requirement that employers not discriminate on the basis of sex in assigning pay to men and women who are doing equal work. The original bill proposed in Congress (which had also been proposed for a number of years previously) and supported by the Kennedy administration called for equal pay for "comparable work" (Williams and Bagby 1984; Booker and Nuckolls 1986). However, during debate, this was changed to require equal work. The statute defines equal work to require that the two jobs entail equal (a) skill, (b) effort, and (c) responsibility, and be (d) performed under similar working conditions (Williams and Bagby 1984). Over time the courts have clarified what they mean by equal work. The existence of two distinct job titles (e.g., maid and janitor) does not guarantee that the court will find the work unequal. The issue is whether the actual work done is equal. Further, courts have decided that the work need not be identical, but merely "substantially equal." For example, if two jobs involve the same tasks 95% of the time, but different tasks on occasion, courts will often find them substantially equal. Yet this softening of the requirement of absolute equality of tasks does not accommodate most comparable worth cases, where completely different jobs (such as nurses versus repair technicians) are compared.

In Equal Pay Act cases, the burden of proof is allocated as follows: Plaintiffs have the burden to prove that women were paid less than men and that the work involved was "substantially equal." If this is shown, plaintiffs are said to have made a *prima facie case*. One way defendants can win the case is to successfully rebut the prima facie case, i.e., to show that the work was not equal or that there really was no pay difference. If the court is convinced that the prima facie case has been made, then defendants can only win the case by proving that the reason for the difference in pay between men and women was one of the four "affirmative defenses" written into the act. A wage differential for equal work is justified if it is shown to be because of (1) seniority, (2) merit, (3) a system that pays according to quality or quantity of production, or (4) any factor other than sex.

B. Title VII of the Civil Rights Act

The Civil Rights Act of 1964 includes sections that deal with discrimination in public accommodations, education, and employment. Title VII deals with employment discrimination. Although both Title VII of the Civil Rights Act and the Equal Pay Act cover sex discrimination in employment, Title VII, passed one year after the Equal Pay Act, is much broader. First, the Equal Pay Act deals only with sex discrimination while Title VII prohibits discrimination on the basis of race, color, religion, sex, or national origin. Second, the Equal Pay Act deals only with pay discrimination where equal work is involved, while Title VII deals with discrimination in pay, hiring, termination, placement, and any other terms of employment. One of the main factors leading to the passage of the Civil Rights Act was the civil rights movement on behalf of the rights of African Americans. The prohibition of sex discrimination resulted from an amendment made by Representative Howard Smith of Virginia, the bill's principal opponent. He is believed to have added the amendment because he felt it would lead to the defeat of the bill as a whole (Williams and Bagby 1984). Because the amendment was added late in the House's deliberations, issues raised by adding sex discrimination to the bill did not have the thorough review of House and Senate committees given the race provisions.

When the act was passed by the House and sent to the Senate with the amendment adding the prohibition of sex discrimination, the senators decided they should clarify the relationship between provisions against sex discrimination in pay in Title VII and in the Equal Pay Act. The Senate thus added the Bennett Amendment to Title VII to avoid conflicts between the two laws. The amendment states that "It shall not be an unlawful employment practice . . . for any employer to differentiate on the basis of sex in determining the amount of wages or compensation paid . . . if such differentiation is authorized by the provisions [of the Equal Pay Act]" (Williams and Bagby 1984, p. 221). The final version of Title VII contains this amendment.

Under Title VII, the Supreme Court has allowed plaintiffs to prove discrimination under two distinct types of theories, "treatment" and "impact" (U.S. Commission on Civil Rights 1985, pp. 41–61). Below I discuss how burdens of proof are assigned under these two models.

The Disparate Treatment Model. To prove differential (or equivalently, disparate) treatment, plaintiffs are required to show that men and women (or blacks and whites, etc.) were treated differently, and that the reason for this differential treatment was intentional discrimination. The treatment at issue may be hiring, placement, promotion, pay, fringe benefits, harassment, or any condition of employment.

In cases alleging differential treatment, plaintiffs sometimes provide evidence of intent of the smoking gun variety. Sometime this is referred to as a *direct* proof of intent. For example, in a hiring case, a written memo by a manager of the firm stating that women will not be hired as carpenters, or persuasive testimony that this was verbally stated, would constitute a smoking gun or direct proof of intentional discrimination. Needless to say, such direct evidence is very hard to come by since employers know they are liable for such statements. Fortunately for plaintiffs, in many kinds of Title VII cases, such direct evidence is not necessary.

In many types of discrimination cases courts have also allowed more circumstantial evidence to suffice as convincing proof of intentional discrimination. Sometimes statistical evidence alone has been sufficient proof in class action cases (*International Brotherhood of Teamsters v. U.S.*, U.S. Supreme Ct. 1977; *Hazelwood School District et al. v. United States*, U.S. Supreme Ct. 1977; *Craik v. Minnesota State University Board*, 8th

Circuit 1984; *Segar v. Smith,* D.C. Circuit 1984). Often anecdotal evidence of intent plus statistical evidence has been sufficient in cases not involving comparable worth (*Bazemore v. Friday,* U.S. Supreme Ct. 1986).

The allocation of burdens in disparate treatment cases under Title VII is as follows: The plaintiff has the burden of proving that disparate treatment occurred due to intentional discrimination. This is called proving a prima facie case. The defendant then has an opportunity to argue that the differential treatment (e.g., of a man and a woman or the class of men and women) that the plaintiff is alleging to be discriminatory really occurred for some legitimate, nondiscriminatory business reason. Here the defendant does not have the burden to *prove* that the nondiscriminatory reason was the real one. The burden is merely one of "production"; the defendant must "articulate" the reason (*Texas Department of Community Affairs v. Burdine,* U.S. Supreme Ct. 1981). If a nondiscriminatory reason is articulated, then the plaintiff has the burden to prove that this reason is a pretext for discrimination, i.e., that intentional discrimination was really the reason.

The Disparate Impact Model.   The disparate impact theory came into being with the 1971 decision of the Supreme Court in *Griggs v. Duke Power Co.* (U.S. Supreme Ct. 1971), a case dealing with race discrimination in hiring. What was novel about the ruling in *Griggs* was that the Supreme Court decided that plaintiffs could prevail even when they did not prove *intentional* discrimination.[3] Rather, *Griggs* decided that a policy of an employer that is nondiscriminatory on its face is nonetheless discriminatory if it has an adverse impact on members of a class protected by Title VII *and* the defendant cannot prove that the policy is job relevant or a business necessity. When plaintiffs make their case in this manner they are using the disparate impact model.

For example, in *Griggs,* plaintiffs showed that requiring a high school diploma disqualified a higher proportion of black than white applicants. The court ruled that this made a prima facie case of discrimination under the disparate impact doctrine that it was newly creating in the case. Educational credentials, test scores, and height requirements have all been challenged under the impact doctrine, often successfully (Burstein and Pitchford 1990).

Griggs said that if plaintiffs prove that an employment policy that appears neutral on its face has a disparate impact, then they have successfully made a prima facie case. The burden of proof then shifts to defendants to show that the policy having the adverse impact is a business necessity. In hiring cases, this consists of presenting compelling evidence that persons with the required credential perform better in the job for which it is a screening device. Giving defendants this burden of proof was a significant change from the way burdens of proof had been and still are allocated under the disparate treatment model reviewed above. For example, it is much easier for a defendant to state that the reason a black plaintiff was not hired is that s/he did not have the required educational credential (an adequate defense under the disparate treatment doctrine) than it is to present convincing evidence that the educational requirement serves to get workers who perform better (the required defense under the disparate impact model).

The burden of proof that *Griggs* assigned to defendants in disparate impact cases in 1971 was changed radically in 1989 with the Supreme Court's decision in *Wards Cove Packing Company v. Antonio*. The decision did not change the rules for how plaintiffs make a prima facie case under the disparate impact theory. The important change in *Wards Cove* was to relieve defendants of a burden of proof they had been given by *Griggs*. After this decision, defendants in disparate impact cases merely had the burden of articulating (not proving) a business reason for the policy that has the disparate impact. If defendants met this (easily met) burden, then plaintiffs could only prevail by proving that the policy having the disparate impact is *not* job related or a business necessity.

In 1991, Congress passed and President Bush signed into law the Civil Rights Act of 1991 (Public Law 102-166). One of its specific aims was to restore the disparate impact doctrine that had, for all practical purposes, been destroyed by the *Wards Cove* decision. After some debate and compromise between Congress and President Bush, legislation was passed that makes employment practices that have a disparate impact on groups protected by Title VII illegal unless the employer can show that the practices are "job-related for the position in question and consistent with business necessity." This essentially restores the *Griggs* ruling, writing it into legislation for the first time.

Let us consider a hypothetical example of a hiring discrimination case to see what the shifts in burden of proof brought about by *Griggs*, *Wards Cove*, and the Civil Rights Act of 1991 imply about the ease with which plaintiffs or defendants can win cases. Consider a situation where an employer requires that applicants pass a physical strength test to be hired as fire fighters. Prior to *Griggs*, the fact that this hiring requirement eliminated more women than men was irrelevant to proving discrimination, since only the differential treatment model was available. Plaintiffs had to show intentional discrimination. After *Griggs*, plaintiffs could show disparate impact by showing that the requirement eliminated a significantly higher proportion of female than male applicants. Under *Griggs* the burden of proof then was on the defendant employer to prove that those who pass the test perform better in the job. If the defendant had no such evidence, the plaintiff prevailed. Under *Wards Cove*, the defendant merely had to state that the test was required because the job of fire fighter requires physical strength. The plaintiff then prevailed only by proving that the test is *not* job relevant. While *Wards Cove* formally left the disparate impact model available to plaintiffs, as a practical matter, it made it very unlikely that plaintiffs could prevail in such cases. The 1991 act essentially restores the burdens of proof articulated by *Griggs*.

Below I will detail how comparable worth cases may be argued by plaintiffs and defended against by employers under either the treatment or impact doctrine. But first I must explain the key case that opened the door to comparable worth litigation under Title VII.

III.   Opening the Door to Comparable Worth: The *Gunther* Decision

The Supreme Court opened the door to comparable worth cases in its decision to uphold the Ninth Circuit Court's decision in *County of Washington, Oregon v. Gunther* (U.S. Supreme Ct. 1981). In *Gunther*, the Supreme Court decided that it is possible for plaintiffs to prevail under Title VII when they claim sex discrimination in pay between two different jobs without meeting the equal work standard of the Equal Pay Act of 1963.

In *Gunther*, the Supreme Court decided that the Bennett Amendment was not intended to limit sex-based wage discrimination cases to those that meet the Equal Pay Act's standard of substantially equal work. Rather, they interpreted the Bennett Amendment to bring into Title VII the four affirmative defenses of the Equal Pay Act but not the equal work standard. Thus, under Title VII, plaintiffs need not prove equal work to show sex discrimination in wages, but employers may defend themselves by showing that the pay differential was due to seniority, merit, a system of rewarding quantity or quality of production, or any factor other than sex. Having decided the question of law about how the Bennett Amendment was to be interpreted, the Court remanded the question of fact of whether the employer had discriminated to the trial court.

Gunther is the only comparable worth case the Supreme Court has heard. (See note 1 to this chapter.) The Court stated that it was not deciding "the precise contours of lawsuits challenging sex discrimination in compensation under Title VII" (*County of Washington, Oregon v. Gunther*, U.S. Supreme Ct. 1981, p. 19). It left unresolved what plaintiffs have to prove in comparable worth cases and what defenses are valid. However, it dropped hints about its future disposition on such matters. Technically speaking, a Supreme Court opinion is only binding on lower courts with respect to the specific points of law on the basis of which the case was appealed and granted certiorari. In *Gunther* this was the question of whether the Bennett Amendment to Title VII should be interpreted to bring the equal work standard from the Equal Pay Act into Title VII in cases alleging sex discrimination in pay. But judicial opinions often contain comments on related issues. Lawyers refer to these comments as *dicta*. Sometimes lower-court judges use these comments as hints to how the Supreme Court might decide an issue in the future and govern their own opinions accordingly. However, the rules of law do not compel them to do so, whereas they are compelled to follow precedent on issues actually decided in a case.

There are three areas of dicta in the *Gunther* opinion that have caused much speculation and confusion. One issue is whether plaintiffs may use the disparate impact model in sex-based wage discrimination cases involving unequal jobs. Writing for the majority, Justice Brennan hinted that disparate impact analysis might not be allowed. However, he made it clear that the court was not deciding the issue. His dictum can be read to suggest that the Equal Pay Act's fourth affirmative defense that the Bennett Amendment brought into Title VII for sex-based wage cases, "any factor other than sex," may preclude using the disparate impact theory of discrimination. The reasoning here is that when a factor is challenged by plaintiffs because it has a disparate impact, it is acknowledged even by the plaintiffs to be a factor other than sex. (For a discussion of this argument see Brilmayer, Hekeler, Laycock, and Sullivan 1980; Laycock 1986a, 1986b.)

A related issue left undecided by *Gunther* is how bringing the four affirmative defenses into Title VII sex-based wage discrimination cases affects burden of proof. Under the Equal Pay Act, if the plaintiff has made out a prima facie case, the burden is on the defendant to *prove* that the reason for the unequal pay was nondiscriminatory. Under Title VII, in disparate treatment cases, as discussed above, if plaintiffs have successfully made a prima facie case, defendants do not have the burden to *prove* that the treatment in question was in fact nondiscriminatory. They simply have to *articulate* a plausible nondiscriminatory reason they are claiming for the treatment. Thus, defendants have a more onerous burden of proof in Equal Pay Act cases than in disparate treatment cases. The burden of proof in Equal Pay Act cases is more like the burden of proof given defendants in disparate impact cases by the 1971 *Gunther* decision. The question has arisen, then, as to whether the Bennett Amendment, by bringing the four affirmative defenses into Title VII, has also brought in the more onerous standard of proof for defendants in sex-based pay cases, whether they are argued under the treatment or impact doctrine. (For prodefense arguments, see Williams and Bagby

1984; U.S. Commission on Civil Rights 1984.) *Gunther* left the issue unresolved.

Another issue formally unresolved by *Gunther* concerns how plaintiffs can prove intentional discrimination when they are proceeding on the disparate treatment theory. The actual case in *Gunther* involved women whose job it was to guard the county's women prisoners. They were paid 70% as much ás men whose job it was to guard the county's male prisoners. The county's system of wage determination involved job evaluation and market surveys. By their own system, the county assessed the women's job to be worth 95% as much as the men's. However, they failed to pay this much to the women. When I first read the *Gunther* opinion, I assumed that the court was ruling that this constituted sufficient evidence to prove intentional discrimination under the disparate treatment model. While the opinion does suggest this, the suggestion has only the status of dicta. The *Gunther* opinion only decided the issue of whether the Bennett Amendment brought the equal work standard into Title VII.

These unresolved issues have led to much confusion and controversy in lower courts since *Gunther*.

IV. Comparable Worth Cases Using the Disparate Treatment Model

What is clear from *Gunther* is that plaintiffs can bring a claim of sex discrimination in pay between different jobs if they are going to provide evidence of intentional discrimination against women, that is, if they are going to use the disparate treatment model. What is not clear is what evidence will meet their burden of proof.

It is clear that smoking gun or direct proofs that employers paid some jobs less than others *for the reason that* those jobs were filled by women will be sufficient. For example, if an employer openly states that some jobs are paid less than others because women hold the jobs, this would demonstrate intent. *International Union of Electrical Workers v. Westinghouse* (1980, 3rd Circuit) is the precedent-setting case here. The case involved distinct jobs in production work at Westinghouse Electric. In the late 1930s Westinghouse established an evaluation system that assigned each job a grade between 1 and 5. Jobs assigned a higher grade were given higher pay. Yet pay in female jobs was less than that in male jobs even when the grade assigned to the female job was higher. The company's written industrial relations manual explicitly attributed such pay differentials to the fact that the lower-paid jobs were held by women. After Title VII was passed, the jobs were no longer explicitly labeled as male and female, but they retained their former sex composition. The jobs filled by women kept their grades of 1 through 5, but all the male jobs were assigned higher grades, although no new job evaluation was performed and the nature of the work had not changed appreciably. The written industrial relations manual was the smoking gun in this case. It stated that the wage differentials had been set on the basis of sex. Although the manual was no longer in force, the interjob wage differentials that had been established by the earlier policy of overt wage discrimination were still in force when the case came to trial (Newman and Owens 1984).

Today, after decades of experience under Title VII, few employers make such explicitly discriminatory statements. Thus, limiting victories for plaintiffs in comparable worth cases to those where there is a "smoking gun" as evidence of discriminatory intent would have the effect of allowing almost no plaintiffs to win such cases.

In what more circumstantial and indirect ways may plaintiffs establish their prima facie case of disparate treatment in comparable worth cases? As discussed above, in Title VII cases involving hiring and promotion, as well as in pay cases other than those involving comparable worth, plaintiffs in class action cases have been allowed to rely on statistics that show different treatments of men and women (or racial groups) when relevant variables have been controlled. Sometimes statistics alone have been sufficient to make a prima facie case (*International Brotherhood of Teamsters v. U.S.*, U.S. Supreme Ct. 1977; *Hazelwood School District v. United States* U.S. Supreme Ct. 1977; *Craik v. Minnesota State University Board*, 8th Circuit 1984; *Segar v. Smith*, D.C. Circuit 1984). In other cases statistics, in combination with anecdotal evidence suggestive of intent to discriminate, have been found adequate (*Bazemore v. Friday*, U.S. Supreme Ct. 1986).

In comparable worth cases, the most relevant sort of statistics would presumably be those from job evaluations that show female jobs to merit more relative to male jobs than the employer is actually paying. There are two ways plaintiffs might possibly proceed here. One way is to use as evidence the employer's own job evaluation, which showed an underpayment of female jobs but which did not result in correction of the inequities. The second way is for plaintiffs to introduce a job evaluation they produced for purposes of the case. The second alternative has not been tested at the circuit court level, but I imagine it would be less compelling to judges than the first. Even the first alternative has not met with success in circuit court cases.

Since the issue of how disparate treatment can be proven is undecided by the Supreme Court, circuit court precedents are binding upon district courts in those circuits where this issue has arisen. The two major cases involving plaintiffs' attempts to use results from an employer's own job evaluation against the employer are *American Federation of State, County, and Municipal Employees v. State of Washington* (hereafter cited as *AFSCME*) (9th Circuit 1985) and *American Nurses' Association et al. v. State of Illinois* (7th Circuit 1986). Both of these cases were decided against the plaintiffs by circuit courts. *AFSCME*, which received extensive press coverage, involved the AFSCME, a national union representing government workers. Some background on the case will help to put it in perspective. Before the case was filed, the state of Washington had hired a consulting firm, Willis, to do a job evaluation. The results showed that female jobs were systematically paid less than male jobs with the same total evaluation points (Remick 1984, forthcoming). A number of state officials, including the governor, made statements admitting that the study showed discrimination, but the legislature did not provide raises for female jobs the study showed to be underpaid. As a result, AFSCME filed a Title VII suit. The trial court (*AFSCME v. State of Washington*, Western District of Washington 1983) found that the evidence from the job evaluation, together with admissions by state officials of discrimination, made a prima facie case of discrimination under both impact and treatment doctrines. But, on appeal, the Ninth Circuit reversed (*AFSCME v. State of Washington*, 9th Circuit 1985), arguing that the job evaluation findings, even in combination with the anecdotal evidence, did not make a prima facie case of discrimination.[4]

American Nurses (*American Nurses' Association et al. v. State of Illinois*, 3rd Circuit 1986) also involved evidence that an employer paid women's jobs less than men's jobs that the employer's own job evaluation found to be of equivalent worth. The Third Circuit ruled that this is not sufficient to make a prima facie case of disparate treatment.

In both of these cases, the employers claimed that they failed to pay women's jobs the same amount as men's jobs that their evaluation found to have equivalent points because they were following market wages. The courts took this as a successful rebuttal of the plaintiffs' prima facie cases. Essentially, the courts said that failure to follow their own job evaluation was not evidence of intentional discrimination if the employer stated that they had a policy of taking both the evaluation and market wages into account in setting wages, or if they claimed that they did the job evaluation but decided not to implement it. Obviously, where even failure to pay male and female jobs consistently in relationship to their value as assessed by the employer's *own* job evaluation was not seen by these circuit courts as proof of discrimination, evidence from a job evaluation that plaintiffs have prepared for trial is likely to be seen as even less compelling.

An interesting aspect of the *AFSCME* case is that the state of Washington was not required to show compelling evidence that it followed market wages. Rather, simply stating that it paid market wages sufficed. After the case was decided, two sociologists obtained access to the state's data and performed an analysis showing that the differences in external market wages between predominantly male and female jobs *did not* entirely explain the wage differentials paid to such jobs by the state. Bridges and Nelson (1989) performed regression analyses predicting state jobs' pay from their points in the job evaluation, their sex composition, and the external market wage of the job the state used as the "benchmark job" for a given job. The external market wage was computed from census data on wages in the state of Washington's overall labor market for the benchmark jobs. Although the lower external market wage of the benchmark jobs keyed to predominantly female jobs explained some of the underpayment of female jobs in relation to their points in the job evaluation, it did not explain it all. There was still a significant effect of jobs' own sex composition on wages even after adjusting for job evaluation points and the market wage of the benchmark job. Thus, Washington state appears to have been engaging in wage discrimination against female employees *in excess of* what can be explained by merely following market wages. This fact never came to light in the trial, in part because the defendant was not required to prove that market wages were the source of the wage disparities but merely to articulate that its policy was to follow market wages.

How can plaintiffs prove differential treatment in cases alleging sex-based wage discrimination involving dissimilar jobs, given these circuit courts' decisions? Examples might be showing that the employer followed a job evaluation in setting wages for male jobs irrespective of market wages, but did not follow the job evaluation in setting wages for female jobs (or vice versa). Another possibility might be showing that the employer used local market surveys to ascertain the market wage and set pay in female jobs, but used market surveys from a larger area to set pay in male jobs (Weals 1984). These might meet the criterion of differential treatment. However, there are no circuit court cases testing this. Thus, to date nothing besides smoking gun proofs of intent have succeeded in comparable worth cases using the disparate treatment model.

V. Comparable Worth Cases Using the Disparate Impact Model

Circuit courts have yet to clarify what (if any) kinds of proofs using the disparate impact model are permitted in comparable worth cases. (For discussion see Loudon and Loudon 1986; U.S. Commission on Civil

Rights 1985, pp. 51–57; Seidenfeld 1982; Laycock 1986a; Pinzler and Ellis 1989; Williams and Bagby 1984.) As discussed above, dicta in the Supreme Court's *Gunther* decision have been interpreted by some writers to mean that disparate impact analysis cannot be used in Title VII cases that involve sex-based wage discrimination.

This reasoning notwithstanding, some circuit courts have allowed disparate impact analysis in cases involving sex-based discrimination in compensation that did *not* involve comparable worth (*Wambheim v. J.C. Penney,* 9th Circuit 1981; *Colby v. J.C. Penney,* 7th Circuit 1987; *Equal Employment Opportunity Commission v. J.C. Penney,* 6th Circuit 1988). In all the cases against J.C. Penney Company, plaintiffs proceeded by showing the adverse impact upon women of Penney's compensation policy of providing health insurance only for employees who were "heads of households," which Penney defined as persons providing more than half of family income. While these were not comparable worth cases, they affect such cases because they show that disparate impact claims are possible in cases about sex discrimination in compensation. These cases establish that, unless the Supreme Court says otherwise, the Bennett Amendment's bringing into Title VII "any factor other than sex" as a defense does not disallow using the disparate impact theory in cases involving sex discrimination in compensation even though they hinge on challenging a policy that is "other than sex" on its face.[5] In effect, they say that not *any* policy but only legitimate business policies may qualify under the "any factor other than sex" clause. Thus, so far, no circuit has disallowed using the disparate impact theory in comparable worth cases in principle. However, neither has it been allowed in a comparable worth case in circuit courts or the Supreme Court.

Even if disparate impact analysis is allowed in principle in comparable worth cases, this may be a moot point for plaintiffs given other restrictions that recent decisions have put on its use. To explore this, let us consider how plaintiffs might prevail in a comparable worth case using disparate impact analysis. To do this, we need to think of *what* employment policy plaintiffs could identify as having a disparate impact on women's wages in a comparable worth case. Two cases have decided that plaintiffs have to identify a specific policy, not the overall compensation system, and that the policy of "following market wages" cannot be found discriminatory because of its disparate impact (*Spaulding v. University of Washington,* 9th Circuit 1984; *AFSCME v. State of Washington,* 9th Circuit 1985). In *Spaulding,* the court stated that the practice of relying on prevailing market wages in each job "is not the sort of 'policy' at which disparate impact analysis is aimed. . . . Employers relying on the market are . . . 'price-takers.' They . . . do not meaningfully have a 'policy' about it in the relevant Title VII sense" (p. 708).

What other policies might be identified as having disparate impact in comparable worth cases? In cases where defendants use a job evaluation system, plaintiffs might try to argue that the choice of compensable factors and the weights given to various factors in an employer's job evaluation system have a disparate impact on women.[6] (See Chapter 4 for definitions of compensable factors and weights in job evaluation systems.) Or they might challenge the use of separate pay lines for various job families. As explained in Chapter 4, many large employers use a formal job evaluation plan for all jobs in the firm. However, often a separate pay line is developed for each of a number of job groups. Different weights or a different intercept may dictate differences in pay lines for the job groups. Often women are concentrated in the job groups with the lower pay lines. As a result, a job scoring 150 points that is in the job family containing many female jobs may well pay less than a job scoring 150 points that is in the job family containing many men's jobs. This clearly has a disparate impact on women's wages. Nonetheless, my prediction is that courts will be reluctant to "second-guess" employers' overall job evaluation systems, given their reluctance to accept virtually any evidence by plaintiffs thus far in comparable worth cases. Thus, it is not clear *what* policy of employers plaintiffs would be allowed to challenge in a comparable worth case even if the courts decide that the Bennett Amendment and *Gunther* do not, in principle, disallow disparate impact claims in sex-based wage cases under Title VII.

If courts were to accept plaintiffs' arguments that job evaluation systems or other aspects of compensation systems have a disparate impact, how easy will it be for defendants to make a defense? This is another confusing and unresolved area. Under the Supreme Court's *Ward Cove* decision of 1989, discussed above, the burdens of proof in disparate impact cases were radically changed from how the 18 years of precedent since *Griggs* had allocated them. Under *Wards Cove*, defendants did not need to *prove* the business necessity of the policy that has been shown to have a disparate impact, as they did between 1971 and 1989 under the *Griggs* decision, but merely to articulate a plausible business reason for the policy. What is unclear is whether the Bennett Amendment renders the *Wards Cove* decision inapplicable to cases involving *sex* discrimination in *compensation*. One case held that the Bennett Amendment means that employers do have this affirmative burden of proof under Title VII if the case involves sex-based wage discrimination (*Kouba v. Allstate Insurance Company*, 9th Circuit 1982). However, this case was decided before the Supreme Court's decision in *Wards Cove* and subsequent legislation has undone some of *Wards Cove*. Thus the issue remains unclear.

If the courts allow disparate impact analysis to plaintiffs in comparable worth cases, and regardless of whether they decide that the defendants have to *prove* or merely *articulate* a business reason for the pay difference, the question arises as to whether paying different jobs according to market wages will suffice as a defense. Plaintiffs have argued that this should not be a defense since market wages are contaminated by discrimination. Again, here, the situation is confusing. On the one hand, courts have allowed defendants' claims that they have based their wage rates for various jobs upon the market rates to rebut plaintiffs' prima facie cases in every circuit that has considered the matter (*AFSCME v. State of Washington*, 9th Circuit 1985; *Craik v. Minnesota State University Board*, 8th Circuit 1984; *Lemons v. City and County of Denver*, 10th Circuit 1980; *Christensen v. State of Iowa*, 8th Circuit 1977; *American Nurses' Association et al. v. State of Illinois*, 3rd Circuit 1986). Yet these cases were argued primarily under the disparate treatment doctrine, leaving unclear whether paying market wages is a legitimate defense in disparate impact cases (whether proven or articulated).

At first glance, one would think that the fourth affirmative defense from the Equal Pay Act, which the Bennett Amendment read into Title VII for sex-based pay cases, would allow paying market wages as a defense since they are a "factor other than sex." However, in one Equal Pay Act case involving equal work in the same or substantially equal jobs, the Supreme Court did *not* allow this defense (*Corning Glass Works v. Brennan*, U.S. Supreme Ct. 1974). *Corning Glass* dealt with payment of different wages to two jobs that the court had found to meet the Equal Pay Act's standard of equal work. The employer argued that the market wage available to most men was higher than that available to most women, and thus that paying more to the males was due to the market, a "factor other than sex." The Supreme Court disallowed this defense. The opinion stated:

> The differential . . . arose simply because men would not work at the low rates paid women . . . , and it reflected a job market in which Corning could pay women less than men for the same work. That the company took advantage of such a situation may be understandable as a matter of economics, but its differential nevertheless became illegal once Congress enacted into law the principle of equal pay for equal work. (*Corning Glass Works v. Brennan*, U.S. Supreme Ct. 1974, p. 188)

The question is whether this same logic applies when the two jobs in question do not meet the equal work standard. I suspect that, *Corning Glass* notwithstanding, the Supreme Court would uphold the market wage defense. One reason for believing this is that the judge who wrote the Ninth Circuit's opinion in *AFSCME*, arguing that comparable worth is incompatible with our free market system of wage setting, Judge Kennedy, has since been appointed to the Supreme Court.

VI.   A Critique of Circuit Court Decisions

In this section I present a critique of the stance that the circuit courts have taken toward comparable worth cases, arguing that it is inconsistent with both the spirit of Title VII and with the evidence from social science I have presented throughout this book. I will argue that what would be most consistent with the broad aims of Title VII would be to allow policy-capturing job evaluation statistics to suffice for plaintiffs' prima facie case, and to disallow market wages as a rebuttal or defense against such a case except where a *temporary* shortage or glut of a particular kind of skill caused the market wage differential. Thus, in my view, the circuit courts have erred in failing to consider job evaluation statistics sufficient for plaintiffs and in seeing articulation of a policy of paying market wages as sufficient for defendants.

First, I must address why I believe comparable worth to be consistent with the broad spirit of Title VII. The animating principle of Title VII regarding sex discrimination is to forbid using sex as a criterion in any employment decision. This includes decisions regarding whom to hire for or assign to a particular job. Title VII also applies to compensation. Section 703(a) states that it is unlawful for an employer "to . . . discriminate against any individual with respect to . . . compensation . . . because of such individual's . . . sex" (U.S. Congress, Civil Rights Act of 1964). Both this language and the principle articulated above imply that sex may not be taken into account when an employer decides whether person A or person B will get paid more in a single job. In addition, both this language and the animating principle of nondiscrimination imply that sex may not lawfully affect a decision about whether job X will pay more than job Y. If job X pays more than job Y for reasons quite apart from the sex composition of the job, there is no sex discrimination. If, however, the sex of those holding the jobs has affected the decision about their relative pay levels, then it is consistent with the principle of nondiscrimination to prevent such discrimination.

This suggests the relevance of policy-capturing job evaluation to comparable worth litigation. In policy-capturing job evaluations the relative weights of each of the compensable factors are determined by a regression analysis showing how important each factor is in predicting what the employer currently pays for each job. The resulting formula of intercept and weights will "capture" the policy the employer is actually using in setting wages. By contrast, in a priori evaluations, whoever is conducting the evaluation decides on nonempirical grounds how to weight each compensable factor. Thus, a priori studies may weight factors in such a way that points correlate less strongly with employers' actual pay practices than is the case for policy-capturing evaluations. (See Chapter 4 for a discussion of a priori and policy-capturing approaches to job evaluation.) In principle, the policy-capturing approach is better suited to identify the employer's actual compensation policies, and to see if sex discrimination is among these. This is true whether it is the employer's own job evaluation or one done by plaintiffs for trial. If policy-capturing studies show a systematic deviation between the pay for male and female jobs with equivalent total points, this is evidence that male and female jobs are being treated differently because of their sex composition. (Clauss 1986 also argues that policy-capturing job evaluations should be probative for disparate treatment proofs in comparable worth cases.)

There are three ways that a policy-capturing regression analysis could show female jobs to be systematically underpaid absent explicit differential treatment by the employer: One possibility is that female jobs were systematically given more points than they warrant (relative to male jobs). The evidence reviewed in the last chapter suggests that, if evaluators are biased, they are more likely to underrate than overrate female jobs. Nonetheless, a plaintiff performing a job evaluation for trial based on job descriptions obtained from the employer in the discovery period of the litigation would need to be careful to use experts whose neutrality was believable to the courts to rate the jobs. In the case where the employer had done such ratings, they would presumably not be suspected of overrating female jobs.

A second possibility is what statisticians call omitted variable bias. Suppose that plaintiff's analysis excluded a factor that, in fact, is correlated with jobs' sex composition, and upon inclusion this factor could be shown statistically to explain all of the putative underpayment of the female jobs. This is the sort of rebuttal by defendants of plaintiffs' prima facie cases that I believe the courts *should* allow in comparable worth cases. Rather, what the courts have been doing is considering the job evaluation statistics to be irrelevant.

A third possible factor other than the *employer's* explicit differential treatment could explain why a policy-capturing job evaluation would show a systematic tendency to underpay female jobs. This is the possibility at issue in the market wage argument. Perhaps the employer has no policy other than to pay prevailing wage rates in each job, and what we are revealing by the policy-capturing analysis is the policy of the aggregation of all employers into market wages rather than deliberate policies of this particular employer. If this is possible, should following market wages be viewed as a nondiscriminatory act? Since this argument is being given so much deference by the courts, and is the principal reason comparable worth is not succeeding in the courts, I need to address how I believe that this issue should be treated in a way that is consistent with the spirit of Title VII and social science evidence.

First, we must distinguish between accepting the limited notion that employers must take market wages into account from the more extreme position that market wages are, in the long run, nondiscriminatory. In its most orthodox form, the neoclassical view asserts both. However, the former is the more reasonable view. The fact that employers are affected by market wages does not imply that market wages are nondiscriminatory, even in the long run. My theoretical reasons for disagreeing with the neoclassical assertion that discrimination will necessarily erode in competitive markets were discussed in Chapter 2. Moreover, Chapters 1 and 3 presented empirical evidence of discrimination in the pay of female jobs from my analysis and other studies. The failure of markets to pay predominantly female jobs commensurate with their skill demands and working conditions must be explained by either crowding and/or discriminatory devaluation of jobs because they are done by women. I argued in Chapter 2 that it is inconsistent to acknowledge the type of sex discrimination in hiring that produces crowding while presuming that discrimination does not also directly affect decisions about the relative pay of jobs. Thus, I argued that the lower average market wages in female jobs (relative to what policy-capturing job evaluation predicts) cannot be explained entirely by crowding, but are also indicative that the average employer has let the sex composition of jobs affect its pay in a discriminatory manner. This discrimination produces lower market wages in female jobs than can be explained by policy-capturing job evaluation studies that otherwise explain employers' pay policies *and* overall market wages remarkably well.

Should the courts consider it lawful under Title VII to follow market wages, given that social scientific evidence suggests that to do so will be to perpetuate the discriminatorily low pay assigned to female jobs? In one sense the issue is whether each individual employer should be able to use discriminatory market wages as an excuse for its own wage-setting practices. There may be some employers who just blindly follow market wages without having consciously treated men's and women's jobs with inconsistent criteria. However, it is unlikely that every employer is doing this or the discriminatory differentials would not have come into being in the first place. Allowing market wages as a defense is tantamount to considering "everybody else is doing it" a valid defense.

If this defense is allowed, then Title VII is powerless to alter the great bulk of this kind of sex discrimination. This does not seem to me to be consistent with the spirit of Title VII.

Still, the courts, following neoclassical economists, have some point when they urge that we do not want to give up all of the benefits of the market wage system in providing signals and incentives about shortages and gluts. For example, if efficient production in response to consumer demand requires an increase in engineers and not enough people are receiving an education to fill this demand at the going wage, the wage will go up according to supply and demand. This will (with some lag time) motivate more people to go into engineering. This decentralized mechanism of equilibration is the great benefit of market wage systems. Their tendency to perpetuate discriminatory wage differentials that originated out of sex bias is a great disadvantage of market wage systems. The dilemma, then, is how the courts, in applying Title VII, could reach decisions that preserve much of the first function but eliminate much of the second. Another way to put the question is to ask how we can know when a deviation between a job's wage and the wage predicted by a policy-capturing job evaluation is indicative of a shortage or glut, and when it is indicative of discrimination. Economic theory tells us that, absent discrimination, shortages and gluts are the short-run determinants of wages whereas human capital requirements and compensating differentials are the long-run determinants. Thus, I take the fact that a systematic underpayment of female jobs vis-à-vis their skill demands and working conditions has been consistently found *over several decades* as evidence that the issue is not simply a temporary shortage in most male fields or a glut in most female fields. (See Chapter 1 for a review of these studies.) I suggest that the courts could use the distinction between short-term versus long-term differentials as a criterion as well, allowing market wages as a defense only when they affect only a short-term deviation from the wages predicted by job evaluation.

I propose, then, that statistical evidence of systematic underpayment of female jobs from a policy-capturing job evaluation be able to make plaintiffs' prima facie case. The case would then hinge upon whether the out-of-line wages appear to be a temporary response to a glut or shortage. If the employer has generally paid the female jobs in question commensurate with the compensable factors it is otherwise using consistently, but has deviated from this because of a temporary glut or shortage, then the defendant's behavior would be lawful because the market differential would be presumed nondiscriminatory. If however, the deviation had consistently been there for a number of years, unlawful discrimination would be presumed in the market wage and in the employer's policy of following market wages.

I have left aside the question of whether this should proceed under a disparate treatment or disparate impact doctrine and of what burden of proof employers should bear. Let me now address these issues. Statistical evidence from a policy-capturing job evaluation finding systematic underpayment of female jobs demonstrates that the employer is *either* simply following discriminatory market wages *or* that the employer's own devaluation of female jobs explains the underpayment, or some combination of the two. The first seems to call for plaintiffs to use disparate impact analysis, and the second for disparate treatment analysis. The statistics alone do not allow us to assess which is the case. When combined with anecdotal evidence of sexist devaluation affecting decisions about how much jobs should pay, job evaluation statistics should constitute evidence of differential treatment of male and female jobs. This should make a prima facie case in a treatment case. The anecdotal evidence would be evidence that the employer's own devaluation was part of the picture, that the employer did not simply follow market wages.

Where plaintiffs present only the statistical evidence, it is possible that the employer did not intend to discriminate but simply followed market wages. Thus, given only statistical evidence, it might be reasonable for the courts to accept such evidence as proof only under the disparate impact doctrine. I do not believe the courts should disallow disparate impact analysis for comparable worth cases. When plaintiffs have made a prima facie case under the disparate impact theory, courts should shift the burden of proof to defendants to show that there was a business necessity for their decision to follow market wages. Here, the precedent developed under Equal Pay Act cases should prevail. Under the Equal Pay Act, where cases involve men and women doing substantially equal work, the notion that being forced to pay higher wages would cost the employer more has not been permitted as a legitimate business defense. The same should hold in a comparable worth case. Also, the "factor other than sex" should not be interpreted to include market wages when social science evidence suggests so persuasively that market wages are systematically discriminatory by sex. However, as I argued above, defendants should be able to meet their burden by showing that this is a *temporary* deviation in their policy, following market wages that are themselves temporarily elevated or depressed. The temporariness of the deviation would be taken as evidence that the market differential was caused by a glut or shortage rather than discrimination. In addition, if the differential relates to compensating differentials or human capital requirements, defendants should prevail if they show that adding compensable factors measuring factors that were omitted from the plaintiff's analysis in fact explains the differentials.

How does this suggested allocation of burdens deal with the argument that employers are price-takers and will be disadvantaged vis-à-vis
other employers if they have to pay above-market wages? If the courts
were to assess the burdens in the way I have suggested is compatible
with social science evidence and the broad spirit of Title VII, no employer would be disadvantaged vis-à-vis any other, because they would
all be simultaneously required to stop following discriminatory market
wage differentials. As a practical matter, some employers might be affected before others, creating temporary disadvantages, but this is no
different than in other areas of the law. For example, the first employers
to be sued after the courts instituted these precedents would be temporarily disadvantaged vis-à-vis other employers against whom lawsuits
had not been filed. But this is no different that what initially occurred
under the Equal Pay Act, where those employers illegally paying wom-
en less than men for the same work were advantaged in profits vis-à-vis
employers who had already been forced by litigation to pay women
equally.

If the courts were to follow my proposals, employers who use some
form of job evaluation consistently to pay male and female jobs would
be at less risk of legal liability, and thus employers who currently do not
use formal job evaluation might feel pressured to do so. This does impose costs on employers. However, this is no different than other areas
of Title VII law, which have imposed costs on employers to use systematic hiring criteria as a protection against possible litigation.

My formulation of the issue, by advocating policy-capturing job evaluation to meet plaintiff's burden of proof, avoids the criticism that jobs
do not have an "intrinsic worth" outside the market, and that comparable worth is trying to mandate payment according to some mythical
intrinsic worth. Policy-capturing job evaluation does not evaluate the
intrinsic worth of jobs. It simply reveals what standards of evaluation
are implicit in the employer's own pay system. There is thus no request
that courts decide what the intrinsic worth of any job is, and no requirement that employers follow any particular formula in translating job
characteristics into pay.

The legal interpretations I have suggested would accomplish something I presume to be in the spirit of Title VII—a mechanism for ridding
the economy of the systematic undervaluation of jobs simply because
they are filled by women. But this is not the road the courts have taken.

However, it is important to note that even if all the positions I have
advocated were adopted by courts, it would not be a panacea for ridding
the economy of the sort of discrimination at issue in comparable worth.
The positions I have advocated merely require that employers use some
set of compensable factors *consistently* to allocate pay to male and female

jobs, i.e., that there not be a direct effect of jobs' sex composition on their pay. Demonstrations of violations of this would be evidence of unlawfulness except where explained by temporary shortages or gluts. However, the formulations I have advocated for the courts would not allow a remedy under Title VII for what I called "indirect sex bias," in which some compensable factors have low or negative weights (net of sex composition) because of the historic association of these types of skills with women's work. An example of this is the deprecation of nurturant social skills found in the analysis in Chapter 3. Another example would be giving the kinds of stress and discomfort common to women's jobs (e.g., exposure to human feces, or to angry clients or customers) less weight as onerous working conditions than the kinds of stress and discomfort common to men's jobs (e.g., exposure to grease or heavy lifting). It would be better for plaintiffs if they could also challenge the weights of defendant's job evaluations as having a disparate impact under Title VII. However, while I firmly believe that the weights of various factors *do* reflect sex bias, I believe it difficult to find a remedy for this *within* Title VII precedents. As discussed in Chapter 4, there is no clear way to know *when* weights in a job evaluation are discriminatory, or when they just happen to disadvantage women. There is no obvious touchstone here that is analogous to the decision in hiring cases that a credential used for screening is legitimate despite a disparate impact when it yields workers who perform better.

Given this, if the precedents I have advocated here were adopted, it would unfortunately give employers an incentive to work backwards from their existing pay scales to find those characteristics of jobs that, when labeled "compensable factors," best explain existing differentials between male and female jobs. Thus, early cases might win more for plaintiffs than later cases when existing market differentials had been embodied into defendants' job evaluation systems. Despite this pessimistic caveat, the precedents I have recommended here would be much more favorable to plaintiffs than the way the circuit courts are currently interpreting Title VII.

VII. Social and Political Factors Affecting Court Decisions

Despite the opening provided by *Gunther*, it has been virtually impossible for plaintiffs to prevail in comparable worth cases under Title VII except when they have written or spoken evidence of intent to discriminate that is of a smoking gun variety. Above I have considered the legal reasoning used by the courts in making it difficult for plaintiffs to prevail, and have given my own critique of this reasoning within the confines of existing legal principles. But, of course, few people believe that judges are only influenced by legal reasoning in coming to their decisions. Their decisions are often affected by their own political leanings and by political and social trends. In this section, I broaden the inquiry and discuss the features of the social and political climate that I believe have most importantly affected the conservative treatment of comparable worth in the federal courts.

One factor is the court's nervousness about comparable worth because it is a new concept, which, if accepted, calls for sweeping change. The evidence in Chapter 3 and my review of prior research in Chapter 1 suggests that this kind of discrimination is pervasive. Thus, to admit its existence is to admit a need for a large amount of change. Also, courts may regard it as a more serious intrusion into private enterprise to tell employers that the pay levels of many of their jobs are discriminatory than to tell them that certain hiring criteria are discriminatory.

The courts' nervousness about comparable worth can be seen in the inconsistent way courts have treated this compared to other types of discrimination. For example, circuit courts have yet to permit disparate impact analysis in comparable worth cases, while they have permitted it in all other types of race and sex discrimination cases, and even in sex-based wage discrimination cases involving issues other than comparable worth.

However, the newness and pervasiveness of the discrimination cannot be the only factors in the courts' conservatism about comparable worth. After all, hiring discrimination by race and sex was extremely pervasive when Title VII cases first started, and that did not stop courts from making decisions with potentially sweeping implications. Nor are the statistical analyses involved in job evaluation more complex than those involved in some hiring and promotion cases.

What other factors might explain the unreceptiveness of the courts to comparable worth? One such factor is the changing composition of the courts. Part of the reason that decisions in many areas of the law—not just comparable worth—are more conservative than a decade ago is that many conservative judges have been appointed since 1980. Today, over half of federal district court judges throughout the nation were appointed by presidents Reagan and Bush (Pinzler and Ellis 1989). Most of the appointees have been conservative Republicans. Since 1980, presidents Reagan and Bush have also made five appointments to the Supreme Court (justices O'Connor, Scalia, Kennedy, Souter, and Thomas), and many appointments to circuit courts. The shifts in criteria being used in cases are less surprising when one realizes the compositional changes that have occurred. For example, the decision in *Wards Cove* that relieved defendants of burden of proof after disparate impact is shown is a reversal of parts of *Griggs*. It probably would not have been decided in the same way by the group of justices that voted on *Griggs*. The general trend has been to limit discrimination cases to those where an identifiable individual was discriminated against by an identifiable employer with an identifiable action that had a clear discriminatory intent. The trend in the courts and federal agencies such as the Equal Employment Opportunity Commission (EEOC), which brings some Title VII cases to court on behalf of plaintiffs, is toward less sympathy toward class action cases or other cases that allow group remedies. Remedies that give preferential treatment toward women or minorities to make up for past unfair group treatment are less likely to be required or allowed by the courts than formerly. All this has made the climate more difficult for using the courts to remove discrimination from the economy.

VIII. Conclusion

Since the *Gunther* case of 1981 it is clear that plaintiffs can bring cases alleging sex-based wage discrimination under Title VII even when the cases involve unequal jobs. But the burdens of proof required in such cases have not been addressed by the Supreme Court directly. This chapter reviewed what circuit courts have established about burdens of proof, and criticized these decisions.

What kinds of proof of wage discrimination can plaintiffs successfully offer in comparable worth cases? Under the disparate treatment theory, plaintiffs have the burden to prove intentional discrimination. Smoking gun proofs in which employers state that wages in a job were set on the basis of the sex of those in the job will be sufficient. But in other areas of Title VII law, plaintiffs have prevailed under the disparate treatment theory without smoking guns; circumstantial proofs, including statistical proofs, have been allowed. I argued that results from a policy-capturing job evaluation showing that female jobs pay less than comparable male jobs should suffice as a proof of disparate treatment. Employers should be able to prevail if their defense shows that a compensable factor that they used consistently in compensating male and female jobs was omitted from the plaintiff's analysis, and that, when added to the analysis, this factor explains the allegedly discriminatory gap between the pay of male and female jobs. However, the circuit courts have not allowed such proofs to suffice, even in combination with anecdotal evidence that the sex of incumbents affected the wages set in various jobs.

The other proof traditionally allowed plaintiffs in Title VII suits is a showing of disparate impact. In principle, use of the disparate impact model may be available in comparable worth suits as well, but none have been successful to date. Courts have explicitly rejected challenges to following market wages under the disparate impact theory.

Employers in comparable worth cases have prevailed in several circuits with the claim that they follow market wages. Although, in the 1970s, the Supreme Court disallowed market wage defenses in Equal Pay Act cases involving substantially equal work, I suspect that they would uphold this as a defense now, given the more conservative Court on the bench now and the circuit courts' discomfort with comparable worth. I argued that the market wage defense should not be permitted when the employer is perpetuating a market wage difference between comparable men's and women's jobs that is itself discriminatory, but that the defense should be allowed when a male job pays more than a comparable female job because of a *temporary* shortage or glut of labor in one job. I suggested that these two situations could be distinguished on the basis of whether the deviation from the usual compensable criteria for jobs' pay is temporary or long-term.

One might summarize the situation by saying that *Gunther* opened the door to comparable worth cases a bit, but circuit courts have prevented any but the most blatant smoking gun proofs of disparate treatment from passing through this narrow space. Plaintiffs have tried to open the door farther by using job evaluations or by arguing that following discriminatory market wages should be illegal. Both of these claims have been rejected. It is clear that, absent new legislation, the federal courts will not be effective vehicles for ending the wage discrimination of the sort at issue in comparable worth in the coming decades.

Notes

1. I am using the term *comparable worth case* differently than some commentators, including the Supreme Court in its opinion in *County of Washington, Oregon v. Gunther* (U.S. Supreme Court 1981). Although Gunther opened the door to such cases, the Supreme Court did not call it a comparable worth case. The majority opinion stated, "Respondents' claim is not based on the controversial concept of 'comparable worth,' under which plaintiffs might claim increased compensation on the basis of a comparison of the intrinsic worth or difficulty of their job with that of other jobs in the same organization or community. Rather respondents seek to prove, by direct evidence, that their wages were depressed because of intentional sex discrimination . . ." (pp. 3–4).

2. Readers should notice the date on each article, however, since several aspects of comparable worth law have been affected by court decisions after some of these pieces were written.

3.   The Constitution does not protect persons from discrimination by private employers. However, in some cases its Equal Protection Clause (in the Fourteenth Amendment) has been found to prohibit sex discrimination in state action, i.e., in the laws or actions of governments, whether local, state, or federal. Such laws or actions may involve employment or other matters. However, unlike in Title VII cases, in Constitutional cases the disparate impact model may not be used. Rather, intentional discrimination must be shown. Furthermore, the Supreme Court has not seen sex discrimination in state action as violating the Fourteenth Amendment as consistently as it has seen race discrimination in state action as a violation. This is why adding an Equal Rights Amendment to the U.S. Constitution would not be entirely redundant to the Equal Protection Clause.

4.   Despite this victory for the defendant, shortly after the Ninth Circuit's decision, the state entered into an out-of-court agreement with plaintiffs to raise pay in female jobs. This settlement prevented plaintiffs from appealing the case to the Supreme Court.

5.   Laycock (1986a) argues that the Supreme Court's decision in *City of Los Angeles v. Manhart*, 9th Circuit, 1978 precludes disparate impact analysis in cases regarding sex discrimination in compensation. The court did not say this explicitly, however.

6.   The decision to omit a compensable factor is merely a special case of a decision about the weight of factors where the factor is given a weight of 0.

6

Feminism and Other Philosophical Positions

I. Introduction

One can be either for or against comparable worth as a basis for wage setting. Taking a position on the matter hinges on both positive and normative beliefs. Positive statements are those that purport to describe or explain what "is," while normative statements make moral or ethical claims about what "should" or "ought" to be the case. Critics of positivism as a philosophy of science point out that positive theories are often influenced by normative values. Positive views influence normative contentions as well. This is sometimes summarized by the phrase "ought implies can," which refers to the belief that one needs to believe that social arrangements are possible in order to advocate them as right. Despite these relationships between normative and positive claims, one can draw a distinction, if not a bright red line, between the two types of claims. In previous chapters I have focused on positive issues, discussing evidence and theories that explain how labor markets work and why predominantly female occupations pay badly. This chapter focuses on normative issues. Since the discussion of normative issues is most explicit within philosophy, I explore positions in social, economic, and political philosophy for their normative implications regarding comparable worth.

Recent feminist scholarship claims that past writings in every field have been biased by seeing things from a perspective more consistent with men's than women's experience, by glorifying the roles and traits traditionally associated with males, by deprecating the roles and traits associated with females, and by a failure to consider gender inequality and its sources. Thus, as I discuss broad theoretical positions, I will also discuss the criticisms and new formulations feminists have suggested.

The positions to be considered are patriarchal views, the libertarian,

253

laissez-faire economic, and egalitarian strands of liberalism, liberal feminism, Marxism, socialist feminism, and radical and cultural feminism.

II.   Patriarchal Views

One can trace a view of gender that I will call "patriarchal" through the history of Western culture. This is not a monolithic view, since I am collapsing over 2000 years of history into one short discussion. Yet, enough common themes are present to make it useful to discuss the view under one heading. Prior to the eighteenth century, largely as a result of Aristotle's influence, women were viewed as patterned on the same model as men, but inferior versions; they were seen as "deficient men" (Tuana forthcoming; 1992). The second view, more common beginning in the eighteenth century, was that women and men are completely different but complementary. However, implicitly if not explicitly, these views see the characteristics they attribute to men to be superior (Tuana forthcoming 1992). Patriarchal views generally see differences in men and women's roles and characteristics as innate and relatively immutable. Women's role in reproduction and nurturing is often seen as the key to all aspects of their inferiority. Given women's inferiority, it is seen as right and just that men have authority over women; this is the sense in which the views advocate patriarchy. This view is articulated in many scientific, religious, and philosophical writings from Aristotle into the twentieth century (Tuana forthcoming). Below, I examine older and newer versions of both religious and secular patriarchal views.

A.   Patriarchal Views Based on Religion

Judeo-Christian creation stories exemplify the deprecation of women (Phillips 1984; Pagels 1988). One might expect that the creativity involved in gestating a life and giving birth would lead theologians to envision female creators and to revere women. This was true in some ancient religions that featured female or both male and female gods creating through natural bodily processes (Sanday 1981; Lerner 1986; Tuana forthcoming). In contrast, the creation stories in the Judeo-Christian tradition cut women out of creation, positing a male God who created through a supernatural, nonbodily process.

Contemporary heirs to patriarchal views of gender based on religion are most visible among Christian fundamentalists. Some patriarchal ideas remain in the doctrines of many "mainstream" denominations as well, although in practice they are less emphasized and even contested. Political expressions of this view are found under the umbrella of the "New Christian Right" (Klatch 1987) in organizations such as the Moral Majority (led by Jerry Falwell) and the Eagle Forum (led by Phyllis Schlafly). The notion that women are inferior to men is undergirded by an interpretation of the Bible that says that women were created by God to be helpers to men, that women's sexuality caused the spiritual downfall of man, and that women should be as obedient to men as the church is to Christ (Daly 1968; Phillips 1984; Pagels 1988). To be sure, many religious writings talk of men and women and their complementary roles as equal in the eyes of God. However, this egalitarianism is undercut by other parts of the view, which see men as more God-like than women (Tuana forthcoming).

What position does patriarchal thinking, based on religion, imply for comparable worth? Writers of the New Christian Right have argued vehemently against comparable worth (Schlafly 1984). But their arguments do not emphasize the question of whether traditionally female jobs should pay more compared to traditionally male jobs. Rather they argue that job segregation results, not from discrimination, but from innate sex differences in preferences, abilities, and childrearing roles. Thus, they do not see the wage gap as discriminatory. But this sidesteps the central question of comparable worth: whether women's jobs are undervalued relative to men's jobs.

Most versions of comparable worth would elevate the pay of jobs expressing the traditionally female value of nurturing and caring. Thus comparable worth can be seen to advance nurturant values that religious thinkers explicitly value. Women's nurturing is explicitly revered by those of the New Christian Right, and liberal feminists are chastised for deprecating the importance of this role (Klatch 1987). Thus, why would religious fundamentalists oppose comparable worth, which would increase the value, or at least the pay, given to jobs involving nurturing? In part it is an opposition to commercializing nurturing via comparable worth wages (Flick 1983). Women of the New Christian Right think that women's nurturing work in the home is valuable, but should be done altruistically, for love and not money (Klatch 1987). Moreover, members of the New Christian Right contend that it is better for mothers not to work outside the home at all. Thus, I have the impression, although they do not make it explicit, that an underlying objection to comparable worth is that higher wages in women's jobs would make it more possible for women to create marriages with egalitarian power relations, or to live without men as childless heterosexual "singles," as lesbians, or as single parents. Another objection is that increased wages for women are seen to undercut men's obligation to support wives as homemakers (Klatch 1987).

B.   Secular Patriarchal Views

Secular views have emphasized rationality, rather than godliness, as that which makes humans valuable and superior to other animals, and that which distinguishes men from women. The early Greek (as well as Judeo-Christian) metaphysical outlook glorified the mental and spiritual and deprecated physicality and emotion. Underlying this view is the assumption that our unchanging mind or spirit is superior to our changeable bodies. Men's spirit is seen as what makes them valuable and distinguishes them from animals. But women are seen to have less spirit or reason than men. Where Greek philosophers had tied spirit and rationality together, the eighteenth-century Enlightenment view narrowed the focus to rationality, but included philosophy, religion, ethics, and the other humanities, as well as science, in the purview of reason. Positivistic science, one heir to the Enlightenment, narrowed the focus still further, excluding nonscientific disciplines from the "highest" realm of reason. Early proponents of all these views saw women as less rational than men; this was an aspect of women's inferiority.

The secular version of patriarchal thinking most prominent today is sociobiology, which includes an evolutionary theory of parental investments (Barash 1977, 1979; Van Den Berge and Barash 1977; Wilson 1978). To understand this theory, one needs to remember two things: (1) To pass on one's genes, one needs to produce offspring, some of whom live long enough to reproduce, and (2) some genes are sex-specific. The theory claims that via evolution men who are dominant and promiscuous are especially likely to pass on their genes, since dominance increases chances of copulation, and promiscuous copulation increases one's number of offspring. The theory holds that females are more likely to pass on their genes if they are nurturant and seek mates who are aggressive providers. The nine months required for pregnancy means that frequent intercourse will not appreciably increase the number of births. Thus, for women, a strategy more likely to increase the number of one's offspring who reproduce is to nurture those already alive to make sure they survive. In short, it takes men less energy to sire a new child than to ensure the survival of an already-born child, whereas for women, given the long gestation period, the opposite may be true. The theory does not hold that people *care* about passing on their genes, but merely that the genetic character of those who produced surviving offspring has determined the genetic predisposition of today's humans. In sum, these sociobiologists believe that men are genetically predisposed to be dominant and promiscuous and women to be nurturant and monogamous. (For a critique of sociobiologists' arguments about sex differences, see Bleier 1984).

In this secular version of patriarchal thinking, it is not men's spiritual authority, but rather their aggressiveness, promiscuity, and technical prowess that explains the inevitability of patriarchy. In the secular view, patriarchy is not normatively endorsed as a positive good. But "ought" is a moot point unless we think a particular set of arrangements is possible. Thus, since secular patriarchal views see egalitarian relations between men and women as impossible, they argue against challenges to patriarchy on the basis of the impossibility of changing it rather than on the basis of a clear normative claim that it is best.

Philosopher Michael Levin (1984, 1987) has used sociobiologists' arguments about sex differences as a basis for arguing against feminist proposals. He sees it as natural and inevitable that women will nurture children and men will be aggressive breadwinners. However, his arguments against comparable worth are borrowed from the laissez-faire tradition of classical liberalism to be discussed below; he does not defend the greater rewards given to men's than women's jobs on the basis of sociobiology. Thus, like the religious patriarchalists, he seems most interested in convincing the reader that it is natural for women to be at home or in less-demanding jobs.

In sum, religious and secular patriarchal views agree on two things: Sex differences are largely innate, and it is either unwise or impossible to change gender inequality in any way, including through comparable worth. The two views have very different ideas of what characteristics are innate to men, but they agree that any attempt to diminish sex differentiation is futile or will lead to problems.

III. Liberalism and Liberal Feminism

Liberalism occupies most of the political spectrum in the contemporary United States. Liberalism is concerned with questions about the relations of individuals to each other and to the state. The liberal tradition spans from John Locke's [1698] (1967) treatises in the seventeenth century through Adam Smith [1776] (1930) in the eighteenth century, John Stuart Mill [1859] (1975) in the nineteenth century, and into the twentieth century. All liberals emphasize the rights of individuals, but they differ in whether they see these rights as primarily held against the state or against other individuals or societal institutions, and in whether they see rights as consisting of a negative freedom *from* particular constraints or freedom *to* certain positive opportunities. The libertarian and laissez-faire strands of liberalism emphasize liberty as negative freedom from interference by the state. This strand is exemplified by twentieth-century writers such as Berlin (1958), Hayek (1960), and Nozick (1974). The egalitarian strand of liberalism emphasizes rights of individuals to equal opportunities and sees these rights as made possible through state action that removes institutional barriers to equality of opportunity constructed by individuals, groups, or societal institutions. This strand is exemplified by twentieth-century writers such as Hobhouse (1911), Green (1941), Rawls (1971), Dworkin (1977), and Ackerman (1980).

I begin by discussing ideas common to all strands of liberalism. Liberals believe that rationality is what is distinctive and especially valuable about humans (Jaggar 1983). This belief is not distinctive to liberalism, but is shared with Western thinkers from the Greeks forward (Schott 1988).

Liberalism is individualist insofar as it sees rights as accruing to individuals (Gray 1986). All versions of liberalism see limits on what governments can rightfully require of individuals; they also see, as a function of government, limiting what individuals can rightfully do to each other (Gray 1986). The notions of limits on government upon which most liberals have agreed include advocacy of constitutional rather than monarchical government, freedom of association and movement, procedural rights to due process, and rights to private property (Sandel 1984; Gray 1986). Given that individuals differ in their notions of the good, the allegiance to individual rights leads liberals to advocate rights of people to engage in behavior that these liberals consider unethical, as long as such behavior is not an infringement on others' fundamental rights (Sandel 1984). Thus, there is a distinction between the "good" and the more limited concept of "justice," the term liberals use to denote a system in which the state upholds fundamental individual rights. Liberals believe that the state's mandate is to uphold justice, not the good.

Liberals have grounded their notions of rights and justice in various things. Locke [1698] (1967) saw natural rights of individuals as part of God-given natural law. Some liberals still advocate natural rights, with or without the theology attached. In the nineteenth century, the utilitarian strain of liberalism emerged with Adam Smith [1776] (1930) and John Stuart Mill [1859] (1975). They believed that the sum of individuals' utilities is greater if the state does not abrogate individuals' liberty and if the state prevents individuals or social institutions from doing so. Still other liberals have grounded rights in Kant's [1797] (1964) notion that persons should only be treated as ends, never as means, because it is their nature to control their destiny rather than to be controlled (Gray 1986).

A.   Laissez-Faire Economics and Libertarianism

Over time, liberalism has split into two major camps. One camp emphasizes individual rights against the state, and thus opposes state action. These liberals see rights as being negative—freedom *from* interference—rather than positive rights to specific opportunities. In this camp are laissez-faire economists, who oppose state regulation of the economy, and libertarians, who oppose most all state action, whether pertaining to the economy or not. The second camp emphasizes rights to *equality* of opportunity or treatment. It is this second camp that is now called liberal in popular discourse, while the former camp is now called conservative. Both, however, are descendants of classical liberalism. I discuss the conservative strands of classical liberalism in this section, and the egalitarian strand in the next.

Libertarianism extends the notion that the state should not interfere in private affairs beyond the economy into areas of civil liberties such as the family, sexual behavior, and speech.[1] Libertarians believe that the state should do virtually nothing except uphold property rights, enforce contracts, and protect individuals' rights to be free from physical assault. Since libertarians want a very limited state, they obviously oppose laws prohibiting discrimination in employment or any other regulation of employment contracts. This would include opposition to the Equal Pay Act and Title VII, whether interpreted to include comparable worth or not, and to any new legislation mandating wages based on the principle of comparable worth.

This liberal impulse to limit state action in the economy developed from the combination of utilitarianism and the marginal revolution (Blaug 1978, pp. 309–342) that led to neoclassical economics. Although neoclassical economics purports to be a positive rather than normative paradigm, it has strong normative leanings. As an example, consider the neoclassical notion of Pareto-optimality, discussed in Chapter 2, which defines efficiency without making interpersonal utility comparisons. In their positive theory, economists take as given some initial distribution of property, goods, and services. By assuming that individuals seek to maximize utility, economists conclude that any two persons who can make themselves better off by an exchange will do so. Economists define an exchange as leading to a Pareto-superior distribution if both parties view themselves as better off after than before the exchange. It follows that if governments do nothing to prohibit exchange or to redistribute resources, a succession of sequentially Pareto-superior moves will occur, leading to a Pareto-optimal distribution. Efficiency is defined in terms of such Pareto-optimality. Using this criterion, redistribution by the state can never improve efficiency, since it is not mutually voluntary exchange. The conclusion that state redistribution cannot increase efficiency also flows from the fact that neoclassical theory sees interpersonal utility comparisons to be impossible. Consider the seemingly uncontroversial assertion that the aggregate amount of utility, and hence efficiency, is increased when the state redistributes the last thousand of a millionaire's dollars to a starving indigent. This assertion rests upon a commonsense interpersonal utility comparison that asserts that the indigent gains more utility from a first thousand dollars than the millionaire gains from an additional thousand. But interpersonal utility comparisons, by assumption, play no part in neoclassical efficiency calculations. This assumption in the positive theory creates strong normative leanings against governmental redistribution and in favor of markets unconstrained by governmental intervention except to enforce explicit contracts and maintain property rights.

How does this apply to comparable worth? In the laissez-faire view, the state should not interfere with an employer's right to pay persons in predominantly female occupations an amount they are willing to accept. Nor should it interfere with a potential employee's right to prefer a badly paying job to no job at all, a trade-off that might exist if forcing employers to pay more in female jobs led them to hire fewer workers in the jobs. Comparable worth is seen to prohibit some exchanges that would move the system toward Pareto-optimality.

Despite these laissez-faire implications of neoclassical theory, there is a range of opinion among neoclassical economists about how much governmental intervention into the economy is warranted. Today most labor economists advocate laws against hiring discrimination, yet they do not advocate governmental action to require that wages meet comparable worth standards. (See, for example, Killingsworth 1984; O'Neill 1984; Polachek 1984.) An exception is Bergmann (1985, 1986, 1989), who sees comparable worth as an antidote to the low wages in female occupations that she sees resulting from hiring discrimination in male occupations leading to crowding and, hence, low wages in female occupations. The opposition of economists to comparable worth is more consistent with the normative leanings of neoclassical theory than is the advocacy by these same people of laws against hiring discrimination. When neoclassical economists advocate laws against hiring discrimination they are stepping outside the neoclassical paradigm and inserting a notion of equity that cannot be found within the efficiency criterion of Pareto-optimality. Thus, to be consistent, when they oppose comparable worth, it cannot be just a result of the paradigm's hostility to governmental intervention, or they would oppose laws against hiring discrimination as well. The reasons for opposing comparable worth have more to do with their positive belief that if there is discrimination at all it must take the form of barriers to entry (i.e., hiring discrimination), and that requiring comparable worth wages would create disemployment that laws against hiring discrimination do not. (These positive claims were explored in Chapter 2.)

B. *The Egalitarian Strand of Classical Liberalism and Liberal Feminism*

Egalitarian Liberalism. Another strand of liberalism has stressed *equality*, in contrast to the emphasis upon individuals' freedom from governmental regulation discussed above. The emphasis in egalitarian liberalism has generally been on equality under the law, equality of opportunity, or equality of treatment, *not* on equality of outcomes. That is, inequalities of income, power, or wealth are accepted by most egalitarian liberals as long as opportunities to ascend these hierarchies are reasonably equal, and as long as the state and other institutions treat all individuals by the same standards (Brenner 1987). Liberals have opposed state-mandated inequalities of opportunity, such as laws limiting access to voting, education, or jobs by race, sex, ethnicity, or property. In this opposition, they have agreed with the laissez-faire and libertarian strands of classical liberalism, including the feminists within these traditions.

Egalitarian liberals have also argued that the state should act to increase equality of opportunity through such things as public schools and universities (so not only the affluent have opportunities for education) and through laws against discrimination by race or sex in employment and other economic transactions. These reforms require state action and regulation that is counter to the laissez-faire or libertarian brands of classical liberalism. In this view, liberty is a right *to* certain basic opportunities, not simply a right to be free from interference. Indeed, such a positive notion of rights *creates* what libertarians would categorize as interference. For example, public education requires that individuals be made to pay taxes to support schools for others' children. Antidiscrimination laws also require taxes for enforcement costs. In addition, they tell employers that they do not have the right to hire whomever they please, that they may not make employment decisions based on race or sex. Thus, the laissez-faire and libertarian strands of classical liberalism conflict with the egalitarian strand over issues of whether the state should intervene to create equalities of opportunity and treatment.

Liberal Feminism. Liberalism has been both friend and foe to women. Early liberal feminists, such as Mary Wollstonecraft [1792] (1975) accepted the belief of some early liberals that rationality is the criterion of natural rights as well as the means of discerning such rights (Donovan 1985, Chapter 1). But where the male writers had generally excluded women from these natural rights because they saw them as less rational than men, feminists such as Wollstonecraft argued that men and women are fundamentally equal in the potential for rationality. Just as Locke [1698] (1967) had argued that men do not need to obey a monarch because men are rational, Wollstonecraft urged that women do not need to obey the authority of men, because women too are rational. Early liberal feminists fought for equal rights under the law for women. These included the right to own property, make contracts, and vote, a right American suffragists achieved in 1919.

Scientific work that challenges claims about innate sex differences is often drawn upon by liberal feminists to buttress their position that women are capable of taking advantage of the same opportunities as men:

First, for example, liberal feminists can point to reviews of psychological evidence that conclude that many alleged sex differences in behavior are illusory (Maccoby and Jacklin 1974; Epstein 1988; but see critique of Maccoby and Jacklin by Block 1976). To the extent that behavioral differences are nonexistent, the question of whether they are innate is moot.

Second, some argue that scientists, because of their sexist biases, have often jumped from inadequate evidence to the conclusion that behavioral differences are innate (Bleier 1984; Fausto-Sterling 1985). The evolutionary theory of parental investment from sociobiology, discussed above, can be attacked this way. Rather than argue that evolutionary theory predicts that aggressiveness is genetically selected for in men because it allows them to compete for women, one could argue that the theory could equally well predict that aggressiveness would be selected for in women because it enables them to defend their young. Given this second prediction from the theory, if we observe that men are more aggressive than women, then the explanation must be social.

Third, feminists have argued that even if sex differences are partly innate, this does not imply a normative conclusion that we should assign roles on the basis of these differences. For example, if men innately had worse eyes than women, we would hardly conclude that women should hold all jobs requiring reading. We would probably decide we should provide men with glasses, despite the costs of doing so.

Fourth, feminists point out that what we call "sex differences," whatever their cause, are differences between the male and female averages. As students of elementary statistics know, but commentators often forget, focusing on differences between averages obscures the variation within each sex. Male and female distributions typically overlap, so that some females are higher than some males even on a trait on which males have a higher average.

A key tenet of liberal thought has always been the notion of a public/private dichotomy paired with the belief that the state should not intervene in what is "private," and that "justice" does not apply to this private sphere. What has continually been under dispute is the location of the boundary between public and private (Jaggar 1983). Gender relations in the family were excluded from the public sphere by the early liberals (Benhabib 1987; Benhabib and Cornell 1987). Locke, for example, saw the domestic sphere as beyond the reach of liberal principles of justice. Even egalitarian liberal theorists of the last twenty years, such as Rawls (1971), Dworkin (1977), and Ackerman (1980), have considered the family as in the private sphere in which liberal principles of state-guaranteed justice do not apply (Okin 1989). For the most part, liberal feminists (unlike socialist feminists and radical-cultural feminists) have not disputed this. Thus they have focused on women's equal rights in nondomestic matters, such as education, politics, and jobs. In general, the notion of equal treatment of men and women in nonhousehold affairs has become the liberal notion of feminism. There are, however, some exceptions to this, as when liberal feminists support enforcement of assault laws to prosecute men who rape or beat their wives at home, or when they argue for public support of child care or for laws mandating that employers give parents the job flexibility they need to combine being parents with employment (Okin 1989).

It is the application of the egalitarian strand of liberalism to the nonhousehold sphere on which liberal feminists have placed most emphasis. Egalitarian liberalism endorses state action in the service of equality of treatment or opportunity outside the family. Feminists have pushed legislative agendas based on this reasoning, supporting the passage and administrative enforcement of laws against discrimination in employment, credit, and educational opportunities.

For many liberal feminists, comparable worth is seen in this same vein. Most liberal-feminist organizations, such as the National Organization for Women and the National Women's Political Caucus, have endorsed comparable worth. They view comparable worth as a tool to achieve nondiscrimination in wage setting. They see the issue as a straightforward equal treatment issue.

Some liberals argue that comparable worth goes beyond equality of opportunity. (See Reynolds 1986 for this argument, and England 1986 for a rebuttal.) In this view, equality of opportunity is limited to access to positions, so that the law should prohibit discrimination in hiring, placement, or promotions. In this view, the equal treatment standard is either not accepted or not seen to require a consistent or unbiased set of criteria for setting wages in both male and female jobs.

If one follows the egalitarian thrust of liberalism far enough, the call for equality of opportunity leads to a call for greater substantive equality by class, race, and gender. This follows from the fact that inequality in outcomes often creates inequality of opportunity. With respect to class or strata, as long as there is inequality among parents, and children receive financial, cognitive, cultural, or social resources from their parents, groups of children will not have equality of opportunity (England 1988). When these facts are realized, the liberal criterion of equality of opportunity, rather than being juxtaposed to a criterion of equality of condition, is seen to require greater equality of condition for its realization. In the case of gender, without equality between men and women in distributions across occupations and earnings, young women cannot have equal opportunity for mentors with similar experiences, role models, and so forth. The argument for race is analogous. Thus, a call for a socialism of sorts can be derived from egalitarian liberalism (Eisenstein 1981). However, most American liberals do not take equality of opportunity this far, either out of fear of the concentration of power in the state required, or because they believe that the possibility of unequal outcomes has incentive-producing effects. It is to a fuller discussion of socialist views, including those derived from Marxism, that I now turn.

IV.   Marxism and Socialist Feminism

In a Marxist view, what is revered and is seen as essentially human is engaging in conscious physical labor directed toward satisfying human needs (Jaggar 1983). This contrasts with the view of liberals such as Locke [1698] (1967) that rationality is the essential characteristic of humanity (Jaggar 1983, Chapter 3). It also contrasts with religious versions of patriarchal views in which being God-like and "nonbodily" are revered (Tuana forthcoming). Harmonizing with Marx's normative valuation of productive labor was his positive assertion that the means and relationships of production are primary to understanding inequality. In capitalism, he thought, the fundamental cleavage is between workers and capitalists, i.e., between those who sell their labor and those who own the nonhuman means of production and can buy others' labor. The normative portion of the theory is the claim that workers are exploited under capitalism. Thus to Marxists, the socialism that flows from egalitarian liberalism is inadequate if it does not abolish capitalism.

Orthodox Marxists see employed women as exploited by capitalists, just as male workers are exploited. In addition, many Marxists see sex discrimination in labor markets, which leads women to have even lower wages than men, as a "side effect" of capitalism. As discussed in Chapter 2, the idea is that discrimination on the basis of workers' sex or race operates to divide and conquer workers by deflecting their attention away from the fact that they have a common enemy, capitalism (Edwards et al. 1975; Reich 1981; Shelton and Agger forthcoming). None of these theorists has specified that the mechanism of sex discrimination that divides and conquers might be the devaluation of women's work that is at issue in comparable worth. However, the theory seems open to the possibility that this could be one mechanism. The theory is equally consistent with exclusion of women from high-paying jobs or payment of unequal wages by sex within jobs as the mechanism of discrimination that serves to divide and conquer.

But what of homemakers? Do Marxists see them as victims of sexism? The most orthodox Marxist position, that of Engels [1884] (1972), has seen women as oppressed by their exclusion from public production and has argued that socialism would liberate women to participate in this by socializing the work women now do in their private homes (Jaggar 1983, Chapter 4). Marxist feminists (James and Dalla Costa 1973; Seccombe 1974; Smith 1978; Vogel 1983) argue that women's unpaid domestic labor serves to maintain and nurture workers and hence produces a commodity, "labor power." Thus, homemakers are exploited in the formal sense of contributing surplus value to capitalists (Shelton and Agger forthcoming). In fact, homemakers are even more exploited than paid workers, since the former are paid nothing for their reproductive labor. This Marxist-feminist view deviates from the orthodox Marxist position, which sees homemakers as oppressed only through their exclusion from public production, a process they see as a function of capitalism. In the orthodox view, homemakers are not exploited as paid workers are because domestic labor is not production and does not contribute to surplus value (Smith 1978). Indeed, household labor is seen by some orthodox Marxists as nonalienated (Zaretsky 1976), making women appear to be less harmed by the capitalist system than men. Despite their differences on whether homemakers are exploited, orthodox Marxists and Marxist feminists both agree that women's subordination is derivative of the class relations between capitalists and workers.

Socialist feminists agree with Marxist feminists' contention that women's household labor creates surplus value for capitalism. However, socialist feminists dispute the claim that gender inequality is entirely derivative of class relations between capitalists and workers (Hartmann 1981; Jaggar 1983, Chapters 6 and 10). But this does not mean that they do not see women's subordination as resulting from material social relations. They argue that women are also oppressed by patriarchy, a system that includes material social relations of male dominance in how reproduction is organized. By "reproduction" they mean some combination of sexuality, procreation, the nurturance of people, and other household labor. Some socialist feminists follow Hartmann (1976, 1981) in also including the power of male employers and male workers over employed women as part of patriarchy. Hartmann (1976, 1981) defines patriarchy as a system involving men's control over women's labor at home and in the paid workplace. Debates within this camp center on whether capitalism and patriarchy are distinct or have become merged into a single system, and, if distinct, whether they are complementary or contradictory. (For reviews of these debates, see Walby 1986, Chapter 2; Shelton and Agger forthcoming.) Regardless of the position they take on this, most socialist feminists and materialist radical feminists see the way in which procreation and reproduction are socially organized as part of a material base. In addition, socialist feminists see household work and paid production as mutually determining, with relations in neither sector more causally prior than the other.

Socialist feminists advocate an abolition of a division of labor based on sex in every aspect of life. Procreation, childrearing, and household work are seen as forms of human labor.

The socialist-feminist position is distinct from the liberal-feminist position in several ways. First, those who follow Marxist theory see labor rather than rationality as the criterion of normative claims (Jaggar 1983). Second, socialist feminists advocate collective struggle to achieve the abolition of the sexual division of labor in the home, while liberal feminists generally eschew interference by any collective in domestic affairs. This is not to say that socialist feminists advocate the intervention of the state into the family in today's capitalist societies; the state in such societies is seen as an instrument of class oppression. But they do see the family as an appropriate target for collective political struggle. Third, socialist feminists, as either Marxist or non-Marxist socialists, challenge many of the hierarchical aspects of the organization of work under capitalism. The unequal distribution of wealth, the hierarchical division of labor, and the extent of inequality in the wage distribution are all challenged. In contrast, most liberals accept these inequalities, and focus their reforms on ensuring that individuals have equality of opportunity to ascend hierarchies or that individuals of equal merit are treated equally within such hierarchies.

What is the Marxist and socialist-feminist position on comparable worth? Socialists, whether they are Marxists or not, are likely to endorse comparable worth as a worthy reform (though not without dangers) but also to see it as inadequately radical. Comparable worth does not challenge the distribution of wealth, the hierarchical division of labor, or inequality in the distribution of wages (Brenner 1987). It simply asks that undervalued female jobs be given wages equal to comparable male jobs. While in practice it tends to narrow the gender gap in wages and compress the overall wage structure, it leaves many other inequalities intact (Acker 1989). Job evaluation, with its complicated statistical formulas, also reinforces the rule of technical experts and obscures the fact that the question of what job characteristics should count more in evaluating jobs is irreducibly political. The superior value of mental over manual skills and the greater importance of supervisory over other kinds of responsibility are often assumed by job evaluators, but are counter to socialist values (Brenner 1987; Acker 1989). Socialists see these as class and perhaps race biases. Thus, Brenner (1987) argues that comparable worth may exacerbate divisions between groups of workers if it does not broaden its discourse to challenge all occupational hierarchies. Indeed, job evaluation, the practical tool of comparable worth, actually legitimates the notion of a hierarchy of jobs with unequal wages proportional to skill and working conditions (Feldberg 1984). That is, it reinforces the idea that people deserve to get paid according to the job evaluation points of their job. This obscures the fact that skill differences between jobs are *created* by employers organizing work in a way that puts skilled and menial tasks in separate rather than the same job. The experience of working in such jobs then contributes to developing skill differences among workers. (For evidence that the mental skill demands of the job affect workers' mental skills, see Kohn and Schooler 1983.)

Thus, because of all the aspects of inequality *not* challenged by comparable worth, some socialist writers have criticized comparable worth as inadequately egalitarian (Brenner 1987; Blum 1987, 1991). These reservations about the adequacy of comparable worth are consistent with both Marxist views and with the non-Marxist view of socialism discussed above as an extension of egalitarian liberalism.

Despite these reservations, many socialists and socialist feminists advocate comparable worth as a reform that could potentially improve the situation of women (Feldberg 1984; Steinberg 1987; Blum 1987, 1991; Acker 1989). Many of the jobs whose pay comparable worth would raise involve nurturant labor, similar to the reproductive labor women do in the home. Thus, there is a normative harmony between the Marxist-feminist and socialist-feminist claim that those who do reproductive labor in the home are doubly exploited and the aim of comparable worth to raise the wages of those who do such reproductive labor in paid employment.

On the question of how comparable worth should be implemented, socialists argue for worker participation in the job evaluation process. This follows from the belief that making decisions about what job characteristics should receive what weights cannot be reduced to a technical value-free formula. Socialists also oppose lowering any workers' wages to provide funds to raise others' wages; thus, they advocate the use of the male line to set wages, bringing the pay of female jobs up to the line that summarizes the relationship between job points and wage among male jobs. (See Chapter 4 for technical details on job evaluation.) Socialist principles suggest using the male line in order to maintain solidarity among all workers as the reform is instituted. Such solidarity would be impeded by paying for women's raises by lowering men's wages. In addition, Marxists' underlying normative theory, following from the labor theory of value, says that labor is exploited by the extraction of surplus value. Thus, any reform that reduced men's wages would heighten their exploitation, something that Marxists could hardly advocate. If comparable worth raises the total wage bill, socialists see this as a plus on the hope that wage increases will come out of profits rather than being passed on to consumers.

V.   Radical and Cultural Feminism

Cultural feminists value traditionally female characteristics, disputing the traditional deprecation of qualities viewed as feminine (Donovan 1985, Chapter 2; Alcoff 1988). Thus, whereas patriarchal and liberal views have elevated the spiritual or rational over the physical, emotional, or intuitive, cultural feminists argue for at least an equal valuation of the latter qualities. Where patriarchal views revere the bravery of risking one's life in hunting, sport, or war, the cultural feminist reveres nurturing for its preservation of life. Whereas patriarchal thinkers, classical liberals, and some Marxists have revered humans for their domination over nature, cultural feminism reveres harmony with nature; this aspect of cultural feminism is sometimes called *ecofeminism.*

The traditionally female characteristics that cultural feminists believe our culture has undervalued include nurturing, nonviolence, sensitivity to the feelings of others, emotional expressiveness, unselfishness, a collective orientation, kinship with rather than domination of nature, acceptance of our physical bodies, humility, flexibility rather than rigid adherence to abstract principles, and intuition of wholes. Cultural feminists argue that people have always benefited from women's practice of these skills and values, but this benefit is seldom acknowledged in patriarchal societies. Rather, these virtues have been seen as weakness, lack of proper individuation, or lack of rationality. Traditionally male characteristics more highly valued in our culture are individual ambition, independence, aggressiveness, abstract and analytical rationality, and repression of emotion. Liberal feminists protest the limitations on women's access to public roles, while not questioning whether traditionally male characteristics are appropriate behavior in these roles. In contrast, cultural feminists argue that traditionally male values are inappropriate for human behavior by *either* men or women in *either* domestic or public roles (Donovan 1985), at least without greater balance from feminine values than currently obtains.

In this discussion, I am choosing to combine cultural feminism and radical feminism, though the match is by no means perfect. Radical feminists see women's subordination to be *the* fundamental inequality, not a side effect of class inequalities as orthodox Marxists believe. Some radical and cultural feminists see the deprecation of women as one part of an ancient historical move to a hierarchical "power-over" model of the relationship between gods and men, men and women, and humans and nature (Starhawk 1987; Eisler 1987; Tuana forthcoming). Radical feminists believe that women's subordination is the result of how sexuality, childbearing, and childrearing have been socially organized (Jaggar 1983). Since activities in these spheres have been seen as female and deprecated, there is a clear link to cultural feminism. Radical and cultural feminists see these very personal areas as political precisely because they are a locus for male dominance.

In their treatment of differences between men and women, some radical-cultural feminists veer toward essentialism (Jaggar 1983; Alcoff 1988). Essentialism is the view that observed differences between men and women are fundamental to their nature. The notion that sex differences in behavior result from inborn, biological differences between men and women is one example of essentialism. Such feminists agree with patriarchal thinkers that many observed sex differences are innate, but they disagree with patriarchal thinkers in that they see female traits to be equal or superior to male traits. For example, radical-cultural feminists who are essentialists see reciprocal nurturing as more valuable than violence and power wielding in human affairs, but see men as inherently less capable of nurturing.

Other radical-cultural feminists reject essentialism. One radical-cultural feminist challenge to essentialism questions the very dichotomy between nature and nurture, arguing that the two can never be disentangled because they are truly interactive, and thus that there are always choices to be made about how much we encourage sex differentiation (Tuana 1983).

Even positions in methodology and epistemology are believed by radical-cultural feminists to be influenced by the tendency to devalue ways of being traditionally associated with women. Western culture extols rationality, and scientists see what they do as the apex of rationality. Scientists value "objectivity," which they see as entailing emotional separation between the knower and the known, assuming that, without such separation, the biases of the knower contaminate the analysis. But some radical-cultural feminists argue that separation was seen as the key to knowing by male scientists and philosophers of science because the way we raise males has encouraged them to value and want separation rather than connection, *not* because separation is really a key to knowledge (Keller 1985). These feminist philosophers of science argue that intimate connection with one's subject matter—what we often think of as subjectivity—may enhance our ability to understand the world (Keller 1985). This is an example of elevating the value of a traditionally female skill.

Radical-cultural feminists argue that the exclusive focus among liberal feminists on allowing women to enter occupational and political positions formerly monopolized by men is misdirected because the underlying values are wrong for *both* men and women. For example, while a liberal feminist might fight to get more women into management, a radical-cultural feminist might be more interested in seeing production organized in a less hierarchal manner so that "manager" and "worker" are no longer job categories, or in increasing the pay and respect given to nonsupervisory workers relative to managers. On this, socialist feminists would agree with radical-cultural feminists. While a liberal feminist might focus on increasing the number of women scientists, a radical-cultural feminist might place equal importance on changing the extent to which separation between scientists and their subject matter is valued in science. For those who are not essentialists, changing the culture to celebrate traditionally female values entails changing men more than changing women, since men now lag behind women in development of positive traditionally female qualities. For example, rather than encouraging women to be more aggressive, a radical-cultural feminist might prefer to see men become more nurturant and altruistic. Those who reject essentialism believe these traditionally female or androgynous values should be taught to both males and females and used to transform the culture. This contrasts with liberal feminists who focus more upon teaching skills consistent with traditionally male roles to women, and see little need to change men or to transform the culture with new values, but rather focus on getting those in power to allow those women who have learned traditionally male skills into already correctly valued spheres.

Some voices within radical-cultural feminism argue that we should question the dichotomization of human traits, rather than simply elevating the traditionally female side to be seen as equal or superior to the traditionally male side of the dichotomies (Hein 1983; Stanley and Wise 1983; Whitbeck 1983; Hare-Mustin and Marecek 1988; Tuana forthcoming). That is, we should question whether pairs of phenomena we have dichotomized are really either opposite or radically distinct. They may, instead, be mutually entailing. These feminists also criticize the tendency to make hierarchies out of dichotomies. Here their position is consistent with poststructuralism (Culler 1982; Weedon 1987; Alcoff 1988; Agger 1991). For example, many patriarchal and liberal thinkers have accepted a dichotomy between reason and emotion and seen reason as more valuable. Men are seen as more reasonable and women as more emotional, and hence men are seen as superior. In addition to criticizing the gender assignment, as liberal feminists do, one could also question the oppositional and hierarchized nature of the dichotomy itself. Might emotion not play into the best reason and reason into the best emotion? For example, some say that part of Einstein's genius was his ability to be intimate with and emotional about his subject matter. Similarly, reason sometimes underlies emotional responses. For example, it may be in part through the intellectual exercise of seeing some similarities in the logics and mechanisms through which women and people of color have been subordinated that one arrives at feelings of empathy for members of oppressed groups of which one is not a member. Rejecting gender-related and other dichotomies entails a notion of rationality that includes emotion and vice versa, a notion of autonomy that sees how it is enhanced by intimacy and vice versa, and a notion of nurturance that sees how it requires power and vice versa.

On one level this rejection of dichotomies is consistent with androgyny, the idea that both men and women should develop both traditionally male and female traits (Vetterling-Braggin 1982). But, taken to its logical extreme, rejecting a dichotomized view of two traits in favor of the view that each is a part of the other entails a profound revision of the traits themselves, and this has eluded many advocates of androgyny. For example, a reason that includes emotion is a new concept of reason. An emotion that includes reason is a new concept of emotion. In some cases, where the oppressiveness of the social domination involved in the traits is too great, we may want to reject the whole system in favor of entirely new traits. For example, Raymond (1975) criticizes androgyny, arguing that if women have been like slaves to men, a postslavery model of liberated men and women can hardly be created out of combining characteristics of slaves and slave masters. Here the need for revising traits is so great as to require starting over.

The theme of separation and connection has organized much recent feminist theorizing. Here, too, we see a dichotomy, and work may be needed to correct the tendency to revere the traditionally male side as well as to refuse the dichotomy. Radical-cultural feminists point out that Western culture has glorified the separative (individuated, autonomous) self, associated this with men, and expressed deprecation toward bonds of emotional connection, associated with women (Gilligan 1982; Keller 1986; Benhabib 1987; Benhabib and Cornell 1987). Patriarchal thinking has failed to imagine forms of connection other than subordination (Keller 1986). Liberal feminists dispute limiting women to realms of connection (such as family, relationships, emotions, and subjective knowing), but they do not dispute the deprecation of connection in comparison with separation.

Catherine Keller (1986) argues that it is a fallacy to see separation and connection as dichotomies. She suggests that everything is connected such that every entity is present in every other, thus ensuring connection. Yet connection need not mean sameness. The connective self is open to the world, but by its unique place in time and space it mirrors a unique view of the world. Thus, one can revere both connection and individuality; individuality does not require an emotionally separative self. In this insistence on respecting differences between individuals, radical-cultural feminists such as Keller (1986) agree with the liberal concern with individuals, but do not base respect for individual differences on a glorification of separation as liberals have (England 1989; England and Kilbourne 1990a, 1990b; England forthcoming). The radical-feminist position also differs from the classical liberal position in the impulse of the former to avoid associating unequal value and reward with individual differences. In this egalitarian impulse, radical-cultural feminists have much in common with socialists, socialist feminists, and some egalitarian liberals.

What position does radical-cultural feminism imply for comparable worth? Radical-cultural feminism is consistent with a version of comparable worth that sees the root of the problem to be a cultural devaluation of some jobs because of their association with traditionally female spheres.

Yet, some proposed methods of implementing comparable worth entail insufficient cultural change for radical-cultural feminists. In particular, policy-capturing approaches to job evaluation do not contest the weights employers give to various job characteristics, and lead to wage changes only when employers' criteria are being used inconsistently. In the radical-cultural feminist view, many traits are now undervalued when they appear in either men's or women's jobs because of their historic association with women's spheres. Thus an a priori approach to job evaluation that explicitly sets out to give more value to traditionally feminine job characteristics such as nurturant skills would be most consistent with the radical-cultural feminist view. (See Chapter 4 for a discussion of job evaluation methods.)

Although the aims of comparable worth reforms are in harmony with radical-cultural feminism, feminists of this persuasion have written and organized little around comparable worth. In part, this is because radical-cultural feminist writers cited in this section have focused on broad theoretical critiques of androcentrism rather than policy debates. It is also because radical-cultural feminist activists have focused upon starting alternative institutions (such as women's cooperative businesses, spiritual groups, and communes) that embody the values they embrace. Few have engaged in political action aimed at persuading the government to mandate comparable worth or unions to bargain for comparable worth. Working through the male-dominated bureaucratic state or unions has been avoided by many radical-cultural feminists, some of whom advocate separatism from male institutions. Nonetheless, there is considerable harmony between the traditionally female and androgynous activities and skills valued by radical-cultural feminists and the traditionally female jobs that would have their pay elevated by comparable worth.

VI. Conclusion

This chapter has related comparable worth to several normative positions in social, economic, and political philosophy. A large part of the chapter was spent explaining the basic philosophies of each position before relating them to comparable worth. We have seen that positions do not always cleanly imply either a pro or con stance toward comparable worth. Yet some positions are much more hospitable to the principles of comparable worth than others, although the several positions harmonious with comparable worth advance it for different reasons. Likewise, the positions hostile to comparable worth oppose it for varying reasons.

Patriarchal thinkers and those adhering to the laissez-faire and libertarian strands of liberalism oppose governmental action to promote wages using principles of comparable worth. In the case of patriarchal thinkers, this seems more rooted in a disapproval of women being employed or having high wages than in an objection to traditionally female tasks being seen as equal to male tasks. In the case of laissez-faire economics and libertarianism, both descendants of classical liberalism, the objection is to state interference in private-sector market processes.

In general, egalitarian liberals, liberal feminists, Marxists, other socialists, socialist feminists, and radical-cultural feminists support comparable worth, although their different underlying philosophies lead them to different notions of how comparable worth should be implemented. Marxists, socialist feminists, and radical-cultural feminists see comparable worth as a very limited reform compared to the larger restructuring of society that is their goal. Thus, comparable worth is not an emphasis in these traditions, though the philosophies are harmonious with at least some principles of comparable worth.

Liberals, including liberal feminists, generally accept capitalist processes except where they involve inequalities of opportunity or treatment, such as sex discrimination in the sense of inconsistent treatment of men and women. Thus, some liberals and many liberal feminists see the inconsistent treatment of male and female occupations at issue in comparable worth to be unfair discrimination warranting governmental intervention. However, liberals and liberal feminists may accept policy-capturing job evaluation as an approach to comparable worth (see Chapter 4), even when it embeds bias against nurturant and other traditionally female skills into wage systems, as long as male and female jobs are evaluated by the same standard. Liberals are also likely to accept processes for arriving at pay equity that are controlled by management and that lack participation by workers.

Many socialists support comparable worth out of opposition to sex discrimination, and out of a desire for greater equality between capital and labor as well as within labor. It follows from this that socialists oppose using comparable worth as an excuse to lower even very highly paid male workers' wages, preferring to bring female jobs' pay up to the male line, and preferring an outcome that raises the overall labor bill. Socialist feminists generally agree with this, but their motivation for endorsing comparable worth also emphasizes the importance of women having decent wages so that male-female equality in the household is more likely and so that women have the option not to be married. Socialists and socialist feminists favor processes for implementing pay equity that involve workers' participation.

Radical-cultural feminists argue that we should elevate the value accorded traditionally female traits and skills, and see them not as opposite to traditionally male traits but as entailed in them. Accordingly, some radical-cultural feminists would support comparable worth because they would see paying a higher wage for traditionally female work as a way of prohibiting the effect if not the underlying animus of the devaluation of female jobs. This reasoning assumes that if employers are forced to pay more to women's jobs, this will lead people over time to come to value these jobs more, a contention that would be rejected by neoclassical economists who see preferences as exogenous to the economy. (See Chapter 2.) Radical-cultural feminists would prefer an a priori approach to job evaluation that explicitly tried to revalue traditionally feminine tasks (such as nurturing skills) to a policy-capturing approach. This is because the latter incorporates whatever devaluation of these skills is present in employers' practices, satisfying itself with applying employers' standards consistently across male and female jobs. Despite the harmony between the values of radical-cultural feminists and the goals of comparable worth reforms, many radical-cultural feminists have avoided political action directed at government or unions, focusing rather on creating small countercultural institutions that embody their values.

My attempts to connect particular views on comparable worth to each of the broad philosophical positions should not be misread to imply that most of those writing or speaking on comparable worth align perfectly with one of these positions. Few individuals follow one of these stylized positions consistently. For example, Schlafly (1984) and Levin (1984, 1987), whom I have called patriarchal thinkers, also advance promarket and antistatist arguments against comparable worth, thus aligning themselves with the laissez-faire strand of classical liberalism. Both patriarchal and laissez-faire arguments would logically lead one to oppose the Equal Pay Act of 1963 as well as Title VII. But business groups, members of the religious right (Schlafly 1984), and economists (O'Neill 1984; Polachek 1984) all now claim to advocate these laws while opposing both interpretations of Title VII that include comparable worth or new legislation to enforce comparable worth. Thus all are being somewhat inconsistent in opposing comparable worth while supporting bans on other kinds of sex discrimination. Similarly, business groups argue against comparable worth based on its interference with market systems of pricing, yet many businesses advocate tariff barriers when it helps their profits, despite the fact that tariffs interfere with market-pricing systems.

My own position on comparable worth draws from several of these positions. I agree with the egalitarian-liberal and liberal-feminist commitment to equality of treatment of men and women in the economy, and see this as a *sufficient* reason to favor governmental intervention for comparable worth. However, I reject the liberal emphasis on rationality as the sole criterion of human rights and the classical liberal glorification of the separative self. On these points, I agree with radical-cultural feminists who want to mend the split between rational and emotional, and want to valorize connection, while respecting but not making hierarchies out of individual differences. The radical-cultural argument that our culture has deprecated traditionally female tasks is another reason to favor comparable worth. I also agree with socialists and socialist feminists in favoring a lessening of all kinds of inequality (including political power, which makes it imperative that socialism be combined with democracy). I do not base these egalitarian ideals on Marxist normative principles; the labor theory of value with its contention that any return to capital (even interest on savings accounts) is exploitative makes no more sense to me than the neoclassical tendency never to question the justice of initial endowments. Thus, my socialist beliefs flow from taking the egalitarian impulse of liberalism much farther than most liberals, and from agreement with the commitment to accepting but not hierarchizing differences in radical-cultural feminism. I reject patriarchal views and the conservative strands of classical liberalism because I believe the level of inequalities they permit are unacceptably painful to those at the bottom of hierarchies, a position that implies that I believe we can make interpersonal utility comparisons. I also reject patriarchal views because I do not believe male dominance to be necessary. In short, I favor comparable worth based on a combination of egalitarian-liberal, socialist-feminist, and radical-cultural feminist principles.

Many of the broad philosophical disagreements discussed in this chapter underlie contemporary policy debates about comparable worth. The specific policy debates are the focus of my final chapter.

Note

1.   Although libertarians are thought to be "right wing" or conservative in the United States, it is their laissez-faire position on economic issues, and the fact that promarket policies conserve the economic inequalities produced by the marketplace, that leads them to be called conservative. In contrast, libertarians' belief that the state should not prohibit subversive speech and should not "establish" religion often allies them with liberal organizations (such as the American Civil Liberties Union).

7

Policy Debates

I. Introduction

Imagine that you are at a party, replete with smart people of various political persuasions, and the topic of comparable worth comes up. In this chapter, I use the points one might hear in such a conversation as a rhetorical device to explore policy debates over comparable worth. In using this device, I will selectively summarize ideas from earlier chapters that inform debates about whether comparable worth is a sensible concept—whether it identifies a consequential form of discrimination to which public policy should be directed.

I owe the idea of presenting the pros and cons of comparable worth in the form of a dialogue to Gold (1983), who presented arguments via a hypothetical debate between an advocate and a critic of the concept. My format, however, will differ from Gold's in that I will insert my own voice, called Author, and give myself the privileged position of adjudicating issues. It is undoubtedly obvious to the reader by now that I am an advocate of comparable worth. Yet, I do not agree with all arguments made by advocates of comparable worth. Additionally, I think some of the opponents' arguments have merit even where they ultimately fail to convince me that comparable worth should be opposed. A second way in which my format will differ from Gold's is that I will identify voices not only as advocates or critics of comparable worth, but also with a disciplinary, political, or philosophical label with which the argument is typically associated. There are multiple and conflicting worldviews among those who oppose comparable worth, as well as among advocates. Thus, the dialogue below features neoclassical critics, libertarian critics, socialist-feminist advocates, sociological advocates, liberal advocates, and many others.

By now a literature has developed that features the arguments for and against comparable worth policies. As I present my version of the dialogue below, I will insert citations where an author entering the policy debate has made more or less this same point. This will serve to direct the interested reader to this literature. However, the person cited may not always be speaking from the point of view to which the comment is attributed in the dialogue. Opinions in this debate are also based on the issues of theory and evidence that have been discussed in Chapters 1–6. To remind the reader of how this debate hinges on what has gone before, I periodically insert parenthetical references to the chapter in which the issue was discussed.

As I have traveled to conferences of academics, policymakers, lawyers, and advocacy groups over the last decade to participate in debates about comparable worth, I have often heard statements that I believe to be factually in error. For example, I have heard opponents of comparable worth say that employed women have less education than men (which Table 1.6 in Chapter 1 shows to be false). Despite the prevalence of factual errors in this (and probably any) policy debate, I have refrained from attributing statements I know to be untrue to participants in the hypothetical debate that follows. As we have seen throughout the book, while facts can resolve some of the debates over comparable worth, other disagreements are about predictions of what would happen under comparable worth policies, how an agreed-upon set of facts is to be theoretically interpreted, or what normative principles policies should embody. Thus there is plenty to argue about even when we agree on most of the facts.

The dialogue will be organized around a set of questions about which advocates and critics of comparable worth often disagree. The questions are the following:

1. Is there a sizable sex gap in pay caused by discrimination?

2. Is the only real problem discrimination in women's access to typically male jobs?

3. Do women need comparable worth and deserve it as simple justice?

4. Does "the market" explain the relative pay of women's and men's jobs, and should public policy seek to change market wages?

5. Is job evaluation a feasible way to achieve comparable worth?

6. Does comparable worth require new legislation or can enforcement of current law achieve it?

7. Can governmental requirements of comparable worth achieve the goal of reducing the sex gap in pay or would there be adverse side effects that would particularly hurt women, the intended beneficiaries of the policy?

8. Would there be other adverse side effects of comparable worth policies that would hurt the economy, polity, or society as a whole?

9. Is comparable worth an inadequately radical reform?

These questions span issues of social science theory, scientific evidence, policy implementation, normative theory, and law, all addressed in preceding chapters. Here, however, the discussion is organized around the central policy question: Is comparable worth a feasible and desirable policy? To explore the question, let us join the hypothetical discussion occurring around the refreshment table at the party. Remember that, in what follows, the voice of Author is not the voice of a participant in the debate at the party, but is my voice as silent commentator telling the reader how I adjudicate the issue under debate.

II. The Sex Gap in Pay and Discrimination

Feminist Advocate: It's pretty obvious to me that we need comparable worth when women who work full-time all year only earn about 65–75 cents for every dollar earned by men (Chapter 1, Tables 1.3 and 1.4), and when job evaluation studies generally find that women's jobs pay about 20% less than men's jobs that are evaluated with the same number of points (Rothchild 1984).

Business Critic: Of course there is a sex gap in pay. But much of it is caused by nondiscriminatory factors. After all the relevant adjustments are made, the gap is much smaller (Williams and Kessler 1984; U.S. Commission on Civil Rights 1984; Equal Employment Advisory Council 1985; Rector 1988; Paul 1989). Some of it results from women's roles as wives and mothers (Berger 1984; O'Neill 1984; Roback 1986), roles that are determined either by biology (Levin 1984) or by socialization (U.S. Commission on Civil Rights 1984). What could be more convincing evidence of the powerful force of family roles on the sex gap in pay than the fact that the sex gap in pay between never-married men and never-married women is much smaller than the overall sex gap in pay (Polachek 1984)? Some of the sex gap in pay undoubtedly results from past discrimination against women by educational institutions, in not admitting women to certain programs, or counseling them in different directions than men. Whether or not you want to call these factors discrimination in some broad sense, employers are certainly not responsible for them (Williams and Kessler 1984; U.S. Commission on Civil Rights, 1984). Even if there was sex discrimination in the labor market in the past, very little remains; women have made tremendous progress (Rector 1988). We can see this by the fact that there is very little difference between the pay of the youngest cohort of men and women workers (Flick 1983; see also Table 1.5 in Chapter 1).

Sociologist Advocate: Well, you are right that women have made some progress, but let's not exaggerate it. If we look at figures on median usual weekly earnings of full-time white workers, adjusted for the slight deviations between the hours worked by male and female full-time workers, we see that women earn 76% of what men do, up from about 67% in 1979 (see Table 1.4). There has been improvement, but the gap is still large. Also, let's not exaggerate how much progress is indicated by the fact that younger cohorts show a smaller sex gap in pay than older cohorts. To some extent, this represents the fact that within each cohort, women's earnings fall farther and farther behind men's over the life cycle, in part because women are concentrated in dead-end jobs that offer fewer promotions and less generous pay increases with seniority. Some of this is certainly indicative of discrimination. You exaggerate when you imply that if we make all the adjustments necessary to get rid of portions of the pay gap not caused by discrimination, we have virtually nothing left.

You make reference to home responsibilities. The most obvious way that women's home responsibilities affect their pay is by reducing their years of employment experience. If we adjust for experience-related forms of human capital, about 45% of the sex gap among whites and 25% of the sex gap among blacks is explained. (See Tables 1.7 and 1.8.) While no measure is perfect, it seems reasonable to conclude that a significant portion of the remainder is indicative of discrimination (Marshall and Paulin 1984). But even some of the portion explained by human capital may be a result of past discrimination, which has discouraged women from staying in the labor force to accumulate experience.

The comment about never-married women and men having more equal earnings is misleading in the extreme. Presumably this is an attempt to choose a comparison that "holds constant" home responsibilities. The problem is that it fails to hold constant some other relevant things. Women with high earning potential are disproportionately single while men with low earning potential disproportionately stay single. Thus, it is not a fair comparison since single women have much more human capital than single men (Steinberg 1986). Besides, even within this group, there is a substantial sex gap in pay (Ehrenberg and Smith 1982, p. 397).

Author: The advocates have the better side of the argument so far, although both are using correct facts. The adjusted pay gap seems non-trivial to me, and the fact that the sex gap is smaller among younger cohorts and among single people does not contradict the notion of substantial discrimination, for the reasons the sociologist gave. (See Chapter 1 for a review of research on the sex gap in pay.)

Neoclassical Critic: Can I join this conversation? I think you are wrong to infer discrimination from the portion of the pay gap that is not explained by other measured factors such as job experience. Perhaps it is explained by some unmeasured but nondiscriminatory factors, such as ambition or assertiveness. I suspect this because there are strong theoretical reasons to doubt that sex (or race) discrimination can persist indefinitely in competitive labor markets. Discrimination in hiring is generally costly to employers (Rector 1988; Paul 1989). (See Chapter 2 on discrimination.)

Socialist-Feminist Advocate: What? Surely capitalists make money by sex discrimination. When they pay women less, they make more profit than if they paid women fairly. This is one reason that capitalism and patriarchy go hand in hand. Sometimes I think you economists can't add and subtract despite your technical training!

Neoclassical Critic: No, the real problem is that you socialists often forget that capitalists compete with each other! The comparison you seem to have in mind is this: A firm that employs men in higher-paying jobs and women in lower-paying jobs makes more money than it would if it employed the same people in the same jobs but paid women more. That's true. But if some employers discriminate against women, any other employer can save money by hiring women in men's jobs for less than they currently pay men in such jobs, but more than the women could make elsewhere in women's jobs. Then both the firm and women would benefit. Surely some profit-maximizing firms will do this, and when enough of them do it, the nondiscriminatory portion of the pay gap will gradually erode to nothing. (See Chapter 2 for an explanation of how neoclassical theory sees this process working.) In this sense, capitalism is women's best friend! So what do we need all this government intervention for? Indeed, I strongly suspect that there isn't much discrimination left these days, that most of it has already eroded through the process I've just described.

New Religious Right Critic: I agree completely. The market works!

Business Critic: Hear, hear.

Author: This argument that competitive markets counteract discrimination is sincerely believed by many neoclassical economists; it follows from their theoretical assumptions. When members of conservative religious and business groups clothe themselves in the same argument, however, I suspect an argument of convenience rather than of principle. After all, fundamentalist religious groups do not take the free-market, laissez-faire position on erotica. Nor do businesses maintain this commitment when their industry is seeking or defending governmental subsidies, such as tariffs. But more important than figuring out who is a hypocrite is assessing whether economists are correct to say that un-aided market forces will destroy discrimination. Let's listen to the rest of the debate on this.

Sociologist Advocate: Well, I have to disagree with my economist friend here. All this talk about competitive markets might make sense, if it weren't for the fact that many firms have internal labor markets, especially in the jobs men hold. Internal labor markets mean that there are structured sequences of promotions into higher-level jobs. Workers not already employed by the firm can't compete for these higher-level jobs. Thus, there is no marketwide competition to tempt employers to look for more economical (female) labor in higher-level jobs, as they would if people were hired into these jobs from the external market. The neoclassical model just doesn't apply for jobs above the bottom rung of these job ladders. (See the discussion of institutional models in Chapter 2.)

New Neoclassical Institutionalist Critic: Wait a minute. I agree with my sociologist friend, and with the old-line institutionalists within my field of economics, that many firms have internal labor markets. We new-neoclassical institutionalists see them as part of implicit contracts. Such arrangements entail trading off low starting wages for steep wage increases, promotions, pensions, and/or protection from layoffs. This makes sense for employers in jobs where the costs of search and on-the-job training make turnover especially expensive. (See Chapter 2 on the new neoclassical institutionalism.) But, roughly speaking, workers look-ing for jobs know what sort of contracts various jobs offer. So there is enough market competition for entry-level jobs to provide the erosion of discrimination my neoclassical colleague alluded to, even if there isn't market competition for the jobs further up mobility ladders.

Author: As I argued in Chapter 2, neoclassical economists have a point about discrimination being bid away by successive wages of profit-maximizing "arbitrageurs." To deny the market pressures in this direc-tion, as many sociologists do, is wrong. However, if some employers are willing to pay above-market-clearing wages to men, it is not clear that competitive markets will erode this discrimination. (See the discussion of Goldberg's model in Chapter 2.) Moreover, even if the market were to "work" to remove discrimination, there is no guarantee it won't take hundreds of years. Indeed, the existence of internal labor markets and implicit contracts makes any erosion of discrimination through market forces much slower, since the process only works through new cohorts entering firms' internal labor markets. Thus even if market forces work against discrimination, as economists suggest, the process is glacial. Women should not have to wait that long for justice.

III. Is Segregation and Hiring Discrimination the Real Problem?

Job-Evaluator Advocate: When a whole establishment or employer is studied with one job evaluation study, predominantly female jobs are generally found to pay about 20% less than comparable male jobs (Rothchild 1984). At least that is what studies from governmental employers, from which we have most of the available data, show. The argument for comparable worth hinges on this portion of the pay gap. Whether or not other kinds of discrimination—for example, not letting women into male occupations—has gone on is really irrelevant to comparable worth.

Liberal Neoclassical Critic: I disagree. Hiring discrimination isn't irrelevant, even to the findings you claim. I presume that the only way female occupations would come to pay less than comparable male occupations is through crowding in women's jobs (O'Neill 1984; Oi 1986). If employers won't hire women in the male jobs, this creates an artificially large supply of labor forced to crowd into female occupations, and it is this large supply relative to demand in those occupations that lowers the wages by the usual forces of supply and demand. When an employer pays a depressed wage to secretaries because of the artificially large supply of people seeking secretarial jobs, this is not discrimination. Rather, it is the unwillingness of employers to hire qualified women in male jobs leading to this oversupply in female jobs that is discriminatory. (See Chapter 2 on crowding.) Comparable worth would not be an issue were there no hiring discrimination. That's one reason comparable worth makes no sense—it doesn't attack the real problem of hiring discrimination (Jacobsen 1989). I'm willing to depart from my neoclassical colleagues who see no discrimination in admitting the presence of hiring discrimination. But let's focus public policy on the real problem—hiring discrimination.

Neoclassical Liberal-Feminist Advocate: I agree that hiring discrimination causes crowding and hence lowers pay in female jobs. But surely my neoclassical colleagues, attuned as they are to issues of efficiency, will see that, while desegregation may be the answer for those now starting their careers, it is inefficient for those who have already been employed for years. How quickly could we move women into male jobs and men into women's jobs and get everyone retrained? The costs would be massive, much greater than the costs of comparable worth policy. Since these retraining costs are prohibitive, to reject comparable worth amounts to denying women now in predominantly female jobs any redress for the discrimination they suffer (Bergmann 1989). Failure to do anything will have a particularly adverse impact on older cohorts of women (Gold 1983).

Radical-Cultural-Feminist Advocate: I can't comment on this crowding theory. But even if it is part of the story, I am sure that there is another factor at work as well. For centuries our culture has devalued all kinds of work traditionally done by women—whether for pay or not. Surely some part of the lower pay in women's jobs results from this devaluation. Just as we haven't appreciated nurturance of children as hard work that is valuable, so we don't value nurturance in paid jobs. Thus, the day-care worker makes less than the janitor although the former has more education and is arguably doing something more important. (See Chapter 6 on radical-cultural feminism.)

Sociologist Advocate: Hear, hear.

Social-Psychologist Advocate: I agree with my feminist friend on this point. Experimental studies have shown that judgments of merit are clouded by sex bias, so there is every reason to think that judgments about the relative worth of jobs would be also. (See Chapter 4.) There is also similar evidence from a new experimental tradition among behavioral economists showing what they call framing effects on judgments. One way these may work is that the current wage in a job frames our perception of the value of the work. Thus, once you get discriminatorily low wages in women's jobs, they will be perpetuated by the effects of the current wages on our perception of what a proper wage is. (See Chapter 2 for discussion of framing models.)

Author: While crowding may explain part of the lower pay in female occupations, devaluation is undoubtedly a factor as well. Even when women are preferred for the job, there is a tendency to pay the job less because women are in it, whether because of a cognitive mistake about the skill requirement or contribution to profit of the job, or because of believing women need or deserve less money than men.

Liberal Critic: Well, I don't know one way or another about whether crowding or devaluation is what makes women's jobs pay less than comparable men's jobs. But I do know that liberals have long favored equality of opportunity. Equality of opportunity is about access to positions. This is why Title VII of the Civil Rights Act was passed in the first place—to ensure minorities and women that discrimination would not block their access to well-rewarded positions. If women have access to all jobs, then they can hardly claim they are discriminated against when they choose a job knowing its low pay. So, for different reasons, I agree with my economist friend's conclusion that hiring discrimination—not comparable worth—should be the focus of antidiscrimination policy. Why do we need comparable worth if women can get into any job (Roback 1986; Paul 1989)?

Author: Many people are moved by the argument that if women don't like the pay of the jobs they are in, they should enter better-paying male jobs, and if they don't do this, they have no legitimate "beef." This argument amounts to the claim that one lacks sympathy for victims of this sort of between-job wage discrimination because they have an alternative route to raising their pay other than correcting the wage discrimination. Of course, in practice this alternative route may require losing much of one's pension, or incurring substantial retraining costs, so it is a much more feasible remedy for a young than an older worker (Gold 1983), and hence may be unfair to expect experienced workers to take it.

In addition, why prohibit discrimination in hiring and in wage setting *within* jobs, but permit discrimination to affect wage setting involving distinct jobs? It makes no sense. All should be prohibited (Grune 1984).

Affirmative action, nondiscrimination in hiring and placement, and comparable worth can be seen as complementary rather than competing strategies (Grune 1984). If we pursue all of them simultaneously, we will reduce the sex gap in pay faster.

IV. Do Women Need and Deserve Comparable Worth as Simple Justice?

Liberal-Feminist Advocate: Comparable worth is simple justice. It is a strategy to reduce a form of discrimination distinct from hiring discrimination or lack of equal pay for equal work in the same job. The discrimination involved in comparable worth is that sex is being taken into account when jobs' wages are set. Nondiscrimination requires that this not be permitted (England 1986; Willborn 1989). It is as simple as that.

Liberal Critic: I can see how women would benefit from higher wages. Who wouldn't? But isn't this reform asking for more than the simple justice of equality of opportunity that our other laws require? To me, equality of opportunity means access to all jobs on equal terms.

Instead, it seems to me that comparable worth is asking for equality of results (Raisin, Ward, and Welch 1986; Paul 1989).

Liberal Advocate: There are two errors underlying this charge. The first error is to imply that our current laws were intended only to address equality of opportunity in the sense of access to positions (England 1986). Both Title VII and the Equal Pay Act explicitly forbid gender discrimination in compensation. The second error is to imply that pay equity seeks to ensure equality of results. No responsible scientist believes that even the most vigilant enforcement of comparable worth to require between-job pay equity would completely close the gender gap in pay. Because not all of the gender gap in pay results from gender discrimination by employers, and only a subset of the portion arising from discrimination results from the sort of wage discrimination at issue in comparable worth, not all of the gap would be eradicated. Thus, to advocate comparable worth cannot be said to demand equality of results (England 1986).

Moreover, comparable worth is friendly to the goal of equal access to positions and thus desegregation. Comparable worth keeps EEO from being a Sisyphean game of hopscotch in which women move into a new occupation, enjoy the benefits of higher pay, but then lose them when the job becomes predominantly female and employers lower the wages, forcing them to move on to yet another occupation for just wages (Gold 1986).

Liberal-Feminist Critic: I think this reform is paternalistic and therefore insulting to women (Paul 1989; McElroy 1990). Women can and should make it on their own, without the government's help in getting them a wage the market can't justify.

Liberal-Feminist Advocate: Nonsense. If you believe that comparable worth is a response to a form of discrimination, and that it is not paternalistic for the government to enforce a prohibition against discrimination in hiring or in wages within the same job, then it is not paternalistic to ask the government to prohibit a newly identified form of sex discrimination in wage setting between jobs. It is simple justice, not a paternalistic gift.

Sociologist Advocate: I agree. Yet some might ask why—other than to serve some abstract notion of justice—it is important that women have access to higher wages. Sociological research is relevant to this question in that it has unearthed a number of the consequences for women having low wages. If women had higher wages, women in abusive marriages would be more able to leave, single women would be better able to support themselves, and single mothers would be better able to support their children (Feldberg 1984). This would help reverse a several-decade decline in children's economic well-being (Preston 1984). Higher wages would give married women something closer to equal power in decision-making in their marriages—on everything from geographical moves, to how money is spent, to whose wishes are important in the couple's sex life. This would include more bargaining power to get men to do their share of housework in dual-job marriages (Feldberg 1984).

Author: My view is that comparable worth is simple justice. Justice requires that one's wage not be lower simply because of one's sex. It requires prohibiting all kinds of sex discrimination, not only sex discrimination in access to positions. Concretely, this justice is very important for the well-being of women, whether married or single.

V. The Market Wage Argument

Business Critic: I think comparable worth is nonsense for two reasons: First, the market, not employers' discriminatory ideas, sets the wages of various occupations. Second, comparable worth is asking us to replace a free-market system with a government-imposed system of setting wages. As an advocate of free markets, I oppose this.

Neoclassical Critic: My business friend is right. Employers are what we call price-takers. Even if they wanted to pay less than the market wage in an occupation, they couldn't. No one would work for them.

Industrial-Psychologist Advocate: You economists stick to your abstract models. I study the behavior of personnel specialists in the real world, and I can tell you that firms have some choice about what they pay in a job. They can choose to be above or below the external market wage average. As the institutionalist economists put it, administrative and institutional factors affect wage setting (Treiman and Hartmann 1981; Bell 1985).

Neoclassical Critic: But if employers choose to pay below the market average, the trade-off is that they don't get as high a quality of worker. For some firms that will be an optimizing decision because, the way they have work organized, the benefit of the extra human capital won't be that great. My statement was intended to be understood under ceteris paribus conditions—holding constant the quality of labor.

Wages in a particular occupation for workers of a particular human capital are set by supply and demand (Williams and Kessler 1984; U.S.

Commission on Civil Rights 1984; Reynolds 1986). Holding demand constant, the more people who want to work in the occupation at any given wage (i.e., the more the supply), the lower the market wage. And, holding supply constant, the more people employers want to hire at any given wage (i.e., the more the demand), the higher the wage. (See Chapter 2 on the orthodox neoclassical model of supply and demand.)

Sociologist Advocate: There are two problems with your argument. First, your theory says that shortages will lead to higher wages, gluts will lead to lower wages, and that this process is gender neutral. But there is substantial evidence that employers respond differentially to shortages in female and male occupations. When there is a shortage in male occupation, the wage is often raised. But when it is a female occupation, often greater effort is expended to find a new source of cheap labor in lieu of raising pay. For example, hospitals have complained of a shortage of nurses for over two decades now, but have often imported foreign nurses instead of raising pay. Surely female workers are no easier to import than male workers, yet employers are more apt to raise pay rather than look for other sources of labor in male occupations (Grune 1984).

There is a second problem with your argument. If discrimination has affected the wage many employers are willing to pay in an occupation because the workers in it are women, then the market wage itself embodies discrimination (Grune 1984; Treiman and Hartmann 1981). Following market wages then is discriminating.

Legal Critic: Well, maybe. But we need to make a distinction between discrimination at some diffuse societal level and discrimination by a particular, identifiable employer (U.S. Commission on Civil Rights 1984). An individual employer can hardly be seen as discriminating when just following market wages, even if other employers' discrimination has gone into determining the market wage.

Feminist Advocate: It certainly seems unfair to me if a type of wage discrimination against women can be practiced by every employer in the market, but no particular employer can be held accountable for it because each one can claim to be following all the rest, i.e., to be following market wages. There is no accountability in such a system.

Author: The feminist advocate has hit the nail on the head. Public policy should not permit each employer to pay women's jobs discriminatorily low wages simply because most other employers are doing the same thing. Calling such a wage a market wage does not change the fact that it is discriminatory.

Business Critic: All right, I'll concede that market wages may sometimes be discriminatory. But let's be practical. How could we ever know when lower wages in women's than men's jobs are due to discrimination and when they are due to other nondiscriminatory market factors, such as shortages and gluts?

Neoclassical Critic: Indeed, there *is* no way to tell. In addition to garden variety shortages and gluts, there's another nondiscriminatory market factor that may affect wage differences between jobs. Economists call this compensating differentials. Jobs differ in how desirable they are on grounds other than their pay. So if a job is particularly dirty, dangerous, stressful, or otherwise onerous, employers will have to pay more to hire workers in that job than they will in a job requiring the same training but with less onerous working conditions (Cameron 1986). (See Chapter 2 for discussion of compensating differentials.)

Job-Evaluator Advocate: But this is no reason to reject comparable worth. Onerous job characteristics that require a higher wage as a compensating differential can be, and often are, built into job evaluation systems as one compensable factor. It is usually called working conditions.

Neoclassical Critic: Okay. But even with all the bells and whistles of job evaluations, it still boils down to the fact that advocates of comparable worth are arguing that there is an inherent value to each job, that the market is mistakenly calibrating this value, and they want to control the wage in accordance with their—necessarily subjective—notion of values. It really amounts to a reversion to the medieval just-wage doctrine or the Marxist labor theory of value (Raisin et al. 1986; Reynolds 1986; Paul 1989; McElroy 1990). But values are intrinsically subjective, and things have no inherent value outside supply and demand. For example, while most of us agree that water is more valuable than diamonds, diamonds cost more. Presumably this is because diamonds are in much shorter supply than water—not because they are inherently more valuable. So too with jobs. They have no inherent value outside supply and demand. So there is no way to determine when their pay deviates from its true value since there is no nonmarket yardstick on which to measure such value.

Institutionalist-Economist Advocate: I agree that jobs have no inherent worth written on stone handed down from heaven. But perhaps there is a kernel of truth in the medieval just-wage doctrine. For all neoclassicals have tried to ignore it, norms and values about status or equity *do* play a role in today's wage setting (Marshall and Paulin 1984).

Unfortunately, since we live in a sexist society, norms that devalue work done by women often creep in. Comparable worth aims to correct this bias, that's all. To say that we can identify systematic sex bias does not imply that we know the inherent value of jobs.

Sociologist Advocate: I agree completely.

Author: I believe that market wages are often discriminatory, and that job evaluation is a useful (albeit imperfect) tool to rid wage systems of such discrimination. Detecting sex bias does not require knowing the inherent value of jobs. If anything, job evaluation may give too few points to women's jobs. Existing research in social psychology suggests that bias, if it exists, works against rather than in favor of women's jobs getting more points. (See Chapter 4.) Nonetheless, advocates of comparable worth must concede that an occasional nondiscriminatory differential will be erroneously identified as discriminatory by a job evaluation. This could happen if there was an idiosyncratic shortage of labor to a male job. But we would expect temporary shortages and gluts to be relatively random in relation to the sex composition of the job.[1] Yet job evaluation studies at many points in time have found women's jobs to be systematically underpaid to relative to men's. (See Chapter 4.) I don't find the prospect that implementing comparable worth will occasionally produce such an error to be a compelling enough argument to let well-documented and systematic patterns of wage discrimination against women persist.

Libertarian Business Critic: You folks are talking about how markets work. I want to shift the argument to fundamental matters of rights. The liberty provided by a market economy is fundamental to American values (Paul 1989). An employer should have the right to set wages on the basis he or she sees fit. Comparable worth means that a *third party* other than the employer and the employee (and other than the employees' bargaining representative—a union) will be able to interfere in wage setting (Williams and Kessler 1984; EEAC 1985). It would be the end of the market wage system as we know it (Northrup 1984; Levin 1984, 1987). Comparable worth allows the government to be used for private "rent seeking" (Paul 1989; Rabkin 1984).

Socialist Advocate: What you call liberty is really letting capitalist property rights override all other rights. Since most Americans own no property to speak of, the liberty they can enjoy as a result of the market system is severely limited!

Liberal Advocate: Besides, comparable worth is not radically different than prior reforms in how much it tells employers what they can and can't do (Grune 1984; Steinberg 1986; England 1986). Every reform from child labor laws to the Equal Pay Act was fought by business groups, each time arguing that this latest reform was somehow *fundamentally* more interventionist than prior reforms (Steinberg 1986). Each time business groups argue that the sky will fall if the reform is instituted. What is amazing is that the ideology of laissez-faire is so strong that people listen to these "Chicken Little" tales every time (Steinberg 1986).

Author: It does come down to values. I place more importance on using public policy to promote gender justice than on preserving an employer's right to be free from any governmental interference.

VI. The Feasibility and Relevance of Job Evaluation

Business Critic: Enough theory. The important question about comparable worth is whether it is practical. I say it isn't. How can you compare apples and oranges? It can't be done. That's why as a practical business man I reject the idea. Job evaluation is inherently subjective (Williams and Kessler 1984; Schwab 1984; U.S. Commission on Civil Rights 1984; Reynolds 1986; Schlafly 1986; Raisin et al. 1986; Paul 1989).

Industrial-Psychologist Advocate: It is ironic that a businessperson finds job evaluation so impractical since large businesses use it all the time to set wages. True, judgments are involved, but that is true in any part of business practice.

Job evaluation involves several steps. (See Chapter 4.) First, descriptions of each job must be written. Second, compensable factors must be chosen. Third, a weight must be chosen for each factor. Sometimes this is done a priori, sometimes empirically via a policy-capturing analysis. Then points must be given for each job on each compensable factor. Finally, a total score is obtained for each job. Jobs are considered comparable if they have the same number of total job evaluation points. If women's jobs are consistently paying lower wages than men's jobs with the same points (for persons of the same seniority), this is evidence of sex discrimination. Job evaluation systems may be imperfect, but they are better than no system at all (Rothchild 1984).

Job evaluation has typically not been performed with an eye to paying comparable male- and female-dominated jobs equally. But it can be used in this way. After evaluating all jobs in a business, one can check to see whether there is a tendency for predominantly female jobs to pay less than predominantly male jobs that the job evaluation gave the same points.

Author: Job evaluation is the best tool we have for comparable worth. It is imperfect, but so are all other solutions, including the market.

Radical-Cultural-Feminist Critic: I'm in favor of comparable worth, but I'm concerned about the amount of bias we leave in wage systems when we use policy-capturing methods of job evaluation. They do have the merit of avoiding subjective decisions about what job characteristics are to have what weights. But I'm concerned that in our zeal to give the benefit of the doubt to employers' own criteria, we may be building in some features of how the market is rewarding things that are discriminatory (Schwab 1984). If the market is giving a low or even a negative weight (return) to types of skills more common in female jobs, such as nurturant social skills, this may be *because* the skill type is associated with women. Policy-capturing evaluation will build this bias into wage systems rather than help us take it out. (See Chapter 3 for evidence that the market does give a negative return to nurturant social skills.)

Author: This is a real dilemma. Job evaluation needs to use weights arrived at either judgmentally (in a priori job evaluation) or empirically (in policy-capturing job evaluation). In the first case, there is a potential for correcting sex bias in the weights; however, there is no empirically derived baseline against which to tell when a weight indicates bias (Treiman and Hartmann 1981; McDowell 1985). If job characteristics most positively correlated with the percentage female in jobs have lower positive or even negative weights, this will adversely impact women's wages, but it may or may not arise from sex discrimination in the setting of the weights. Policy capturing objectively reflects whatever weights are currently being used, gives the employer the benefit of the doubt that they are not a result of bias, and then uses the resulting job evaluation formula to assess whether female jobs are paid as much as male jobs with the same number of points. Although this removes direct gender bias (nonconsistency), it doesn't remove bias in the weights themselves. Thus policy capturing may build in some parts of bias. But, as an empirical matter, policy capturing almost always finds bias (nonconsistency) and leads to gains for women. Actually, both policy capturing and the commonly used management-decided a priori methods (such as the Hay system) tend to find, at least in government workplaces, that women's jobs are underpaid by about 20% (Rothchild 1984). Thus, they are much better than nothing. A priori systems of job evaluation with weights decided by management-labor committees on which workers from female jobs are adequately represented are another possibility, one with more potential to remove sexist bias in the weights themselves.

Industrial-Psychologist Critic: Job evaluation builds in more features of market wages than just the weights. It also builds in elements of market wages when multiple plans are used for different job families and each plan has different weights and intercepts (Schwab 1980). For example, many firms have separate evaluation plans for management, clerical, and blue-collar jobs. The tendency is to give the predominantly male groups—management and blue-collar jobs—higher point-to-pay lines, leading to higher wages for male jobs than female jobs with the same points. However, these discrepancies are not corrected because adjustments are not made across job families, only within them.

Author: This is a major reason that the use of job evaluation by many large firms coexists with discriminatory wages in female jobs. Because of this, any legal requirement of comparable worth should mandate one single plan for an establishment.

VII.   Legal Issues

Legal Critic: Comparable worth is not required by Title VII of the Civil Rights Act of 1964, which was passed to ensure equal opportunity in access to positions and equal pay for equal work within positions. (See Chapter 5 on legal issues.)

Feminist Legal Advocate: I disagree. The legal form of the argument for comparable worth goes like this: The animating principle of Title VII regarding gender discrimination is to forbid using gender as a criterion in any employment decision. This includes decisions regarding whom to hire for or assign to a particular job. Title VII also applies to compensation, stating that it is unlawful for an employer "to . . . discriminate against any individual with respect to . . . compensation . . . because of such individual's . . . sex." Both this language and the simple principle of nondiscrimination imply that gender may not be taken into account when an employer decides whether person A or person B will get paid more in a single job (equal pay for equal work) *and* that it not be taken into account in a decision about whether job X will pay more than job Y (comparable worth). If job X pays more than job Y for reasons quite apart from the gender composition of the job, there is no gender discrimination. If, however, the gender of those holding the jobs has affected the decision about their relative pay levels, then it is consistent with the spirit of Title VII to prohibit such discrimination.

Legal Critic: But employers don't decide what to pay in each job; they often follow market wages. And all the circuit courts that have ruled on the issue have been quite clear in permitting paying the market wage as a rebuttal or a defense in comparable worth cases (Williams and Kessler 1984; U.S. Commission on Civil Rights 1984).

Feminist Legal Advocate: True, but this has not been tested by the Supreme Court, and I think the circuit courts have erred. Permitting the market wage defense amounts to deciding that each individual employee is allowed to engage in gender discrimination in setting wages as long as s/he is merely following the discrimination practiced by everyone else! There is Supreme Court precedent for rejecting a somewhat analogous market wage defense in an Equal Pay Act case (Newman and Owens 1984). However, today's Supreme Court is, unfortunately, much more conservative than the Court that made this decision.

If the market wage defense fails when it finally reaches the Supreme Court, as I hope it will, then the interesting legal question becomes what burden of proof plaintiffs have in comparable worth cases. I think that a policy-capturing job evaluation showing inconsistent treatment of male and female jobs should constitute a differential treatment proof of discrimination (England 1986). Disparate impact cases could be used to challenge biased weights for comparable factors. The most optimistic scenario I can paint for getting comparable worth implemented in the private sector without new legislation is that the Supreme Court will reject the market wage defense and then lower courts will permit results from policy-capturing job evaluations as evidence of differential treatment.

Legal Critic: Well, I doubt that today's Supreme Court will reject the market wage defense. But even if this happened, you can't use a policy-capturing job evaluation as proof of differential treatment. This would be a disparate impact proof, but disparate impact proofs are not permitted in comparable worth cases (McDowell 1985; U.S. Civil Rights Commission 1984). Cases alleging wage discrimination involving different jobs are allowable where intent can be clearly shown, as, for example, where an employer openly states in a smoking-gun memo that a job was paid more because it contained men (U.S. Commission on Civil Rights 1984). Other than this, plaintiffs can't win comparable worth cases under Title VII.

Author: I agree with the advocate, that it would be consistent with the antidiscrimination spirit of Title VII to reject market wage defenses, to permit job evaluation to constitute a differential treatment proof (of the non–smoking-gun variety), and to permit challenges to weights as disparate impact proofs. However, the circuit courts have not seen the issue this way, and I doubt that the current Supreme Court will, given its conservative composition. Thus, I think legal approaches to comparable worth cases, except those of the smoking-gun variety, require new legislation. In addition, legislation can get governments to reevaluate their own jobs; this is already happening in many states and localities. (See Table 4.1.) Another strategy for comparable worth is organizing through unions to push for wage increases for those in predominantly female jobs.

VIII. Could Comparable Worth Achieve Its Goals?

Businessperson: Let's get practical again. I'll assume, for the sake of argument, that job evaluation can be used to identify when jobs' wages are discriminatory. What would comparable worth policy look like? What do the advocates envision as a law or policy? How would it be enforced?

Liberal-Feminist Advocate: The law should require that the gender composition of jobs not affect what the jobs are paid. This wouldn't absolutely require every firm to do a job evaluation, but it would encourage most to do so. Consulting firms might sell systems that are easy to implement. Either a regulatory agency, such as the OFCCP (in the case of federal contractors) or the EEOC, or plaintiffs in a court case could allege discrimination. A job evaluation would be needed to prove guilt or innocence. Title VII as it is written now should be interpreted to require this. But since, so far, the courts have not interpreted Title VII this way, new federal legislation is needed. We advocates also favor the strategy of states and localities legislating job evaluation for their own employees. However, this doesn't affect the private sector (except indirectly, as, for example, increases in clerical pay in state capitals would affect what businesses have to pay secretaries to prevent the best from going to work for the state). Hence we also endorse new federal legislation that applies to all employers, public or private.

Neoclassical Critic: But there would be all sorts of ways for employers to get around these requirements. They could subcontract out the work currently done in female jobs to small firms. Small firms are less likely to be worth suing and below some size they would probably be exempted from the legislation (Oi 1986). In firms covered by the legislation, continual vigilance would be needed to prevent employers from letting wages in male jobs creep up above those in comparable female jobs after initial equity adjustments (Levin 1984; Cameron 1986). Besides, it is not clear how much all this effort will reduce the sex gap in pay, because some of this gap results from women's concentration in smaller, marginal firms and industries that pay lower wages. Comparable worth policy won't touch these interfirm differentials since it will apply only within firms.

Author: To be sure, comparable worth is not a panacea. But still, evaluation studies generally find women's jobs underpaid by about 20%. This means that women's wages would be increased by about 25% if comparable worth were fully implemented within organizations across the economy ($100 - 20 = 80$, $20 = 25\%$ of 80). This is not trivial! Barring a supreme Court decision favorable to interpreting Title VII to require comparable worth, we need new legislation to bring comparable worth to the private sector.

Neoclassical Critic: We've discussed the direct effects of comparable worth—raising wages in women's occupations. But we must also look at possible unintended, but harmful, consequences. (See Chapter 2 for a discussion of neoclassical views of comparable worth.) Economic theory suggests that there would be many adverse effects. We might start with the effects on women, the supposed beneficiaries of the policies. Requiring employers to raise the wage in female occupations will reduce the number of people employers hire in those occupations. This follows from standard principles of supply and demand. This will lead to some unemployment and some people who stop looking for work because the best pay they can get is not worth working for (Hildebrand 1980; EEAC 1985; Cameron 1986; Schlafly 1986; O'Neill 1984). Much of this burden will be borne by women since they are the ones now in the female jobs and may be at some disadvantage in getting male jobs.

Naive Advocate: Are you saying that firms will fire people because of comparable worth wage adjustments? Surely regulations could be written so employers aren't allowed to do this.

Neoclassical Critic: True, but that won't stop the disemployment. Even if employers covered by the regulations don't fire any of the people in the female jobs whose wages they are forced to increase, they may decline to replace workers who leave. Then people who otherwise would have gotten hired in female jobs will not get them. This will be happening economywide.

Naive Advocate: That's absurd. If they need 50 secretaries in the firm, they are going to have to keep 50 to get the work done.

Neoclassical Critic: Not really. For example, if secretaries get more expensive, firms may decide it is worthwhile to invest in more time-saving equipment (e.g., a collating machine), so they can have fewer, more efficient secretaries. When secretaries were cheaper, it may not have been cost-effective to buy the equipment. And disemployment is not the only undesirable side effect of comparable worth; it may also lower some women's wages. This is ironic since the whole point of comparable worth is to raise the wages of women (and the occasional man) in female jobs. While it *will* do so in those firms covered by the reform, it may indirectly lower the wages of women in other firms. This happens because there are always firms not covered by the law, an uncovered sector, either because the law exempts firms below a certain size from coverage, or because, even if they are formally covered, as a practical matter, there is less enforcement in such firms. Those who otherwise would have gotten jobs in the covered sector will be forced into the uncovered sector (if not into unemployment or out of the labor force). Because the uncovered sector will now contain more workers than previously, this crowding will lower wages. This will hit particularly hard in female occupations in the uncovered firms, since women displaced from the uncovered firms will probably seek similar jobs in the uncovered sector (Cameron 1986; Oi 1986; Smith 1988). And those in the uncovered section of small firms with little capital investment per worker already earn less (Smith 1988). So the women already paid the least may be hurt the most. (See Chapter 2 for neoclassical views of consequences of comparable worth.)

Liberal-Neoclassical Advocate: A lot turns on the magnitude of the disemployment and crowding caused by comparable worth. I agree that some will occur. However, if the magnitude is small, this may just mean slightly longer spells of unemployment during search. Also, some of the critics act as if there are two distinct groups of women: a first group that benefits from the mandated wage increases in female jobs in the covered sector, and a second group trying to enter such jobs but finding themselves unemployed or forced into a lower-wage job in the uncovered sector. In reality, there is considerable overlap between the two groups. So the net benefit to women must be seen in terms of an averaging between the positive and adverse effects of the reform (Bergmann 1989).

Author: I have to agree with the liberal neoclassical advocate here. Comparable worth might well cause some disemployment, but this cost has to be weighed against the substantial benefits. But the critic's point should remind us that any reform that raises wages makes full employment policies all the more important.

Classical Liberal-Feminist Critic: The adverse impact of comparable worth that really bothers me is something different. Women won't be as motivated to seek entry into the male jobs as they are now (O'Neill 1984;

Reynolds 1986; Schlafly 1986; Gethman 1987; Rector 1988; Paul 1989). The "pink-collar ghetto" will be perpetuated. Feminists should not be advocating this.

Sociologist Advocate: The critic is right that the higher wages in female jobs may make more women decide to enter or stay in such jobs than would otherwise have been the case. But so what? Why should we want female jobs worth as much as male jobs to continue to be devalued because of their gender just to provide a motivation for women to integrate men's jobs? Women seeking higher pay will still be attracted into those male occupations that, for nondiscriminatory reasons, continue to pay more than female occupations even after the wage adjustments. Moreover, if integration is a good thing, and I agree that it is, then we should also be concerned about men being motivated to enter female occupations. Here comparable worth will help; if the wages in women's occupations go up, more men will be motivated to take those jobs. This may eventually change men's tastes and values in favor of traditionally female tasks—and it will provide the cognitive input and role models for the next generation of boys to see this as well. Perhaps this will even help make it acceptable for men to do female tasks in the home, another much needed reform for women. (See Chapter 2 for a discussion of sociological views of how changing structural positions changes one's tastes and values.)

Feminist Advocate: It is so ironic that the same groups that have fought affirmative action and Title VII tooth and nail the last 30 years are suddenly its biggest advocates, claiming to be terribly concerned that comparable worth could undermine these efforts (Steinberg 1986). In fact, comparable worth and job integration have considerable complementarity. For example, if men don't fear that more women in their job will lower wages, because paying according to gender composition is illegal, men will be more sympathetic to women entering their jobs (Steinberg 1986).

Sociologist Advocate: This is important since there is a lot of evidence that it is male workers who have often convinced employers to discriminate against women trying to get into their jobs, both out of their own sexism and out of fear of their wages going down. (See Chapter 1.)

Legal Advocate: Comparable worth also gives employers a motivation to eliminate segregation because they can hardly be liable for comparable worth discrimination if most of their jobs are sex integrated.

Author: The advocates have the better argument here. Comparable worth will aid desegregation in many ways. It will impede desegregation only where the former wage advantage to male jobs that was motivating women's entry was itself discriminatory.

IX.   Possible Adverse Effects on the Economy, Polity, and Society

Neoclassical Critic: Unfortunately, there are other adverse effects of comparable worth. (These too are discussed in the section on neoclassical views of comparable worth in Chapter 2.) So far we've been arguing about those that would hurt women's wages or employment chances. But comparable worth would also have effects on the whole economy. The unemployment rate may increase as employers demand fewer workers in female jobs. But this won't hit only women; it will hurt whatever workers are most disadvantaged in getting jobs (Reynolds 1986; Rector 1988). If employers raise wages in female jobs without lowering them in male jobs, they will have to increase the price of their products, thus making American products less competitive in international markets (EEAC 1985; Raisin et al. 1986). The per capita gross national product will fall if labor costs rise with no increase in productivity (Reynolds 1986; Rector 1988).

Labor Advocate: Employers always resist reforms that cost them something. Business groups fought the Equal Pay Act, Title VII, and all job safety regulations tooth and nail (Steinberg 1986). Costs shouldn't be an issue if this is a matter of basic justice (Williams and Kessler 1984). You could make a cost argument against all of Title VII, but I don't hear these critics doing it. Why then make the argument against comparable worth? Besides, let's not exaggerate the costs. The costs can be kept manageable if the wage changes are spread out over time (Sape 1985; Steinberg 1986). Even if they are done all at once they have generally been only between 2 and 5% of payroll (McEntee 1986; Steinberg 1986).

Business Advocate: The funds for gradual increases could come out of funds for regular raises. This would not entail lowering wages in any male jobs, but would dictate slower raises in these jobs than would otherwise have been the case (Bergmann 1986).

Business Critic: But the relevant costs aren't only the actual costs of the wage increases. There are also enforcement and administrative costs, such as the taxes required to support governmental regulatory agencies, and the salaries required for firms to hire extra personnel professionals to do job evaluations. The federal courts will have their caseloads increased—something taxpayers will have to pay for (Rabkin

1984). In addition, firms and employee groups will spend money lobbying to change regulations and hiring lawyers to initiate and fight lawsuits. All these costs reduce the per capital productivity of the economy (Reynolds 1986; Jacobsen 1989) and absorb funds that could otherwise be used to improve the infrastructure of our economy (Cameron 1986; Rector 1988).

Political Scientist Critic: In addition to all these costs, labor-management strife will increase, and our political culture will see increased conflict (Rabkin 1984).

Feminist Advocate: Gee, you make it sound like the sky is falling. Why are all these issues suddenly brought up when the reform in question would help women achieve economic independence? I don't hear these arguments when the reform is helpful to business, labor, farmers, or even minority men. Besides, if all you business people and economists are really so concerned with efficiency, then why haven't you considered the search and retraining costs of moving massive numbers of women from female to male occupations in a short period of time? The costs of fully integrating all occupations by sex would be much greater than the costs you are talking about. And the political strife that would result from millions of men having to move to female jobs when women out-qualify them for male jobs would hardly be trivial! It seems to me that what you really advocate is either no change or making the victims of discrimination bear the costs of the change. If the economy is in trouble, why fix it on the backs of women?

Business Advocate: Besides, we haven't looked at some of the benefits to taxpayers of comparable worth. Comparable worth will save taxpayer's money in that some low-income women receiving noncash public assistance such as food stamps will no longer be eligible for these benefits (Gleason 1985). Since the issue won't go away, businesses should voluntarily undertake the reform (Sape 1985), using job evaluation. It is a tool many large firms have used for decades, although generally not in a consistent manner across all job families. This will be much cheaper than spending decades in litigation or in fights with women's unions.

Author: There are costs of any reform, and it is good to realize this, enough though we can't calculate them exactly. Still, I fail to see that the costs of comparable worth are qualitatively different from those involved in other antidiscrimination reforms. For me, the prospect of ending the unfair and systematic devaluation of work because it is done by women makes the reform worthwhile.

X. Is Comparable Worth an Insufficiently Radical Reform?

Leftist Critic: As much as I hate to agree with conservative economists, I too think this reform is the wrong way to go, though my reason for opposition is completely different than that of the conservatives. There is a real danger that comparable worth could exacerbate the losses workers have been taking during the last two decades. It works against the solidarity the working class so desperately needs to move toward economic democracy. Men may legitimately fear that if women get raises, men's wages will be lowered—or the raises for women will be taken from a pool that would have gone to future raises for men (Feldberg 1984). If so, comparable worth will pit men and women workers against each other.

Socialist-Feminist Advocate: True, these are dangers, but it is also true that women's currently low wages divide the working class. When women earn so much less, men don't want to include women in their unions because of the fear that it would take so much effort to get women's wages up to their level, that not enough energy would go into trying to increase men's wages. Whether comparable worth becomes a basis of solidarity or men fight it depends a lot on the responses of organized labor at the local grass-roots level (Feldberg 1984). It can go either way. (See Chapter 6 for a discussion of socialist feminism.)

Socialist Critic: Well, maybe. But another problem I have with comparable worth is that it seems always to end up rewarding educational credentials and cognitive knowledge, and devaluing physical labor and blue-collar jobs (Schlafly 1986; Berger 1984). This isn't fair to working-class men, particularly men of color who are most concentrated in this hard, dirty work.

Socialist-Feminist Advocate: Comparable worth need not be biased against manual work. The weights could give more reward to blue-collar work than they do. I agree that managerial work is currently overpaid, relative to manual work. But why should manual labor that gets dirt and grease under the fingernails pay more than jobs that expose workers to human vomit and feces and involve interpersonal stress? These are common in women's service sector jobs. Women of color are concentrated in such jobs, with the lowest pay of all workers. Thus, they would be helped a good deal by comparable worth (Malveaux 1986). Sexism has surely affected the valuation of these jobs.

Socialist-Feminist Critic: These issues should remind us that job evaluation is never an entirely apolitical, neutral technical practice. Neither is the decision to follow market wages. The decision to reward managerial power with higher pay rather than see it as rewarding in its own right is political. Comparable worth is a sham unless workers, including women, get to participate in the inherently political decisions of how it is carried out. Otherwise, there is a real potential for abuse here. Technocrats working for management can find a formula to reify and legitimate virtually any set of criteria for pay that management wants. Even if the government provides regulations, the capitalist class has the resources to lobby for implementation strategies that make it look like women are being helped when very little change is going on. It seems a better socialist and feminist strategy to me to rely on organizing women into unions.

Radical-Feminist Advocate: I have a similar concern—that the process needs to be consistent with feminist values that argue for mutual respect, empowerment of participants, and accepting differences in views. But this doesn't lead me to oppose comparable worth. For me, it is all the more reason to argue for democratic processes in the implementation of comparable worth in every workplace.

Socialist-Feminist Advocate: I agree. Perhaps we will decide, when we approach this democratically, that many low-paid jobs deserve more, relative to managerial and professional jobs, than they are now paid because they rob the worker of their very chance to develop human capabilities (Amott and Matthai 1984). Comparable worth need not embrace liberal, meritocratic principles of justice and need not say that wages for white men are fair. It simply requires the claim that men's wages are less exploitative than the rate received by women and minorities (Shrage 1987). Comparable worth, although certainly an inadequate reform by socialist standards, may set the stage for attacks on other forms of inequity (Feldberg 1984). Moreover, since critics are viewing comparable worth as an attack on the market, it forces a rethinking of the dominance of the market (Feldberg 1984; Steinberg 1986). All in all, it seems a reform worth supporting.

Radical-Cultural-Feminist Critic: I'm concerned that comparable worth doesn't do much to change the devaluation of traditionally female values such as altruism and nurturance when they are present in work. This is particularly true when policy capturing is used, since it takes the weights for factors the employer is using as given, and merely allows us to see that they are applied consistently in men's and women's jobs. (See Chapter 6 for a discussion of radical-cultural feminism.)

Radical-Cultural-Feminist Advocate: True. But we can push for democratically controlled a priori discussions of factor weights. But even if we only get policy capturing, if significantly more women became economically independent, that would be a radical change (Feldberg 1984) that does threaten traditional notions of masculinity. I see that the reform is inadequate, but it's much better than nothing. We radical feminists have tended to choose the strategy of developing women's culture in (sometimes separatist) women's communities where we seek to reward those traditionally female values, like mutual nurturance, that are not merely a result of subordination under patriarchy. I think this continues to be of value to the women's movement. But the reality is that millions of women, married and single, parents and nonparents, lesbian and heterosexual, are going to continue to work in mainstream organizations. Many have little choice. It seems that we should be in favor of a reform that gives more value to traditionally women's work in these settings. My hope is that this will contribute to changing values in the culture at large in a feminist direction.

Behavioral-Economist Advocate: Well, this is one place that neoclassical economists would disagree with my feminist friend, but I would agree. Most economists would say that forcing employers to pay more in female jobs won't change their values about those kinds of tasks. But the framing theory developed in behavioral economics suggests that it may indeed change their perceptions of what is of value. (See Chapter 2.) Present wages provide part of the frame within which we assess the value of a job and what wages it should pay.

Sociologist Advocate: This is consistent with research from social psychology showing that current arrangements of who is rewarded tend, over time, to be seen by societal members as right. Thus, comparable worth probably would change values.

Author: As I argued in Chapter 6, one can find grounds for support for comparable worth in any of the three major feminist positions. Yet the reform is dissonant with aspects of each position, as well. It is endorsed by groups called liberal feminist, such as NOW and National Women's Political Caucus, yet is inconsistent with the laissez-faire roots of the classical liberalism from which liberal feminism grew. Versions of comparable worth that have much likelihood of adoption are insufficiently radical for socialist feminists or radical feminists, although they speak to some of the egalitarian concerns of each. In my view, all feminists should agree that making gender less a basis for pay is a reform to be supported.

XI. Conclusion

Let me provide a final summing up of the chapter and the book as a whole. There is a still sizable sex gap in pay. Much of it results from women's concentration in lower-paying occupations. Traditional interpretations of EEO have focused on women gaining access to all occupations and on their procuring equal pay for equal work in all jobs. Comparable worth, sometimes called pay equity, adds a third strategy to these. Its aims are policies that ensure that the pay level of a job is not lower simply because the work is done mainly by women. Evidence of this sort of discrimination abounds, in results of job evaluations done within organizations, as well as in national data. Such studies find that the sex composition of a job affects its pay, net of the job's skill demands and working conditions, and that demands typical of the jobs women are in, such as nurturing social skills, often receive low and even negative returns. Ideally, comparable worth would eradicate these types of gender bias in wage setting as employers use job evaluation to set wages in a consistent and nonbiased manner. I see no evidence that the tendency of employers to take the sex composition of jobs into account in setting wages has declined.

Neoclassical economists argue that all sorts of discrimination will eventually erode in competitive markets. I agree such a tendency exists, but there are many institutional facts that make the process glacial in speed. Thus, governmental action is warranted on comparable worth, as well as other forms of discrimination.

Some opponents of comparable worth argue that the real problem is occupational segregation, and that policy should be directed toward ensuring that women have fair access to higher-paying (typically male) jobs. Some take this argument even farther and say that if women's jobs are underpaid relative to their skill levels, this must be due to crowding in female jobs, itself caused by women's exclusion from male jobs. I argued that, while crowding may be a factor, the cultural devaluation of work that is done by women contributes to the low pay in female jobs as well. Comparable worth speaks directly to this devaluation in a way that desegregation does not, although desegregation is also an important goal. As a matter of justice, women should not have to change jobs to have access to a wage not contaminated by gender bias. Moreover, it would be extremely costly for women already trained for traditionally female jobs to retrain and change jobs. If one is against discrimination, it makes sense to be against all forms of it.

Lower wages for women have grave consequences. The ability of the growing number of single and divorced women to support themselves and their children hinges on progress in women's earnings. Sociological evidence also shows that women's earnings affect their marital power. Low wages for women reinforce the patriarchal nature of the family; raising women's wages would promote egalitarian marriages.

One of the most tendentious parts of the debate over comparable worth is the issue of whether "the market" explains the lower wages in women's jobs, and whether employers who follow market wages are innocent of discrimination. Critics of comparable worth answer yes to both questions, while advocates answer no. To be sure, markets create some wage differentials between jobs for nondiscriminatory reasons such as human capital requirements and compensating differentials. But, if many employers discriminate, then *even if* market processes eventually erode discrimination, market wages will transmit discriminatory differentials before this erosion is complete, perhaps for decades. Thus an employer who simply pays the "going rate" in a female job is adopting a discriminatory wage. I agree with advocates of comparable worth that employers should be prohibited from paying discriminatory wages.

Comparable worth would not make every male job pay the same as every female job. Job evaluation would be used to assess which jobs are deemed comparable. Part of the debate over comparable worth hinges on its feasibility. Opponents call job evaluation "subjective," seeing this as a pejorative term. Job evaluation is undoubtedly an imperfect tool that involves human judgments; all decision-making processes used by either businesses or government have this property. It is ironic that businesses groups attack job evaluation as overly subjective, since many large employers have used job evaluation for decades. However, employers often do not use one consistent system for all job families within an establishment, and hence the pay awarded per point is often lower in the job families (e.g., clerical) containing mostly female jobs. To achieve comparable worth, it is important that employers use a single system for all jobs.

To use job evaluation, an employer must choose either a policy-capturing or an a priori system. At issue is whether the only requirement should be that employers use a system of weights for compensable factors consistently across male and female jobs, or whether the weights themselves can be contested as gender biased. In practice, with consultants and management in charge, policy-capturing and a priori systems generally achieve similar results. But a priori systems have the *potential* to contest aspects of hierarchy not touched by policy-capturing systems. If a democratic process is used to set the weights, for example, the hegemony of mental over manual skills, or of managerial social skills over nurturant social skills could be contested. This is what many advocates suggest, but it is a harder version of the reform to achieve, in part because it allows more of what employers do to be contested.

Would comparable worth really help women, its intended beneficiaries? In one sense it obviously would—wages would be raised in women's jobs. But economists contend that there would also be unintended, adverse effects. Disemployment from firms covered by the regulations and crowding in other firms would affect some women, although these effects would be shared by whoever is lowest in the employment queue.

In addition, critics point to the costs of regulation. These are arguments that have been raised by business groups against every reform that proposes regulating employers' actions. This includes past anti-discrimination legislation, legislation that those opposing comparable worth now claim to favor. One can understand employers' rational preference for less regulation. But the prospect of raising women's wages seems also to strike a deep irrational core of hysteria because it threatens men's entitlement to have whatever they do accorded more importance than what women do, and to higher wages than women of their race and class.

Comparable worth is insufficiently radical for many socialists, socialist feminists, and radical-cultural feminists. It preserves many aspects of hierarchical arrangements, even elements of gender hierarchies, and may even serve to legitimate them. Yet, at the same time, by contesting employers' absolute authority to set wages, by contesting laissez-faire market policies, it sets the stage for other questions to be raised. It is, nonetheless, a limited reform. I argued that because comparable worth would work toward removing one particular source of gender discrimination from wage systems, it deserves feminist support.

Where does the law now stand on comparable worth? My view is that it would be consistent with the animating principle of Title VII—non-discrimination—to consider violations of comparable worth to be violations of law. However, the appellate circuit courts have not interpreted Title VII this way. They have allowed paying market wages as a defense. This point has not yet been tested at the Supreme Court. Given the current makeup of the Supreme Court, I believe it would support the market wage defense and reject comparable worth. Thus, the future of comparable worth hinges upon political efforts at the federal, state, and local levels to pass laws that require the governmental units to perform job evaluations and pay according to comparable worth principles, an effort already underway in many states and localities. However, to have large-scale effects, comparable worth needs to be required in the private sector as well. If the courts will not interpret Title VII to require this, then new legislation is needed.

Comparable worth refers to a kind of discrimination that has proven surprisingly difficult to explain to scholars, judges, policymakers, or citizens. It is invisible even to most of its victims. In our culture, it is easier to see that (1) women are discriminated against when they are not allowed into predominantly male jobs, than to see that (2) women are discriminated against when entire occupations are devalued and paid less because they are done by women and/or involve traditionally female skills. The first suggests that feminism is about women entering nontraditional activities. The second suggests that feminism is about revaluing and increasing the rewards of traditionally female activities. I believe that feminism should be simultaneously about both; its goals should be to open activities to people irrespective of gender and to value activities irrespective of the gender of those who now do them or have traditionally done them. In the scholarly understanding of gender as well as the practical politics of feminism, much hinges on recognizing both types of sexism.

Notes

1. The crowding thesis argues that women's jobs systematically have gluts and men's have shortages. (See Chapter 2.) This criticism of comparable worth policies has been dealt with in an earlier section of this chapter's dialogue.

References

Abowd, John and Mark Killingsworth. 1983. "Sex, Discrimination, Atrophy, and the Male-Female Wage Differential." *Industrial Relations* 22(3):387–402.

Acker, Joan. 1987. "Sex Bias in Job Evaluation: A Comparable Worth Issue." Pp. 183–196 in *Ingredients for Women's Employment Policy*, edited by C. Bose and G. Spitze. Albany: State University of New York Press.

———. 1989. *Doing Comparable Worth: Gender, Class and Pay Equity.* Philadelphia: Temple University Press.

Ackerman, Bruce A. 1980. *Social Justice in the Liberal State.* New Haven, CT: Yale University Press.

Agger, Ben. 1991. "Critical Theory, Poststructuralism, Postmodernism: Their Sociological Relevance." Pp. 105–132 in *Annual Review of Sociology,* vol. 17, edited by W. Richard Scott and Judith Blake. Palo Alto, CA: Annual Reviews.

Aigner, D. J. and G. G. Cain. 1977. "Statistical Theories of Discrimination in Labor Markets." *Industrial and Labor Relations Review* 30:1975–1987.

Akalin, Mustafa T. 1970. *Office Job Evaluation.* Des Plaines, IL: Industrial Management Society.

Akerlof, George A. 1982. "Labor Contracts as Partial Gift Exchange." *Quarterly Journal of Economics* 97:543–569.

———. 1984. "Gift Exchange and Efficiency Wages: Four Views." *American Economic Review* 74:79–83.

Akerlof, George and H. Miyazaki. 1980. "The Implicit Contract Theory of Unemployment Meets the Wage Bill Argument." *Review of Economic Studies* 47:321–338.

Akerlof, George A. and Janet L. Yellen. 1986. *Efficiency Wage Models of the Labor Market.* Cambridge: Cambridge University Press.

Alcoff, Linda. 1988. "Cultural Feminism Versus Post-Structuralism: The Identity Crisis in Feminist Theory." *Signs* 13:405–436.

Aldrich, Mark and Robert Buchele. 1986. *The Economics of Comparable Worth.* Boston: Ballinger.

———. 1989. "Where to Look for Comparable Worth: The Implications of Efficiency Wages." Pp. 11–28 in *Comparable Worth: Analyses and Evidence,* edited by M. Anne Hill and Mark Killingsworth. Ithaca, NY: ILR Press.

Alexander, Jeffrey C., ed. 1985. *Neofunctionalism.* Beverly Hills, CA: Sage.

309

Althauser, Robert P. and Arne L. Kalleberg. 1981. "Firms, Occupations, and the Structure of Labor Markets: A Conceptual Analysis." Pp. 119–149 in *Sociological Perspectives on Labor Markets*, edited by Ivar Berg. New York: Academic Press.

Althusser, Louis. 1970. *For Marx*. New York: Vintage.

———. 1971. *Lenin and Philosophy*. New York: Monthly Review Press.

American Federation of State, County, and Municipal Employees v. State of Washington. 1983. Western District of Washington, Tacoma.

American Federation of State, County, and Municipal Employees v. State of Washington. 1985. 770 F. 2d 1401. 9th Circuit.

American Medical Association. 1986. *Physician Characteristics and Distribution in the U.S.* Annual. Chicago: American Medical Association.

American Nurses' Association et al. v. State of Illinois et al. 1986. No. 85-1766. USCA. 7th Circuit.

Amott, Teresa and Julie Matthai. 1984. "Comparable Worth, Incomparable Pay." *Radical America* 18(5):26.

Anderson, Charles H. and Daniel B. Corts. 1973. *Development of a Framework for a Factor-Ranking Benchmark System of Job Evaluation*. Washington, DC: U.S. Civil Service Commission, Personnel Research and Development Center.

Arrow, Kenneth, 1972. "Models of Job Discrimination." Pp. 83–102 in *Racial Discrimination in Economic Life*, edited by A. Pascal. Lexington, MA: Lexington Books, Heath.

———. 1973. "Social Responsibility and Economic Efficiency." *Public Policy Review* 21:303–317.

———. 1974. "Limited Knowledge and Economic Analysis." *American Economic Review* 64:1–10.

Arthur Young and Company. 1981. *A Comparable Worth Study of the Michigan Job Classifications*. Lansing: Office of Women and Work, Michigan Department of Labor.

Arvey, R. D. 1979. "Unfair Discrimination in the Employment Interview: Legal and Psychological Aspects." *Psychological Bulletin* 86:736–765.

———. 1986. "Sex Bias in Job Evaluation Procedures." *Personnel Psychology* 39:315–335.

Arvey, Richard D. and Katherine Holt. 1988. "The Cost of Alternative Comparable Worth Strategies." *Compensation and Benefits Review* 20(5):37–46.

Arvey, R. D., S. E. Maxwell, and L. M. Abraham. 1985. "Reliability Artifacts in Comparable Worth Procedures." *Journal of Applied Psychology* 70:695–705.

Arvey, R. D., E. M. Passino, and J. W. Lounsbury. 1977. "Job Analysis Results as Influenced by Sex of Incumbent and Sex of Analyst." *Journal of Applied Psychology* 62:411–416.

Ash, P. 1948. "The Reliability of Job Evaluation Rankings." *Journal of Applied Psychology* 32:313–320.

Atchison, T. and W. French. 1967. "Pay Systems for Scientists and Engineers." *Industrial Relations* 7:44–56.

Averitt, Robert T. 1968. *The Dual Economy*. New York: McGraw-Hill.

———. 1988. "The Prospect of Economic Dualism: A Historical Perspective." Pp. 23–42 in *Industries, Firms and Jobs: Sociological and Economic Perspectives*, edited by George Farkas and Paula England. New York: Plenum.

Azariadis, Costas. 1975. "Implicit Contracts and Underemployment Equilibria." *Journal of Political Economy* 83:1183–1202.

Azariadis, C. and J. E. Stiglitz. 1983. "Implicit Contracts and Fixed Price Equilibria." *Quarterly Journal of Economics* 98:1–22.

Bachman, J. G., L. D. Johnston, and P. M. O'Malley. 1980. *Monitoring the Future: Questionnaire Responses From the Nation's High School Seniors.* Ann Arbor: Institute for Social Research, University of Michigan.

Baily, Martin, 1974. "Wages and Unemployment under Uncertain Demand." *Review of Economic Studies* 41:37–50.

Barash, D. 1977. *Sociobiology and Behavior.* New York: Elsevier.

———. 1979. *The Whisperings Within.* New York: Harper & Row.

Barnes, William and Ethel Jones. 1974. "Differences in Male and Female Quitting." *Journal of Human Resources* 9(4):439–451.

Barnett, Edith. 1986. "Comparable Worth: What Plaintiffs Face in Sex-Based Pay-Discrimination Suits." *Trial* (Dec):22–26.

Baron, James N. and William T. Bielby. 1980. "Bringing the Firm Back In: Stratification, Segmentation, and the Organization of Work." *American Sociological Review* 45:737–755.

Baron, James and Andrew Newman. 1989. "Pay the Man: Effects of Demographic Composition on Prescribed Wage Rates in the California Civil Service." Pp. 107–130 in *Pay Equity: Empirical Inquiries,* edited by Robert Micahel, Heidi Hartmann, and Brigid O'Farrell. Washington, DC: National Academy Press.

———. Forthcoming. "For What It's Worth: Organizational and Occupational Factors Affecting the Value of Work Done by Women and Nonwhites. *American Sociological Review.*

Barrett, Michele. 1980. *Women's Oppression Today: Problems in Marxist Feminist Analysis.* London: Verso.

Barrett, Nancy. 1991. "Women." Pp. 69–94 in *Human Capital and America's Future,* edited by David W. Hornbeck and Lester M. Salamon. Baltimore: Johns Hopkins Press.

Barron, John M., Dan A. Black, and Mark Loewenstein. 1990. "Gender Differences in Training, Capital, and Wages." Paper presented at the 1990 Annual Meetings of the Western Economic Association.

Barry, J. 1985. "Women Production Workers—Low Pay and Hazardous Work." *American Economic Review* 75:262–265.

Bazemore v. Friday. 1986. 106 S. Ct. 3000.

Beatty, Richard W. and James R. Beatty. 1984. "Some Problems with Contemporary Job Evaluation Systems." Pp. 59–78 in *Comparable Worth and Wage Discrimination,* edited by H. Remick. Philadelphia: Temple University Press.

Beck, E. M. 1980. "Labor Unionism and Racial Income Inequality: A Time-Series Analysis of the Post–World War II Period." *American Journal of Sociology* 85:791–891.

Beck, E. M., Patrick M. Horan, and Charles M. Tolbert II. 1978. "Stratification in a Dual Economy: A Sectoral Model of Earnings Determination." *American Sociological Review* 43:704–720.

———. 1980. "Industrial Segmentation and Labor Market Discrimination." *Social Problems* 28:113–130.

Becker, F. M. 1934. *Administration of the Personnel Program in the State of California.* Sacramento: State of California Archives (Administration, Personnel Board-Historical).

Becker, Gary. 1957. *The Economics of Discrimination,* 1st ed. (2nd ed., 1971). Chicago: University of Chicago Press.

_____. 1962. "Investment in Human Capital: A Theoretical Analysis." *Journal of Political Economy* 70:9–49.

_____. 1976. *The Economic Approach to Human Behavior.* Chicago: University of Chicago Press.

_____. 1981. *A Treatise on the Family.* Cambridge, MA: Harvard University Press.

_____. 1985. "Human Capital, Effort, and the Sexual Division of Labor." *Journal of Labor Economics* 3:S33–S58.

Belcher, C. W. 1974. *Compensation Administration.* Englewood Cliffs, NJ: Prentice-Hall.

Bell, Carolyn Shaw. 1985. "Comparable Worth: How Do We Know It Will Work?" Paper presented at annual meetings of the American Statistical Association.

Bellak, Alvin O. 1984. "Comparable Worth: A Practitioner's View." Pp. 75–82 in *Comparable Worth: Issue for the 80's: A Consultation of the U.S. Commission on Civil Rights.* Washington, DC: U.S. Commission on Civil Rights.

Beller, Andrea. 1979. "The Impact of Equal Employment Opportunity Laws on the Male-Female Earnings Differential." Pp. 304–330 in *Women in the Labor Market,* edited by Cynthia Lloyd, Emily Andrews, and Curtis Gilroy. New York: Columbia University Press.

_____. 1982a. "Occupational Segregation by Sex: Determinants and Changes." *Journal of Human Resources* 17:371–392.

_____. 1982b. "The Impact of Equal Opportunity Policy on Sex Differentials in Earnings and Occupations." *American Economic Review* 72:171–175.

_____. 1984. "Trends in Occupational Segregation by Sex and Race, 1960–1981." Pp. 11–26 in *Sex Segregation in the Workplace: Trends, Explanations, Remedies,* edited by Barbara F. Reskin. Washington, DC: National Academy Press.

Benge, Eugene J. 1941. "The Factor Comparison Method, Its Characteristics, and Its Advantages." Pp. 41–55 in *Manual of Job Evaluation: Procedures of Job Analysis and Appraisal.* New York: Harper and Brothers.

_____. 1984. "Using Factor Methods to Measure Jobs." Pp. 242–255 in *Handbook of Wage and Salary Administration,* edited by Milton Rock. New York: McGraw-Hill.

Benhabib, Seyla. 1986. *Critique, Norm, and Utopia: A Study of the Foundations of Critical Theory.* New York: Columbia University Press.

_____. 1987. "The Generalized and the Concrete Other: The Kohlberg-Gilligan Controversy and Feminist Theory." Pp. 77–95 in *Feminism as Critique: On the Politics of Gender,* edited by Seyla Benhabib and Drucilla Cornell. Minneapolis: University of Minnesota Press.

Benhabib, Seyla and Drucilla Cornell, eds. 1987. "Introduction: Beyond Politics of Gender." Pp. 1–15 in *Feminism as Critique: On the Politics of Gender.* Minneapolis: University of Minnesota Press.

Berger, Brigitte. 1984. "Comparable Worth at Odds with American Realities." Pp. 65–74 in *Comparable Worth: Issues for the 80's: A Consultation of the U.S. Commission on Civil Rights.* Washington, DC: U.S. Commission on Civil Rights.

Berger, Joseph, Bernard P. Cohen, and Morris Zelditch, Jr. 1972. "Status Characteristics and Social Interaction." *American Sociological Review* 37:241–255.

Berger, Joseph, Thomas L. Conner, and M. Hamit Fisek. 1974. *Expectation States Theory: A Theoretical Research Program*. Cambridge, MA: Winthrop.

Bergesen, Albert. 1988. "The Rise of Semiotic Marxism." Paper presented at the annual meetings of the American Sociological Association, Atlanta, GA.

Bergmann, Barbara. 1974. "Occupational Segregation, Wages and Profits When Employers Discriminate by Race and Sex." *Eastern Economic Journal* 1:103–110.

––––––. 1985. "The Economic Case for Comparable Worth." Pp. 70–85 in *Comparable Worth: New Directions for Research*, edited by Heidi Hartmann. Washington, DC: National Academy Press.

––––––. 1986. *The Economic Emergence of Women*. NY: Basic Books.

––––––. 1989. "Does the Market for Women's Labor Need Fixing?" *Journal of Economic Perspectives* 3(1):43–60.

Bergmann, Barbara and William Darity. 1981. "Social Relations in the Workplace and Employee Discrimination." *Proceedings of the Industrial Relations Research Association:* 155–162.

Berk, Richard A. and Sarah Fenstermaker Berk. 1979. *Labor and Leisure at Home: Content and Organization of the Household Day*. Newbury Park: Sage.

Berlin, Isaiah. 1969. *Four Essays on Liberty*. Oxford: Oxford University Press.

Bernstein, Aaron. 1986. "Comparable Worth: It's Already Happening." *Business Week* April 28:52, 56.

Bianchi, Suzanne and Daphne Spain. 1986. *American Women in Transition: The Population of the United States in the 1980s*. New York: Russell Sage Foundation.

Bielby, William and James Baron. 1984. "A Woman's Place Is with Other Women: Sex Segregation within Organizations." Pp. 27–55 in *Sex Segregation in the Workplace: Trends, Explanations, Remedies*, edited by Barbara F. Reskin. Washington, DC: National Academy Press.

––––––. 1986. "Men and Women at Work—Sex Segregation and Statistical Discrimination." *American Journal of Sociology* 91:759–799.

Bielby, Denise D. and William T. Bielby. 1988. "She Works Hard for the Money." *American Journal of Sociology* 93:1031–1059.

Blank, Rebecca. 1989. "The Role of Part-Time Work in Women's Labor Market Choices over Time." *American Economic Review* 79(2):295–299.

Blau, Francine. 1977. *Equal Pay in the Office*. Lexington, MA: Heath.

––––––. 1984. "Occupational Segregation and Labor Market Discrimination." Pp. 117–143 in *Sex Segregation in the Workplace: Trends, Explanations, Remedies*, edited by Barbara F. Reskin. Washington, DC: National Academy Press.

––––––. 1988. "Occupational Segregation by Gender: A Look at the 1980's." Paper presented at the annual meetings of the American Economic Association, New York.

Blau, Francine and Marianne A. Ferber. 1986. *The Economics of Women, Men, and Work*. Englewood Cliffs, NJ: Prentice-Hall.

Blau, Francine D. and C. L. Jusenius. 1976. "Economic Dimensions of Occupational Segregation—Economists' Approaches to Sex Segregation in Labor Market Appraisal." *Signs* 1:181–199.

Blau, Francine D. and Lawrence M. Kahn. 1981. "Race and Sex Differences in Quits by Young Workers." *Industrial and Labor Relations Review* 34:563–577.

Blau, P. M. and O. D. Duncan. 1967. *The American Occupational Structure.* New York: Wiley.

Blaug, Mark. 1978. Third Edition. *Economic Theory in Retrospect.* Cambridge: Cambridge University Press.

Bleier, Ruth. 1984. *Science and Gender: A Critique of Biology and Its Theories on Women.* New York: Pergamon Press.

Block, Jeanne H. 1976. "Issues, Problems, and Pitfalls in Assessing Sex Differences: A Critical Review of the Psychology of Sex Differences." *Merrill-Palmer Quarterly* 22:283–308.

Blum, Linda. 1987. "Possibilities and Limits of the Comparable Worth Movement." *Gender and Society* 1:380–399.

———. 1991. *Beyond Feminism and Labor: The Significance of the Comparable Worth Movement.* Berkeley: University of California Press.

Bonacich, Edna. 1972. "A Theory of Ethnic Antagonism: The Split Labor Market." *American Sociological Review* 37:547–549.

———. 1976. "Advanced Capitalism and Black-White Relations in the U.S.: A Split Labor Market Interpretation." *American Sociological Review* 41:34–51.

Bonjean, Charles M., Billye J. Brown, Burke D. Grandjean, and Patrick O. Macken. 1982. "Increasing Work Satisfaction through Organizational Change: A Longitudinal Study of Nursing Educators." *Journal of Applied Behavioral Science* 18:357–369.

Booker, Sharon and L. Camille Nuckolls. 1986. "Legal and Economic Aspects of Comparable Worth." *Public Personnel Management* 15:189–206.

Borjas, George J. and Matthew S. Goldberg. 1978. "Biased Screening and Discrimination in the Labor Market." *American Economic Review* 68(5):918–922.

Bourdieu, P. 1977. "Cultural Reproduction and Social Reproduction." Pp. 487–511 in *Power and Ideology in Education,* edited by J. Karabel and A. H. Halsey. New York: Oxford University Press.

Bourdieu, P. and J. Passeron. 1977. *Reproduction—In Education and Society.* Beverly Hills, CA: Sage.

Bowles, Samuel. 1985. "The Production Process in a Competitive Economy: Walrasian, Neo-Hobbesian, and Marxian Models." *American Economic Review* 75:16–36.

Bowles, Samuel and Herbert Gintis. 1976. *Schooling in Capitalist America: Educational Reform and the Contradictions of Economic Life.* Princeton, NJ: Princeton University Press.

Braverman, Harry. 1974. *Labor and Monopoly Capital: The Degradation of Work in the Twentieth Century.* New York: Monthly Review Press.

Brenner, Johanna. 1987. "Feminist Political Discourses: Radical Versus Liberal Approaches to the Feminization of Poverty and Comparable Worth." *Gender & Society* 1:447–465.

Brenner, O. C. and Joseph Tomkiewicz. 1979. "Job Orientation of Males and Females: Are Sex Differences Declining?" *Personnel Psychology* 32:741–750.

Bridges, William P. and Robert L. Nelson. 1989. "Markets in Hierarchies: Organizational and Market Influences on Gender Inequality in a State Pay System." *American Journal of Sociology* 95(3):616–658.

Brilmayer, Lea, Richard W. Hekeler, Douglas Laycock, and Teresa A. Sullivan. 1980. "Sex Discrimination in Employer-Sponsored Insurance Plans: A Legal and Demographic Analysis." *University of Chicago Law Review* 47:505–560.

Brinton, Mary C. 1988. "The Social-Institutional Bases of Gender Stratification: Japan as an Illustrative Case." *American Journal of Sociology* 94:300–334.

Brown, Charles. 1980. "Equalizing Differences in the Labor Market." *Quarterly Journal of Economics* 94:113–134.

Bull, Clive. 1983. "Implicit Contracts in the Absence of Enforcement and Risk Aversion." *American Economic Review* 73:658–671.

Bulow, Jeremy I. and Lawrence H. Summers. 1986. "A Theory of Dual Labor Markets with Application to Industrial Policy, Discrimination, and Keynesian Unemployment." *Journal of Labor Economics* 4:376–414.

Burawoy, Michael. 1990. "Marxism as Science: Historical Challenges and Theoretical Growth." *American Sociological Review* 55(6):775–793.

Bureau of National Affairs. 1981. *The Comparable Worth Issue.* Washington, DC: Bureau of National Affairs.

Burkhauser, Richard V. and Greg J. Duncan. 1989. "Economic Risks of Gender Roles: Income Loss and Life Events over the Life Course." *Social Science Quarterly* 70(1):3–23.

Burstein, Paul. 1985. *Discrimination, Jobs, and Politics.* Chicago: University of Chicago Press.

Burstein, Paul and Susan Pitchford. 1990. "Social-Scientific and Legal Challenges to Education and Test Requirements in Employment." *Social Problems* 37:243–257.

Burtless, Gary, ed. 1990. *A Future of Lousy Jobs? The Changing Structure of U.S. Wages.* Washington, DC: The Brookings Institution.

Butz, William P. and Michael P. Ward. 1979. "The Emergence of Countercyclical U.S. Fertility." *American Economic Review* 69:318–327.

Cain, Pamela S. and Donald J. Treiman. 1981. "The DOT as a Source of Occupational Data." *American Sociological Review* 46:253–278.

Cameron, Trudy Ann. 1986. "Some Reflections on Comparable Worth." *Contemporary Policy Issues* 4:32–39.

Camic, Charles. 1986. "The Matter of Habit." *American Journal of Sociology* 91:1039–1087.

Carmichael, H. Lorne. 1985. "Can Unemployment Be Involuntary?: Comment." *American Economic Review* 75:1213–1214.

———. 1990. "Efficiency Wage Models of Unemployment: A Survey." *Economic Inquiry* 28:296–306.

Center for Human Resources Research. 1983. *The National Longitudinal Surveys Handbook, 1983–84.* Columbus: Center for Human Resources Research, Ohio State University.

Cherlin, Andrew J. 1981. *Marriage, Divorce, Remarriage: Social Trends in the United States.* Cambridge, MA: Harvard University Press.

Chesler, David J. 1948. "Reliability and Comparability of Different Job Evaluation Systems." *Journal of Applied Psychology* 32:465–475.

Chi, Keon. 1986. "Comparable Worth in State Government: Trends and Issues." *Policy Studies Review* 5:800–814.

Christensen v. State of Iowa. 1977. 563 F. 2d 353. 8th Circuit.

City of Los Angeles v. Manhart. 1978. 435 U.S. 702. 9th Circuit.

Clauss, Carin A. 1986. "Comparable Worth: The Theory, Its Legal Foundation, and the Feasibility of Implementation." *University of Michigan Journal of Law Reform* 20:7–97.

Cohn, Samuel. 1985. *The Feminization of Clerical Labor in Great Britain.* Philadelphia: Temple University Press.

Colby v. J. C. Penney Co. 1987. 811 F. 2d 1119. 7th Circuit.

Collett, Merrill J. 1983. "Comparable Worth: An Overview." *Public Personnel Management* 12:325–331.

Collins, Randall. 1975. *Conflict Sociology: Toward an Explanatory Science.* New York: Academic Press.

Colwill, N. 1982. *The New Partnership: Women and Men in Organizations.* Palo Alto, CA: Mayfield.

Cook, Alice. 1985. *Comparable Worth: A Case Book of Experiences in States and Localities.* Manoa: University of Hawaii, Industrial Relations Center.

———. 1986. *Comparable Worth: A Case Book of Experiences in States and Localities— 1986 Supplement.* Manoa: University of Hawaii, Industrial Relations Center.

Corcoran, Mary and Greg J. Duncan. 1979. "Work History, Labor Force Attachments, and Earnings Differences Between the Races and Sexes." *Journal of Human Resources* 14:3–20.

Corcoran, Mary, Greg Duncan, and Michael Ponza. 1984. "Work Experience, Job Segregation, and Wages." Pp. 171–191 in *Sex Segregation in the Workplace: Trends, Explanations, Remedies,* edited by Barbara F. Reskin. Washington, DC: National Academy Press.

Corning Glass Works v. Brennan. 1974. 417 U.S. 188. U.S. Supreme Court.

County of Washington, Oregon v. Gunther. 1981. 452 U.S. 161. U.S. Supreme Court.

Coverdill, James E. 1988. "The Dual Economy and Sex Differences in Earnings." *Social Forces* 66(4):970–993.

Craik v. Minnesota State University Board. 1984. 731 F. 2d 465. 8th Circuit.

Crane, M. and R. Hodson. 1984. "Job Satisfaction in Dual Career Families: Gender Differences in the Effects of Job and Family Characteristics and Personal Expectations." University of Texas–Austin. Mimeo.

Culler, J. 1982. *On Deconstruction: Theory and Criticism after Structuralism.* Ithaca, NY: Cornell University Press.

Daly, Mary. 1968. *The Church and the Second Sex.* New York: Harper & Row.

Davis, Kingsley and Wilbert Moore. 1945. "Some Principles of Stratification." *American Sociological Review* 10:242–249.

Daymont, Thomas and Paul Andrisani. 1984. "Job Preferences, College Major, and the Gender Gap in Earnings." *Journal of Human Resources* 19(3):408–428.

Deaux, Kay. 1985. "Sex and Gender." *Annual Review of Psychology* 36:49–81.

Deaux, Kay and Tim Emswiller. 1974. "Explanations of Successful Performance on Sex-Linked Tasks: What Is Skill for the Male Is Luck for the Female." *Journal of Personality and Social Psychology* 29:80–85.

Delphy, Christine. 1984. *"Close to Home": A Materialist Analysis of Women's Oppression.* Amherst: University of Massachusetts Press.

Desai, Sonalde and Linda J. Waite. 1991. "Women's Employment during Pregnancy and after the First Birth: Occupational Characteristics and Work Commitment." *American Sociological Review* 56:551–566.

Dex, S. 1985. *The Sexual Division of Work*. New York: St. Martin's.

Diamond, Peter and Michael Rothschild, eds. 1989. *Uncertainty in Economics: Readings and Exercises*. Second revised edition. New York: Academic Press.

Dickens, William T. 1986. "Wages, Employment, and the Threat of Collective Action by Workers." National Bureau of Economic Research, Cambridge, MA. Working paper.

Dickens, William T. and Lawrence Katz. 1987. "Industry Wage Patterns and Theories of Wage Determination." National Bureau of Economic Research, Cambridge, MA. Working paper.

DiMaggio, Paul. 1979. "Review Essay: On Pierre Bourdieu." *American Journal of Sociology* 84:1460–1474.

DiPrete, Thomas and Whitman Soule. 1988. "Gender and Promotion in Segmented Job Ladder Systems." *American Sociological Review* 53(1):26–40.

Doeringer, Peter and Michael Piore. 1971. *Internal Labor Markets and Manpower Analysis*. Lexington, MA: Heath.

Donohue, John J. 1987. "The Changing Relative Hazard Rates of Young Male and Female Workers." Northwestern University School of Law, American Bar Foundation, Chicago, Illinois. Unpublished paper.

Donovan, Josephine. 1985. *Feminist Theory: The Intellectual Traditions of American Feminism*. New York: Frederick Ungar.

Doverspike, D. A. and G. V. Barrett. 1984. "An Internal Bias Analysis of a Job Evaluation Instrument." *Journal of Applied Psychology* 69:648–662.

Doverspike, D., A. M. Carlist, G. V. Barrett, and R. A. Alexander. 1983. "Generalizability Analysis of a Point-Method Job Evaluation Instrument." *Journal of Applied Psychology* 68:476–483.

Dresang, Dennis L. Forthcoming. "Gender and Pay: The Politics of Pay Equity in Wisconsin." in *The Politics and Practice of Pay Equity*, edited by Ronnie Steinberg. Philadelphia: Temple University Press.

Duncan, Greg J. and Bertil Holmlund. 1983. "Was Adam Smith Right After All? Another Test of the Theory of Compensating Wage Differentials." *Journal of Labor Economics* 1:366–379.

Duncan, Greg J. and Frank P. Stafford. 1980. "Do Union Members Receive Compensating Wage Differentials?" *American Economic Review* 70:355–371.

Dworkin, Ronald. 1977. *Taking Rights Seriously*. Cambridge, MA: Harvard University Press.

Edgeworth, F. Y. 1922. "Equal Pay to Men and Women." *Economics Journal* 32:431–457.

Edwards, Richard, Michael Reich, and David Gordon, eds. 1975. *Labor Market Segmentation*. Lexington, MA: Heath.

Ehrenberg, Ronald G. 1979. *The Regulatory Process and Labor Earnings*. New York: Academic Press.

———. 1989. "Empirical Consequences of Comparable Worth." Pp. 90–106 in *Comparable Worth: Analyses and Evidence*, edited by M. Anne Hill and Mark R. Killingsworth. Ithaca, NY: ILR Press.

Ehrenberg, Ronald G. and Robert S. Smith. 1982. *Modern Labor Economics*. Glenview, IL: Scott, Foresman.

———. 1987. "Comparable-Worth Wage Adjustments and Female Employment in the State and Local Sector." *Journal of Labor Economics* 5:43–62.

Eisenstein, Zillah R. 1981. *The Radical Future of Liberal Feminism*. New York: Longman.

Eisler, Riane. 1987. *The Chalice and the Blade: Our History, Our Future*. New York: Harper & Row.

Elster, Jon. 1979. *Ulysses and the Sirens: Studies in Rationality and Irrationality*. Cambridge: Cambridge University Press.

Engels, Friedrich, [1884] 1972. *The Origin of the Family, Private Property, and the State*. New York: International Publishers.

England, Paula. 1979. "Women and Occupational Prestige: A Case of Vacuous Sex Equality." *Signs: Journal of Women in Culture and Society* 5:252–265.

———. 1981. "Assessing Trends in Occupational Sex Segregation, 1900–1976." Pp. 273–295 in *Sociological Perspectives on Labor Markets*, edited by Ivar Berg. New York: Academic Press.

———. 1982. "The Failure of Human Capital Theory to Explain Occupational Sex Segregation." *Journal of Human Resources* 18:358–370.

———. 1984. "Wage Appreciation and Depreciation: A Test of Neoclassical Economic Explanations of Occupational Sex Segregation." *Social Forces* 62:726–749.

———. 1986. "A Dissenting View in Favor of Pay Equity." *Harvard Journal of Law & Public Policy* 9:99–106.

———. 1988. "Equality of Opportunity, Inequality of Reward, and the Hierarchical Division of Labor." *Free Inquiry in Creative Sociology* 16:137–142.

———. 1989. "A Feminist Critique of Rational-Choice Theories: Implications for Sociology." *American Sociologist* 20:14–28.

———. Forthcoming. "The Separative Self: Androcentric Bias in Neoclassical Assumptions." In *Beyond Economic Man*, edited by Marianne Ferber and Julie Nelson. Chicago: University of Chicago Press.

England, Paula, Marilyn Chassie, and Linda McCormick. 1982. "Skill Demands and Earnings in Female and Male Occupations." *Sociology and Social Research* 66:147–168.

England, Paula and Dana Dunn. 1988. "Evaluating Work and Comparable Worth." *Annual Reviews of Sociology* 14:227–248.

England, Paula and George Farkas. 1986. *Households, Employment, and Gender: A Social, Economic and Demographic View.* Hawthorne, NY: Aldine de Gruyter.

England, Paula, George Farkas, Barbara Stanek Kilbourne, and Thomas Dou. 1988. "Explaining Occupational Sex Segregation and Wages: Findings from a Model with Fixed Effects." *American Sociological Review* 53:544–558.

England, Paula and Barbara Stanek Kilbourne. 1989. *Occupational Measures from the Dictionary of Occupational Titles for 1980 Census Detailed Occupations*. Machine-readable dataset and documentation ICPSR #8942. Ann Arbor, MI: Inter-university Consortium for Political and Social Research.

———. 1990a. "Feminist Critiques of the Separative Model of Self: Implications for Rational Choice Theory." *Rationality and Society* 2:156–171.

_____. 1990b. "Does Rational Choice Theory Assume a Separative Self? Response to Friedman and Diem." *Rationality and Society* 2:522–525.

_____. 1990c. "Markets, Marriages, and Other Mates: The Problem of Power." Pp. 163–189 in *Beyond the Marketplace: Rethinking Economy and Society,* edited by Roger Friedland and A. F. Robertson. Hawthorne, NY: Aldine de Gruyter.

England, Paula and Steven McLaughlin. 1979. "Sex Segregation of Jobs and Male-Female Income Differentials." Pp. 189–213 in *Discrimination in Organizations,* edited by R. Alvarez, K. Lutterman, and Associates. San Francisco: Jossey Bass.

Epstein, Cynthia. 1988. *Deceptive Distinctions: Sex, Gender and the Social Order.* NY: Russell Sage Foundation.

Equal Employment Advisory Council. 1985. "Twenty Questions on Comparable Worth." *Personnel Administrator:*64–68.

Equal Employment Opportunity Commission v. J. C. Penney. 1988. 843 F. 2d 249. 6th Circuit.

Eulberg, J. R. 1987. "An Examination of the Measurement Properties and Role of Gender-Related Biases in the Evaluation of Non-Exempt Jobs." Ph.D. Dissertation, School of Management, University of Texas at Dallas.

Evans, Sara M. and Barbara J. Nelson. 1989. *Wage Justice: Comparable Worth and the Paradox of Technocratic Reform.* Chicago: University of Chicago Press.

Farkas, George, Paula England, and Margaret Barton. 1988. "Structural Effects on Wages: Sociological and Economic Views." Pp. 93–112 in *Industries, Firms, and Jobs: Sociological and Economic Approaches,* edited by George Farkas and Paula England. New York: Plenum.

Fausto-Sterling, Anne. 1985. *Myths of Gender: Biological Theories About Women and Men.* New York: Basic Books.

Feagin, J. R. and C. B. Feagin. 1978. *Discrimination American Style: Institutional Racism and Sexism.* Englewood Cliffs, NJ: Prentice Hall.

Featherman, David and Robert Hauser. 1978. *Opportunity and Change.* New York: Harcourt, Brace, Jovanovich.

Feldberg, Roslyn L. 1984. "Comparable Worth: Toward Theory and Practice in the United States." *Signs: Journal of Women in Culture and Society* 10:311–328.

Ferber, Marianne A. and Helen M. Lowry. 1976. "The Sex Differential in Earnings: A Reappraisal." *Industrial And Labor Relations Review* 29:377–387.

Ferber, Marianne A. and Joe L. Spaeth. 1984. "Work Characteristics and the Male-Female Earnings Gap." *American Economic Review* 74:260–264.

Figart, Deborah, Heidi Hartmann, Eleanor Hinton Hoytt, and Janice Hamilton Outtz. 1989. "The Wage Gap and Women of Color." Pp. 25–33 in *Proceedings from the First Annual Women's Policy Research Conference.* Washington, DC: Institute for Women's Policy Research.

Filer, Randall. 1983. "Sexual Differences in Earnings: The Role of Individual Personalities and Tastes." *Journal of Human Resources* 18(1):82–99.

_____. 1985. "Male-Female Wage Differences: The Importance of Compensating Differentials." *Industrial and Labor Relations Review* 38(3):426–437.

_____. 1989. "Occupational Segregation Compensating Differentials and Comparable Worth." Pp. 153–170 in *Pay Equity: Empirical Inquiries,* edited by

Robert T. Michael, Heidi I. Hartmann, and Brigid O'Farrell. Washington, DC: National Academy Press.

———. 1990a. "Compensating Differentials and the Male-Female Wage Gap: A Comment." *Social Forces* 69(2):469–474.

———. 1990b. "The Usefulness of Predicted Values for Prior Work Experience in Analyzing Labor Market Outcomes for Women." Department of Economics, Hunter College, City University of New York. Unpublished manuscript.

Flammang, Janet A. 1986. "Effective Implementation: The Case of Comparable Worth in San Jose." *Policy Studies Review* 5:815–837.

Flanagan, Robert J., Robert S. Smith, and Ronald G. Ehrenberg. 1984. *Labor Economics and Labor Relations*. Glenview, IL: Scott, Foresman.

Flick, Rachel. 1983. "The New Feminism and the World of Work." *Public Interest* 71:33–44.

Folbre, Nancy. Forthcoming. "Micro, Macro, Choice, and Structure." In *Theory on Gender/Feminism on Theory*, edited by Paula England. Hawthorne, NY: Aldine de Gruyter.

Fraser, S. L., S. F. Cronshaw, and R. A. Alexander. 1984. "Generalizability Analysis of a Point Method Job Evaluation Instrument: A Field Study." *Journal of Applied Research* 69:643–647.

Friedman, Debra and Carol Diem. 1990. "Comments on England and Kilbourne." *Rationality and Society* 2:517–521.

Fuchs, Victor R. 1988. *Women's Quest for Economic Equality*. Cambridge, MA: Harvard University Press.

Gethman, Barton R. 1987. "The Job Market, Sex Bias, and Comparable Worth." *Public Personnel Management* 16(2):173–180.

Gibbard, A. 1986. "Interpersonal Comparisons, Preference, Good, and the Intrinsic Rewards of a Life." Pp. 165–194 in *Foundations of Social Choice Theory*, edited by Jon Elster and Aanund Hylland. Cambridge: Cambridge University Press.

Gilligan, Carol. 1982. *In a Different Voice: Psychological Theory and Women's Development*. Cambridge, MA: Harvard University Press.

———. 1990. "The Impact of Occupational Segregation on Employment Conditions." *Social Forces* 68(3):779–796.

Glass, Jennifer, Marta Tienda, and Shelley A. Smith. 1988. "The Impact of Changing Employment Opportunity on Gender and Ethnic Earnings Inequality." *Social Science Research* 17:252–276.

Gleason, Sandra E. 1985. "Comparable Worth: Some Questions Still Unanswered." Paper presented at annual meetings of American Statistical Association.

Glenn, N. and C. Weaver. 1982. "Further Evidence on Education and Job Satisfaction." *Social Forces* 61:46–55.

Gold, Michael Evan. 1983. *A Dialogue on Comparable Worth*. Ithaca, NY: ILR Press.

———. 1986. "The Case for Comparable Worth." *Humanist* May–June:14–17.

Goldberg, Matthew S. 1982. "Discrimination, Nepotism, and Long-Run Wage Differentials." *Quarterly Journal of Economics* 97:308–319.

Goldin, Claudia. 1986. "Monitoring Costs and Occupational Segregation by Sex: A Historical Analysis." *Journal of Labor Economics* 4:1–27.

_____. 1990. *Understanding the Gender Gap: An Economic History of American Women.* New York: Oxford University Press.

Gomez-Mejia, L. R., R. C. Page, and W. W. Tornow. 1982. "A Comparison of the Practical Utility of Traditional, Statistical, and Hybrid Job Evaluation Approaches." *Academy of Management Journal* 25:790–809.

Gordon, David M. 1972. *Theories of Poverty and Unemployment.* Lexington, MA: Heath.

Gordon, Donald F. 1974. "A Neoclassical Theory of Origins of Keynesian Unemployment." *Economic Inquiry* 12:431–459.

Gorz, Andre. 1978. *The Division of Labor: The Labor Process and Class Struggle in Modern Capitalism.* London: Harvestor Press.

Grams, R., and D. P. Schwab. 1985. "An Investigation of Systematic Gender-Related Error in Job Evaluation." *Academy of Management Journal* 28:279–290.

Gramsci, A. 1971. *Selections from the Prison Notebooks.* New York: International Publishers.

Gray, John. 1986. *Liberalism.* Milton Keynes: Open University Press.

Gray, Louis N. and Irving Tallman. 1987. "Theories of Choice: Contingent Reward and Punishment Applications." *Social Psychology Quarterly* 50:16–23.

Green, T. H. 1941. *Lectures on the Principles of Political Obligation.* London: Longmans.

Greenberger, Ellen and Laurence Steinberg. 1983. "Sex Differences in Early Labor Force Experience: Harbinger of Things to Come." *Social Forces* 62:467–487.

Greenwood, Daphne. 1984. "The Institutional Inadequacy of the Market in Determining Comparable Worth: Implications for Value Theory." *Journal of Economic Issues* 18:457–463.

Gregory, Robert G., Roslyn Anstie, Anne Daly, and Vivian Ho. 1989. "Women's Pay in Australia, Great Britain, and the United States: The Role of Laws, Regulations, and Human Capital." Pp. 222–242 in *Pay Equity: Empirical Inquiries,* edited by Robert T. Michael, Heidi I. Hartmann, and Brigid O'Farrell. Washington, DC: National Academy Press.

Gregory, R. G. and R. C. Duncan. 1981. "Segmented Labor Market Theories and the Australian Experience of Equal Pay for Women." *Journal of Post Keynesian Economics* 3:403–428.

Griggs v. Duke Power Co. 1971. 401 U.S. 424. U.S. Supreme Court.

Gronau, Reuben. 1988. "Sex-Related Wage Differentials and Women's Interrupted Labor Careers—The Chicken or the Egg?" *Journal of Labor Economics* 6(3):277–301.

Gross, E. 1968. "Plus ca change . . . ?: The Sexual Structure of Occupations Over Time." *Social Problems* 16:198–208.

Grossman, Sanford J. and Oliver D. Hart. 1981. "Implicit Contracts, Moral Hazard, and Unemployment." *American Economic Review* 71:301–307.

Grossman, Sanford J., Oliver D. Hart, and Eric S. Maskin. 1983. "Unemployment with Observable Aggregate Shocks." *Journal of Political Economy* 91:907–928.

Grune, Joy Ann. 1984. "Pay Equity Is a Necessary Remedy for Wage Discrimination." Pp. 165–176 in *Comparable Worth: Issues for the 80's: A Consultation of the*

U.S. Commission on Civil Rights. Washington, DC: U.S. Commission on Civil Rights.

Gruneberg, Michael M. 1979. *Understanding Job Satisfaction.* New York: Mac-Millan.

Gunderson, Morley. 1989. "Male-Female Wage Differentials and Policy Responses." *Journal of Economic Literature* 27(1):46–72.

Haber, Sheldon E., Enrique J. Lamas, and Gordon Green. 1983. "A New Method of Estimating Job Separation by Sex and Race." *Monthly Labor Review* June:20–27.

Hall, R. E. and D. M. Lilien. 1979. "Efficient Wage Bargains under Uncertain Supply and Demand." *American Economic Review* 69:868–879.

Hare-Mustin, Rachel T. and Jeanne Marecek. 1988. "The Meaning of Difference: Gender Theory, Postmodernism, and Psychology." *American Psychologist* 43:455–464.

Hartmann, Heidi. 1976. "Capitalism, Patriarchy and Job Segregation by Sex." Pp. 137–170 in *Women and the Workplace: The Implications of Occupational Segregation,* edited by Martha Blaxall and Barbara Reagan. Chicago: University of Chicago Press.

_____. 1981. "The Unhappy Marriage of Marxism and Feminism: Toward a More Progressive Union." Pp. 1–41 in *Women and Revolution,* edited by Lydia Sargent. Boston: South End Press.

Hartmann Heidi, Patricia A. Roos, and Donald J. Treiman. 1985. *Comparable Worth: New Directions for Research.* Washington, DC: National Academy Press.

Hartmann, Heidi I. and Donald J. Treiman. 1983. "Notes on the NAS Study of Equal Pay for Jobs of Equal Value." *Public Personnel Management* 12:404–417.

Hashimoto, Masanori. 1981. "Firm-Specific Human Capital as a Shared Investment." *American Economic Review* 71:475–482.

Hauser, Robert M. 1980. "On 'Stratification in a Dual Economy.'" *American Sociological Review* 45:702–712.

Hayek, F. A. 1960. *The Constitution of Liberty.* Chicago: Henry Regnery.

Hazelwood School District et al. v. United States. 1977. 433 U.S. 299. U.S. Supreme Court.

Heen, M. 1984. "A Review of Federal Court Decisions under Title VII of the Civil Rights Act of 1964." Pp. 197–218 in *Comparable Worth and Wage Discrimination,* edited by H. Remick. Philadelphia: Temple University Press.

Hegtvedt, Karen. 1989. "Fairness Conceptualizations and Comparable Worth." *Journal of Social Issues* 45:81–97.

Heilman, Madeline. 1979. "High School Students' Occupational Interest as a Function of Projected Sex Ratios in Male-Dominated Occupations." *Journal of Applied Psychology* 64(3):275–279.

Hein, Hilde. 1983. "Liberating Philosophy: An End to the Dichotomy of Matter and Spirit." Pp. 123–141 in *Beyond Domination: New Perspectives on Women and Philosophy,* edited by Carol C. Gould. Totowa, NJ: Rowman & Allanheld.

Held, David. 1980. *Introduction to Critical Theory: Horkheimer to Habermas.* Berkeley: University of California Press.

Hensen, Mary F. 1990. "Trends in Income, by Selected Characteristics: 1947 to 1988. Table 21 in *Current Population Reports*. Series P-60, No. 167. Washington, DC: Government Printing Office.

Herzog, A. R. 1982. "High School Students' Occupational Plans and Values: Trends in Sex Differences 1976 through 1980." *Sociology of Education* 55:1–13.

Higginbotham, Elizabeth. 1987. "Employment for Professional Black Women in the Twentieth Century." Pp. 73–92 in *Ingredients for Women's Employment Policy*, edited by Christine Bose and Glenna Spitze. Albany: State University of New York Press.

Hildebrand, George. 1980. "The Market System." Pp. 79–106 in *Comparable Worth: Issues and Alternatives*, edited by E. Robert Livernash. Washington, DC: Equal Employment Advisory Council.

Hill, Martha. 1980. "Authority at Work: How Men and Women Differ." Pp. 107–146 in *Five Thousand American Families: Patterns of Economic Progress*, edited by Greg Duncan and James Morgan. Ann Arbor, Michigan: Institute for Survey Research, University of Michigan.

Hirshleifer, Jack. 1984. *Price Theory and Applications*. Third edition. Englewood Cliffs, NJ: Prentice-Hall.

Hobhouse, L. T. 1911. *Liberalism*. New York: Oxford University Press.

Hochschild, Arlie. 1989. *The Second Shift*. New York: Viking Penguin.

Hodson, Randy. 1983. *Workers' Earnings and Corporate Economic Structure*. New York: Academic Press.

———. 1984. "Companies, Industries, and the Measurement of Economic Segmentation." *American Sociological Review* 49:335–348.

Hodson, Randy and Paula England. 1986. "Industrial Structure and Sex Differences in Earnings." *Industrial Relations* 25:16–32.

Hodson, Randy and Robert L. Kaufman. 1982. "Economic Dualism: A Critical Review." *American Sociological Review* 47:727–739.

Hoffman, Saul D. 1981. "On-the-Job Training: Differences by Race and Sex." *Monthly Labor Review* July:34–36.

Holmstrom, Bengt. 1983. "Moral Hazard and Observability." *Bell Journal of Economics* 14:74–91.

Horan, Patrick. 1978. "Is Status Attainment Research Atheoretical?" *American Sociological Review* 43:534–541.

Humphries, J. 1976. "Women: Scapegoats and Safety Values in the Great Depression." *Review of Radical Economics* 8:98–121.

Hutner, Frances C. 1986. *Equal Pay for Comparable Worth: The Working Woman's Issue of the Eighties*. New York: Praeger.

International Brotherhood of Teamsters v. U.S. 1977. 431 U.S. 324. U.S. Supreme Court.

International Union of Electrical Workers v. Westinghouse. 1980. 631 F. 2d 1094. 3rd Circuit.

Jackson, L. 1989. "Relative Deprivation and the Gender Wage Gap." *Journal of Social Issues* 45:117–133.

Jacobs, Jerry A. 1985. "Sex Segregation in American Higher Education, 1948–1980." Pp. 191–214 in *Women and Work: An Annual Review*, edited by Laurie Larwood, Ann H. Stromberg, and Barbara Gutek. Beverly Hills, CA: Sage.

————. 1989a. "Long-Term Trends in Occupational Segregation by Sex." *American Journal of Sociology* 95(1):160–173.

Jacobs, Jerry. 1989b. *Revolving Doors: Sex Segregation and Women's Careers.* Stanford, CA: Stanford University Press.

Jacobs, Jerry A. and Ronnie J. Steinberg. 1990a. "Compensating Differentials and the Male-Female Wage Gap: Evidence from the New York State Comparable Worth Study." *Social Forces* 69(2):439–468.

————. 1990b. "Compensating Differentials and the Male-Female Wage Gap: A Reply." *Social Forces* 69(2):475–478.

Jacobsen, Joyce P. 1989. "The Economics of Comparable Worth: Theoretical Considerations." Pp. 36–50 in *Comparable Worth: Analyses and Evidence,* edited by M. Anne Hill and Mark R. Killingsworth. Ithaca, NY: ILR Press.

Jaffee, David. 1989. "Gender Inequality in Workplace Autonomy and Authority." *Social Science Quarterly* 70(2):375–390.

Jaggar, Alison M. 1983. *Feminist Politics and Human Nature.* Totowa, New Jersey: Rowman & Allanheld.

James, Selma and Mariarosa Dalla Costa. 1973. *The Power of Women and the Subversion of the Community.* Bristol, UK: Falling Wall Press.

Jaussaud, Danielle P. 1984. "Can Job Evaluation Systems Help Determine the Comparable Worth of Male and Female Occupations?" *Journal of Economic Issues* 18:473–482.

Johnson, George and Gary Solon. 1984. "Pay Differences Between Women's and Men's Jobs: The Empirical Foundations of Comparable Worth Legislation." National Bureau of Economic Research, Cambridge, MA. Working paper no. 1472.

————. 1986. "Estimates of the Direct Effects of Comparable Worth Policy." *American Economic Review* 76(5):1117–1125.

Johnson, Miriam M. 1989. "Feminism and the Theories of Talcott Parsons." Pp. 101–118 in *Feminism And Sociological Theory,* edited by Ruth A. Wallace. New York: Sage.

————. Forthcoming. "Functionalism and Feminism: Is Estrangement Necessary?" In *Theory on Gender/Feminism on Theory,* edited by Paula England. Hawthorne, NY: Aldine de Gruyter.

Jones, A. M. 1948. "Job Evaluation of Non-Academic Work at the University of Illinois." *Journal of Applied Psychology* 32:15–19.

Jones, F. L. and Jonathan Kelley. 1984. "Decomposing Differences Between Groups: A Cautionary Note on Measuring Discrimination." *Sociological Methods & Research* 12:323–343.

Kahn, Shulamit, 1986. "Economic Implications of Public-Sector Comparable Worth: A Case Study of San Jose." Paper presented at the annual meetings of the American Economic Association.

Kahn, Shulamit and Harriet Griesinger. 1989. "Female Mobility and the Returns to Seniority: Should EEO Policy Be Concerned with Promotion?" *American Economic Review* 79(2):300–304.

Kahneman, Daniel and Richard Thaler. 1991. "Economic Analysis and the Psychology of Utility: Applications to Compensation Policy." *American Economic Review* 81(2):341–346.

Kahneman, Daniel and Amos Tversky. 1979. "Prospect Theory: An Analysis of Decision Making Under Risk." *Econometrica* 47:263–291.

Kalleberg, Arne, Michael Wallace, and Robert Althauser. 1981. "Economic Segmentation, Worker Power, and Income Inequality." *American Journal of Sociology* 87:651–683.

Kant, Immanuel. [1797] 1964. *The Metaphysical Principles of Virtue*. New York: Bobbs-Merrill.

Kanter, Rosabeth. 1977. *Men and Women of the Corporation*. New York: Basic Books.

Katz, Lawrence. 1986. "Efficiency Wage Theories: A Partial Evaluation." *Macroeconomic Annual*. Cambridge, MA: National Bureau of Economic Research.

Katz, Paul A. 1984. "The Federal Civil Service." Pp. 14/1–14/10 in *Handbook of Wage and Salary Administration*, edited by Milton Rock. New York: McGraw-Hill.

Keller, Catherine. 1986. *From a Broken Web: Separation, Sexism, and Self*. Boston: Beacon Press.

Keller, Evelyn Fox. 1985. *Reflections on Gender and Science*. New Haven, CT: Yale University Press.

Kerbo, Harold R. 1983. *Social Stratification and Inequality: Class Conflict in the United States*. New York: McGraw-Hill.

Kilbourne, Barbara Stanek. 1991. *Occupational Skill, Gender, and Earnings*. Ph.D. dissertation, Program in Political Economy, University of Texas-Dallas.

Kilbourne, Barbara Stanek, Paula England, George Farkas, and Kurt Beron. 1990. "Skill, Compensating Differentials, and Gender Bias in Occupational Wage Determination." Paper presented at the Annual Meetings of the American Sociological Association.

Killingsworth, Mark R. 1984. "Statement on Comparable Worth." Testimony before the Joint Economic Committee, U.S. Congress.

———. 1985. "The Economics of Comparable Worth: Analytical, Empirical, and Policy Questions." Pp. 86–115 in *Comparable Worth: New Directions for Research*, edited by Heidi Hartmann. Washington, DC: National Academy Press.

———. 1986. "The Economics of Comparable Worth: A Comment on Hartmann." Pp. 186–195 in *The Moral Foundations of Civil Rights*, edited by Robert K. Fullinwider and Claudia Mills. Totowa, NJ: Rowman & Littlefield.

———. 1990. *The Economics of Comparable Worth*. Kalamazoo, MI: Upjohn Institute.

Killingsworth, Mark R. and James J. Heckman. 1986. "Female Labor Supply: A Survey." Pp. 103–204 in *Handbook of Labor Economics*, Volume I, edited by O. Ashenfelter and R. Layard. New York: Elsevier.

Klatch, Rebecca E. 1987. *Women of the New Right*. Philadelphia: Temple University Press.

Kohn, Melvin and Carmi Schooler (with J. Miller, K. Miller, and R. Schoenberg). 1983. *Work and Personality: An Inquiry into the Impact of Social Stratification*. Norwood, NJ: Ablex.

Kokkelenberg, Edward C. and Donna R. Sockell. 1985. "Union Membership In

The United States, 1973–1981." *Industrial and Labor Relations Review* 38:497–543.

Kouba v. Allstate Insurance Company. 1982. 691 F. 2d 873. 9th Circuit.

Krueger, Alan B. and Lawrence H. Summers. 1988. "Efficiency Wages and the Inter-Industry Wage Structure." *Econometrica* 56:259–293.

Kuhn, Peter. 1991. "Gender-Based Personnel Policy." Paper presented at the Annual Meetings of the American Economic Association.

LaClau, E. and C. Mouffe. 1985. *Hegemony and Socialist Strategy.* London: Verso.

Landes, E. M. 1977. "Sex Differences in Wages and Employment: A Test of the Specific Capital Hypothesis." *Economic Inquiry* 15:523–538.

Lang, Kevin. 1988. "A Sorting Model of Statistical Discrimination." Department of Economics, Boston University. Unpublished Manuscript.

———. 1991. "Persistent Wage Dispersion And Involuntary Unemployment." *Quarterly Journal of Economics* 106:181–202.

Lang, Kevin and William Dickens. 1988. "Neoclassical Perspectives on Segmented Labor Markets." Pp. 65–88 in *Industries, Firms and Jobs: Sociological and Economic Approaches,* edited by George Farkas and Paula England. New York: Plenum.

Lawshe, C. H., Jr. and P. C. Farbo. 1949. "Studies in Job Evaluation: 8. The Reliability of an Abbreviated Job Evaluation System." *Journal of Applied Psychology* 33:158–166.

Lawshe, C. H., Jr. and R. F. Wilson. 1947. "Studies in Job Evaluation: 6. The Reliability of Two Point Rating System." *Journal of Applied Psychology* 31:355–365.

Laycock, Douglas. 1986a. "Continuing Violations, Disparate Impact in Compensation, and Other Title VII Issues." *Law and Contemporary Problems* 49:53–61.

———. 1986b. "Statistical Proof and Theories of Discrimination." *Law and Contemporary Problems* 49:97–106.

Lazear, Edward. 1979. "Why Is There Mandatory Retirement?" *Journal of Political Economy* 87:1261–1284.

———. 1981. "Agency, Earnings Profiles, Productivity, and Hours Restrictions." *American Economic Review* 71:606–620.

Lehrer, Evelyn L. and Houston Stokes. 1985. "Determinants of the Female Occupational Distribution: A Log-linear Probability Analysis." *Review of Economics and Statistics* 67(3):395–404.

Lemons v. City and County of Denver. 1980. 620 F. 2d 228. 10th Circuit.

Leonard, Jonathan S. 1984. "The Impact of Affirmative Action on Employment." *Journal of Labor Economics* 2:439–463.

Lerner, Gerda. 1986. *The Creation of Patriarchy.* New York: Oxford University Press.

Levin, Michael. 1984. "Comparable Worth: The Feminist Road to Socialism." *Commentary* 78:13–19.

———. 1987. *Feminism and Freedom.* New Brunswick, NJ: Transaction Books.

Levinson, Richard. 1975. "Sex Discrimination and Employment Practices: An Experiment with Unconventional Job Inquiries." *Social Problems* 22:533–543.

Levy, Frank. 1987. *Dollars and Dreams: The Changing American Income Distribution.* New York: Russell Sage Foundation.

———. 1988. "Incomes, Families, and Living Standards." Pp. 108–153 in *American Living Standards: Threats and Challenges,* edited by Robert Litan, Robert Lawrence, and Charles L. Schultze. Washington, DC: The Brookings Institute.

Light, Audry L. and Manuelita Ureta. 1989. "Panel Estimates of Male and Female Turnover Behavior: Can Female Non-Quitters Be Identified?" Dept. of Economics, State University of New York at Stony Brook, Working paper.

Lippman, Steven and John J. McCall. 1986. "The Economics of Job Search: A Survey." *Economic Inquiry* 14:155–189.

Livy, Bryan. 1975. *Job Evaluation: A Critical Review.* New York: Wiley.

Lloyd, Cynthia B. 1975. "The Division of Labor Between the Sexes: A Review." Pp. 1–24 in *Sex, Discrimination, and the Division of Labor,* edited by Cynthia B. Lloyd. New York: Columbia University Press.

Lloyd, Cynthia and Beth Niemi. 1979. *The Economics of Sex Differentials.* New York: Columbia University Press.

Locke, John. [1698] 1967. *Two Treatises of Government.* New York: Cambridge University Press.

Loudon, J. P. and T. D. Loudon. 1986. "Applying Disparate Impact to Title VII Comparable Worth Claims: An Incomparable Task." *Indiana Law Journal* 61:165–187.

Lueck, Marjori, Ann Orr, and Martin O'Connell. 1982. "Trends in Childcare Arrangements of Working Mothers." CPS Special Studies P-23, No. 117. Washington, D.C.: Government Printing Office.

Lueptow, L. B. 1980. "Social Change and Sex-Role Change in Adolescent Orientations Toward Life, Work, and Achievement: 1964–1975." *Social Psychology Quarterly* 43:48–59.

Lundberg, Shelly J. and Richard Startz. 1983. "Private Discrimination and Social Intervention in Competitive Labor Markets." *American Economic Review* 73:340–347.

Lynch, Lisa M. 1991. "The Role of Off-the-Job vs. On-the-Job Training for the Mobility of Women Workers." *American Economic Review* 81(2):151–156.

Maccoby, Eleanor E. and Carol N. Jacklin. 1974. *The Psychology of Sex Difference.* Stanford, CA: Stanford University Press.

Madden, Janice F. 1973. *The Economics of Sex Discrimination.* Lexington, MA: Lexington Books.

Madigan, R. M. 1985. "Comparable Worth Judgments: A Measurement Properties Analysis." *Journal of Applied Psychology* 70:137–147.

Madigan, R. M. and D. J. Hoover. 1986. "Effects of Alternative Job Evaluation Methods on Decisions Involving Pay Equity." *Academy of Management Journal* 29:84–100.

Major, Brenda. 1989. "Gender Differences in Comparisons and Entitlements: Implications for Comparable Worth." *Journal of Social Issues* 45:99–115.

Major, Brenda and Blythe Forcey. 1985. "Social Comparisons and Pay Evaluations: Preferences for Same-Sex and Same-Job Wage Comparisons." *Journal of Experimental Social Psychology* 21:393–405.

Major, Brenda and E. Konar. 1984. "An Investigation of Sex Differences in Pay

Expectations and Their Possible Causes." *Academy of Management Journal* 27:777–792.

Malveaux, Julianne. 1986. "Comparable Worth and Its Impact on Black Women." *Review of Black Political Economy* 14(2–3):47–62.

Marglin, S. 1978. "What Do Bosses Do? The Origins and Functions of Hierarchy in Capitalist Production." Pp. 13–54 in *The Division of Labor: The Labor Process and Class Struggle in Modern Capitalism,* edited by Andre Gorz. London: Harvestor.

Marini, Margaret M. and Mary Brinton. 1984. "Sex Typing in Occupational Socialization." Pp. 192–232 in *Sex Segregation in the Workplace: Trends, Explanations, Remedies,* edited by Barbara F. Reskin. Washington, D.C.: National Academy Press.

Marini, Margaret M. and E. Greenberger. 1978. "Sex Differences in Occupational Aspirations and Expectations." *Sociology of Work and Occupations* 5:147–178.

Marshall, Ray and Beth Paulin. 1984. "The Employment and Earnings of Women: The Comparable Worth Debate." Pp. 196–214 in *Comparable Worth: Issues for the 80's: A Consultation of the U.S. Commission on Civil Rights.* Washington, DC: U.S. Commission on Civil Rights.

Martin, Teresa Castro and Larry L. Bumpass. 1989. "Recent Trends in Marital Disruption." *Demography* 26(1):37–50.

Marx, Karl. [1852] 1963. *The Eighteenth Brumaire of Louis Bonaparte.* New York: International Publishers.

———. [1867] 1967. *Capital, Volume I.* New York: International Publishers.

———. [1885] 1967. *Capital, Volume II.* New York: International Publishers.

———. [1894] 1967. *Capital, Volume III.* New York: International Publishers.

———. [1844] 1975. "Economic and Philosophical Manuscripts." Pp. 279–400 in *Early Writings.* New York: Viking Press.

McArthur, L. Z. 1985. "Social Judgment Biases in Comparable Worth Analysis." Pp. 53–70 in *Comparable Worth: New Directions for Research,* edited by Heidi I. Hartmann. Washington, DC: National Academy Press.

McArthur, L. Z. and S. W. Obrant. 1986. "Sex Biases in Comparable Worth Analyses." *Journal of Applied Social Psychology* 16:757–770.

McCormick, E. J., P. R. Jeanneret, and R. C. Mecham. 1972. "A Study of Job Characteristics and Job Dimensions as Based on the Position Description Questionnaire." *Journal of Applied Psychology* 56:547–562.

McDowell, Douglas. 1985. "An Analysis of the National Academy of Sciences' Comparable Worth Study." Pp. 267–282 in *Comparable Worth: Issues and Alternative,* second edition, edited by Robert Livernash. Washington, DC: Equal Employment Advisory Council.

McElroy, Wendy. 1990. "Comparable Worth: Feminism Turning to Paternalism." *Freeman* 40,10:380–381.

McEntee, Gerald W. 1986. "Comparable Worth: A Matter of Simple Justice." *Humanist* May–June:18–45.

McLanahan, Sara S., Annemette Sorensen, and Dorothy Watson. 1989. "Sex Differences in Poverty: 1950–1980." *Signs* 15(1):102–122.

Milkman, Ruth. 1987. *Gender at Work.* Urbana: University of Illinois Press.

Mill, John Stuart. [1859] 1975. *On Liberty.* New York: Norton.

Miller, Ann R., Donald J. Treiman, Pamela S. Cain, Patricia A. Roos, eds. 1980. *Work, Jobs, and Occupations: A Critical Review of the Dictionary of Occupational Titles*. Washington, DC: National Academy Press.

Mincer, Jacob and Haim Ofek. 1982. "Interrupted Work Careers: Depreciation and Restoration of Human Capital." *Journal of Human Resources* 17:3–24.

Mincer, Jacob and Soloman Polochek. 1974. "Family Investments in Human Capital: Earnings of Women." *Journal of Political Economy* 82:S76–S108.

———. 1978. "Women's Earnings Reexamined." *Journal of Human Resources* 13:118–134.

Molm, Linda D. 1991. "Affect and Social Exchange: Satisfaction in Power-Dependence Relations." *American Sociological Review* 56:475–493.

Montgomery, James D. 1991. "Equilibrium Wage Dispersion and Inter-industry Wage Differentials." *Quarterly Journal of Economics* 106(1):163–180.

Mott, Frank L. and Sylvia Moore. 1983. "The Tempo of Remarriage among Young American Women." *Journal of Marriage and the Family* 45:427–436.

Mount, Michael K. and Rebecca A. Ellis. 1987. "Investigation of Bias in Job Evaluation Ratings of Comparable Worth Study Participants." *Personnel Psychology* 40:85–96.

Murray, M. and T. Atkinson. 1981. "Gender Differences in Correlates of Job Satisfaction." *Canadian Journal of Behavioral Science* 13:44–52.

Nakamura, A. and M. Nakamura. 1989. "Predicting Effects of Comparable Worth Programs on Female Labor Supply." *Journal of Social Issues* 45:191–208.

Nalebuff, Barry and Richard Zeckhauser. 1981. "Involuntary Unemployment Reconsidered: Second-best Contracting with Heterogeneous Firms and Workers." Institute for Research on Poverty, University of Wisconsin, Madison. Discussion paper 675–681.

National Academy of Sciences. 1981. *Fourth Edition Dictionary of Occupational Titles (DOT) Scores for 1970 Census Categories, Codebook*. Washington, DC: Committee on Occupational Classification and Analysis, National Academy of Sciences.

National Committee on Pay Equity. 1987. *Pay Equity: An Issue of Race, Ethnicity and Sex*. Washington, DC: National Committee on Pay Equity.

———. 1989. *Pay Equity in the Public Sector, 1979–1989*. Washington, DC: National Committee on Pay Equity.

Newman, Winn and C. Owens. 1984. "Race- and Sex-based Discrimination Is Illegal." Pp. 131–47 in *Comparable Worth: Issue for the 80's: A Consultation of the U.S. Commission on Civil Rights*. Washington, DC: U.S. Commission on Civil Rights.

Nieva, V. F. and Barbara A. Gutek. 1980. "Sex Effects on Evaluation." *Academy of Management Review* 5:267–276.

Northrup, Herbert R. 1980. "Wage Setting and Collective Bargaining." Pp. 107–136 in *Comparable Worth: Issues and Alternatives*, edited by E. R. Livernash. Washington, DC: Equal Employment Advisory Council.

———. 1984. "Comparable Worth and Realistic Wage Setting." Pp. 93–98 in *Comparable Worth: Issues for the 80's: A Consultation of the U.S. Commission on Civil Rights*. Washington, DC: U.S. Commission on Civil Rights.

Norwood, Janet. 1982. "The Female-Male Earnings Gap: A Review of Employment and Earnings Issues." U.S. Department of Labor, Washington, DC. Bureau of Labor Statistics report.

Nozick, John. 1974. *Anarchy, State and Utopia.* New York: Basic Books.

O'Farrell, Brigid and Sharon Harlan. 1982. "Craftworkers and Clerks: The Effect of Male Co-Worker Hostility on Women's Satisfaction with Non-Traditional Jobs." *Social Problems* 29(3):252–265.

O'Neill, June A. 1981. "A Times-Series Analysis of Women's Labor Force Participation." *American Economic Review* 71:76–80.

———. 1983. "The Determinants and Wage Effects of Occupational Segregation." Urban Institute, Washington, DC. Working paper.

———. 1984. "An Argument Against Comparable Worth." Pp. 177–186 in *Comparable Worth: Issues for the 80's: A Consultation of the U.S. Commission on Civil Rights.* Washington, DC: U.S. Commission on Civil Rights.

———. 1985. "The Trend in the Male-Female Wage Gap in the United States." *Journal of Labor Economics* 3(January Supplement):S91–S116, Tables 3 and 5.

Oi, W. Y. 1986. "Neglected Women and Other Implications of Comparable Worth." *Contemporary Policy Issues* 4:21–32.

Okin, Susan Moller. 1989. *Justice, Gender, and the Family.* New York: Basic Books.

Okun, Arthur. 1981. *Prices and Quantities: A Macroeconomic Analysis.* Washington, DC: Brookings Institution.

Olson, Craig A. 1981. "An Analysis of Wage Differentials Received by Workers on Dangerous Jobs." *Journal of Human Resources* 16:167–185.

Oppenheimer, Valerie Kincade. 1970. *The Female Labor Force in the United States: Demographic and Economic Factors Governing Its Growth and Changing Composition.* Berkeley: Regents of the University of California.

———. 1982. *Work and Family.* New York: Academic Press.

Orazem, P. F. and P. Mattila. 1987. *Comparable Worth and the Structure of Earnings: The Iowa Case.* Iowa State University, Ames. Unpublished manuscript.

———. 1989. "Comparable Worth and the Structure of Earnings: The Iowa Case." Pp. 179–199 in *Pay Equity: Empirical Inquiries,* edited by Robert Micahel, Heidi Hartmann, and Brigid O'Farrell. Washington, DC: National Academy Press.

Osterman, Paul. 1982. "Affirmative Action and Opportunity: A Study of Female Quit Rates." *Review of Economics and Statistics* 64:604–612.

Pagels, Elaine. 1988. *Adam, Eve, and the Serpent.* New York: Random House.

Parcel, Toby. 1989. "Comparable Worth, Occupational Labor Markets, and Occupational Earnings: Results from the 1980 Census." Pp. 134–152 in *Pay Equity: Empirical Inquiries,* edited by Robert Michael, Heidi Hartmann, and Brigid O'Farrell. Washington, DC: National Academy Press.

Parsons, Talcott. 1954. *Essays in Sociology Theory.* Revised edition. Glencoe, IL: Free Press.

———. 1966. *Societies: Evolutionary and Comparative Perspectives.* Englewood Cliffs, NJ: Prentice-Hall.

Parsons, Talcott and Robert F. Bales. 1955. *Family Socialization and Interaction Process.* New York: Free Press.

Patten, T. 1987. "How Do You Know If Your Job Evaluation System Is Working?" Pp. 10–19 in *New Perspectives on Compensation,* edited by D. B. Balkin and L. R. Gomez-Mejia. Englewood Cliffs, NJ: Prentice-Hall.

Paul, Ellen Frankel. 1989. *Equity and Gender: The Comparable Worth Debate.* New Brunswick, NJ: Transaction Publishers.

Peng, S. S., W. B. Fetters, and A. J. Kolstad. 1981. *High School and Beyond: A Capsule Description of High School Students.* Washington, DC: National Center for Education Statistics.

Pfeffer, Jeffrey and Alison Davis-Blake. 1987. "The Effect of the Proportion of Women on Salaries: The Case of College Administrators." *Administrative Science Quarterly* 32:1–24.

Phelps, Edmund. 1972. "The Statistical Theory of Racism and Sexism." *American Economic Review* 64:59–61.

Phillips, Anne and Barbara Taylor. 1980. "Sex and Skill: Notes Toward a Feminist Economics." *Feminist Review* 6:79–83.

Phillips, John A. 1984. *Eve: The History of an Idea.* New York: Harper and Row.

Pierson, David A., Karen S. Koziara, and Russell Johannesson. 1983. "Equal Pay for Jobs of Comparable Worth: A Quantified Job Content Approach." *Public Personnel Management* 12:445–460.

———. 1984. "A Policy-Capturing Application in a Union Setting." Pp. 118–136 in *Comparable Worth and Wage Discrimination,* edited by Helen Remick. Philadelphia: Temple University Press.

Pinzler, Isabelle Katz and Deborah Ellis. 1989. "Wage Discrimination and Comparable Worth: A Legal Perspective." *Journal of Social Issues* 45:51–65.

Polachek, Solomon W. 1975. "Discontinuous Labor Force Participation and Its Effect on Women's Market Earnings." Pp. 90–124 in *Sex, Discrimination, and the Division of Labor,* edited by Cynthia B. Lloyd. New York: Columbia University Press.

———. 1979. "Occupational Segregation Among Women: Theory, Evidence, and a Prognosis." Pp. 137–157 in *Women in the Labor Market,* edited by Cynthia B. Lloyd, Emily S. Andrews, and Curtis L. Gilroy. New York: Columbia University Press.

———. 1981. "Occupational Self Selection: A Human Capital Approach to Sex Differences in Occupational Structure." *Review of Economics and Statistics* 58:60–69.

———. 1984. "Women in the Economy: Perspectives on Gender Inequality." Pp. 34–53 in *Comparable Worth: Issue for the 80's: A Consultation of the U.S. Commission on Civil Rights.* Washington, DC: U.S. Commission on Civil Rights.

Poulantzas, Nicos. 1974. *Classes in Contemporary Capitalism.* London: New Left Books.

———. 1978. *State, Power and Socialism.* London: New Left Books.

Preston, Samuel. 1984. "Children and the Elderly: Divergent Paths for America's Dependents." *Demography* 21:435–458.

Preston, Samuel H. and McDonald, John. 1979. "The Incidence of Divorce within Cohorts of American Marriages Contracted Since the War." *Demography* 16:1–25.

Price, James L. 1977. *The Study of Turnover.* Ames: Iowa State University Press.

Quinn, R. P. and G. L. Staines. 1979. *Quality of Employment Survey, 1977: Cross Section.* Ann Arbor, MI: Interuniversity Consortium for Political and Social Research.

Rabkin, Jeremy. 1984. "Comparable Worth as Civil Rights Policy: Potentials for

Disaster." Pp. 187–195 in *Comparable Worth: Issues for the 80's: A Consultation of the U.S. Commission on Civil Rights*. Washington, DC: U.S. Commission on Civil Rights.

Raisin, John, Michael P. Ward, and Finis Welch. 1986. "Pay Equity and Comparable Worth." *Contemporary Policy Issues* IV(2):4–20.

Rawls, John. 1971. *A Theory of Justice*. Cambridge, MA: Belnap Press of the Harvard University Press.

Raymond, Janice. 1975. "The Illusion of Androgyny." *Quest* 2:57–66.

Rebitzer, James B. 1989. "Efficiency Wages and Implicit Contracts: An Institutional Evaluation." Pp. 16–40 in *Microeconomic Issues in Labour Economics: New Approaches*, edited by Robert Drago and Richard Perlman. New York: Harvester Wheatsheaf.

Rector, Robert. 1988. "The Pseudo-Science of Comparable Worth: Phrenology for Modern Times." In *The Heritage Foundation Backgrounder*, February.

Reich, Michael. 1978. "Who Benefits from Racism?: The Distribution among Whites of Gains and Losses from Racial Inequality." *Journal of Human Resources* 13:524–544.

————. 1981. *Racial Inequality: A Political-Economic Analysis*. Princeton, NJ: Princeton University Press.

Reichenberg, Neil E. 1986. "Pay Equity in Review." *Public Personnel Management* 15:211–231.

Remick, Helen. 1980. "Beyond Equal Pay for Equal Work: Comparable Worth in the State of Washington." Pp. 405–419 in *Equal Employment Policy for Women*, edited by Ronnie Steinberg Ratner. Philadelphia: Temple University Press.

————. 1984. "Major Issues in a Priori Applications." Pp. 99–117 in *Comparable Worth and Wage Discrimination*, edited by Helen Remick. Philadelphia: Temple University Press.

————. Forthcoming. "Considerations in the Long-run Implementation of Comparable Worth." In *The Politics and Practice of Pay Equity*, edited by Ronnie Steinberg. Philadelphia: Temple University Press.

Reskin, Barbara F. 1988. "Bringing the Men Back In: Sex Differentiation and the Devaluation of Women's Work." *Gender & Society* 2:58–81.

Reskin, Barbara F. and Patricia Roos. 1990. *Job Queues, Gender Queues: Explaining Women's Inroads into Male Occupations*. Philadelphia: Temple University Press.

Reynolds, William Bradford. 1986. "Comparable Worth: Bad Policy and Bad Law." *Harvard Journal of Law & Public Policy* 9:89–94.

Richardson, John G. and Brenda Wooden Hatcher. 1983. "The Feminization of Public School Teaching, 1870–1920." *Work and Occupations* 10(10):81–99.

Ridgeway, Cecilia. Forthcoming. "Gender, Status, and the Social Psychology of Expectations." In *Theory on Gender/Feminism on Theory*, edited by Paula England. Hawthorne, NY: Aldine de Gruyter.

Roback, Jennifer. 1986. *A Matter of Choice: A Critique of Comparable Worth by a Skeptical Feminist*. New York: Priority Press Publications.

Robinson, D. D., O. W. Wahlstrom, and R. C. Mecham. 1974. "Comparison of Job Evaluation Methods: A Policy-Capturing Approach Using the Position Analysis Questionnaire (PAQ)." *Journal of Applied Psychology* 59:633–637.

Roemer, John E. 1979. "Divide and Conquer: Microfoundations of a Marxian Theory of Wage Discrimination." *Bell Journal of Economics* 10:695–705.

———. 1988. *Free To Lose: An Introduction to Marxist Economic Philosophy.* Cambridge, MA: Harvard University Press.

Roos, Patricia A. 1985. *Gender and Work: A Comparative Analysis of Industrial Societies.* New York: State University of New York Press.

Roos, Patricia and Barbara F. Reskin. 1984. "Institutional Factors Contributing to Sex Segregation in the Workplace." Pp. 235–260 in *Sex Segregation in the Workplace: Trends, Explanations, Remedies,* edited by Barbara F. Reskin. Washington, DC: National Academy Press.

Rosen, Benson. 1982. "Career Progress of Women: Getting In and Staying In." Pp. 70–99 in *Women in the Work Force,* edited by H. J. Bernardin. New York: Praeger.

Rosen, B. and Jerdee, T. H. 1974. "Effects of Applicant's Sex and Difficulty of Job on Evaluations of Candidates for Managerial Positions." *Journal of Applied Psychology* 59:511–512.

———. 1978. "Perceived Sex Differences in Managerially Relevant Behavior." *Sex Roles* 4:837–843.

Rosen, Sherwin. 1986. "The Theory of Equalizing Differences." *Handbook of Labor Economics* 1:641–692.

Rosenbaum, James. 1980. "Hierarchical and Individual Effects on Earnings." *Industrial Relations* 19(1):1–14.

Rosenfeld, Rachel and Arne L. Kalleberg. 1990. "A Cross-national Comparison of the Gender Gap in Income." *American Journal of Sociology* 96(1):69–106.

Ross, Catherine E. 1987. "The Division of Labor at Home." *Social Forces* 65:816–833.

Rothchild, Nina. 1984. "Overview of Pay Initiatives, 1974–1984." Pp. 119–128 in *Comparable Worth: Issues for the 80's: A Consultation of the U.S. Commission on Civil Rights.* Washington DC: U.S. Commission on Civil Rights.

Rynes, Sara L. and George T. Milkovich. 1986. "Wage Surveys: Dispelling Some Myths About the 'Market Wage.'" *Personnel Psychology* 39:71–90.

Rynes, Sara L., Caroline L. Weber, and George T. Milkovich. 1989. "Effects of Market Survey Rates, Job Evaluation, and Job Gender on Job Pay." *Journal of Applied Psychology* 74:114–123.

Sanday, Peggy Reeves. 1981. *Female Power and Male Dominance.* Cambridge: Cambridge University Press.

Sandel, Michael J., ed. 1984. *Liberalism and Its Critics.* Oxford: Basil Blackwell.

Sandell, Steven H. and Shapiro, David. 1978. "A Re-examination of the Evidence." *Journal of Human Resources* 13:103–117.

Sape, George P. 1985. "Coping with Comparable Worth." *Harvard Business Review* May–June:145–152.

Schlafly, Phyllis, ed. 1984. *Equal Pay for Unequal Work.* Washington, DC: Eagle Forum Education & Legal Defense Fund.

———. 1986. "Comparable Worth: Unfair to Men and Women." *Humanist* May–June:12–30.

Schott, Robin May. 1988. *Cognition and Eros: A Critique of the Kantian Paradigm.* Boston, MA: Beacon Press.

Schroedel, Jean Reith. 1985. *Alone in a Crowd: Women in the Trades Tell Their Stories.* Philadelphia: Temple University Press.

Schultz, T. P. 1981. *The Economics of Population.* Reading, MA: Addison-Wesley.

Schwab, Donald P. 1980. "Job Evaluation and Pay Setting: Concepts and Practices." Pp. 49–78 in *Comparable Worth: Issues and Alternatives,* edited by E. Robert Livernash. Washington, DC: Equal Employment Advisory Council.

———. 1984. "Using Job Evaluation to Obtain Pay Equity." Pp. 83–92 in *Comparable Worth: Issues for the 80's: A Consultation of the U.S. Commission on Civil Rights.* Washington, DC: U.S. Commission on Civil Rights.

———. 1985. "Job Evaluation Research and Research Needs." Pp. 37–52 in *Comparable Worth: New Directions for Research,* edited by Heidi I. Hartmann. Washington, DC: National Academy Press.

Schwab, D. P. and R. Grams. 1985. "Sex-Related Errors in Job Evaluation: A Real-World Test." *Journal of Applied Psychology* 70:533–539.

Schwab, D. P. and H. G. Heneman III. 1986. "Assessment of a Consensus-Based Multiple Information Source Job Evaluation System." *Journal of Applied Psychology* 71:354–356.

Schwab, D. P. and D. W. Wichern. 1983. "Systematic Bias in Job Evaluation and Market Wages: Implications for the Comparable Worth Debate." *Journal of Applied Psychology* 31:353–364.

Seccombe, Walter. 1974. "The Housewife and Her Labor Under Capitalism." *New Left Review* 83:3–24.

Segar v. Smith. 1984. 738 F. 2d 1249. D.C. Circuit.

Seidenfeld, M. B. 1982. "Sex-based Wage Discrimination under the Title VII Disparate Impact Doctrine." *Stanford Law Review* 34:1083–1103.

Seidman, Laurence S. 1979. "The Return of the Profit Rate to the Wage Equation." *Review of Economics and Statistics* 61:139–142.

Shapiro, C. and J. E. Stiglitz. 1984. "Equilibrium Unemployment as a Worker Discipline Device." *American Economic Review* 74:433–444.

Shelton, Beth Anne and Ben Agger. Forthcoming. "Shotgun Wedding, Unhappy Marriage, No-Fault Divorce? Rethinking the Feminism-Marxism Relationship." In *Theory on Gender/Feminism on Theory,* edited by Paula England. Hawthorne, NY: Aldine de Gruyter.

Shepala, S. T. and A. T. Viviano. 1984. "Some Psychological Factors Affecting Job Segregation and Wages." Pp. 47–58 in *Comparable Worth and Wage Discrimination,* edited by Helen Remick. Philadelphia: Temple University Press.

Sheppard, Harold L. and Herrick, Neal. 1972. *Where Have All the Robots Gone?* New York: Free Press.

Shorey, John. 1983. "An Analysis of Sex Differences in Quits." *Oxford Economic Papers* 35:213–227.

Shrage, Laurie. 1987. "Some Implications of Comparable Worth." *Social Theory and Practice* 13(1):77–102.

Smith, Adam. [1776] 1930. *Wealth of Nations.* London: Methuen.

Smith, Catherine Begnoche. 1979. "Influence of Internal Opportunity Structure and Sex of Worker on Turnover Patterns." *Administrative Science Quarterly* 24:362–381.

Smith, James P. and Michael P. Ward. 1984. *Women's Wages and Work in the Twentieth Century.* R-3119-NICHD. Santa Monica: Rand.

Smith, Paul. 1978. "Domestic Labour and Marx's Theory of Value." Pp. 198–219 in *Feminism and Materialism,* edited by Annette Kuhn and Annmarie Wope. London: Routledge and Kegan Paul.

Smith, Robert S. 1979. "Compensating Wage Differentials and Public Policy: A Review." *Industrial Labor Relations Review* 32:339–352.

_____. 1988. "Comparable Worth: Limited Coverage and the Exacerbation of Inequality." *Industrial and Labor Relations Review* 41:227–239.

Snelgar, R. J. 1983. "The Comparability of Job Evaluation Methods in Supplying Approximately Similar Classifications in Rating One Job Series." *Personnel Psychology* 36:371–380.

Snyder, David and Paula M. Hudis. 1976. "Occupational Income and the Effects of Minority Competition and Segregation: A Reanalysis and Some New Evidence." *American Sociological Review* 41:209–234.

Sorensen, Elaine. 1987. "Effect of Comparable Worth Policies on Earnings." *Industrial Relations* 26:227–239.

_____. 1989a. "Measuring the Effect of Occupational Sex and Race composition on Earnings." Pp. 49–69 in *Pay Equity: Empirical Inquiries,* edited by Robert Micahel, Heidi Hartmann and Brigid O'Farrell. Washington, DC: National Academy Press.

_____. 1989b. "The Wage Effects of Occupational Sex Composition: A Review and New Findings." Pp. 57–79 in *Comparable Worth: Analyses and Evidence,* edited by M. Anne Hill and Mark Killingsworth. Ithaca, NY: ILR Press.

_____. 1991a. "Review of Mark R. Killingsworth's Book: The Economics of Comparable Worth." Washington, DC, The Urban Institute. Unpublished manuscript.

_____. 1991b. "Wage and Employment Effects of Pay Equity: Evidence from the United States." Washington, DC, The Urban Institute. Unpublished manuscript.

Spaulding v. University of Washington. 1984. 740 F. 2d 686. 9th Circuit.

Stafford, F. P. and Duncan, G. J., 1980. "The Use of Time and Technology by Households in the United States." Pp. 335–375 in *Research in Labor Economics,* Volume 3, edited by R. G. Ehrenberg. Greenwich, CT: JAI Press.

Stanley, Liz and Sue Wise. 1983. *Breaking Out: Feminist Consciousness and Feminist Research.* London: Routledge & Kegan Paul.

Starhawk. 1987. *Truth or Dare: Encounters with Power, Authority, and Mystery.* San Francisco: Harper & Row.

Steinberg, Ronnie. 1986. "The Debate on Comparable Worth." *New Politics* 1(1):108–126.

_____. 1987. "Radical Challenges in a Liberal World: The Mixed Success of Comparable Worth." *Gender & Society* 1:466–475.

_____. 1990. "Social Construction of Skill: Gender, Power, and Comparable Worth. *Work and Occupations* 17:449–482.

_____, ed. Forthcoming. *The Politics and Practice of Pay Equity.* Philadelphia: Temple University Press.

Steinberg, Ronnie J. and Lois Haignere. 1987. "Equitable Compensation: Methodological Criteria for Comparable Worth." Pp. 157–182, in *Ingredients for Women's Employment Policy*, edited by Christine Bose and Glenna Spitze. Albany: State University of New York Press.

Steinberg, Ronnie J., Lois Haignere, C. Possin, C. H. Chertos, and D. Treiman. 1986. *The New York State Pay Equity Study: A Research Report*. Albany, NY: Center for Women in Government, State University of New York Press.

Steuerle, Eugene. Forthcoming. *The Tax Decade: 1981–1990*. Washington, DC: Urban Institute Press.

Steuerle, Eugene, and Paul Wilson. 1987. "The Taxation of Poor and Lower-Income Workers." *Tax Notes* (February):695–711.

Stevenson, Mary. 1988. "The Persistence of Wage Differences Between Men and Women: Some Economic Approaches." Pp. 87–100, in *Women Working*, edited by A. Stromberg and S. Harkess. Palo Alto, CA: Mayfield.

Stigler, C. J. and Gary Becker. 1977. "De Gustibus non est Disputandum." *American Economic Review* 67:76–90.

Stigler, George. 1961. "The Economics of Information." *Journal of Political Economy* 69:213–225.

———. 1962. "Information in the Labor Market." *Journal of Political Economy* 70:94–105.

Stiglitz, Joseph. 1987. "The Causes and Consequences of the Dependence of Quality in Price." *Journal of Economic Literature* 25:1–48.

Strober, Myra H. 1984. "Toward a General Theory of Occupational Segregation: The Case of Public School Teaching." Pp. 144–56 in *Sex Segregation in the Workplace*, edited by Barbara Reskin. Washington DC: National Academy Press.

Subich, Linda, Gerald Barrett, Dennis Doverspike, and Ralph Alexander. 1989. "The Effects of Sex-Role-Related Factors on Occupational Choice and Salary." Pp. 91–106 in *Pay Equity: Empirical Inquiries*, edited by Robert Micahel, Heidi Hartmann, and Brigid O'Farrell. Washington, DC: National Academy Press.

Szymanski, A. 1976. "Racial Discrimination and White Gain." *American Sociological Review* 41:403–414.

Taeuber, Cynthia, ed. 1991. *Statistical Handbook on Women in America*. Phoenix, AZ: Oryx Press.

Texas Department of Community Affairs v. Burdine. 1981. 450 U.S. 248. U.S. Supreme Court.

Thurow, Lester. 1975. *Generating Inequality*. New York: Basic Books.

———. 1983. *Dangerous Currents*. New York: Random House.

Tigges, Leann. 1988. "Dueling Sectors: The Role of Service Industries in the Earnings Process of the Dual Economy." Pp. 281–301 in *Industries, Firms, and Jobs: Sociological and Economic Approaches*, edited by George Farkas and Paula England. New York: Plenum.

Tittle, C. I. 1981. *Careers and Family: Sex Roles and Adolescent Life Plans*. Beverly Hills, CA: Sage.

Tolbert, Charles II, Patrick Horan, and E. M. Beck. 1980. "The Structure of

Economic Segmentation: A Dual Economy Approach." *American Journal of Sociology* 85:1095–1116.

Tool, Marc R. 1988. *Evolutionary Economics, Volume I: Foundations of Institutional Thought.* New York: M. E. Sharpe.

Treiman, D. J. 1979. *Job Evaluation: An Analytic Review.* Interim Report to the Equal Employment Opportunity Commission. Washington, DC: National Academy of Sciences.

Treiman, Donald J. and Heidi Hartmann. 1981. *Equal Pay for Jobs of Equal Value.* Washington, DC: National Academy Press.

Treiman, Donald J. and Kermit Terrell. 1975a. "Sex And The Process of Status Attainment: A Comparison Of Working Women And Men." *American Sociological Review* 40:174–200.

———. 1975b. "Women, Work and Wages—Trends in the Female Occupational Structure since 1940." Pp. 157–200 in *Social Indicator Models,* edited by Kenneth C. Land and Seymour Spilerman. New York: Russell Sage Foundation.

Tuana, Nancy. 1983. "Re-Fusing Nature/Nurture." *Women's Studies International Forum* 6:621–632.

———. 1992. *Woman And The History of Philosophy.* New York: Paragon Press.

———. Forthcoming. *The Misbegotten Man: Scientific, Religious, And Philosophical Images Of Woman's Nature.* Bloomington: University of Indiana Press.

Tucker, Robert, ed. 1978. *The Marx-Engels Reader.* New York: Norton.

Tversky, Amos and Daniel Kahneman. 1987. "Rational Choice and the Framing of Decisions." Pp. 67–94 in *Rational Choice: The Contrast Between Economics and Psychology,* edited by R. M. Hogarth and M. W. Reder. Chicago: University of Chicago Press.

U.S. Bureau of the Census. 1983a. *Census of Population and Housing, 1980: Public-Use Microdata Samples Technical Documentation.* Washington, DC: U.S. Government Printing Office.

———. 1983b. *Child Support and Alimony: 1981* (Advance Report). Current Population Reports, Special Studies, Series P-23, No. 124. U.S. Government Printing Office.

———. 1984a. *1980 Census of Population, Volume 2, Subject Reports: Earnings by Occupation and Education.* PC80-2-8B. U.S. Government Printing Office.

———. 1984b. *1980 Census of Population, Volume 2, Subject Reports: Occupation by Industry.* PC80-2-7C. Washington, DC: U.S. Government Printing Office.

———. 1985. *1980 Census of Population, Occupation By Industry Technical Documentation.* Washington, DC: U.S. Government Printing Office.

———. 1987. *Male-Female Differences in Work Experience, Occupation, and Earnings: 1984.* Current Population Reports, Series P-70, No. 10. Washington, DC: U.S. Government Printing Office.

U.S. Commission on Civil Rights. 1984. *Comparable Worth: Issue for the 80's: A Consultation of the U.S. Commission on Civil Rights* Washington, DC: U.S. Commission on Civil Rights.

———. 1985. *Comparable Worth: An Analysis and Recommendations.* Washington, DC: U.S. Commission on Civil Rights.

U.S. Department of Labor. 1967–1989. *Employment and Earnings.* January. Washington, DC: U.S. Government Printing Office.

———. 1987b. *News.* Washington, DC: U.S. Government Printing Office.

———. 1989b. *Handbook of Labor Statistics.* Bulletin 2340. Washington, DC: U.S. Government Printing Office.

Van Den Berghe, P. L. and D. P. Barash. 1977. "Inclusive Fitness and Human Family Structure." *American Anthropologist* 79:809–823.

Vetterling-Braggin, Mary, ed. 1982. *"Femininity," "Masculinity," and "Androgyny": A Modern Philosophical Discussion.* Totowa, NJ: Littlefield, Adams.

Viscusi, W. Kip. 1980. "Sex Differences in Worker Quitting." *Review of Economics and Statistics* 62:388–398.

Vogel, Lise. 1983. *Marxism and the Oppression of Women: Toward a Unitary Theory.* New Brunswick, NJ: Rutgers University Press.

Wachter, Michael and Oliver Williamson. 1978. "Obligational Markets and the Mechanics of Inflation." *Bell Journal of Economics* 6:250–278.

Waite, Linda and S. Berryman. 1985. "Women in Nontraditional Occupations: Choice and Turnover." The Rand Corporation, Santa Monica, CA. Rand Report R-3106-FF.

Walby, Sylvia. 1986. *Patriarchy at Work: Patriarchal and Capitalist Relations in Employment.* Minneapolis: University of Minnesota Press.

Walker, Jon, Curt Tausky, and Donna Oliver. 1982. "Men and Women at Work: Similarities and Differences in Work Values within Occupational Groupings." *Journal of Vocational Behavior* 21:17–36.

Wallace, Michael and Arne L. Kalleberg. 1981. "Economic Organization of Firms and Labor Market Consequences: Toward a Specification of Dual Economy Theory." Pp. 77–117 in *Sociological Perspectives on Labor Markets,* edited by Ivar Berg. New York: Academic Press.

Wambheim v. J. C. Penney. 1983. 705 F. 2d 1492. 9th Circuit.

Ward, Kathryn B. and Charles M. Mueller. 1985. "Sex Differences in Earnings: The Influence of Industrial Sector, Authority Hierarchy, and Human Capital Variables." *Work and Occupations* 12:437–463.

Wards Cove Packing Company v. Antonio. 1989. U.S. Supreme Court.

Weals, Christopher A. 1984. "AFSCME v. State of Washington: Rethinking Comparable Worth." *Northwestern University Law Review* 79:809–846.

Weedon, Chris. 1987. *Feminist Practice and Poststructuralist Theory.* New York: Basil Blackwell.

Weiss, Andrew. 1980. "Job Queues and Lay-offs in Labor Markets with Flexible Wages." *Journal of Political Economy* 88:526–538.

Weitzman, Martin L. 1989. "A Theory of Wage Dispersion and Job Market Segregation." *Quarterly Journal of Economics* 104(1):121–138.

Whitbeck, Caroline. 1983. "A Different Reality: Feminist Ontology." Pp. 64–88 in *Beyond Domination: New Perspectives on Women and Philosophy,* edited by Carol C. Gould. Totowa, NJ: Rowman & Allanheld.

Willborn, Steven L. 1989. *A Secretary and a Cook: Challenging women's Wages in the Courts of the United States and Great Britain.* Ithaca, NY: ILR Press.

Williams, Robert E. and Thomas R. Bagby. 1984. "The Legal Framework." Pp.

197–265 in *Comparable Worth: Issues and Alternatives,* 2nd edition, edited by E. Robert Livernash. Washington, DC: Equal Employment Advisory Council.

Williams, Robert E. and Lorence L. Kessler. 1984. *A Closer Look at Comparable Worth: A Study of the Basic Questions to Be Addressed in Approaching Pay Equity.* Washington, DC: National Foundation for the Study of Equal Employment Policy.

Williamson, Oliver. 1975. *Markets and Hierarchies.* New York: Free Press.

_____. 1981. "The Economics of Organization: The Transaction Cost Approach." *American Journal of Sociology* 87:548–577.

_____. 1985. *The Economic Institutions of Capitalism.* New York: Free Press.

_____. 1988. "The Economics and Sociology of Organization: Promoting a Dialogue." Pp. 159–186 in *Industries, Firms, and Jobs: Sociological and Economic Approaches,* edited by George Farkas and Paula England. New York: Plenum.

Williamson, Oliver, Michael Wachter, and Jeffrey Harris. 1975. "Understanding the Employment Relationship: The Analysis of Idiosyncratic Exchange." *Bell Journal of Economics* 6:250–278.

Wilson, E. O. 1978. *On Human Nature.* Cambridge, MA: Harvard University Press.

Wilson, John. 1983. *Social Theory.* Englewood Cliffs, NJ: Prentice-Hall.

Witt, Mary and Patricia K. Naherny. 1975. *Women's Work—Up from 878: Report on the DOT Research Project.* Madison: Women's Education Resources, University of Wisconsin-Extension.

Wolf, Wendy C. and Neil D. Fligstein. 1979. "Sex and Authority in the Workplace: The Causes of Sexual Inequality." *American Sociological Review* 44:235–252.

Wollstonecraft, Mary. [1792] 1975. *A Vindication of Rights of Woman.* Baltimore: Penguin.

Wright, E. O. 1978. "Race, Class and Income Inequality." *American Journal of Sociology* 83:1368–1397.

Wright, Erik Olin, David Hachen Costello, and Joey Sprague. 1982. "The American Class Structure." *American Sociological Review* 47:709–726.

Yellen, Janet L. 1984. "Efficiency Wage Models of Unemployment." *American Economic Review* 74:200–205.

Zaretsky, Eli. 1976. *Capitalism, the Family and Personal Life.* London: Pluto Press.

Zellner, Harriet. 1975. "The Determinants of Occupational Segregation." Pp. 125–145 in *Women in the Labor Market,* edited by Cynthia B. Lloyd, Emily S. Andres, and Curtis L. Gilroy. New York: Columbia University Press.

Zucker, Lynne G. and Carolyn Rosenstein. 1981. "Taxonomies of Institutional Structure: Dual Economy Reconsidered." *American Sociological Review* 46:869–884.

Index